ELEMENTS

OF

MICROPROGRAMMING

DILIP K. BANERJI
Jawaharlal Nehru University
New Delhi, India

JACQUES RAYMOND
University of Ottawa
Ottawa, Ontario, Canada

Prentice-Hall, Inc., Englewood Cliffs, New Jersey   07632

Library of Congress Cataloging in Publication Data

BANERJI, DILIP K.
  Elements of microprogramming.

  (Prentice-Hall software series)
  Includes bibliographies and index.
  1. Microprogramming. I. Raymond, Jacques.
II. Title. III. Series.
QA76.6.B347   001.64'2   81-10566
ISBN 0-13-267146-8   AACR2

© 1982 by Prentice-Hall, Inc., Englewood Cliffs, N.J.   07632

Prentice-Hall Software Series
Brian W. Kernighan, advisor

Editorial/production supervision and interior design
  by *Aliza Greenblatt*

Cover Design
  by *Judith A. Matz*

Manufacturing buyer
  Gordon Osbourne

Printed in the United States of America

10 9 8 7 6 5 4 3 2 1

To our students

PRENTICE-HALL INTERNATIONAL, INC., *London*
PRENTICE-HALL OF AUSTRALIA PTY. LIMITED, *Sydney*
PRENTICE-HALL OF CANADA, LTD., *Toronto*
PRENTICE-HALL OF INDIA PRIVATE LIMITED, *New Delhi*
PRENTICE-HALL OF JAPAN, INC., *Tokyo*
PRENTICE-HALL OF SOUTHEAST ASIA PTE. LTD., *Singapore*
WHITEHALL BOOKS LIMITED, *Wellington, New Zealand*

Contents

Preface   *xv*

PART ONE   REVIEW

Chapter One   Basics of Microprogramming   **3**

   1.1   Introduction   3
   1.2   The Control Unit   4
   1.3   Concepts of Microprogramming   9
   1.4   Advantages and Disadvantages of Microprogramming   12
       Summary   15
       References   16
       Further Readings   16

Chapter Two   Historical Evolution of Microprogramming   *17*

2.1   Introduction   17
2.2   History of Growth   19
2.3   User-Microprogrammable Machines   20
2.4   History of Applications   21
      Summary   22
      References   23
      Further Readings   23

Chapter Three   Basic Computer Organization: an Overview   *25*

3.1   Introduction   25
3.2   CPU Organization   26
      3.2.1 Index Registers 28;   3.2.2 Base Register 29;
      3.2.3 General-Purpose Registers 30;
      3.2.4 Input/Output Register 32;
      3.2.5 Return Address Stack (RAS) 33
3.3   Instruction Formats   33
3.4   Control Flip-Flops and Their Functions   36
      3.4.1 Fetching and Execution of Instructions 37;
      3.4.2 Program State Flip-Flops 41;
      3.4.3 Interrupt Mechanism and Flip-Flop 42;
      3.4.4 I/O Interrupt Handling 44;
      3.4.5 Direct Memory Access (DMA) and DMA Flip-Flop 47;
      3.4.6 Traps and Trap Flip-Flop 50;
      3.4.7 Programmed Interrupt 51;   3.4.8 Hard Errors 51
3.5   Instruction Classification   52
      3.5.1 Arithmetic Instructions 53;   3.5.2 Logical Instructions 53;
      3.5.3 Shift/Rotate Instructions 53;
      3.5.4 Comparison Instructions 55;   3.5.5 Branch Instructions 55;
      3.5.6 Subroutine Linkage Instructions 56;
      3.5.7 Data Movement Instructions 56;
      3.5.8 I/O and Privileged Group of Instructions 57;
      3.5.9 Control Group Instructions 59;
      3.5.10 Miscellaneous Instructions 59
3.6   A Proposed Microinstruction Format   60
      Summary   61
      References   62

illustrated by an example implemented on the Microdata 1600* machine. Finally, Chapter 13 describes some of the other applications of microprogramming: virtual memory implementation, microdiagnostics, implementation of specialized functions for computer graphics, and implementation of a communications controller. These are only a few representative examples of the other applications.

Three appendices provide useful background information to the reader. Appendix A provides a summary of the features of an emulated (target) machine discussed in Chapter 9, whereas Appendix B describes the features of the microprogrammable host machine. Appendix C provides a complete microprogram listing of the emulator discussed in Chapter 9. The References and Further Readings at the end of chapters provide a useful guide to relevant literature in the field.

The book is intended for use at Computer Science/Electrical Engineering senior and graduate levels. Chapters 1 through 8 are suitable for seniors, whereas the inclusion of Chapters 9 through 13 would make it suitable for graduate level. Some background in computer organization and some exposure to assembly language programming would be helpful in reading the book. The book can also be used as a handy reference for practicing engineers and computer professionals. It can be used either as a primary text for a full course on microprogramming or as a supplementary text in a course on computer architecture/organization. The introductory chapters can be used to supplement a basic computer organization course, while other chapters can supplement a more advanced course on architecture/organization. At the University of Ottawa it is to be used as a primary text for a full course on microprogramming.

No book can be completed without the authors receiving active support from various sources. In this context we would like to thank Data General Corporation, Microdata Corporation, and Intel Corporation for giving us permission to use some of their technical literature in the book. Many of our colleagues and students both at the University of Ottawa & JNU have helped in the preparation of the manuscript. In particular, the assistance of Peter Hickey at Ottawa in testing many of the microprograms is acknowledged. At JNU, Prasenjit Biswas, Abir Bhattacharya, and Arun Majumdar have helped a good deal. Without the assistance of these individuals, it would have been difficult to complete the book. Throughout the course of writing the book, our families have been very patient and have consistently rendered moral support. Finally, our special thanks are due to Claudette Henderson for her excellent typing.

DILIP K. BANERJI   **JACQUES RAYMOND**
Jawaharlal Nehru University   *University of Ottawa*
New Delhi, India   *Ottawa, Ontario, Canada*

*Reprinted with permission of Microdata Corporation, Irvine, California.

PART TWO   MICROPROGRAMMING HARDWARE AND MICROINSTRUCTIONS

Chapter Four   Hardware for Microprogramming   **65**

4.1   Microprogramming Control Unit   65
    4.1.1 Functional Units 65;
    4.1.2 Control Memory Sequencing Schemes 67;
    4.1.3 Other Hardware Facilities 70

4.2   Review of Control Memory Technology   71
    4.2.1 Read/Write Memories 71;
    4.2.2 Read-Only Memories (ROM) 72;   Future Outlook 77

4.3   Levels of Control   78
    4.3.1 Concepts of Levels 78;
    4.3.2 The Machine-Language Level 80;
    4.3.3 The Microprogram Level 80;   4.3.4 Further Levels 81

    References   83
    Further Readings   83
    Exercises   85

Chapter Five   Microinstructions   **86**

Introduction   86

5.1   Microinstruction Structure   87
    5.1.1 Horizontal Microinstructions 87;
    5.1.2 Vertical Microinstructions 88;
    5.1.3 Diagonal Microinstructions 89;
    5.1.4 Encoding of Microinstruction Fields 92

5.2   Microinstruction Execution   93
    5.2.1 Basic Microinstruction Cycle 93;
    5.2.2 Vertical Microinstruction Execution Example 96;
    5.2.3 Horizontal Microinstruction Execution Example 97;
    5.2.4 Diagonal Microinstruction Execution Example 97

5.3   Microinstruction Design: Some Considerations   98
    5.3.1 Vertical versus Nonvertical Format 98;
    5.3.2 Minimization of Microinstruction Size 100;
    5.3.3 Other Considerations 105

    References   107
    Exercises   109

PART THREE   MICROPROGRAMMING PRACTICE

Chapter Six   Developing a Microprogram   *113*

6.1   Direct Microprogramming   113
      6.1.1 Writing Absolute Code 113;
      6.1.2 Testing a Microprogram 115;
      6.1.3 Obtaining the Firmware 119
6.2   Assemblers   120
      6.2.1 Microassembler Language 120;
      6.2.2 The Assembly Process 122;
      6.2.3 Extra Features of Assemblers 123
6.3   High Level Microprogramming Languages   125
      6.3.1 Necessity and Advantages 125;
      6.3.2 Disadvantages and Trade-Offs 126;
      *6.3.3 Considerations in the Design of a Microprogramming
            Language 127;*
      6.3.4 High Level Languages for Microprogramming 128
6.4   Micro Operating Systems   131
      6.4.1 Introduction 131;   6.4.2 Components 131
      References   132
      Further Readings   132
      Exercises   136

*Chapter Seven   Implementation of Some Common Machine
                 Instructions and Functions*   *137*

7.1   Introduction   137
7.2   Some Common Machine Instructions   141
7.3   Specialized Instructions   146
7.4   Examples of I/O Instructions   156
      7.4.1 Microdata 1600 I/O System 156;   7.4.2 Examples 158
7.5   Interrupt Handling   162
      7.5.1 Microdata 1600 Interrupt System 163;
      7.5.2 Examples of Interrupt Handling 166
7.6   Stack Processing   169
      References   173
      Further Readings   173
      Exercises   174

Chapter Eight   Performance and Optimization   *175*

8.1   Introduction   175
8.2   Control Store Optimization   176
      8.2.1 Use of Parallelism 176;
      8.2.2 Dynamic Address Modification 177;
      8.2.3 Use of Subroutines 179;   8.2.4 Common Segments 180;
      8.2.5 Extending the Control Store 180;
      8.2.6 Formal Techniques 184
8.3   Execution Time Optimization   190
      8.3.1 Use of Parallelism 190;
      8.3.2 Use of Suitable Programming Methodology 192;
      8.3.3 Algorithms 193
      References   195
      Further Readings   195
      Exercises   196

PART FOUR   MICROPROGRAMMING APPLICATIONS

Chapter Nine   Microprogramming and Emulation   *199*

9.1   Basic Concepts   199
      9.1.1 Introduction 199;
      9.1.2 Characteristics of Host and Target Machines 200;
      9.1.3 Strategy for Emulation 201
9.2   CPU Emulation   202
      9.2.1 Data Path Structure 202;
      9.2.2 Functional Processing Unit 203;
      9.2.3 Mapping of Registers, Local Storage, and Main
            Memory 205;
      9.2.4 Example of CPU Emulation 206
9.3   Emulation of Input/Output Systems   213
      9.3.1 I/O Device Mapping 216;
      9.3.2 Device Operational Characteristics 216;
      9.3.3 Data Formatting 217;   9.3.4 I/O Bus Structure 217;
      9.3.5 I/O Interrupt Structures 217;
      9.3.6 Timing Considerations 217

9.4   Emulation of Interrupt Systems   218
    9.4.1 Mapping of Interrupt Systems 218;
    9.4.2 Interrupt Handling 219;
    9.4.3 Example: Emulation of Nova I/O System on the
       Microdata 1600 220

9.5   General Remarks   232
    9.5.1 Hardware, Firmware, Software Trade-offs in
       Emulation 232;
    9.5.2 Universal Host Machine 233;
    9.5.3 Emulation of Front Panel Operation 234
    References   235
    Further Readings   235
    Exercises   237

**Chapter Ten   Microprogramming Support for Operating Systems
and High Level Languages**   **238**

10.1   Operating System Support   239
    10.1.1 Review of Operating System Concepts 239;
    10.1.2 OS Overhead 241;
    10.1.3 Improvements Expected From Firmware
       Support 241;
    10.1.4 General Considerations in Firmware Support 242

10.2   Implementation   244
    10.2.1 Identification of Primitives 244;
    10.2.2 Criteria For Firmware Implementation 246;
    10.2.3 Selection of Primitives for Firmware
       Implementation 246;
    10.2.4 Firmware Implementation 247;
    10.2.5 Firmware Support 248

10.3   Examples   248
    10.3.1 Microprogramming of a Scheduler 248;
    10.3.2 Microprogramming Some Basic Operations 250;
    10.3.3 Other Examples 252

10.4   Firmware Support for High-Level Languages   254
    10.4.1 The Problem 254;
    10.4.2 An Overview of the Work Done 257
    References   264
    Further Readings   265
    Exercises   267

PART FIVE   EXAMPLES

Chapter Eleven   Microprogrammable Microprocessors:
An Example   *271*

11.1   Introduction   271
11.2   The Intel Series 3000   275
 11.2.1 3001 Microprogram Control Unit 277;
 11.2.2 Functional Description of the MCU 280;
 11.2.3 Extended Addressing 287;
 11.2.4 3002 Central Processing Element (CPE) 288;
 11.2.5 Functional Description of the 3002 CPE 290
11.3   Cross Microprogramming System (CROMIS)   297
 11.3.1 XMAS Language 298;
 11.3.2 XMAP Language and Control Language 312;
 11.3.3 Microprogramming Techniques for Series 3000 313
11.4   Additional Support: In-Circuit Emulation   321
 References   323

Chapter Twelve   A Firmware Implementation
of Block-Structured Programming   *324*

12.1   Top-down Structured Programming at Machine
 Level (TDSP)   325
 12.1.1 Primitives and Control Programs 325;
 12.1.2 The Hierarchy of Control 327;   12.1.3 Arguments 328;
 12.1.4 Machine Instructions for Control 329;
 12.1.5 Overview of the Execution of One Instruction 329
12.2   Description of the Control Program Instructions   331
 12.2.1 Writing a Control Program 331;
 12.2.2 Description of the Execution of a Control Instruction 338
 References and Further Readings   345
 Exercises   346

Chapter Thirteen   Other Examples of Applications   *347*

13.1   Virtual Memory Implementation Through
 Microprogramming   347
 13.1.1 Concept of Virtual Memory 348;
 13.1.2 An Example of DAT Implementation 348

13.2   Microdiagnostics   355
    13.2.1 Introduction 355;
    13.2.2 Advantages of Microdiagnostics 356;
    13.2.3 Microdiagnostics Implementation 357

13.3   Firmware Implementation of Some Functions
of a Graphics Terminal   358
    13.3.1 Introduction 358;
    13.3.2 A Microprogrammed Graphics Terminal 359;
    13.3.3 Architecture of the Graphics Terminal 361;
    13.3.4 Operation of the Terminal 362

13.4   A Communications Controller   362
    13.4.1 Introduction 362;
    13.4.2 Example of a Microprogrammed Controller 363

    References   376
    Further Readings   376
    Exercises   378

Appendix A   The Nova Computer   *379*

Appendix B   The Microdata 1600   *396*

Appendix C   Nova Emulator   *414*

Index   *431*

Preface

This book has essentially evolved out of the course CSI 4114/ELG 5189, "Microprogramming and Machine Architecture," that the authors have offered at the University of Ottawa since 1971. Since the material for the course is derived from various sources, including some of our own work, our students repeatedly urged us to put it all together as a package, which eventually took the form of a manuscript.

The book is intended to provide a comprehensive coverage of the basic principles, practices, and applications of microprogramming. We have endeavored to stick to this objective as much as possible. Admittedly, however, as in any book, there may be a few shortcomings. For the positive aspects of the book the authors would like to share the credit with their students and colleagues who have consistently provided encouragement and support; for any shortcomings, the buck stops at our desks.

We have deliberately avoided case studies of specific microprogrammed/microprogrammable machines. With rapidly changing computer technology, machines tend to be outdated relatively quickly, thus rendering the books containing case studies out-of-date. By concentrating on basic concepts and applications of microprogramming, we hope that this book will remain useful for a longer period. Throughout the book we have used only one microprogrammable machine, the Microdata 1600,* available at the University of Ottawa, to develop and illustrate microprogramming examples. Some readers may not agree with our choice of the machine, but this choice was motivated by the availability of the machine and by our desire to list tested microprograms.

Chapter 1 is purely introductory in nature; its main objective is to introduce the basic concepts of microprogramming. Chapter 2 traces the historical growth of microprogramming since the introduction of the concept in 1951 by Wilkes. The evolution of microprogramming up to the present stage as an integral part of computer architecture is discussed briefly. Chapter 3 reviews the basic concepts of computer organization. It is primarily intended as a refresher course in computer organization and can be skipped by readers familiar with computer hardware and organization. Chapter 4 discusses both the hardware resources required to support microprogramming and the basic schemes for implementing microprogram control and technologies used therein. Chapter 5 analyzes, in depth, the various aspects of micro-instruction design, formats, and execution. It also discusses various design tradeoffs in microinstruction design.

Chapters 6 through 8 are concerned with microprogramming practice. In Chapter 6 we discuss the various aspects of developing microprograms. Starting with absolute coding, we discuss the need for a micro-assembly language, and then the need and availability of high-level languages for microprogramming. In Chapter 7 we are concerned with the microprogram implementation of some common machine instructions and functions. The example microprograms have been written for and tested on the Microdata 1600 machine. Chapter 8 discusses the effect of various factors on the performance of a microprogrammed system. In addition, it presents techniques for optimizing the size of a microprogram.

Chapters 9 through 13 essentially cover the various applications of microprogramming. In Chapter 9 we discuss the concept of emulation and show how this is achieved through microprogramming. A novel feature of this chapter is the section on I/O emulation which is generally not available in the existing texts. The emulation of an existing machine on the Microdata 1600 is described in some detail. Chapter 10 is concerned with microprogramming support for operating systems as well as high-level language processing. General principles of how this is achieved are discussed, along with a few specific examples of such applications. In Chapter 11, we discuss microprogrammable (bit-slice) microprocessors. The discussion is centered around the Intel 3000† microprocessor family which can be micro-programmed to suit user requirements. Chapter 12 describes the use of microprogramming to support block structured programming. This is

---

*Reprinted with permission of Microdata Corporation, Irvine, California.
†Reprinted by Permission of Intel Corporation, Copyright 1976.

PART ONE

Review

CHAPTER ONE

Basics
of Microprogramming

1.1 INTRODUCTION

Since the introduction of the concept in 1951 by Wilkes [1], microprogramming has attained a great deal of acceptance and significance, not only as an alternative method of control unit design in a computer*, but also as a powerful tool in the hands of designers and users alike. The main reason for using this technique in computer control implementation is the tremendous flexibility attainable at a relatively small cost, which has made user-restructuring of computer architecture a reality. Also as Husson [2] has observed, "microprogramming has made it economically feasible to have the same comprehensive instruction set built into a whole line of new computers, even the smallest ones. Thus we now have computers that are architecturally compatible, yet their internal hardware, organization, and structure are drastically different." Besides offering the so-called upwards and downwards

*Although we talk of the control of a computer, the concept applies to any digital controller.

compatibility in computer systems, microprogramming offers the possibility of user-defined instruction sets. Thus a collection of basic hardware can be tailored to meet specific requirements for a system.

1.2 THE CONTROL UNIT

In order to fully understand the meaning and role of microprogramming, we must look at the control unit of a computer and its function within the computer system. Any computer can be thought of as consisting of the following five basic functional units.

1. Input.
2. Output.
3. Memory.
4. Arithmetic and Logic Unit (ALU).
5. Control Unit.

The interconnection of and information flow between these units is shown in Fig. 1.1.

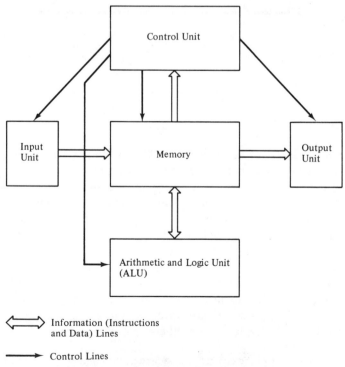

Figure 1.1 Functional Organization of a Computer

It is evident from the functional arrangement that the control unit directs all the hardware activity inside the system. The control unit causes an instruction to be fetched from memory, analyzes (decodes) the instruction to determine the operation to be performed, determines the source and destination of data, causes the movement of data and the required operation to be performed, and then repeats the entire process until a halt operation is executed. Thus the control unit is the source from which commands emanate, directing the hardware to perform various operations required for executing a single machine instruction. In this sense, the control unit can be viewed as the message and command center for the hardware system of a machine; this is where the concept of microprogramming comes in, as we shall see shortly.

The conventional approach to the design of a control unit is to put together a logic network that generates timing and control signals in a pre-determined sequence for each machine-level instruction. This is often called **hardwired** or **conventional control,** since the control unit logic is permanently "wired in" once the machine is built and it cannot be changed without a nontrivial amount of effort and expense. Figure 1.2 shows part of the data flow path of a hypothetical machine. The control points in this figure have been numbered and circled. We shall use this data flow path to illustrate how conventional control logic is derived for a typical instruction.

In this machine, a register bank can be accessed and the contents of the register specified by the A-address or the B-address can be copied onto the A- or the B-bus and be operands of the ALU. The ALU output goes on the D-bus, which has contents that can be copied in a register as specified by the B-address. Control signals are provided to select A (1), select B (2), copy output of ALU (3), read or write register (4), and specify ALU operation (5–8).

Suppose an ADD instruction for this machine has the format

OPCODE 'ADD'	A-field	B-field

where A- and B-fields refer to two registers in the register bank of Fig. 1.2. The ADD instruction could be defined as follows.

> Add the contents of the register designated by the A-field to the register designated by the B-field and store the result in the register specified in the B-field.

Assume that the instruction is already available in a register (usually the instruction register of the computer). The timing sequence necessary to

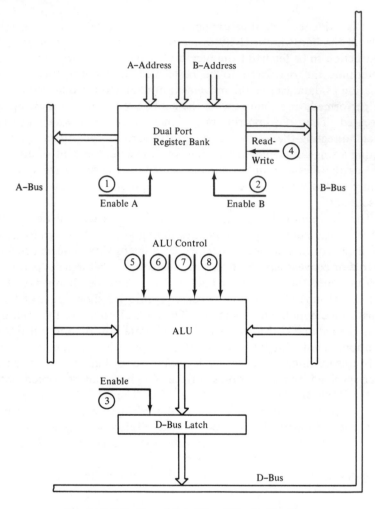

Figure 1.2 Section of Data Flow Path of a Machine

implement this instruction is shown in Fig. 1.3, along with the master clock (MC) and four clock pulses, which are labeled ϕ_1, ϕ_2, ϕ_3, and ϕ_4.

For the ADD operation to be completed, the following sequence of events must take place.

ϕ_1 a. Enable A-address: This sets the first operand into ALU.
     b. Enable B-address: This sets the second operand into ALU.
     c. Set ALU control: This specifies the operation to be performed.

ϕ_2 a. Enable A-address: Keep A-value.
     b. Enable B-address: Keep B-value.
     c. Latch enable: Get result onto D-bus.
     d. Set ALU control: Keep OPCODE for ALU.

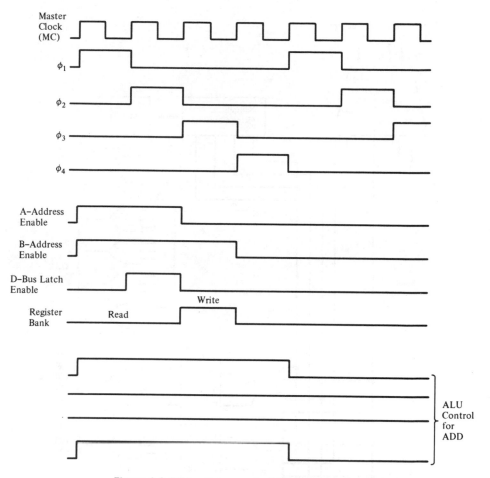

Figure 1.3 Timing Sequence for ADD Instruction

ϕ_3 a. Disable A-address: Not required any more.
        b. Enable B-address: Required to write D-bus contents.
        c. Latch disable: Not required anymore.
        d. Write enable: Specifies a copy of D-bus contents.
ϕ_4 Disable all signals: End of operation.

The master clock in any machine is the chief source from which other timing and sequencing signals are generated. In fact, ϕ_1 through ϕ_4 are outputs of a four-stage ring counter driven by the master clock. The details of the ring-counter logic are not shown here; this information should be available in any book on digital logic design (see, for example, Baron [3]).

Figure 1.4 shows a control logic schematic diagram to generate the necessary timing signals in order to implement the ADD instruction. Note

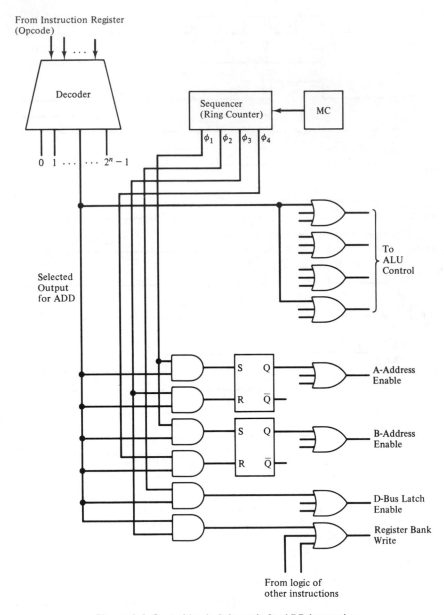

From Instruction Register
(Opcode)

Decoder

0   1 ···|··· $2^n - 1$

Sequencer
(Ring Counter)

MC

ϕ_1 ϕ_2 ϕ_3 ϕ_4

To
ALU
Control

Selected
Output
for ADD

S   Q

R $\bar{Q}$

A-Address
Enable

S   Q

R $\bar{Q}$

B-Address
Enable

D-Bus Latch
Enable

Register Bank
Write

From logic of
other instructions

Figure 1.4 Control Logic Schematic for ADD Instruction

that this control logic is by no means unique; modifications or improvements
to this arrangement can be made, depending on the ingenuity of the designer.

As we can see from Fig. 1.4, the A-address enable signal is set when
the ADD opcode is present and ϕ_1 phase is on. It is reset via the flip-flop

for an ADD signal and ϕ_3 as required in Fig. 1.3. As Fig. 1.4 shows, the control lines are driven by a set of OR functions; this is because more than one instruction may require a specific control line to be activated. Hence the other inputs to these OR gates are from the control logic of other instructions that require these control lines.

In this way, for *each* of the machine instructions, the control sequence is determined by the designer and then an appropriate logic network is specified to implement the instruction. Thus the logic designer figures out how the various logic elements are to be arranged for generating the control pulses for each instruction. Much of this process is intuitive and involves a fair deal of trial and error on the part of the designer before finalizing the design. For example, after designing a particular control logic network, the designer may find ways to reduce the execution time for an instruction by devising another network that utilizes some possible parallelism in the operation of the control lines. Furthermore, once a design has been finalized and the machine wired, it requires expensive design changes if a new instruction is to be added to the machine instruction set or if an existing instruction is to be modified in any significant way. Of course, it is always possible to add a new instruction at the software level through the use of a macroinstruction. However, a software-implemented instruction cannot be executed as fast as a hardware-implemented instruction.

Programmers will attest to the fact that the manufacturer-supplied instruction set often does not meet all their requirements; ideally, they would like to specify their own instruction set or add to the existing one. Any such modification or extension of the instruction repertoire is not possible in a machine with a conventional control unit. However, the fact remains that there are situations where flexibility in the instruction set definition is desirable. By allowing the user to alter the instruction set without involving any circuit design changes, microprogramming plays a major role in such situations.

1.3 CONCEPTS OF MICROPROGRAMMING

We can now ask the question, what is microprogramming? As we mentioned in Sec. 1.1, the term was introduced by Professor Wilkes at Cambridge Mathematical Laboratory in 1951. He conceived it as a "systematic and orderly approach for designing the control section of any computing system."

We can see that the execution of a machine instruction requires inter-register movement of data; some of this data movement is, of necessity, sequential, whereas other data movement can be parallel. We can now envision an "inner machine" which executes simple instructions, causing inter-register transfers of data; these instructions for the inner machine are called **microinstructions.** Thus, execution of a machine-level instruction, in effect, consists of executing an associated **sequence of microinstructions** or a **microprogram.** Each microinstruction consists of one or more commands to the control lines in order to effect the inter-register movement of data; these commands are known as **microcommands.** An operation controlled or effected by a microcommand is known as a **microoperation.**

We shall now illustrate how a microprogram can be developed for the ADD instruction discussed in Sec. 1.2. Figure 1.2 contains eight control points; the microoperations required for executing the various machine instructions can be effected by activating or inhibiting the necessary control points. The ON/OFF (active/inactive) state of each control point can be represented by a single bit in a memory. The states of these control points at the time of executing a particular microinstruction can then be represented by a word in this memory; a block of such words will represent a complete microprogram, which executes a single machine-level instruction. The memory containing the microprograms is generally referred to as the **control memory** or **control store.** In the most straightforward implementation of microprogrammed control, the control store associated with Fig. 1.2 will have to contain at least eight-bit words. Referring to the ADD instruction, we now write down the microoperation sequence, and identify the control points which must be turned on or off at each step.

MICROOPERATIONS	CONTROL POINT AFFECTED
1. Enable A-address.	1
Enable B-address.	2
Set up ALU for addition.	5, 6, 7, 8
2. Keep A-address on.	1
Keep B-address on.	2
Keep ALU in addition mode.	5, 6, 7, 8
Enable D-bus latch.	3
3. Disable A-address.	1
Keep B-address on.	2
Disable D-bus latch.	3
Write D-bus to register bank.	4
4. Disable B-address.	2
Disable write.	4

This completes the microoperation sequence. Figure 1.5 schematically shows the control-store contents corresponding to the microprogram for the ADD instruction. Each word in this control store is a microinstruction, and each bit of a word directly controls the corresponding control point. In this arrangement, each microinstruction contains eight microcommands. More details on control-store organization and sequencing will be discussed in Chap. 4.

The reader can now appreciate the difference between conventional

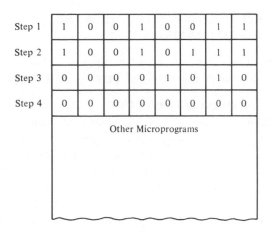

Step 1	1	0	0	1	0	0	1	1
Step 2	1	0	0	1	0	1	1	1
Step 3	0	0	0	0	1	0	1	0
Step 4	0	0	0	0	0	0	0	0

Other Microprograms

Figure 1.5 Microprogram Representation for ADD Instruction

(hardwired) control and microprogrammed control. In conventional control—as mentioned earlier—the microoperation sequence required for executing a machine instruction is wired in, and this, in turn, results in a fixed instruction set once the machine is wired. In microprogrammed control, the microprograms for the various machine instructions are stored in a control store, which *usually* is distinct from the program store. This, however, is not necessary; in fact, there are machines in which control and program stores are physically the same units. In earlier days of microprogramming practice, economic and security reasons dictated that control stores be of read-only type. However, much of the power of the concept can be best exploited when the control store—or a part of it—is of read and write type. The impact of this feature will be discussed in more detail in the subsequent chapters.

Finally, one may feel an aura of mysticism surrounding microprogramming in the computing community. However, microprogramming is not in the exclusive realm of "super programmers" or designers. Anyone familiar with machine or assembly language programming can learn to write microcode in a reasonably short time. In fact, writing microcode is just programming at another (lower) level, which gives the programmer much more direct control over the hardware resources of the machine than assembly language or high-level language programming. In addition, microprogramming is often confused with the programming of microprocessors. Although this confusion is unfortunate, it is not surprising. To alleviate this confusion, the reader should keep in mind that microprogramming is basically a vehicle for implementing the control functions in a machine.

1.4 ADVANTAGES AND DISADVANTAGES OF MICROPROGRAMMING

This section discusses some of the advantages and disadvantages of using microprogrammed control in a machine. First the advantages are considered.

1. Systematic Design of Control Unit

Systematic design was, in fact, the chief motivation of Wilkes in proposing the concept of microprogrammed control. The conventional control unit design results in a very unsystematic, random logic structure which is difficult for persons other than the designer to understand. This is primarily because conventional control design involves a fair amount of trial and error before a suitable sequencing network is designed. In principle, one should be able to use the systematic design procedures from the sequential machine theory. In practice, however, the number of states in a computer is so large that it is extremely difficult to apply any formal design procedures for control unit synthesis. The logic designer, therefore, derives sequencing logic for one machine instruction at a time or, at best, for a group of similar instructions while trying to share logic between various instructions. The result is a random logic network which has little systematic structure even though it may be efficient in terms of execution speed of machine instructions.

In comparison, microprogrammed control is much more systematic and easier to understand. Microoperation sequences for a machine instruction are identified and a corresponding microprogram can be created immediately. Conversely, by examining the microprogram for an instruction, one can easily determine the associated microoperation sequence. This makes it easier to understand the control logic and reduces training periods for maintenance personnel.

2. Architectural Changeability

The *architecture* of a computer system can be defined as the external characteristics of the system as seen by a programmer. Since a set of microprograms defines the user level machine, it is possible to alter the external characteristics of the machine (such as instruction set or word size) by altering the microprograms. If the control store is a ROM, the machine architecture can be changed by plugging in a new ROM; in case of a read/write control store, the new microprograms are simply written into the control store. In this sense, microprogrammed control allows the possibility of defining a "soft" architecture, which can be changed if necessary.

3. Flexibility

Microprogramming allows a great deal of flexibility during system design, in that the repertoire of machine instructions need not be fixed before hardware design is undertaken. As a matter of fact, the machine order code and hardware developments can proceed in parallel. Once the microlevel machine has been designed (a set of hardware resources that can execute a given set of microinstructions), it can be microprogrammed to support any order code. This feature allows system designers to experiment with various instruction sets before deciding on an optimum set according to some criteria. Even this instruction set need not be final, and as pointed out in the second advantage, it can be altered by suitably changing the microprograms. This kind of flexibility is not offered by conventional control.

4. Adaptability

This advantage is related to the second and third advantages. Through the use of microprogramming, a machine can be adapted to user requirements. This can be done either by enhancing an existing instruction set by adding a few more application-oriented instructions or by designing a completely new instruction set. In this manner, the same basic hardware resources can be custom-tailored to different user requirements.

5. Software Compatibility

Microprogramming can help maintain software compatibility when one computer system is replaced by another. For example, a computer manufacturer can market a new machine and yet maintain compatibility with the older systems through the use of microprogramming. This allows all the existing software to be run on the new machine without any modifications. Compatibility is achieved by providing a set of microprograms—an **emulator**—that executes the older system's instruction set on the new system's hardware. This is a very important advantage of microprogramming, because the major cost of changing from one system to another is the cost of software conversion. Without any compatibility feature, it may be an economic disaster for a user to convert to a new system because the cost of software conversion can be far greater than any economy achieved by using a better machine.

Microprogramming can also be used to achieve instruction-set compatibility within a whole family of computers. This appears to be the primary motivation for the use of microprogramming in some machines of the same family, especially in the lower-numbered models. In effect, each microprogrammed machine emulates the same basic instruction set, even though the internal organization of these machines may be widely different. It is worth noting that software compatibility does not necessarily mean compatibility at microprogram level; that is, microprograms written for one machine need not necessarily be executable on another machine.

The compatibility feature can also be created by a user if a writable control store is available with the machine. By writing appropriate microprograms, the same basic hardware can be used to emulate a variety of machines, which, in turn, would allow the software for different machines to be executed on the same hardware. This aspect of microprogramming will be discussed in greater detail in Chap. 9.

6. Economy

It has been established [2] that except for a very simple machine, the hardware logic for conventional control is more expensive than that for microprogram control. As a machine instruction set becomes more and more comprehensive, it becomes more economical to implement it via microprogramming. Even though the cost of hardware is continually dropping, the use of microprogramming has other economic advantages as discussed next.

7. Diagnosibility

Microprogramming allows easier diagnosis and maintenance of the machine hardware. The control unit itself has a much more regular structure as compared to its hardwired version. This makes it easier to generate diagnostic tests for the control unit and to train the maintenance personnel. Diagnostic microprograms can help to pinpoint hardware errors much more precisely than is possible otherwise.

These factors make it easier to maintain a microprogram-controlled machine, which has its associated economic advantages.

8. Ease of Experimentation

This is related to some of the advantages mentioned earlier. Through the use of emulation, it is possible to test and evaluate new machine architectures. Of course, the same thing can be done on a nonmicroprogrammed machine through the use of software simulation; however, with the use of microprogramming, special machine instructions can be defined which better facilitate the process of evaluating a new architecture.

The following are some of the possible disadvantages of microprogramming:

1. Uneconomical for Simple Systems

For machines that are very simple in design and perform a dedicated task, microprogramming tends to be more expensive than conventional control. The hardwired control logic for such systems is simpler and cheaper, compared to the basic hardware facilities that must exist to support microprogramming.

2. Possible Loss of Speed

It is questionable whether microprogramming can be used to achieve the goal of a high instruction-execution rate. Even though high-speed bipolar memories are available for use as control stores, it is possible to design hardwired control logic, with high speed components, that works faster.

3. Cost of Support Software

This is a disadvantage of microprogramming that is often ignored in any economic considerations. Development of microprograms requires some software support packages that have to be developed either by the manufacturer or by the user (the details of this aspect are presented in Chap. 6). In either case, the cost associated with this software development is usually paid for by the user indirectly through the manufacturer or directly in the form of programmers' salaries.

SUMMARY

This chapter has introduced the concept of microprogramming and pointed out the difference between conventional control and microprogrammed control. To put microprogramming in its proper perspective, the possible advantages and disadvantages of using it in machine design were listed.

REFERENCES

[1] WILKES, M. V., W. RENWICK, and D. J. WHEELER, "The Design of the Control Unit of an Electronic Digital Computer," *Proc. of IEE* (June 1958), pp. 121–28.

[2] HUSSON, SAMIR S., *Microprogramming: Principles and Practices* (Englewood Cliffs, N.J.: Prentice-Hall, Inc., 1970), Ch. 1 and 2.

[3] BARON, ROBERT C., and ALBERT T. PICCIRILLI, *Digital Logic and Computer Operations*, (New York: McGraw-Hill Book Company, 1967), pp. 87–92.

FURTHER READINGS

1. BROADBENT, J. K., "Microprogramming and System Architecture," *The Computer Journal*, 17, no. 1 (January 1974), 2–8.

2. JONES, L. H., "An Annotated Bibliography on Microprogramming," *SIGMICRO Newsletter*, 6, no. 2 (July 1975), 8–31.

3. JONES, L. H., "Bibliography," in *Microprogramming and Systems Architecture*, Infotech State of the Art Report 23, ed. C. Boon. Infotech Information Ltd., 1975, pp. 573–90.

4. JONES, L. H., "A Survey of Current Work in Microprogramming," *Computer*, 8, no. 8 (August 1975), 33–38.

5. WILKES, M. V., "Microprogramming Principles and Development," in *Microprogramming and Systems Architecture*, Infotech State of the Art Report 23, ed. C. Boon. Infotech Information Ltd., 1975, pp. 163–79.

CHAPTER TWO

Historical Evolution
of Microprogramming

2.1 INTRODUCTION

As mentioned in Sec. 1.1, Wilkes and his associates were the originators of
the concept of microprogramming. They developed and applied this technique
for the design of the control unit of the EDSAC computer built at Cambridge
University [1, 2]. The main purpose in developing this concept was to sys-
tematize the ad hoc procedures used for the control unit design of a digital
computer.

Sec. 1.3 illustrated how the states of various control points within a
machine, at the time of executing a microinstruction, can be represented by
a corresponding word in the control memory of the machine. Figure 2.1
schematically shows the basic control memory organization proposed by
Wilkes. The output of the control matrix CM is used to activate the various
control points within the machine, whereas the output of the sequencing
matrix SM is used to sequence through a microprogram in the control
memory. A dot at the intersection of a horizontal and a vertical line indicates

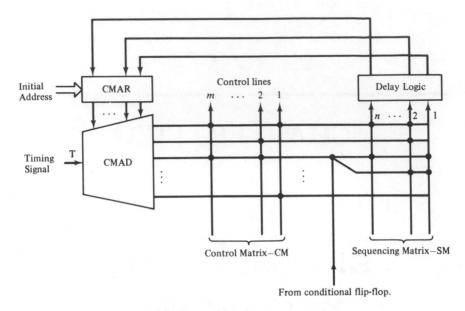

Figure 2.1 Wilkes' Microprogram Control Organization

that when the horizontal line carries a signal, the associated vertical line will get activated. Wilkes' original proposal mentioned the use of either diodes or ferrite cores to achieve this coupling between the horizontal and vertical lines [1]. The microprogrammed control of Fig. 2.1 operates as follows: Initially, the operation code is mapped to a control memory address and this address is put into the control memory address register (CMAR); this address is the beginning address of the microprogram that would execute the machine instruction in question. From CMAR, the address is gated to the control memory address decoder CMAD, which then selects one of the output (horizontal) lines over which the timing signal T is to be sent. Application of the timing signal T activates the selected horizontal line which, in turn, activates a subset of the vertical lines in CM and SM. The output of CM activates a subset of the control points, thus causing the corresponding microoperations to be performed. The output of SM is fed, via a delay network, to CMAR in order to prepare for addressing the next microinstruction; the delay is required to allow sufficient time for the current microinstruction to be executed. Once the new address from the sequencing matrix is loaded into CMAR, the entire cycle is repeated. In this way, microinstructions are executed in a predetermined sequence until the microprogram corresponding to a machine instruction terminates.

The set of output lines from CM and SM taken together form a microinstruction. Thus each microinstruction in this arrangement contains the address of its successor microinstruction. Therefore it is not necessary for the microinstructions of a microprogram to occupy contiguous locations in the control memory.

Like any conventional program, microprograms also require the facility of **conditional branching**. This is schematically shown in Fig. 2.1, where a horizontal line is shown to be split into two lines before entering SM. Only one of the two paths going into SM is selected, depending on whether a specified condition is satisfied or not; this, in turn, selects one of the two possible successor microinstructions. An extension of this scheme can test for more than one condition simultaneously and select one out of many successor microinstructions. It follows quite logically that if a horizontal line is split before it enters CM, then the current as well as the successor microinstruction selection will depend on the condition(s) being tested. There have been many modifications proposed to the basic scheme of Wilkes. An excellent review of these modifications is given by Husson [3].

2.2 HISTORY OF GROWTH

Even though the concept of microprogramming was introduced in 1951, during the 1950s it did not receive any widespread attention or acceptance; only a handful of researchers in laboratories scattered around the world paid any attention to it. The main reason for this was that with the available technology at that time, the cost of control memory was very high. Consequently, microprogrammed implementation of a reasonably complex repertoire of machine instructions would have been very expensive.

Technological breakthroughs of the 1960s resulted in lower memory costs, which made the implementation of microprogrammed control economically feasible. As a result, microprogramming received a much greater amount of attention in the 1960s than it did earlier.

The major thrust for the acceptance of microprogramming as a valuable and viable technique seems to have come with the announcement of the System/360 series of machines by IBM. This corporation used microprogrammed control in the lower numbered models of System/360 (Models 30, 40, 50, and so on) in order to achieve instruction set compatibility across the entire System/360 series. The control units for the larger, high-performance models are hardwired for reasons of speeed. Thus IBM's main motivation for using microprogramming in System/360 machines was to achieve instruction-set compatibility between machines of varying capabilities and internal organizations.

Other major manufacturers, notably Honeywell and RCA, also came forward with their microprogrammed machines; for example, RCA SPECTRA 70/45 was announced as a microprogrammed machine.

Even though the machines mentioned in the preceding paragraphs were among the first commercially available microprogrammed machines, they did not provide any user microprogramming capability. There appear to be two main reasons for this.

1. A reluctance on the part of manufacturers to allow the users to tamper with the repertoire of machine instructions, since it might result in a catastrophic effect on the system software.
2. Fast read-write memories of adequate size, required to support user microprogramming, were relatively expensive until the beginning of the 1970s.

2.3 USER-MICROPROGRAMMABLE MACHINES

Towards the end of the 1960s and the beginning of the 1970s, several machines with user-microprogramming capability appeared on the market. With the continually declining memory costs, more and more user-microprogrammable machines continue to be offered by various manufacturers. Most of these machines fall under the category of minicomputers; some of the manufacturers are Perkin-Elmer, Univac, Hewlett-Packard, Microdata, Data General, and Digital Equipment Corporation.

The basic vehicle for microprogramming by the user in these machines is a writable control store (WCS), which is a fast read/write memory used for storing user-generated microprograms. Conceptually, the control memory in these machines is divided into two parts, as shown in Fig. 2.2. The **read-only memory** (ROM) part of the control memory contains the microcode for executing the basic instruction set of the machine as specified by the manufacturer. The basic instruction set is thus protected, as the ROM contents cannot normally be altered by the user. The **random-access memory** (RAM) part of the control memory is referred to as writable control store (WCS) or *alterable control memory* (ACM). The usual method for loading user-defined microcode into the WCS consists of logically treating the WCS module as an input/output (I/O) device during loading. If the user-defined microcode is used to enhance the existing machine instruction set, then the WCS can be treated as an extension of the ROM control memory. However, if the user microcode defines a completely new machine architecture, the WCS can be logically treated as a replacement for the existing ROM. The implementation details of this scheme may vary from one machine to another; the basic philosophy, however, remains the same.

In addition to the WCS, the manufacturers of user-microprogrammable machines also supply some support software to assist the user in developing microcode. Such support can vary from a simple microassembler to sophisticated debuggers or monitors, simulators with extensive trace features, high-level microprogramming language compilers, and so on. A detailed discussion on developing user microprograms is provided in Chap. 6.

In the mid-1970s, some semiconductor manufacturers introduced microprogrammable microprocessors on the market; these devices are also

Control Memory

```
┌─────────────────────────┐
│                         │
│          ROM            │
│                         │
│   (Microcode for Basic  │
│    Instruction Set)     │
├─────────────────────────┤
│          RAM            │
│                         │
│                         │
│    (User Microcode)     │
└─────────────────────────┘
```

Figure 2.2 Control Memory for User Microprogramming

known as *bit-slice* microprocessors. These microprocessors do not come with any predefined machine instruction set. Instead, they support a manufacturer-specified microinstruction set which is to be used by the system designer (user) to support the instruction set. Another feature that differentiates these devices from the normal user-microprogrammable machines is the absence of any "resident" support software to aid the user in the development of microprograms. This absence occurs because the system on which any software can be run is left to the user to define. However, support software that can run on another (host) machine is usually available to assist the user. In addition, combined hardware and software support systems such as "in-circuit emulators" and "ROM simulators" are also available as user aids. Bit-slice microprocessors will be discussed in more detail in a subsequent chapter.

2.4 HISTORY OF APPLICATIONS

When the concept of microprogramming was introduced, it was considered only as an alternate and more systematic method for designing the control unit of a machine. During the 1950s and early 1960s, the only application of microprogramming consisted of providing some flexibility in the instruction set definition of a machine. The first major application of microprogramming by IBM seems to have led naturally to the next application, *emulation*. Although there are differences of opinion regarding the definition of an *emulator*, in this book we define it as a set of microprograms running on one (host) machine that enables the host to execute programs for another (target) machine. The availability of an emulator is of great help when converting from one machine to another, because it allows the existing software to run on the new machine, thus saving a major conversion cost. As a matter of fact, when the System/360 was introduced, IBM also made available emulators for several of their previous generation machines (for example, 1620, 1401, and 7090). Thus a System/360 with an IBM 1401 emulator, for example, can run either in its native (S/360) mode for System/360 programs or in the emulator (1401) mode when required to run 1401 programs. In fact, it can be argued that a given microprogrammed machine with a specified architecture is just a collection of hardware resources that emulates the given architecture. Thus the various microprogrammed models of System/360, for example, emulate a common architecture. Emulation has also been used between machines of two different manufacturers; an example of this is presented in Chap. 9.

Another application area that has evolved since the late 1960s is microprogramming support for operating systems [4, 5, 6]. There are two basic approaches that have been followed for this purpose. The first one consists of identifying those functions of an operating system that are used very frequently. These functions are then microprogrammed in order to increase the overall speed of the operating system. The second approach consists of defining a set of primitives that are microprogrammed; these primitives are then used as building blocks to construct an operating system.

Microprogramming has also been used for the support of high-level programming languages—both in terms of processing and execution of these languages [7–11]. For support in the processing of high-level languages, it can be used to create special instructions to assist the compiler writer. For the execution of a high-level language via microprogramming, three possible approaches can be used.

1. The language can be compiled into microcode instead of being compiled into the usual machine code.
2. The language can be compiled into some intermediate-level language that is designed to be interpreted efficiently by the lower-level microcode.
3. The language can be directly *interpreted* by microcode, bypassing any compilation at all.

Some of the other areas in which microprogramming has found applications are in the implementation of instructions or functions or both in microprocessors and calculators, in the design of peripheral controllers, in graphics, and in teleprocessing.

SUMMARY

This chapter traced the historical growth of microprogramming since the introduction of the concept in 1951 by Wilkes. It also attempted to show how microprogramming has evolved from an alternate technique for the control unit design of a computer to a powerful concept which not only allows one to define a flexible machine architecture but also finds applications in other areas of design and application of computer systems.

REFERENCES

[1] WILKES, M. V., W. RENWICK and D. J. WHEELER, "The Design of the Control Unit of an Electronic Digital Computer," *Proceedings of IEE* (June 1958), pp. 121–28.

[2] WILKES, M. V., "The Growth of Interest in Microprogramming," *ACM Computing Surveys*, 1, no. 3 (September 1969), 139–45.

[3] HUSSON, SAMIR S., *Microprogramming: Principles and Practices*, (Englewood Cliffs, N.J.: Prentice-Hall, Inc., 1970) pp. 22–38.

[4] WERKHEISER, A. H., "Microprogrammed Operating Systems," *Third Annual Workshop on Microprogramming Preprints*, ACM (October 1970).

[5] BURKHARDT, W. H. and R. C. RANDELL, "Design of Operating Systems with Microprogrammed Implementation," Report No. PIT–CS–BU–73–01 University of Pittsburg, (September 1973).

[6] LISKOV, B. H., "The Design of the Venus Operating System," *Communications of the ACM*, 15, no. 3 (March 1972), 144–49.

[7] WEBER, H., "A Microprogrammed Implementation of EULER on IBM System/360 Model 30," *Communications of the ACM*, 10, no. 9 (September 1967), 549–58.

[8] HASSITT, A., J. LAGESCHULTE, and L. E. LYON, "Implementation of a High Level Language Machine," *Communications of the ACM*, 16, no. 4 (April 1973), 199–212.

[9] BROCA, F. R., and R. E. MERWIN, "Direct Microprogrammed Execution of Intermediate Text from a High Level Language Compiler," *Proceedings of ACM National Conference* (1973), pp. 57–63.

[10] MOULTON, P., "Microprogrammed Subprocessors for Compilation and Execution of High Level Languages," *Seventh Annual Workshop on Microprogramming* (Preprints), ACM (September 1974), pp. 74–79.

[11] HASSIT, A., and L. E. LYON, "An APL Emulator on System/370," *IBM Systems Journal*, no. 4 (1976), pp. 358–78.

FURTHER READINGS

1. BROADBENT, J. K., "Microprogramming and System Architecture," *The Computer Journal*, 17, no. 1 (January 1974), 2–8.

2. JONES, L. H., "An Annotated Bibliography on Microprogramming," *SIG-MICRO Newsletter*, 6, no. 2 (July 1975), 8–31.

3. JONES, L. H., "Bibliography," in *Microprogramming and Systems Architecture*, pp. 573–90. Infotech State of the Art Report 23, ed. C. Boon, Infotech Information Ltd., 1975.

4. JONES, L. H., "A Survey of Current Work in Microprogramming," *Computer*, 8, no. 8 (August 1975), 33–38.
5. WILKES, M. V., "Microprogramming Principles and Development," in *Microprogramming and Systems Architecture*, pp. 163–79. Infotech State of the Art Report 23, ed. C. Boon, Infotech Information Ltd., 1975.

CHAPTER THREE

Basic Computer Organization: an Overview

3.1 INTRODUCTION

The previous two chapters introduced the basic notion of microprogramming and traced its historical evolution to the present stage, where it has become an accepted tool in defining a computer system's architecture. This chapter provides a brief overview of computer organization to place the role of microprogramming in a proper perspective later on. The chapter can serve as a refresher for those readers who have studied computer organization before but would like a review before proceeding further. Readers unfamiliar with the basic concepts of computer organization may not find the chapter detailed enough; if so, they should refer to the literature in the references for further details [1–15]. The goal, however, is to provide enough information for this latter class of readers so that they can proceed to the subsequent chapters without referring to additional literature.

Microprogramming has been introduced as a somewhat more orderly procedure than the hardwired method of control for controlling the operations of a digital computer. The following sections talk about hardware resources and discuss how the organization of a computer system depends on these resources. **Resources,** in computer organization jargon, are the objects (such as the arithmetic and logic unit (ALU), registers, and control flip-flops) operated on by the control mechanism (either microprogrammed or hardwired).

3.2 CPU ORGANIZATION

The central processing unit (CPU) performs the basic processing of all information in a computer system. Figure 3.1 schematically shows the organization of a typical register-oriented CPU, which can perform all the basic functions of a modern computer system. The following *resources* are shown in Fig. 3.1.

1. Instruction register (IR) and control registers (CTRG 1–CTRG 5).
2. Program counter (PC).
3. General purpose registers (GPR 1–GPR 4).
4. Memory address register (MAR).
5. Memory data register (MDR).
6. Input/output register (IOR).
7. Arithmetic and logic unit (ALU) and associated output latch.
8. Control flip-flops.
9. Return address stack (RAS).

Each of these elements will be discussed in the context of the role it plays in the various design considerations of a computer system. The number of registers in a CPU depends largely on the goals of the system design and—to some extent—on the designer. The number of registers shown in Fig. 3.1 is sufficient to present the basic concepts of computer organization without any loss of generality.

The four elements (resources) discussed in the following paragraphs, ALU, PC, MAR, and MDR, form the core of a stored program or von Neumann machine.

ALU:

This is the pivotal element in the CPU; all the registers serve either as a source or destination of information to this element. The functional operation of the ALU can be represented by the notation

$$C \longleftarrow A \quad OP \quad B$$

where OP denotes an arithmetic or logical operation performed by the ALU on the inputs A and B and C denotes the output of ALU. The number of

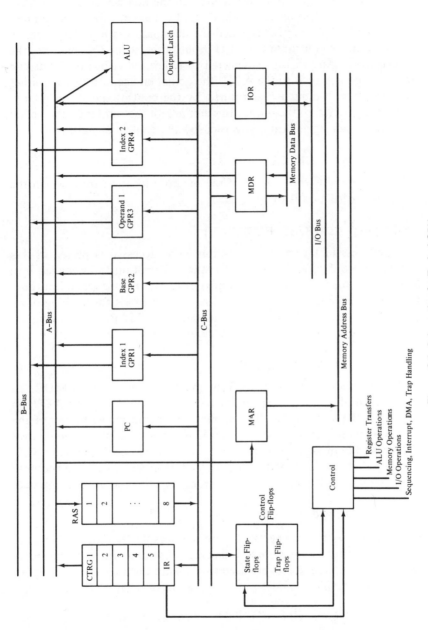

Figure 3.1 Schematic of a Typical CPU

27

bits constituting the inputs A or B depends on the number of bits the ALU has been designed to handle at a time. Output C also has the same number of bits as A or B. This number is called the **data path width** of the machine. The inputs A and B constitute the ALU input buses, while C constitutes the ALU output bus. Any register connected to either the A-bus or B-bus can provide the inputs A or B to the ALU; the actual choice of a register either as the A-input or B-input is determined by the control signals. Similarly, any register connected to the output bus can accept the output C, the actual choice of a register again being governed by the control signals.

PROGRAM COUNTER:

The PC contains the address of the memory location from which the next machine instruction is to be fetched.

MEMORY ADDRESS REGISTER:

The address of the memory location to be accessed is placed in this register. In the configuration in Fig. 3.1, the information to be loaded into the MAR can come from any of the control registers, PC, or general purpose registers. For example, PC contents are loaded into MAR for fetching of an instruction, whereas GPR 4 may be loaded into MAR for fetching an operand. Different examples of how MAR is loaded are shown in Fig. 3.9.

MEMORY DATA REGISTER:

The information that is read from memory is available in MDR. In Fig. 3.1, the MDR contents can be moved to the A-input of the ALU; in some other configurations, MDR contents can be transferred to any of the registers. Depending on the type of instruction being executed, the control may either modify or keep the data unchanged as it passes through the ALU and then load it into one of the registers as required. For memory-write operation, data is loaded into the MDR before the write operation is initiated.

3.2.1. Index Registers

Figure 3.1 shows that two general purpose registers, GPR 1 and GPR 4, are used as index registers in the system. Index registers are useful in the memory-address calculation process and are used to sequence through a set of memory locations. For example, suppose a memory address is calculated as

$$\text{MAR} \longleftarrow (\text{Index/GPR 1}) + (\text{Control/CTRG 1})$$

where (T/X) denotes the contents of register X of type T. Now, suppose

$$(\text{CTRG 1}) = n$$

where (R) denotes the contents of register R. If (GPR 1) = 0 at the beginning of a program loop, then the initial effective memory address is given by

$$(MAR) = n + 0 = n$$

If GPR 1 is incremented by 1 each time through the program loop, that is, if

$$GPR\ 1 \longleftarrow (GPR\ 1) + 1$$

then the successive values of MAR would be n + 1, n + 2, n + 3, . . . , until the program comes out of the loop according to some prespecified criterion. It is clear, therefore, that successive memory locations are addressed by manipulating the contents of the index register. A data structure stored in memory in the form of a linear array can be accessed in this manner. Multiple indexing with more than one index register (for example, GPR 1 and GPR 4) can be used for accessing more complex data structures such as multidimensional arrays.

3.2.2. Base Register

In Fig. 3.1, GPR 2 is also called a **base register.** A base register is a very useful resource in the CPU and is used primarily for two purposes.

1. Economizing on the address field of an instruction.

To illustrate how a base register is used for this purpose, we consider the instruction format shown in Fig. 3.2. The OPCODE field specifies the type of operation (add, subtract, and so on) to be performed by the CPU. Considering a minimal set of operations, say eight, we need a 3-bit field for specifying the OPCODE. For this particular instruction, assume that Operand 1 is fetched from a GPR and the result of the operation is routed back to the same GPR. Since there are four GPRs in the configuration shown in Fig. 3.1, 2 bits are needed to specify the Operand 1/destination address field uniquely. Suppose Operand 2 is fetched from the memory whose size is assumed to be 256 K, requiring 18 bits to address any location. Therefore an instruction with the format shown in Fig. 3.2 would require 3 + 2 + 18 = 23 bits for encoding. With the use of a base register, however, the bit size of the instruction can be reduced.

OPCODE	(Operand 1)/(Destination Address)	Operand 2 Address

Figure 3.2 An Instruction Format

Suppose that instead of specifying the Operand 2 address directly in an instruction, it is computed as follows:

Effective Operand 2 address = Contents of a GPR (base register)
+ Contents of Operand 2 field
in the instruction

In this scheme, the base register would contain an **initial address**(*base address*), whereas the Operand 2 field would specify the location of Operand 2 *relative* to the base address. For this reason, the Operand 2 field in such a scheme is named the **displacement field.** Thus

$$\text{MAR} \longleftarrow (\text{Base register}) + (\text{Displacement field})$$

If only one GPR is used as a base register, as in Fig. 3.1, then it need not be explicitly specified in an instruction. The size of the displacement field can be chosen to allow access to a memory block of reasonable size, say 256 words. In this case, an instruction of the type shown in Fig. 3.2 would require $3 + 2 + 8 = 13$ bits for encoding. However, if we decide that any of the four GPRs shown in Fig. 3.1 can be used as a base register, then the instruction would require an additional 2-bit field to specify a base register, increasing its size to 15 bits. Either of these two cases represents a substantial reduction in the bit size of an instruction requiring a memory reference for an operand. The use of the "base-displacement" addressing technique generally results in instructions that are more memory efficient than the instructions that use "direct" addressing of a memory location.

2. Program Relocatability.

Economy in the size of an instruction is not the only advantage offered by a base register. In case of very large programs—for example, an operating system—different segments of the program do not reside in memory at the same time. Before the time of *actual* loading from some auxiliary storage (such as a disk), it is not known where in the memory a particular program segment would be loaded. The base register is used to advantage in such a situation by loading a base address in it and by loading the program segment *relative* to this base address. Changing the contents of the base register does not change the instructions, but it changes all the relative addresses in the program segment. As an example, Fig. 3.3 shows the values in the base register and displacement field of an instruction when the program segment containing the instruction is loaded at different places in the memory; the displacement field contents remain identical in both the cases.

3.2.3. General-Purpose Registers

As the name implies, GPRs can be used for a variety of purposes, such as index or base registers, operand (source) registers, or result (destination) registers—in fact, for any purpose permitted by the instruction formats of a

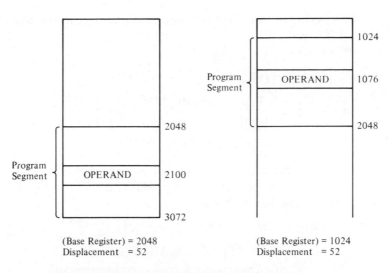

(Base Register) = 2048
Displacement = 52

(Base Register) = 1024
Displacement = 52

Figure 3.3 Use of Base Register for Relative Addressing

particular computer system. It is the programmer who specifies the use of these registers for the intended purpose.

In certain architectures, some of the GPRs are logically organized in the form of a **stack** in addition to their normal mode of operation; this is depicted in Fig. 3.4. In this mode of operation, one of the GPRs can be used as a stack pointer, which points to the next register available for information storage. If the GPRs are organized in the form of a **last in, first out**

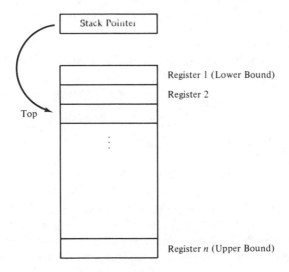

Figure 3.4 A Register Stack

(LIFO) stack, then the stack pointer conceptually points to the top of the stack. In a LIFO stack, the operation of data stacking—known as the *PUSH operation*—can be described as follows.

> PUSH: TOP ← TOP +1
>
> If TOP ≤ UPPER BOUND
>
> THEN STACK [TOP] ← OPERAND
>
> ELSE SET STACK OVERFLOW

where TOP denotes the contents of the stack pointer register. Similarly, the operation of removing an item from the top of the stack, known as the *POP operation*, can be described as follows:

> POP: IF TOP < LOWER BOUND
>
> THEN SET STACK UNDERFLOW
>
> ELSE REGISTER X ← STACK [TOP]
>
> TOP ← TOP − 1

where X denotes the register that receives the contents of the top of the stack. STACK OVERFLOW and STACK UNDERFLOW are two control flags (flip-flops) required for monitoring when the stack is full or empty, respectively.

3.2.4. Input/Output Register

Typically, any communication from the CPU to an external input/output (I/O) device entails the following sequence of operations.

1. Selection of a particular device.
2. Determining the status of the device, for example, whether it is ready for operation or busy with an I/O operation.
3. Executing a control operation, such as positioning the carriage in a console typewriter, if necessary.
4. Sending or receiving information to or from the device.
5. Signaling the end of the operation or the inability to perform the operation due to some reason.

For all such dialogue between the CPU and an I/O device, the IOR is the register through which the CPU sends its commands or data to a device and receives information from the device. In some architectures, the control and data transfer activities of I/O operations are separated and two different registers are provided for these functions—an I/O control register (IOCR) for exchange of control information and an I/O data register (IODR) for data transfer purposes.

3.2.5. Return Address Stack

This is a LIFO stack of eight registers used for storing return addresses during subroutine calls. Its use is explained in Sec. 3.5.6.

3.3 INSTRUCTION FORMATS

An instruction format essentially specifies the "layout" of an instruction; that is, information about the various parts (fields) of an instruction, the size of these fields, and the kind of information these fields are to contain. With reference to the CPU organization of Fig. 3.1, the general instruction format would be as shown in Fig. 3.2.

Section 3.2 discussed the index and base register methods of addressing. It shows that there are variations in the method of address formation for operand fetching; a **mode** field in the instruction format represents this variability. This mode field can be combined either with the opcode field or the operand field to yield two variations of the general instruction format of Fig. 3.2. These variations will be referred to as Type 1 format and Type 2 format, respectively, in the subsequent discussion. Figure 3.5 and 3.6 show Type 1 and Type 2 instruction formats, respectively, for the configuration shown in Fig. 3.1; the numbers on top of the various fields indicate the bit sizes of these fields. As a matter of fact, the formats shown are somewhat more general than Fig. 3.1 requires. The base, index, and register operand fields are all 4 bits wide, whereas a 2-bit field would be enough in the context of Fig. 3.1. These formats could be used for a CPU with up to 16 GPRs. The bit size of the instructions in these formats is a multiple of 8; this is in conformity with the organization of most present day computers. For both these formats, the secondary fields (shown in the figures) of an instruction are interpreted after the analysis of the mode bits in the primary fields.

The main characteristics of Type 1 format are as follows.

1. Larger instruction repertoire (64 instructions in our example).
2. Less flexibility in operand addressing (4 modes in our example).

The chief characteristics of Type 2 format are the following.

1. Smaller instruction repertoire (16 instructions in our example).
2. Greater flexibility in addressing (16 modes in our example).

The various instruction types belonging to the Type 1 format are now briefly described.

1. Register/Register (RR) Type
   a. Operand 1 is in the register specified by Reg. 1 field.
   b. Operand 2 is in the register specified by Reg. 2 field.
   c. Result of the operation is routed to the Operand 1 register.

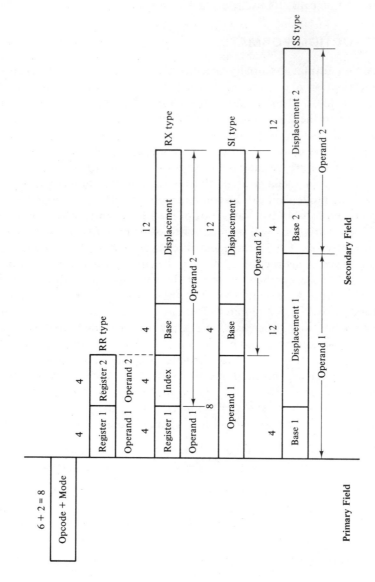

Figure 3.5 Type 1 Instruction Format

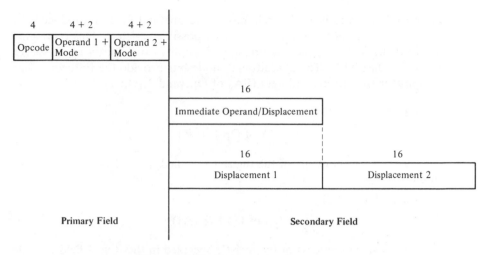

Figure 3.6 Type 2 Instruction Format

2. Register/Index (RX) Type
   a. Operand 1 is in the register specified by Reg. 1 field.
   b. Operand 2 is fetched from a memory location with address (Index) + (Base) + Displacement; that is, the contents of the register specified in the index field, the contents of the register specified in the base field, and the contents of the displacement field are added together to form the Operand 2 address.
   c. The result of the operation is routed to the Operand 1 register.
3. Storage/Immediate Operand (SI) Type
   a. Operand 1 is specified as part of the instruction (immediate operand).
   b. Operand 2 is fetched from a memory location with an address that is obtained by adding the contents of the register specified in the base field with the contents of the displacement field.
   c. The result of the operation is stored in Operand 2 location.
4. Storage/Storage (SS) Type
   a. Operand 1 is fetched from a memory location with an address that is obtained by adding the contents of the register specified in Base 1 field with the contents of the Displacement 1 field.
   b. Operand 2 is fetched from a memory location whose address is obtained by adding the contents of the register specified in Base 2 field with the contents of the Displacement 2 field.
   c. The result of the operation is stored in Operand 1 location.

Let us consider the simplest of these instruction types, the RR type, and see how its addressing flexibility can be increased by introducing some additional mode information in the format. Let the modified RR type format be:

8	4	2	2
Opcode + mode	R1	Mode	R2

Here we have introduced 2 mode bits in the operand field and reduced the range of Reg. 2 specification from 16 to 4 possible registers. This represents a direct tradeoff between addressing flexibility and hardware resource utilization flexibility. The 2 additional mode bits provide the following four options for the effective address (EA) of Operand 1 (Op 1):

1. *Normal mode*

$$\text{EA of Op } 1 = R1$$

That is, the contents of the register specified in the Reg. 1 field constitute Operand 1.

2. *Indirect mode*

$$\text{EA of Op } 1 = (R1)$$

That is, the contents of the register specified in the Reg. 1 field provide the *address* of Operand 1.

3. *Autoincrementing mode*

$$\text{EA of Op } 1 = (R1)$$
$$R1 \longleftarrow (R1) + 1$$

That is, the contents of the register specified in the Reg. 1 field provide the address of Operand 1; at the end of the operation, the contents of this register are incremented by 1.

4. *Autodecrementing mode*

$$\text{EA of Op } 1 = (R\ 1)$$
$$R1 \longleftarrow (R\ 1) - 1$$

That is, the contents of the register specified in the Reg. 1 field provide the address of Operand 1; at the end of the operation, the contents of this register are decremented by 1.

All these modes can be extended to both the operands as well as to the other instruction types belonging to the Type 1 format. In this manner, the system designer can tailor the instruction formats according to the system design requirements or goals.

3.4 CONTROL FLIP-FLOPS AND THEIR FUNCTIONS

This section describes the various flip-flops or "flags" that are generally required in a computer system for control purposes.

3.4.1. Fetching and Executing Instructions

Different instruction formats have been explained in the previous section. The locations of some of the fields shown in these formats make them a bit cumbersome to manipulate in the fetch/execute control that will be described in this section. For the sake of convenience, therefore, the locations of the fields can be redefined to suit this control structure. This is shown in Fig. 3.7, where R is a register, X is an index register, B is a base register, D is the displacement value, and I represents an "immediate" operand. The indices 1 and 2 are associated with the first and second operand, respectively. The redistribution of fields does not in any way change the function of a particular instruction. In the subsequent discussion, it is assumed that 32 bits are read from or written into the memory in a single memory operation. This, however, does not represent any limitation on the generality of the discussion since any other memory word size—for example, 8 or 16 bits—can be accomodated quite easily with minor changes in the control structure.

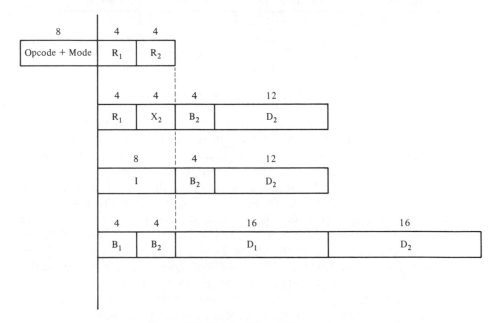

Figure 3.7 Redefined Type 1 Format

Figure 3.8 shows the master clock used for synchronizing the various operations in the CPU; the master clock is used to generate five phase signals t_1 through t_5, as shown in the figure. Also, T_1 through T_5 represent five time slots between the beginning of one phase to the beginning of the next. Figure

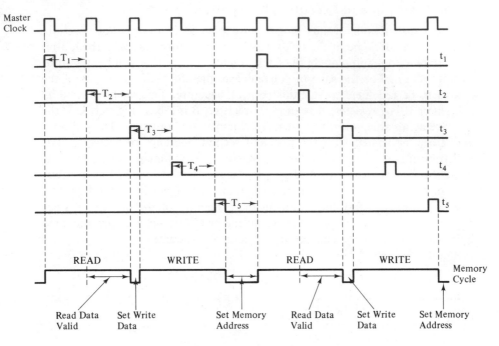

Figure 3.8 CPU and Memory Timing Signals

3.8 also shows the memory cycle timing for this machine. Control functions consist basically of activities; some of these can occur concurrently, while others depend on the successful completion of a set of activities. Concurrent activities are grouped together in the same clock phase, while dependent activities occur in different clock phases according to a predetermined sequence. Figure 3.9 shows an operation sequence for the fetching and execution of instructions in different formats. As illustrated, for the RR format, the contents of MDR are moved to IR and the contents of PC are incremented by 1 concurrently in the T_2 slot since they are nonconflicting activities. In the T_3 slot, the actual operation is performed as the instruction becomes available in IR only during the previous time slot.

For the SS format, PC is incremented in two steps. This is because a SS-type instruction is more than one word long and the memory has to be accessed twice to fetch the full instruction. Since the time taken by different operations within the *same* format may be different, the loading of the result in the destination location is not generally shown in Fig. 3.9. According to this control structure, the result is available in the first T_4 slot after the particular operation is completed. In the SS format, writing the result in the first operand location has been shown with a time discontinuity after the beginning of the operation to be performed. In order to implement

Figure 3.9 Fetch/Execute Operations

Time	RR	RR (R2 indirect)	RX	SI	SS
T5	MAR ← (PC)	MAR ← (PC)	MAR ← (PC)	MAR ← (PC)	MAR ← (PC)
T1	Read	Read	Read	Read	Read
T2	IR ← (MDR); PC ← (PC) +1	IR ← (MDR); PC ← (PC) +1	IR ← (MDR); PC ← (PC) +1	IR ← (MDR); PC ← (PC) +1	IR ← (MDR); PC ← (PC) +1
T3	R 1 OP R 2 → R 1	No op	CTRG 1 ← (B 2) + D 2	CTRG 1 ← (B 2) + D 2	CTRG 1 ← (B 1) + D 1
T4	End	No op	CTRG 1 ← (CTRG 1) + (X 2)	No op	No op
T5		MAR ← (R 2)	MAR ← (CTRG 1)	MAR ← (CTRG 1)	MAR ← (CTRG 1)
T1		Read	Read	Read	Read
T2		R 2 ← (MDR)	CTRG 2 ← (MDR)	CTRG 2 ← (MDR)	CTRG 2 ← (MDR)
T3		R1 OP R2 → R1	R 1 OP CTRG 2 → R 1	RI OP CTRG 2 → CTGR2	No op
T4		End	End	MDR ← (CTRG 2)	No op
T5				No op	MAR ← (PC)
T1				No op	Read
T2				No op	CIRG 3 ← (MDR), PC ← (PC) + 1
T3				Write	CTRG 3 ← (B 2) + D 2
T4				End	No op
T5					MAR ← (CTRG 3)
T1					Read
T2					CTRG 4 ← (MDR)
T3					CTRG 2 OP CTRG 4 → CTRG 2
T4					No op
T5					MAR ← (CTRG 1)
T1					MDR ← (CTRG 2)
T2					No op
T3					Write
T4					End

the control logic for the fetch and execute cycles of an instruction, some signals and state flip-flops are needed in the CPU; these are briefly described as follows.

1. SYSTEM RESET (SR)

When the machine is turned on or when the system RESET switch is pressed, this signal is generated. It brings the control unit to a predetermined initial state.

2. RUN

This is a flip-flop set by the START switch when the signal SR is low. The flip-flop is reset by the HALT condition.

3. STOP

This flip-flop is set by the STOP switch and reset by the START switch.

4. END

Though synchronized by the master clock, the time required for the execution of different instructions varies according to the complexity of the function performed by the instruction. The END flip-flop is set asynchronously when the operation specified by the opcode of the instruction is completed, and by the SR signal. It is reset when the FETCH flip-flop is reset.

5. TYPE

This flip-flop is set by the *mode* field of an instruction; it helps distinguish between one-word and multiple-word instructions. It is reset when the EXECUTE flip-flop is set.

6. FETCH

Setting of this flip-flop starts the sequence of fetch and execution cycles. During the fetch cycle, an instruction at the memory location to which the PC points is fetched and placed in the instruction register (IR). The set and reset conditions of the flip-flop are given by

$$(\text{FETCH}) \text{ set } = \text{RUN. END. } t_1$$
$$(\text{FETCH}) \text{ reset } = \text{TYPE. } t_3$$

7. EXECUTE

Setting of this flip-flop starts the execution cycle of an instruction; during this time, the IR contents are analyzed by the control unit and the operation specified by the opcode is performed. Therefore this flip-flop controls the execution of operations required by the instruction. The set and reset conditions for this flip-flop are given by

$$(\text{EXECUTE}) \text{ set } = \overline{\text{FETCH}}. \, t_3$$

$$(\text{EXECUTE}) \text{ reset } = \text{END}. \, t_5 + \text{SR}$$

8. HALT

The setting of this flip-flop stops the sequence of fetch and execution cycles. It can be set only after the end of the current execution cycle. The set and reset conditions of this flip-flop are given by

$$(\text{HALT}) \text{ set } = \text{END}. \text{ STOP}. \, t_5$$

$$(\text{HALT}) \text{ reset } = \text{START}$$

3.4.2. Program State Flip-Flops

Apart from the flip-flops discussed in Sec. 3.4.1 that represent the machine states, there are other necessary flip-flops that represent the various conditions arising out of a given ALU operation. These are briefly described as follows.

1. CARRY

This flip-flop is set when there is a carry out of the most significant position of the ALU. For example, if two n-bit numbers are added in the ALU and the result is $(n + 1)$ bits wide, then the CARRY flip-flop would be set.

2. ZERO

This flip-flop is set when the result of an ALU operation is zero. For example, if the ALU performs the operation $A - B$ when A and B are equal, the result would be zero and the ZERO flip-flop would be set.

3. SIGN

This flip-flop indicates the sign of the result of an ALU operation. If the sign of the result is positive (leftmost bit 0) the flip-flop is reset, whereas if the result is negative (leftmost bit 1), the flip-flop is set.

4. EVEN/ODD

This flip-flop indicates whether the result of an ALU operation represents an even number or an odd number. If the rightmost (least significant) bit of the result is 0, then the result is an even number (multiple of two) and the flip-flop is reset; if the rightmost bit is 1, then the result is an odd number and the flip-flop is set.

Each of these flip-flops—sometimes referred to as **flags**—can act as a decision variable for the conditional branch class of instructions described later.

3.4.3. Interrupt Mechanism and Flip-Flop

Interrupt is a general mechanism which disrupts the execution of a program at the current location specified by the PC. It arises out of some condition requiring immediate attention of the CPU. When an interrupt occurs, the instruction currently in execution is completed and control transfers to some location in memory that is the address of the interrupt service routine; this address is not specified in the interrupted program. The interrupt service routine is subsequently executed and once the interrupt has been "serviced," control is transferred back to the interrupted program. Since an interrupt forces a branch to a location not specified in the interrupted program, this mechanism is program independent and is thus a feature of the system.

Interrupts can be categorized by two main types.

1. Programmed.
2. Naturally occurring asynchronous events consisting of the following.
   a. Input/output.
   b. Hard errors.
   c. Traps.

Each of these terms will be explained during the course of discussion in this section.

In a computer system, interrupts are arranged in an order of priority, which means some interrupts take precedence over others; an interrupt with higher priority must be serviced before one with a lower priority even if the processor has to temporarily abandon servicing the lower-priority interrupt. An example of this phenomenon is frequently found in servicing I/O interrupts, where devices with widely different data transfer rates generate interrupt signals for processor attention. If the processor is servicing an interrupt from a slow device (such as a teletypewriter) and a high-speed device (such as a disk) generates an interrupt signal, the processor must suspend the servicing of the former interrupt and begin servicing the latter. Interrupts caused by high-speed devices have a greater priority in comparison with those caused by slower devices because a high-speed device can wait for a relatively small amount of time for the CPU to grant its service request. If the CPU takes too long to respond to this request, the data from the device would be lost because it arrives at the fixed data-transfer rate of the device.

Depending on a computer system's design, the priority structure among the interrupts can either be **static** (preassigned) or **dynamic** (program alterable). Figure 3.10 shows a schematic diagram for a dynamic-priority interrupt system. Each individual interrupt line representing a distinct

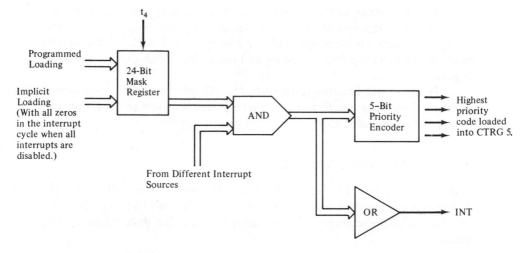

Figure 3.10 Dynamic Priority Interrupt System Schematic

interrupt source is ANDed with the corresponding bit of a mask register. This example uses a 24-bit mask register, which is determined by the format of the ENIM instruction discussed in Sec. 3.5.8. Masking is necessary because subsequent interrupts from a particular source or level and from all other sources or levels with lower priority are not recognized until the first interrupt request is serviced. The mask register can either be loaded under program control with a specified masking pattern or implicitly loaded with an all-zero pattern. Masking operation is discussed in connection with the ENIM instruction in Sec. 3.5.8; the mask register is loaded at time phase t_4. As shown in Fig. 3.10, 24 mask lines go to a priority encoder, which encodes the current highest priority interrupt into a 5-bit binary code. This code is loaded into the control register CTRG 5.

The masked lines going into the encoder are also ORed to generate the signal INT, which sets the INTERRUPT flip-flop signaling the presence of an interrupt. The FETCH and EXECUTE equations presented in Sec. 3.4.1 can now be modified to accomodate the interrupt mechanism.

$$(\text{INTERRUPT) set} \quad = \text{INT. END. } t_5$$

$$(\text{INTERRUPT) reset} = \text{INTERRUPT. } t_4 + \text{SR}$$

$$(\text{FETCH) set} \quad\quad = \overline{\text{INTERRUPT}}. \text{ RUN. END. } t_1$$

$$(\text{FETCH) reset} \quad = \text{TYPE. } t_3$$

$$(\text{EXECUTE) set} \quad = \overline{\text{FETCH}}. \overline{\text{INTERRUPT}}. t_3$$

$$(\text{EXECUTE) reset} \quad = \text{END. } t_5 + \text{SR}$$

Thus the setting of the INTERRUPT flip-flop at t_5 prevents the setting of the FETCH flip-flop at t_1 (thereby temporarily stopping an instruction fetch) and starts an interrupt cycle. When the INTERRUPT flip-flop is reset, the FETCH flip-flop can be set and the normal fetch-execute sequence begins.

The interrupt handling procedure for I/O interrupts will be discussed in detail. Once the principles of I/O interrupt handling are grasped, they can be applied or extended to any type of interrupt handling.

3.4.4. I/O Interrupt Handling

Suppose a data byte is to be sent from an I/O device to the IOR. When the device is ready for data transfer, a particular status flag from the device is set. The following sequence of steps describes how the data transfer takes place.

1. Read device status.
2. Check if the device is ready to send data. If ready, proceed to Step 3; else go to 1.
3. Input data from device to IOR.
4. Move data from IOR to desired destination.

Until the device is ready to transfer data, the CPU loops between Steps 1 and 2; these two steps, in fact, represent the overhead required for the actual objective of moving data from the device to the CPU. For noncritical data processing requirements, this method merits attention because of its simplicity. It is known as the **polling method** or **programmed I/O**. However, the disadvantage of the method is that the CPU gets tied up in status checking until the device is ready for data transfer. Meanwhile, therefore, the CPU cannot perform any other useful task. For this reason, another method for I/O is frequently preferred; namely, **interrupt-driven I/O**. In this method, the CPU does not waste its time in a status checking loop. Instead, it carries on with the program under execution *until* a device is ready for data transfer, at which time it signals its readiness to the CPU by generating an interrupt signal. When such an interrupt occurs, the CPU suspends the program under execution and services the I/O interrupt, that is, it performs the I/O operation and then returns to the original program to continue processing until another interrupt occurs.

Figure 3.11 shows a partial map of the main memory of a machine. Initially, the CPU executes instructions in the part of the memory labeled *Main Segment*. When an interrupt occurs, the following actions take place during the interrupt cycle.

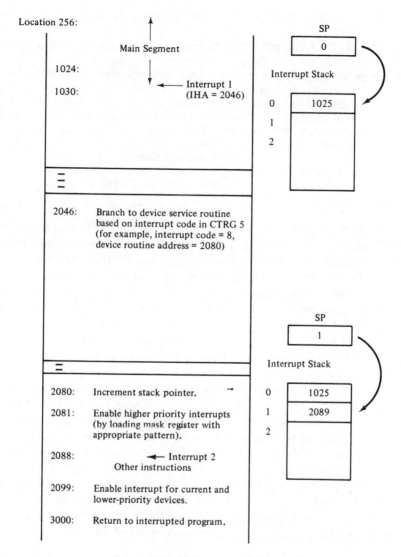

Figure 3.11 I/O Interrupt Handling

1.   (Stack Pointer) ←— (PC)

That is, the PC content—the return address—is stored in a stack location with address given by the stack pointer.

2.   Mask Register ←— 0

That is, all further interrupts are (temporarily) masked.

3.   PC, MAR ← Interrupt Handler Address

That is, the CPU gets ready to execute the interrupt service routine.

There are generally two options used to implement this scheme.

1. The stack pointer and interrupt handler address can be stored in two CPU control registers that have been previously loaded with proper values. In addition, the interrupt stack (for storing return addresses) is also implemented as a set of CPU hardware registers. In this case, the interrupt cycle takes only one (t_1-t_5) time slot before the fetch cycle is restarted. This, in fact, is the scheme assumed in this example; the scheme is reflected in the modified set/reset equations for the INTERRUPT and FETCH flip-flops outlined in Sec. 3.4.3.

Referring to Fig. 3.11, suppose the stack pointer (SP) and interrupt handler address (IHA) register contents are initially zero and 2046, respectively. The figure shows that the first interrupt occurs while the instruction at location 1024 is being executed. When this happens, the return address (1025) is stored in stack location zero, which is initially the top of the stack, all further interrupts are masked by loading the mask register with zeros (this has to be built into the hardware), and IHA register contents are moved to PC and MAR. The CPU then starts executing the interrupt handler and a branch is taken to the particular device service routine. The latter routine first updates the stack pointer and enables higher-priority interrupts. When a second interrupt occurs at location 2088, the return address (2089) is stored in stack location 1 and the rest of the procedure already outlined follows. The interrupt stack is a LIFO stack; when the interrupt service routine of a particular device finishes execution, a return is made to the interrupted program by moving the last entry in the interrupt stack to PC. This entry is then deleted from the stack. In the case of the example in Fig. 3.11, control will transfer to location 2089 after the second interrupt is serviced; eventually control will transfer to location 1025 after the first interrupt has been completely serviced. The LIFO characteristic of the interrupt stack ensures that the interrupts are serviced in the decreasing order of priority.

2. Two fixed memory locations (usually 0 and 1) contain the SP and the IHA, respectively; a block of memory is used as the interrupt stack. In this case, the interrupt cycle requires multiple (t_1-t_5) time slots before restarting the fetch cycle. For example, one memory cycle—or (t_1-t_5) slot—is required to get the stack pointer from location 0. Another memory cycle is required to store the return address in the interrupt stack, and so on. This scheme is generally used in machines with very limited hardware resources within the CPU.

In servicing I/O interrupts, one should ensure that the maximum service delay for any particular device is never exceeded.

3.4.5. Direct Memory Access (DMA) and DMA Flip-Flop

As pointed out in Sec. 3.4.4, when an I/O device causes an interrupt, a branch is taken to the interrupt handler; eventually control transfers to the particular device service routine. The time taken for executing these steps of the interrupt service program is called the **minimum interrupt service time** for the device; this time is computed on the assumption that no higher priority interrupt arises while executing that service routine. If, however, a higher priority interrupt occurs, naturally the service time for the former device increases, and it continues to increase if other higher priority interrupts occur. For relatively slow devices (teletypewriter or card reader, for example) this increased service time is almost insignificant compared to the device data transfer rate. For devices such as high-speed disk drives, however, the interrupt service time may prove to be critical. Too much delay in servicing a device can result in the loss of some data since data transfer takes place at a fixed rate determined by the device. Figure 3.12 graphically represents this situation, in which the request for transmission of the next data byte is lost because the previous interrupt has not been serviced in time.

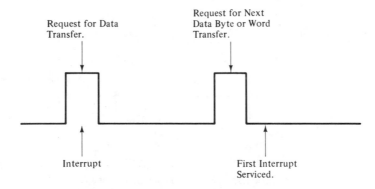

Figure 3.12 Effect of Interrupt Service Delay

A solution to this problem is to set up a *direct path* between the memory and a high-speed device, without routing the data through the CPU as required by the normal interrupt handling procedure. This method of data transfer is called direct memory access, or DMA. An associated flip-flop known as the **DMA flip-flop** is set by the device in need of data transfer, and the device generates the timing signals at which it can send or receive data.

When the DMA flip-flop is set, the CPU is "frozen" after the current memory cycle and the interrupting device has priority access to the memory. This phenomenon is called **cycle stealing** since the DMA mechanism, in effect, "steals" memory cycles from the CPU.

In order to implement the DMA mechanism, the MAR and MDR are duplicated on the device side, as shown in Fig. 3.13, and these registers control the memory buses during the DMA operation. It should be noted that the help of the CPU is still required to *start* the DMA operation, but once started, the operation goes on without further CPU intervention. The device MAR (DMAR) is initially loaded by the CPU by executing I/O instructions with the particular device code, the number of words or bytes to be transferred is loaded in a counter in the device controller, and the I/O operation is started by the CPU. As the data words or bytes are transferred, the DMAR and the counter contents are automatically modified until the data transfer is completed or some error occurs, resulting in the termination of the DMA operation prematurely. While the DMA operation is going on, the CPU can continue with operations not requiring memory references. When there is no pending DMA request, the memory cycle is handed over to the CPU. Thus, except for starting the DMA operation, there is no other instruction overhead for transferring data as required with the normal interrupt handling procedure.

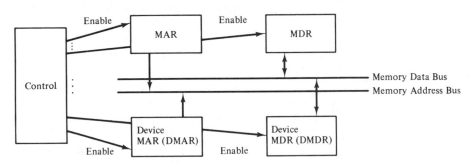

Figure 3.13 DMA Implementation Mechanism

Figure 3.14 schematically shows the principle of DMA operation. Multiple DMA requests are shown to occur at different points on the operation axis. Device 1 requests are assumed to have priority over Device 2 requests. A DMA request from the same device is not entertained unless the previous request has been serviced. This is implemented by means of a DMA acknowledge signal to the requesting device. A DMA controller resolves the priority of requests, decides on cycle stealing, generates appropriate DMA acknowledge signals, and restores the memory cycle to CPU upon the completion of DMA operations.

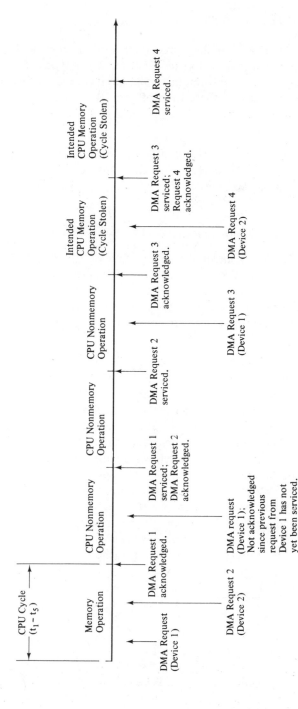

Figure 3.14 Principle of DMA Request Servicing

3.4.6. Traps and Trap Flip-Flop

The discussion of interrupt handling procedure concentrated on I/O interrupts; however, the scheme can be generalized for other types of interrupts as well, each handled by a routine uniquely suited to its needs. The occurrence of following events can trigger the setting of the TRAP flip-flop.

1. Illegal Opcode

Not all possible binary combinations in the opcode field of an instruction may be used as *actual* opcodes. In this case, any combination that does not represent an opcode becomes an illegal opcode, resulting in an error condition which sets the TRAP flip-flop.

2. Privileged operation in user mode

When the machine is under the supervision of an operating system, some instructions—such as the I/O instructions or instructions for changing the state of the CPU—are reserved by the operating system for its own use. If one tries to use these instructions, a program error is signaled. However, for a stand-alone program that does not utilize a resident operating system, this error is masked.

3. Protection

When a computer system is operating in a multi-user environment, the safety of the memory area of every user must be guaranteed. In addition, the operating system itself must be protected from direct user access in order to ensure its integrity. There are many schemes that can be devised to implement this protection mechanism. Figure 3.15 shows a simple scheme for this purpose. Register L specifies the lower bound, and Register U specifies the upper bound of addresses for a particular user program. These registers are loaded by the operating system before a user program begins execution. If there is any trespassing of these boundaries, even inadvertently, the TRAP is set. For the operating system, this range covers the entire memory so that it can access any area of memory without violating the protection feature.

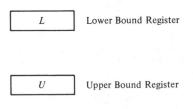

Figure 3.15 A Simple Protection Scheme

4. Addressing

This error is signaled—and TRAP set—if more than the existing memory is addressed.

5. Overflow/underflow

This condition arises when the CARRY and SIGN flip-flops, defined in Sec. 3.4.2, have opposite values at the end of an arithmetic operation in 2's complement arithmetic. This means that either the result of an arithmetic operation is too large (overflow) or too small (underflow) to be represented by the finite word size of the machine.

6. Divide interrupt

This occurs in case of an attempted division by zero.

These are not the only traps that can occur in a system. For a particular system architecture, it is possible to specify other traps as well.

3.4.7. Programmed Interrupt

Programmed interrupt is generated by a type of instruction executed by the CPU, called the SVC (supervisory call) instruction in IBM360/370 organization. The general format used by this type of instruction is as follows.

Opcode	Interrupt code

After the execution of such an instruction, the next instruction in sequence is not executed, but a new instruction is executed instead. Its location is determined by the interrupt code field of the SVC instruction.

An example of its use is found where, for instance, a user program uses system routines for initiating an I/O operation. The user program and the system routines do not occupy contiguous memory locations. The user program utilizes a SVC XX instruction to access the I/O initiating routine in this case. At the end of the latter routine, a RETURN instruction transfers the control back to the user routine, just as in the case of I/O interrupts. Figure 3.16 illustrates the use of programmed interrupt in this case.

3.4.8. Hard Errors

A **hard error** makes the operation of the computer system unreliable. For checking the reliability of operations being carried out, error-checking schemes are employed in various places within a computer system. Following are some typical checks.

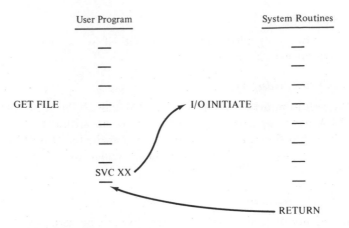

Figure 3.16 An Example of Use of Programmed Interrupt

1. Parity check

This is employed for all program-related information—instructions and data both in memory and in registers. The information is stored in memory along with its parity bit. When it is brought to CPU from memory, its parity is recomputed and matched with the existing parity to check if an error occurred during the transfer.

2. Cyclic redundancy check (CRC)

This check is employed for *blocks* of data transferred between memory, devices, and CPU. The details of the CRC mechanism are discussed in Chap. 7.

3. Expected sequence of signals at certain checkpoints of the system

When any error is detected, special diagnostic routines are called in order to identify the source of error. If there is no provision for such a scheme, the machine simply stops.

3.5 INSTRUCTION CLASSIFICATION

The instruction set of any general purpose computer can be classified according to the following.

1. Addressing method employed for fetching of operands.
2. The functions performed by the instructions.

The former classification was discussed in Sec. 3.3. This section categorizes the instructions according to the functions performed. In describing the function performed by an instruction, a slightly modified ISP (instruction set processor) notation of Bell and Newell [4] is used in which EA denotes the effective address of an operand, independent of the instruction format; that is, whether it is an RR, RX, SI, or SS instruction.

3.5.1. Arithmetic Instructions

Instructions that perform the operations of add, subtract, multiply, and divide fall in this category. Operands can be either binary-coded decimal, binary fixed point (integer), or floating point type; both the operands must be of the same type. A typical example of an arithmetic instruction is

$$\text{ADD EA 1, EA 2} :: \text{EA 1} \longleftarrow (\text{EA 1}) + (\text{EA 2})$$

where : : is the instruction delimiter; on the right hand side of : : is a description of the operation performed by the instruction. Here the operands are added and the result is placed in the first operand location.

3.5.2. Logical Instructions

Instructions in this class perform binary logical operations such as AND, OR, EXCLUSIVE OR, and so on, on operands that are binary strings. Corresponding bits of each operand are used in the operation. A typical instruction in this class is

$$\text{AND EA 1, EA 2} :: \text{EA 1} \langle r \rangle \longleftarrow \text{EA 1} \langle r \rangle \text{ AND EA 2} \langle r \rangle$$

where EA $\langle r \rangle$ denotes the r th bit of the operand with effective address EA.

3.5.3. Shift/Rotate Instructions

There are basically two types of shift instructions—**logical** shift and **arithmetic** shift. In logical shift, the *entire* bit string is shifted; the most significant bit (MSB) or the least significant bit (LSB) is lost depending on whether it is a left shift or a right shift, respectively. In the following discussion, EA $\langle n_1 : n_2 \rangle$ will denote all the bits from n_2 to n_1 of the operand at effective address EA and $\square$ will denote the concatenation operator.

1. Logical shift left

$$\text{LSL EA} :: \text{EA} \langle 30 : 0 \rangle \square 0$$

The operand at effective address EA is shifted left by one position.

2. Logical shift right

$$\text{LSR EA} :: 0 \square \text{EA} \langle 31 : 1 \rangle$$

The operand at effective address EA is shifted right by one position.

In arithmetic shift, the most significant bit, which usually denotes the sign of an operand, remains unchanged. The other bits are shifted by one position.

3. Arithmetic shift left

$$\text{ASL EA} :: \text{EA} \langle 31 \rangle \square \text{EA} \langle 29:0 \rangle \square 0$$

All the bits except the sign bit of the operand at effective address EA are shifted left by one position.

4. Arithmetic shift right

$$\text{ASR EA} :: \text{EA} \langle 31 \rangle \square \text{EA} \langle 31:1 \rangle$$

All the bits of the operand at effective address EA are shifted right by one position while the sign bit remains unchanged.

In rotate instructions, bits are not lost in the process. A bit that is shifted out of the least significant position enters the most significant position in right rotation, and vice versa for left rotation.

5. Rotate right

$$\text{RR EA} :: \text{EA} \langle 0 \rangle \square \text{EA} \langle 31:1 \rangle$$

The operand at effective address EA is rotated right by one position; the rightmost bit is moved to the leftmost position.

6. Rotate left

$$\text{RL EA} :: \text{EA} \langle 30:0 \rangle \square \text{EA} \langle 31 \rangle$$

The operand at effective address EA is rotated left by one position; the leftmost bit is moved to the rightmost position.

Some machines provide rotate instructions involving the carry bit also. If C denotes the carry bit, then we can define the **rotate with carry** instructions as follows.

7. Rotate right with carry

$$\text{RRC EA} :: C \square \text{EA} \langle 31:1 \rangle, \ C = \text{EA} \langle 0 \rangle$$

The operand is rotated right by one position; the present value of the C-bit is moved to the leftmost position of the operand while the rightmost operand bit is moved to C.

8. Rotate left with carry

$$\text{RLC EA} :: \text{EA} \langle 30:0 \rangle \ \square \ C, \ C = \text{EA} \langle 31 \rangle$$

The operand is rotated left by one position; the present value of the C-bit is moved to the rightmost position of the operand, while the leftmost operand bit is moved to C.

3.5.4. Comparison Instructions

These are instructions that create decision points in a program by executing comparison operations and setting different state flip-flops (Sec. 3.4.2) according to the relationship between the operands. The general functional format of these instruction is

$$\text{CMP EA 1, EA 2} :: \text{If (EA 1)} < \text{(EA 2), set SIGN} = 1, \text{ZERO} = 0$$
$$\text{If (EA 1)} = \text{(EA 2), set SIGN} = 0, \text{ZERO} = 1$$
$$\text{If (EA 1)} > \text{(EA 2), set SIGN} = 0, \text{ZERO} = 0$$

The combination of these two flip-flops (SIGN and ZERO) provides the condition codes for some sequence-control instructions discussed next.

3.5.5. Branch Instructions

Instructions of this type allow a programmer to alter the sequence of instruction execution either unconditionally or conditionally. In unconditional branch instructions, the PC is loaded with the branch address irrespective of any condition code; the functional format of such an instruction is

$$\text{BR EA} :: \text{PC} \longleftarrow \text{EA}$$

For conditional branch instructions, a particular setting of condition codes is necessary for a successful branch to take place. Otherwise the program continues its normal execution sequence. Some typical conditional branch instructions are as follows.

1. Branch on carry

$$\text{BRC EA} :: \text{PC} \longleftarrow \text{EA if } C = 1; \text{ else PC} \longleftarrow \text{(PC)} + 1$$

A branch to the effective address occurs if the carry bit is 1; otherwise normal sequence of instruction execution continues.

2. Branch on zero

$$\text{BRZ EA} :: \text{PC} \longleftarrow \text{EA if flag ZERO} = 1; \text{ else PC} \longleftarrow \text{(PC)} + 1$$

3. Branch on negative

$$\text{BRN EA} :: PC \longleftarrow EA \text{ if SIGN} = 1; \text{ else } PC \longleftarrow (PC) + 1$$

This certainly is not an exhaustive list of conditional branch instructions. Utilizing the various program state flip-flops discussed in Sec. 3.4.2, other such instructions can be defined.

3.5.6. Subroutine Linkage Instructions

In the normal branch instructions, there is no return point implicit in the instruction. However, in the case of a branch to a subroutine it is necessary to store the return address, which is $(PC) + n$, where n denotes the instruction length in terms of number of bytes or words, as the case may be.

$$\text{BSU EA} :: \text{Top [RAS]} \longleftarrow (PC) + n$$
$$PC \longleftarrow EA$$

In our example, the return address is stored in the RAS. Since the number of registers in RAS is eight (Fig. 3.1), the level of **nesting** of subroutine calls is limited to eight, that is, at most eight subroutine calls can be allowed without completing any of the subroutines entered.

In some systems—for example, in IBM 360/370 and Nova 1200—the return address is stored initially in a general-purpose register. With a very elementary programming effort, the register contents can be stored in memory, thereby increasing the subroutine nesting capability substantially.

The return from a subroutine to the calling program is accomplished by an instruction with the functional description

$$\text{RTN} :: PC \longleftarrow \text{Top [RAS]}$$

Since RAS is a LIFO stack, the most recent return address is restored to the PC; at the same time this address is removed from the stack.

In the case where a return address is stored in memory, the subroutine can transfer control to the calling program by finally executing an **indirect** jump or branch through the memory location.

3.5.7. Data Movement Instructions

A major overhead in any program consists of moving data from register to memory, memory to register, and memory to memory. The functional formats of instructions for performing these operations are as follows:

1. $\text{LOAD R, EA} :: R \longleftarrow (EA)$

The operand at effective address EA is loaded into register R.

2.   STORE EA, R : : EA ⟵ (R)

The contents of register R are stored at effective address EA.

3.   MOVE EA 1, EA 2 : : EA 2 ⟵ (EA 1)

The operand at effective address EA 1 is moved to the location with effective address EA 2.

3.5.8. I/O and Privileged Group of Instructions

These instructions are used for input/output and interrupt servicing facilities of a computer system. Since any program involving input/output devices requires specialized knowledge about the devices, a problem program usually leaves the device handling task to special routines available as a system facility. Thus only the system programs are allowed the privilege of using these instructions. For this reason, these are referred to as a **privileged group of instructions.** As pointed out in Sec. 3.4.6, any user program trying to utilize these instructions causes a particular trap designed for this purpose to be set. Since the I/O instructions are generally not a user facility, there is much less standardization in these as compared to the CPU instructions.

    Functionally, I/O instructions can be implemented either as a part of the instruction set of a conventional CPU, or the portion of the CPU that is responsible for executing the I/O instruction set can be separated as a dedicated I/O processor. In the latter case, it is the I/O processor that interrupts the CPU program flow, rather than an interrupting device as in the case of a conventional CPU. Since the I/O processor, in general, may have to handle devices with widely different characteristics, it is desirable to build enough flexibility into it—a feature which is conveniently provided if it is microprogram controlled. Furthermore, since the I/O processor now deals directly with devices, it should have its own facility for handling interrupts.

    Whether the I/O operations are performed by the CPU or by a dedicated I/O processor, the time required for handling I/O operations is almost the same because the I/O operations are basically sequential in nature. Hence there is very little parallelism that can be exploited in either approach. However, the I/O processor concept is very useful in a multiprogramming context in which the CPU is left free for carrying out other operations while I/O is in progress. The functional format of I/O instructions designed to satisfy the I/O architecture as defined in Sec. 3.2.7, 3.4.3, and 3.4.4 is as follows.

⟵——— IOR ———⟶

1.   SEL | DEVICE CODE | : : Select Device

The device code part of the instruction is loaded into the IOR to select a particular I/O device.

2.   STC | FUNCTION CODE | : : Set Code

A function code is loaded into the IOR to perform one of the following operations:

Read status.
Read data.
Write-control information.
Write data.

3.   INP

Depending on the function code specified in the STC instruction, either status information or data is read from the selected device into the IOR.

4.   OUT

Depending on the function code specified in the STC instruction, either write-control information or data from IOR is sent to the selected device.

5.   ENIM MASK : : Enable Interrupt with Mask

MASK is a 24-bit field that is loaded into the mask register shown in Fig. 3.10. The use of enabling interrupts selectively is illustrated in Fig. 3.11. When the MASK field contents are all 1's, it enables all the interrupt lines to contend for the setting of INTERRUPT flip-flop; when the MASK field contains a pattern of zeros and 1's, the lines corresponding to the zero-bits are disabled from causing an interrupt and the lines corresponding to 1-bits are enabled. A pattern of all zeros in the MASK field disables all interrupts.

6.   RTN : : Return

With the help of this instruction, the interrupted program is reenterred. The RAS in which the return address had been stored in a LIFO scheme is popped (unstacked) and the address is loaded into the PC. The (previous) second entry from the top of the stack now becomes the top entry.

7.   SVC : : Supervisory Call

This is already explained in Sec. 3.4.7.

8.   HALT

This halts any further operations from being performed by the CPU and sets the HALT flip-flop described in Sec. 3.4.1.

3.5.9. Control Group Instructions

This group of instructions does not need any explicit operand field. The operand is implicit in the instruction. Some examples of instructions belonging to this group are the following.

1.   CLC : : Clear Carry

This instruction causes the CARRY flag to be reset or cleared.

2.   CMC : : Complement Carry

This instruction causes the CARRY flag to be logically complemented.

3.   CLS : : Clear Sign

This instruction causes the SIGN flag to be reset.

4.   CMS : : Complement Sign

This instruction causes the SIGN flag to be logically complemented.

5.   COV : : Clear Overflow

This instruction causes the OVERFLOW flag to be reset.

This is not an exhaustive list of control group instructions. Depending on the design of the machine, other instructions of this type can be defined.

3.5.10. Miscellaneous Instructions

1.   NOP : : No Operation, PC $\longleftarrow$ (PC) $+$ 1

This instruction does not cause any operation to be performed; the PC is simply incremented to point to the next instruction.

2.   CVB EA 1, EA 2 : : Convert to Binary

This instruction converts the radix or base of the second operand at effective address EA 2 from decimal to binary and stores the result at effective address EA 1.

3.   CVD EA 1, EA 2 : : Convert to Decimal

This instruction converts the radix of the second operand at effective address EA 2 from binary to decimal and stores the result at effective address EA 1.

4.   PUSH : : Push into stack

5.   POP : : Pop from stack

The PUSH and POP instructions are used for stacking and unstacking operations, respectively, in those machine organizations that allow stack operations directly. The details of these operations were discussed in Sec. 3.2.3.

3.6 A PROPOSED MICROINSTRUCTION FORMAT

Using the functional classification of instructions outlined in Sec. 3.5 and the organization defined in Fig. 3.1, a microinstruction format consistent with the specified requirements can be proposed and is shown in Fig. 3.17. The various fields of the proposed format perform the following functions.

Opcode	Source 1	Source 2	Destination	Memory Operation	MAR Source	Control Functions	Condition Field	Next Address Field

Figure 3.17 A Proposed Microinstruction Format

OPCODE: This field specifies a microoperation to be performed, such as add, subtract, shift, or move.

SOURCE 1: This field specifies the source of one of the operands in a binary microoperation or the source of data in a "move" microoperation with the destination of the move specified in the DESTINATION field.

SOURCE 2: This field specifies the second operand in a binary microoperation; for microoperations not requiring a second operand, this field is left blank.

DESTINATION: This field specifies the destination of data after the microoperation specified in the OPCODE field has been performed.

MEMORY OPERATION: This field indicates whether a memory operation (read or write) is to be performed or not —possibly in parallel with other nonmemory microoperations.

MAR SOURCE: This field specifies a register containing the memory address for an intended memory operation.

CONTROL FUNCTIONS: This field specifies any control functions to be performed by the microinstruction, such as setting or clearing of flags either independently or depending on the result of some operation performed by the microinstruction.

CONDITION FIELD: This field specifies whether some or all of the micro-operations specified by the microinstruction are to be performed unconditionally or conditionally. For example, it can specify that a binary microoperation utilizing SOURCE 1 and SOURCE 2 fields would be performed only if the OVERFLOW flag is clear.

NEXT ADDRESS FIELD: This field is optional and, depending on the microinstruction designer, it can either be included in the format or deleted. If it is included, it specifies the control store address of the successor microinstruction. If it is not included in the format, then the successor microinstruction is assumed to be located in the next sequential control store location unless the current microinstruction specifies a branch (conditional or unconditional) to a specific location.

We have proposed a fairly simple microinstruction format, capable of utilizing the hardware resources shown in Fig. 3.1. It should be emphasized that this format is neither unique nor necessarily the best one that can be conceived for the resources shown in Fig. 3.1. The "goodness" of a microinstruction format, in terms of meeting the goals of system design, depends on such factors as the ingenuity of the microinstruction designer, the system resources, the amount of parallelism that the hardware can support, and the ease of writing microcode. It should be clear that system resources and parallelism play a major role in determining a suitable format.

SUMMARY

This chapter provided an overview of computer organization. It should be appreciated by the reader that the subject area of computer organization is so wide that an entire volume can be written on this alone! All the same, the main features of this topic have been covered for the reader.

Beginning with a description of basic hardware resources in a computer, typical instruction formats, classified both according to operand addressing schemes and according to functions performed by the instructions, were discussed. Interrupt mechanism and its role in I/O was described. In addition, other types of interrupts not concerned with I/O were discussed. A microinstruction format, consistent with the schematic diagram of Fig. 3.1, was proposed.

REFERENCES

[1] ABD-ALLA, ABD-ELFATTAH, and ARNOLD C. MELTZER, *Principles of Digital Computer Design* (Englewood Cliffs, N.J.: Prentice-Hall, Inc., 1976), Vol. I.

[2] ABRAMS, M. D., and P. G. STEIN, *Computer Hardware and Software: An Interdisciplinary Introduction*, (Reading, Mass.: Addison-Wesley Publishing Co., Inc., 1973).

[3] AMDAHL, G. M., G. A. BLAAUW, and F. P. BROOKS, JR., "Architecture of the IBM System/360," *IBM Journal of Research and Development*, 8 (April 1964), 87–101.

[4] BELL, C. GORDON, and A. NEWELL, *Computer Structures: Readings and Examples* (New York: McGraw-Hill Book Company, 1971).

[5] BOOTH, TAYLOR L., *Digital Networks and Computer Systems* (New York: John Wiley & Sons, Inc., 1971).

[6] CHU, YAOHAN, *Computer Organization and Microprogramming* (Englewood Cliffs, N.J.: Prentice-Hall, Inc., 1972).

[7] CHU, YAOHAN, *Introduction to Computer Organization* (Englewood Cliffs, N.J.: Prentice-Hall, Inc., 1970).

[8] DIETMEYER, D. L., *Logical Design of Digital Systems* (Boston, Mass.: Allyn & Bacon, Inc., 1971).

[9] HAYES, JOHN P., *Computer Architecture and Organization* (New York: McGraw-Hill Book Company, 1978).

[10] HILL, F. J., and G. R. PETERSON, *Introduction to Switching Theory and Logical Design* (New York: John Wiley & Sons, Inc., 1968).

[11] HILL, F. J., and G. R. PETERSON, *Digital Systems: Hardware Organization and Design* (New York: John Wiley & Sons, Inc., 1973).

[12] PEATMAN, J. B., *The Design of Digital Systems* (New York: McGraw-Hill Book Company, 1972).

[13] SCOTT, N. R., *Electronic Computer Technology* (New York: McGraw-Hill Book Company, 1970).

[14] SOBEL, H. S., *Introduction to Digital Computer Design* (Reading, Mass.: Addison-Wesley Publishing Co., Inc., 1970).

[15] STONE, HAROLD S., *Introduction to Computer Organization and Data Structures* (New York: McGraw-Hill Book Company, 1972).

PART TWO

Microprogramming Hardware and Microinstructions

CHAPTER FOUR

Hardware
for Microprogramming

4.1 MICROPROGRAMMING CONTROL UNIT

4.1.1. Functional Units

In order to implement microprogrammed control, certain hardware facilities must be provided to store the microinstructions and to execute the microoperations in a desired sequence for each machine-level instruction. A general functional schematic for a microprogram-controlled machine is shown in Fig. 4.1. As the figure shows, the heart of the control unit in a microprogrammed machine consists of a **control memory,** as opposed to a hardwired sequencer in a conventionally controlled machine. In other words, the microoperation sequencing information for executing a machine instruction is contained in the control memory. In order to get this sequencing information, the opcode portion of a machine instruction is mapped to a corresponding control memory address. This address is the starting address of the associated microprogram for executing the machine instruction. The microinstructions are read out from the control memory in a sequence and

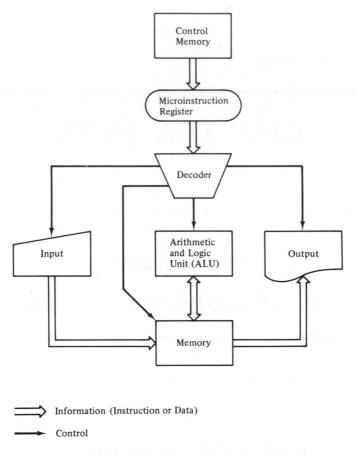

Information (Instruction or Data)

Control

Figure 4.1 General Schematic of a Microprogram Controlled Machine

are used to perform the required microoperations. On termination of a microprogram, the entire cycle is repeated for the next machine instruction [1]. Therefore the main difference between a conventionally controlled machine and a microporgram-controlled machine is the way the control unit is implemented.

Conceptually, control memory can be of any type, such as a random-access memory. However, considerations of cost and protection of a basic machine instruction set may require it to be a read-only memory. Furthermore, control memory should be fast enough to provide a reasonable execution rate for machine instructions. This is more easily obtained through ROMs than RAMs. In user-microprogrammable machines, the control memory can consist of both ROMs and RAMs, with the ROM supporting a basic machine instruction set and the RAM supporting any user extensions.

Other considerations involving the design and organization of control memories are discussed later on.

Microprogram-controlled operation of a machine requires certain support hardware units, as follows.

1. Control Memory Location Counter (CMLC)

This register contains the address of the next microinstruction to be fetched from the control memory. It also functions as the control memory address register (CMAR) because microinstruction execution does not involve fetching of data from control memory; hence there is no need for another distinct address register. The size of CMLC is dependent on the size of maximum addressable control memory space. Depending on the control memory sequencing scheme—to be discussed in detail later—the CMLC can function as a counter that is incremented with every microinstruction execution cycle or changed as a result of a branch microinstruction.

2. Microinstruction Register (MIR)

This register contains the microinstruction currently being executed. It doubles as the control memory data register because there is no need to fetch data from control memory or write data into it during execution.

3. Other Registers

Apart from these two registers, there are various other registers that are necessary for data manipulation and for temporary storage of information, that is, for "scratch pad" purposes. This category includes status registers, I/O registers, operational or file registers, and so on, which are not necessarily accessible to the machine language programs but are used by the microprogrammer for various purposes.

4.1.2. Control Memory Sequencing Schemes

This section describes some commonly used schemes for determining the address of the next microinstruction to be executed after the execution of the current one.

1. Basic Schemes

There are two basic techniques used for sequencing through the control memory: **implicit** addressing and **explicit** addressing.

In the implicit addressing scheme, the CMLC is automatically incremented by one after fetching the current microinstruction. This is based on the premise that microinstructions constituting a microprogram are *normally* sequential; this sequential flow is altered by **jump** or **skip** microinstructions.

In the case of a *jump* microinstruction, the jump address is put into the CMLC and then normal sequencing proceeds. In the case of a *skip* instruction, the CMLC is incremented by a fixed value if the skip condition is satisfied and normal sequencing is again resumed. The main advantage of implicit addressing is that it helps reduce the size of a microinstruction. As an example, this scheme would reduce the size of a microinstruction for a 4K control memory by 12 bits that would otherwise be needed if an explicit next address is to be carried with each microinstruction.

In the explicit addressing scheme, each microinstruction carries the address of its successor, which is loaded into the CMLC for fetching the next microinstruction. Thus there is an implied jump executed with each microinstruction. Therefore, the microinstructions need not be arranged in a sequential manner. This linked-list organization of microinstructions allows easier editing of microprograms in a writable control store.

In machines that have microinstructions containing only a few microcommands, several microinstructions are needed to perform any significant processing. This results in relatively long microinstruction sequences, requiring few jumps. Such machines, therefore, tend to use the implicit address scheme since the next address field would be redundant most of the time. On the other hand, when a single microinstruction provides for many parallel microoperations, significant processing can be done using relatively short microinstruction sequences. More jump instructions would have to be used in order to proceed with other processing. Such machines use the explicit scheme to avoid wasting time and control memory for repeated use of the jump microinstruction.

2. Variations

In the explicit addressing scheme described, the address of the successor microinstruction is an absolute address. However, in order to reduce the number of bits in each microinstruction—especially for large control stores—relative addressing can be used. In this case, the address of the successor microinstruction is obtained by either adding or concatenating the microinstruction address field with an address contained in a base register. This base register can be viewed as pointing to a page or a bank in the control memory. The value in the base register is set or modified by special microinstructions for this purpose. This register is set whenever control is transferred to another page or bank of the control memory.

With any of the addressing schemes, microinstruction fetch and execution cycles can be overlapped in order to increase the effective execution rate of microinstructions. Figure 4.2 shows a timing diagram for this scheme. In order to implement this overlapping, an additional register—the microinstruction buffer register (MIBR)—is needed, as shown in Fig. 4.3. At the beginning of every execution cycle, the MIBR contents are transferred to

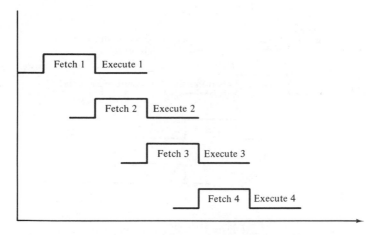

Figure 4.2 Microinstruction Overlap Timing Diagram

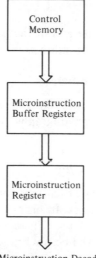

To Microinstruction Decoder

Figure 4.3 Register Arrangement
for Overlapping

MIR so that the next microinstruction can be fetched and loaded into MIBR, while the current one is being executed from MIR. However, if the current microinstruction is a conditional branch or skip type of instruction and the branch condition is satisfied, then the execution of the microinstruction held in MIBR must be aborted and a new microinstruction must be fetched. This is shown in the timing diagram of Fig. 4.4. In this particular situation, overlapping does not provide any advantage. However, the overall

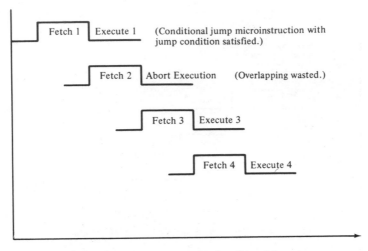

Figure 4.4 Overlapping with Conditional Branch

microinstruction execution rate is still increased since the majority of the instructions in a typical microprogram are not of conditional jump type.

4.1.3. Other Hardware Facilities

There are other hardware facilities that can be provided to assist the micro-programmer. In the following paragraphs, we describe the most common of these facilities.

1. Subroutine Linkage Facility

One of the most convenient features for writing microprograms is the ability to call (micro) subroutines. In order to implement this feature, some extra facilities should be available. These consist of a special register in which the return address is saved before branching to the subroutine and the associated CALL and RETURN microinstructions. If no special return address register is provided, then some facility for saving the contents of CMLC, such as a microinstruction to copy CMLC into a file register, must be available.

The availability of one return address register allows only one level of subroutine call. However, by using a stack of return registers, the subroutine calls can be nested, with the number of nesting levels determined by the size of the stack. This scheme necessitates the use of an extra register, called the **stack pointer,** which points to the next free return register in the stack. Some machines provide special microinstructions to increment or decrement the stack pointer, allowing greater control over subroutine nesting.

2. Dynamic Microinstruction Modification

This feature refers to modification of microinstructions at execution time. Such a modification is performed according to some variables with values known only at execution time and not at the time the microprograms are written. In order to implement this feature, the MIR must be modifiable prior to the microinstruction execution. Some machines provide a special register with contents that are combined with the MIR contents when microinstruction modification is required, generating an **effective** micro-instruction, which is then executed. This technique of combining a static value in a register with a microinstruction is sometimes referred to as **residual control.** Generally, this feature is very useful for saving control store; some examples of this are provided in Chap. 8. Note that the microinstruction in control memory is not modified in any way.

4.2 REVIEW OF CONTROL MEMORY TECHNOLOGY

A control memory can be implemented either as a read-only memory (ROM), read/write memory (commonly, although incorrectly, known as random-access memory or RAM), or as a combination of these two types; that is, partly as a ROM and partly as a read/write memory. In addition, some memory that combines the characteristics of the two types, such as a programmable read-only memory (PROM), can also be used for this purpose.

4.2.1. Read/Write Memories

Basically, any read/write memory technology can be used for implementing a control memory. This includes the use of magnetic core or any other magnetic technology [2]. Primarily because of considerations of speed and technological compatibility with the rest of the processor, however, semiconductor technology is better suited for control memory implementation.

Semiconductor read/write memories can be implemented either using metal oxide semiconductor (MOS) technology or bipolar technology [3]. The latter provides faster access times but dissipates more power compared to MOS memories and is generally more expensive. The very fast bipolar memories are based on emitter-coupled logic (ECL) and operate at an access time of less than 10 ns. These memories are relatively expensive and they dissipate milliwatts of power per bit. Next in order are memories based on transistor transistor logic (TTL) devices, which have a typical access time of 50 ns and are slightly less expensive than ECL memories.

Metal oxide semiconductor memories generally have an access time of hundreds of nanoseconds, although some newer types have access times of less than 100 ns. Among this latter type is the MOS static RAM, which is challenging bipolar RAMs both in terms of speed and cost. Because MOS memories have greater bit density, fewer memory chips are required to implement a control memory of a given size.

Another type of bipolar memory available in the market is the **current injection logic** or **integrated injection logic** (I^2L) memory. This type of memory combines the speed advantages of bipolar memories with the low power-dissipation and high chip-density characteristics of MOS memories. One of the most interesting characteristics of I^2L technology is that the speed-power product is practically constant. Thus, for example, an I^2L gate can operate with a propagation delay of 1 μs and power dissipation of 5 μw. On the other hand, the gate can be operated with a delay of 10 ns and dissipation of 0.5 mw. This means that I^2L memories can be powered down by a factor of 100 or more without losing their contents (data).

4.2.2. Read-Only Memories (ROM)

Historically, control memories were implemented with ROMs mainly because of cost and speed considerations; the initial writing of the memory contents was done either at the time of manufacture or by a separate manual or semimanual process.

All of the ROM implementations share a common matrixlike structure as shown in Fig. 4.5, in which a **word line** is activated, in turn activating a subset of **bit lines**. A bit line is activated if a **coupling** exists between it and the activated word line. At the intersection of a word line and a bit line, the existence of a coupling (shown by a heavy line) defines a logical 1, while

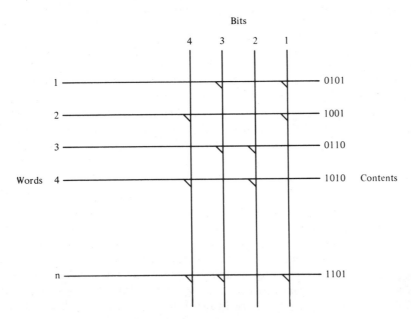

Figure 4.5 ROM Organization

the absence of a coupling defines a logical zero. The entire set of bit lines represents a microinstruction. In the past, the coupling has been established by the presence of resistors, capacitors, or something similar, at the intersections of the various word and bit lines.

Some rather innovative schemes have been used for providing a degree of programmability in these memories; a brief review of these follows.

1. Card Resistor Read-Only Memory (CRROM)

In this type of ROM [4], the word and bit lines and the coupling elements (resistors) were embedded in punched cards of standard size, usually made of plastic—although paper was also tried. The physical geometry of these cards was arranged so that they would fit the regular card-punching equipment. By punching holes at selected places on the card, the resistors could be selectively removed. This allowed identical memory cards to be manufactured and then individually tailored as required. These cards also had the required electrical contacts available and were inserted manually into individual card holder slots in the assembly that contained the drive and sense electronics. Using this resistive coupling technology, IBM was able to construct a ROM of 500 words of up to 60 bits, with a cycle time of 5 to 10 μs.

2. Card Capacitor Read-Only Memory (CCROM)

The CCROM is similar to the CRROM; here capacitive, instead of resistive, coupling is used between the word and bit lines (Fig. 4.6). When a

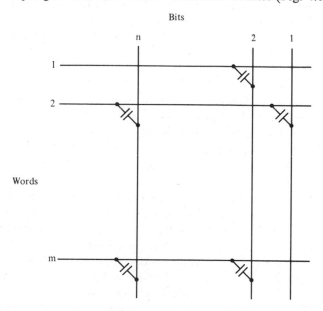

Figure 4.6 Capacitively Coupled ROM

drive current is sent along a word line, the corresponding (capacitively coupled) bit lines are energized, thus transmitting a logical 1. Husson [4] has provided a good description of this technology, developed for the IBM S/360 Model 30 computer; this computer used a ROM of 4032 words of 60 bits each, with a cycle time of 1 μs.

A refinement of this technology was used in the IBM S/360 Models 50, 65, and 67, in which a "balanced" capacitive coupling arrangement was used to eliminate the unwanted coupling (noise) from other words and sense lines. However, in this refined technology, the memory contents were etched into the array during manufacture, thus eliminating the possibility of easy alteration of memory contents. The IBM balanced capacitor memory had a total capacity of 2816 words of 100 bits each, with a cycle time of 200 ns and an access time of 90 ns.

3. Inductively Coupled ROM

In this type of ROM, the coupling element is inductive, including such coupling as magnetic core, magnetic bar, and transformer [2, 4]. This technology is very similar to the conventional core-memory technology. One important distinction is that for control memories, this technology was used to make magnetic read-only memories—as opposed to read/write memories—by means of geometric or physical differences between bit positions programmed to be zeros and 1's. The other distinction was that ROM technology, being physically simpler than read/write memory technology, was easier to operate at higher speeds. Observe that the programming of these ROMs was fixed at the time of manufacture. Furthermore, there was not the same opportunity to mass-produce identical pieces of memory for subsequent programming. A transformer like ROM was used for storing microprograms in IBM S/360 Models 20 and 40.

4. Diode/Transistor Coupled ROM

Diodes or transistors can be used as coupling elements between word and bit lines. Figure 4.7 shows the schematic of a diode ROM array. Normally, the diodes are reverse-biased and, hence, in a nonconducting state. When a word line is selected, a positive voltage of sufficient magnitude is applied to it; this causes the corresponding coupling diodes to conduct, activating the corresponding bit lines. As Husson [4] has pointed out, the idea of using diodes as coupling elements in a ROM has been around since 1949.

Instead of diodes, transistors can be used for coupling by connecting a word line to the base of a transistor [4, 5]; the emitter is connected to the corresponding bit line, while the collector is connected to a supply voltage. The use of transistors has the advantage that the word and bit lines are electrically isolated. A prime example of transistor-coupled ROM for control memory is found in the Illiac IV machine.

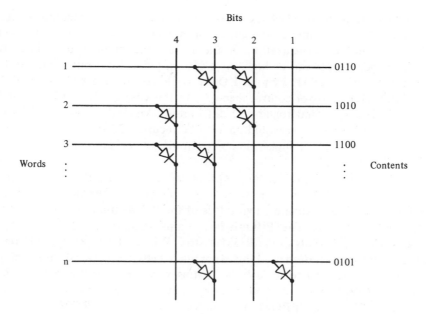

Figure 4.7 Diode ROM Array

As far as the method of establishing a coupling is concerned, these diode and transistor arrays were the forerunners of the present day semiconductor integrated circuit ROMs and PROMs. The following are the main advantages of these semiconductor memories.

1. Technological compatibility with the rest of the processor logic elements.
2. High reliability.
3. Small size.
4. Relatively small power requirements.
5. Fast access and cycle times.
6. On-chip address decoding and reduced interconnection complexity.

There are basically two types of read-only memories—the conventional ROM and the programmable ROM, or PROM. The first type, implemented using either bipolar or metal-oxide–semiconductor technology, is programmed during the manufacturing process by creating specifically tailored masks from user-supplied data. This data, consisting of the desired ROM contents, is usually provided on such devices as magnetic tape, paper tape, punched cards, and microprogram object listing. These masks are used in the final stages of the manufacturing process to achieve the desired memory contents. It should be noted that obtaining a mask-programmed ROM can represent a substantial cost factor to the control memory designers unless the ROM contents are stable (not subject to further changes) and the required volume

75

is sufficiently high to offset the mask generation costs. Depending on the number of bits per microinstruction, the number of words in the control memory, and the organization of the ROM, the number of differently programmed ROMs can be high. As a case in point, for a microinstruction of 40 bits, the use of 1K by 8-bit ROMs would require five different ROMs per 1024 (1K) words of control memory. In this case, a 4K word by 40-bit control memory would require 20 different ROMs and, consequently, the costs of mask generation would have to be incurred 20 times. Clearly, this cost must be offset by high-volume requirements for the control memory with stable contents.

In contrast to ROMs, the PROMs are field programmable, and for this reason they have become extremely popular with the designers. It is estimated that approximately two-thirds of the ROMs used by designers are field programmable. The PROMs are manufactured with the couplings established at *all* points in the ROM matrix. Wherever a 0 (zero) is desired, the coupling is either destroyed (fused) or made highly resistive; the remaining couplings correspond to logical 1's. In this way, the user "programs" the PROM to achieve the desired memory contents; this process is usually carried out using a "PROM programmer" before the PROM chips are plugged into the control memory board.

The PROMs are very well suited for implementing control memory during the development phase of a system and for systems with low-volume requirements. First of all, their speed and size characteristics are comparable with the mask-generated ROMs. Secondly, PROMs have a much lower initial cost than mask ROMs. This cost factor is very significant during the development phase of a computer system because any microprogrammed or microprogrammable machine would need at least some microinstructions in a ROM, for example, for an elementary bootstrap loader, even though the machine may have a writable control store as the main development tool for microprograms. It may well be argued that with the availability of a WCS, the initial few microinstructions can be toggled into the control memory. However, from a user's viewpoint, the availability of at least one basic program in a ROM (or PROM) is certainly very convenient.

The low initial cost is also an important consideration if the basic ROM contents are subject to change or addition, because the PROM does not have to be completely programmed at one time. Thus, if the initial set of microprograms does not completely fill the PROM, the remaining words can be used for additional microprograms later on. Clearly, this facility is not available with mask-programmed ROMs. In the present fast-paced and competitive computer industry, the development phase of a system often tends to overlap the early production phase; the relatively low investment required for programming a PROM makes it specially attractive to the designers. In addition, the manufacturers of semiconductor memories have recognized the need for PROMs during the development phase of a product and the conversion to ROMs after the memory contents have been "frozen." For this reason, PROMs are usually available with corresponding pin-compatible ROMs, making the transition to ROMs relatively painless.

The only problem faced by the designer in using ROMs and PROMs is that they are not reprogrammable. For those applications where an alterable, yet nonvolatile, control memory is required, there exists another type of PROM—the alterable, programmable ROM. The first such erasable PROMs were developed by the Intel Corporation in 1970; they are known as **ultraviolet-erasable PROMs**, often called EPROMs. The contents of these PROMs are erased by a dose of ultraviolet light applied through a window in the package. The other types of erasable PROMs are the electrically alterable ROMs, widely known as EAROMs. These devices can be programmed like the ultraviolet-erasable PROMs and can be erased in circuit simply by applying an electrical impulse to the programming pins.

The erasable PROMs are all implemented with MOS technology, and all of them have about the same speed. They are slow compared to mask ROMs and, as a result, they are not suitable for use as control memories in production model computers. However, they are quite handy for prototyping computer systems. A system designer can use them to check out the integrity of the microprograms; once the microcode has been debugged and optimized, a switch can be made to a cheaper and faster conventional ROM.

Future Outlook

Initially, control stores were basically ROMs because the hardware designers treated the control memory as a direct replacement for hardwired logic. As computer system technology evolved, the analogy between microprogramming and normal programming became apparent. This, naturally, led to a desire for writable control stores that would allow microprogram development to be implemented with greater ease. At the time of initial WCS development, economic considerations made it feasible for use only by the manufacturer during product development, with the ROM storing the firmware in the final product. Today, however, the technology of semiconductor memories has evolved to a stage where it is economically and technologically feasible to provide a WCS for the user. At the same time, ROM technology is still evolving towards greater capacity and higher speed. Mainly as a result of advances in the technology of semiconductor memories [3], quite a few user-microprogrammable computers are now available on the market; it is expected that the number of such machines will grow as users gain an understanding of the full potential of user-microprogrammability.

4.3 LEVELS OF CONTROL

4.3.1. Concept of Levels

The widespread use and application of computers has provided each end-user with a specialized machine to perform particular tasks. The user is usually unaware of the details of how these tasks are performed. For example, in an airline reservation system, the reservation agent (the end-user) enters information (such as passenger name, flight number, date, and time of departure) related exclusively to a flight without any concern for how this information is processed. This data can be entered via a teletypewriter and sent to a central reservation agent. On the other hand, the central office may have a computer system to process reservation requests and to send back the response. In either case, the reservation agent communicates with a system designed to make seat reservations; the agent is not concerned with the implementation aspects of the system. Furthermore, for a mechanized reservation system, the end-user thinks that there exists a reservation machine (Fig. 4.8a). In a computerized reservation system, however, there is no "seat-reservation machine" as such, but rather a general-purpose computer

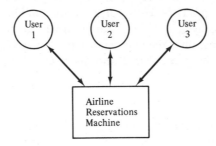

Figure 4.8a Single-Level Machine

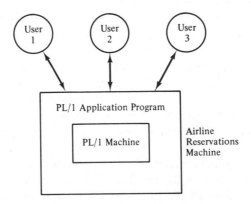

Figure 4.8b Two-Level Machine

programmed to behave like such a machine. In this case, the system can be pictured as a two-level system, as shown in Fig. 4.8b. The outer level, which interfaces with the end-user, is supported by the inner-level machine, on which the software is run.

The same considerations apply to the inner level. If the outer level

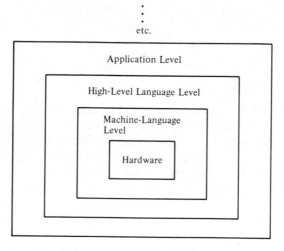

Figure 4.8c Multilevel Machine

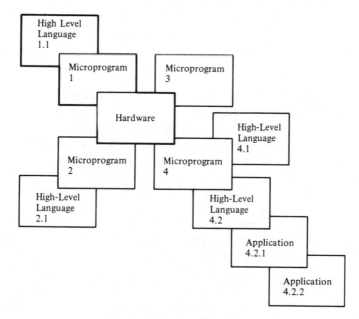

Figure 4.8d Virtual Machines

is implemented in a high-level language such as PL/1, then for the application programmer, there exists a virtual PL/1 machine (Fig. 4.8b), and again the programmer need not know the implementation details of the PL/1 machine. Unless this high-level language is directly executed by the hardware, this concept of hierarchy of levels can be extended until we reach a level which is the actual hardware of the machine. This is shown in Fig. 4.8c, where each outer level is supported by its preceding inner level. This hierarchical level concept of a system remains valid in general for any kind of application; Level 0 represents the actual hardwired machine, whereas Levels 1 to n represent virtual machines [1].

4.3.2. The Machine-Language Level

For machines with conventional (hardwired) control, the machine-language instructions are executed directly by the hardware. Therefore the machine-language level can be thought of as Level 1. However, for microprogrammed machines, the machine-language instructions are not directly executed by the hardware but are, instead, interpreted by microprograms. The microinstructions are directly executed by the hardware. Level 1 thus now consists of the microprogram level, while Level 2 consists of the machine-language level. The definition of a machine language therefore depends on whether the machine under consideration has hardwired control or microprogrammed control. Because of this, it is necessary to clearly define the concept of a machine language. In terms of the hierarchy of levels (Fig. 4.8c), the machine-language level is the level directly supported by the hardware, although for the sake of consistency with the existing terminology, this definition will not be used in this book.

4.3.3. The Microprogram Level

In a microprogram-controlled machine, the microprogram level normally occupies Level 1 of Fig. 4.8c and its instructions (microinstructions) are directly executed by the hardware. This level interprets and executes the higher-level instructions, which could be the traditional machine language instructions or higher-level instructions such as PL/1 instructions. In the extreme case, the microprogram level can be used directly to interpret the application-oriented commands or instructions such as the reservation system commands. In this way, the microprogram level can be used to support any virtual machine level, where the "machine language" for such a virtual machine can occupy any level of Fig. 4.8c. As a matter of fact, the microprogram level can support a *number* of virtual machine levels, providing the capability of executing different machine languages on the same hardware; these machine languages can, in turn, support other higher-level languages. This concept is illustrated graphically in Fig. 4.8d, where the microprogram level is used to support four different virtual machine levels. For example, the three levels enclosed within heavy lines in the figure make up a virtual high-level language machine. It is feasible to support the various virtual machine levels concurrently, with the system switching from one virtual machine to another according to some predetermined scheme.

4.3.4. Further Levels

Just as the microprogramming level is used to enable a flexible definition of the machine-language level, so can further lower levels be used to provide a flexible definition of the microprogram level. In other words, the microprogram level is not necessarily the ultimate level supported by the hardware. Flexibility in the definition of the microprogram level is a convenient feature when the host hardware is to be used to support any arbitrary virtual machine structure; that is, when it is to be used as a "universal host" (see Sec. 9.5.2).

The following example further illustrates this concept. Suppose a virtual machine with a 36-bit virtual data path has been defined; the hardware data path is only 32 bits wide and appropriate microinstructions use this data path. In this case, a machine-level instruction such as

LDA A,B   * Load Register A from Register B

will be interpreted using such microinstructions as

MOV 1,3   * Copy low-order 32 bits of Register B into
               Register A.

MOV 2,4   * Copy remainder of B into A.

AND 2,X'0000000F'   * Mask high-order 28 bits of Register 2.

where Registers A and B are mapped into hardware file registers, as shown in Fig. 4.9. If, however, the microprogram level could be redefined to operate on a virtual data path of 18 bits (the number must be less than the width of the hardware data path), then

LDA A,B

would be interpreted using the microinstructions

MOV 1,3   * Copy low order.

MOV 2,4   * Copy high order.

where the file registers at the microprogram level are now 18 bits wide.

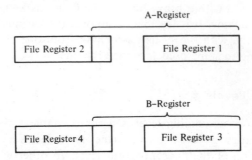

Figure 4.9 Mapping of A- and B-Registers

This flexibility in the definition of the microprogram level has been used in some machines and is generally known as **nanoprogramming.** It allows greater leeway in tailoring the host machine to support an arbitrary target machine.

REFERENCES

[1] TANENBAUM, ANDREW S., *Structured Computer Organization* (Englewood Cliffs, N.J.: Prentice-Hall, Inc., 1976).

[2] RILEY, WALLACE B., *Electronic Computer Memory Technology* (New York, N.Y.: McGraw-Hill Book Company, 1971).

[3] BURSKY, D., "Special Report: Memories Pace Systems Growth," *Electronic Design* (September 27, 1980), pp. 63–74.

[4] HUSSON, SAMIR S., *Microprogramming: Principles and Practices* (Englewood Cliffs, N.J.: Prentice-Hall, Inc., 1970).

[5] BOULAYE, GUY G., *Microprogramming*, English translation of *La Microprogrammation*, Dunod, Paris, 1971 (London: The MacMillan Press Ltd., 1975).

FURTHER READINGS

1. BOULAYE, G. G., "Realization of Control Units with Associative Memories," in *Microarchitecture of Computer Systems*, ed. R.W. Hartenstein and R. Zaks. North-Holland/American Elsevier, 1975, pp. 181–84.

2. CASAGLIA, G. F., "Nanoprogramming vs. Microprogramming," *Computer*, 9, no. 1 (January 1976), 54–58.

3. CORNELL, R. G. and TORNG, H. C., "A Cellular General Purpose Computer," *Proceedings of the Second Annual Symposium on Computer Architecture*, (January 20–22, 1974), pp. 207–13.

4. DAHLBERG, B., "On Hardware Implementation of Branching Conditions in Microprogramming," *IEEE Computer Society Repository* R74-137.

5. DALEY, L. N., "Architectural Considerations in the Design of Special-purpose Machines," *IEEE Computer Society Repository*, R75-318, 87 pages.

6. DOUGLAS, J. R., "Large Scale Systems Architectures," in *Microprogramming and Systems Architecture*, ed. C. Boon. Infotech State of the Art Report 23, Infotech Information Ltd., 1975, pp. 181–203.

7. GARON, G. and M. KRIEGER, "Address Driven Microprogramming," *IEEE Computer Society Repository*, R74-58, 14 pages.

8. HOFF, G., "Design of Microprogrammed Control for General Purpose Processors," *SIGMICRO Newsletter*, 3 (July 1972), 57–64.

9. JONES, L. H., "Instruction Sequencing in Microprogrammed Computers," *AFIPS Conference Proceedings*, 44 (1975 NCC.), 91–98.

10. JONES, L. H., "Microinstruction Sequencing and Structured Microprogramming," in *Microprogramming and System Architecture*, ed. C. Boon. Infotech State of the Art Report 23, Infotech Information Ltd., 1975, pp. 433–53.

11. KARTASHEV, S. I., "A Microcomputer with a Shift-Register Memory," *IEEE Trans. Comput.*, C–25, 5 (May 1976), 470–84.

12. MARTEAU, D. J., "Indirection Feature in Control Address at Micro Level—A

Facility for Macro Interpreting," *EUROMICRO Newsletter*, 1, no. 1 (October 1974), 29–34.

13. NOGUEZ, G. L. M., "A Standardized Microprogram Sequencing Control with a Push Down Store," *Preprint of the Fifth Workshop on Microprogramming* (September 1972), Urbana, Ill.

14. RAMAMOORTHY, C. V. and M. TSUCHIYA, "Analysis of Microprogrammed Processor Design Trade-offs," *Proceedings of the Sixth Annual IEEE Computer Society International Conference* (September 1972), San Francisco, Ca.

15. STIGALL, P. D., "Memory Utilization for a Dynamically Microprogrammed Computer," *Preprints of the Sixth Workshop on Microprogramming* (September 1973), College Park, Maryland.

16. THOMAS, R. T., "Organization for Execution of User Microprograms from Main Memory: Synthesis and Analysis," *IEEE Trans. Comput.*, C–23, 8 (August 1974), 783–91.

17. WAKERLY, J. F., C. R. HOLLANDER, and D. DAVIES, "Placement of Microinstructions in a Two-dimensional Address Space," *Proceedings of the Eighth Annual Workshop on Microprogramming*, September 21–23, 1975, pp. 46–51.

EXERCISES

4.1 Use a table to summarize the advantages and disadvantages (cost, speed, flexibility, ease of manufacture, and so on) of the various technologies to implement the read-only memories mentioned in Sec. 4.2.

4.2 Given a microinstruction size of n bits and an explicit address field of m bits, assume that an average of j microinstructions perform a significant function. What is the control memory size necessary to house such a microprogram? Draw the curve representing this size when n and j vary (m can be assumed constant).

4.3 Repeat Exercise 4.2 with a microinstruction using the implicit address scheme. Compare the two results. Evaluate the crossover point and determine when one scheme is cheaper in terms of memory size than the other.

4.4 Under what conditions can overlapping be wasted in a machine using the explicit address scheme?

4.5 What are the hardware resources necessary to implement a nanoprogrammed machine, as presented in Sec. 4.3?

CHAPTER FIVE

Microinstructions

INTRODUCTION

This chapter is concerned with the various aspects of microinstruction design, formats, and execution, as well as trade-offs involved in the design of microinstructions. Microinstruction structures vary widely from machine to machine; this chapter attempts to provide an insight into the various factors involved [22].

So far, the term *microinstruction* has been used rather loosely; however, it will now be defined more precisely. As mentioned in Sec. 1.3, the register transfer operations required for executing a machine instruction are called *microoperations*. Each microoperation execution is controlled by a corresponding *microcommand*. The set of microcommands is directly related to the hardware structure of a machine that determines the microoperations which can be performed. In general, there exist sets of microoperations that can be performed in parallel and other sets in which this is not the case. A **microinstruction** can now be defined as a group of microcommands that can be executed simultaneously.

5.1 MICROINSTRUCTION STRUCTURE

5.1.1. Horizontal Microinstructions

A **horizontal** microinstruction is a microinstruction that allows one to specify *all* possible parallel microoperations that can be performed by the machine. Note, however, that generally only a few microoperations need be specified in a microinstruction since all hardware resources do not have to be controlled at the same time. For example, when writing a microprogram to interpret a machine language CPU instruction, there is usually no need to specify I/O microoperations. Furthermore, some microoperation combinations, such as two microoperations gating two different registers onto the same bus simultaneously, represent invalid microinstructions.

The chief advantage of horizontal microinstructions is that the microprogrammer has ultimate flexibility in utilizing the hardware resources of the machine and parallelism of data paths can be exploited to the fullest extent. There are two main disadvantages of horizontal microinstructions.

1. Inefficient utilization of control memory, because most of the time only a few microoperations are specified.
2. Relative difficulty of programming, because several functions must be specified within a microinstruction in order to fully utilize the data path parallelism. This makes it difficult for a compiler to generate optimum horizontal microcode.

As an example, consider a section of the data flow path of a machine, as shown in Fig. 5.1. The bank of 16 registers (0–15) can be gated onto A- and B-buses, forming two inputs to the ALU. The output of the ALU is gated onto the C-bus, which is then written into one of the registers. We assume the ALU inputs and outputs are latched; that is, they remain un-

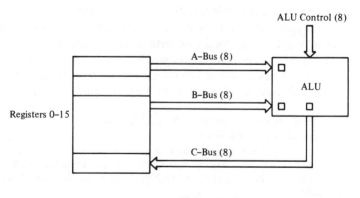

□ Input/Output Latches

Figure 5.1 An Example Data Path

changed until new data are stored in them. The ALU has eight control lines, one for each of the eight distinct functions—for instance, add, subtract, transfer A-bus to C-bus—that it can perform. The following microoperations are associated with the data path.

1. A-Bus ⟵ Register.
2. B-Bus ⟵ Register.
3. Select ALU operation.
4. Register ⟵ C-Bus.

These yield a horizontal microinstruction format.

55	48 47	32 31	16 15	0
ALU operation	A-bus field	B-bus field	C-bus field	

where the A- and B-bus fields specify 1 of 16 registers to be gated to the A- and B-bus, respectively, the C-bus field specifies 1 of 16 registers into which C-bus contents are written, and the ALU operation field specifies one of eight operations to be performed in the ALU. Any field specified by all zeros means a no operation (NOOP) for that particular field. For example, the following microinstruction represents (in hexadecimal notation) the addition of the contents of Registers 4 and 5, with the result stored in Register 6.

01	0010	0020	0040

A-bus ⟵ Register 4
B-bus ⟵ Register 5
Add
Register 6 ⟵ C-bus

5.1.2. Vertical Microinstructions

A **vertical** microinstruction specifies only one microoperation to be performed. This, however, represents an extreme case and, generally, more than one microoperation must be specified to create a meaningful microinstruction. For example, an ALU microinstruction would specify an ALU operation to be performed, as well as selection of source and destination operands. The main advantages of vertical microprogramming are the following.

1. The microinstruction fields are fully utilized since only the microoperation to be performed is specified.
2. The microinstructions are very easy to write because of their simple format. This makes it relatively easy to write a compiler to produce vertical microcode since there is no need to worry about the full utilization of all microoperation fields.

There are two disadvantages of vertical microprogramming.

1. A microprogram requires relatively long sequences of microinstructions, resulting in a longer execution time for the microprogram.
2. No advantage is taken of any possible parallel execution of microoperations.

For the example of Fig. 5.1 and the microoperations mentioned in Sec. 5.1.1, four vertical microinstructions would be defined.

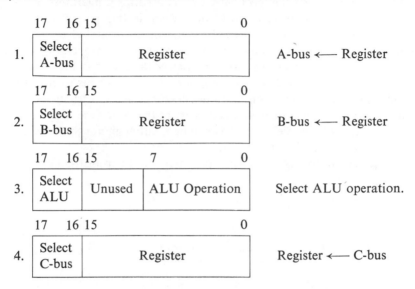

Using this format, the following microprogram could be used to represent (in hexadecimal notation) the addition of the contents of Registers 4 and 5, with the result stored in Register 6.

0	0	0	1	0	A-bus ←— Register 4
1	0	0	2	0	B-bus ←— Register 5
2	0	0	0	1	Select ADD operation in ALU.
3	0	0	4	0	Register 6 ←— C-bus

5.1.3. Diagonal Microinstructions

Most microprogrammed machines use a microinstruction format somewhere between the horizontal and vertical formats, in order to achieve a compromise between the two. For lack of a better name, this format is generally referred to as a **diagonal** format.

The definitions of horizontal and vertical microinstructions represent two extreme cases, and would leave most machines in the diagonal microinstruction category. However, in general usage, the term *vertical* is used for a microinstruction containing one to three different fields (microoperations and operands) with a typical length of 16 bits; the term *diagonal* is used for a microinstruction containing four to six different fields with a typical length of 24 to 36 bits, and the term *horizontal* is used for a microinstruction containing more than six fields with more than 48 bits per microinstruction. Note, however, that the vertical, diagonal, or horizontal characteristic of a microinstruction is dependent on the number of microoperations specified and not on the number of bits per microinstruction, as the latter is also dependent on the degree of encoding used for the various microinstruction fields. Like vertical microinstructions, diagonal microinstructions are fairly easy to write or generate with a compiler; at the same time, they allow some of the data-path parallelism to be exploited, although not to the same extent as horizontal microinstructions do.

Referring to Fig. 5.1 again, two diagonal microinstructions could be defined as follows.

1.

32	31	16 15	0
Select ALU Operands	Select A-bus Operand	Select B-bus Operand	

A-Bus ⟵ Register
B-Bus ⟵ Register

2.

32	31	16 15	8 7	0
Operate	C-Bus to Register field	Select ALU Operation	Unused	

Operate, and store result in register.

Using these two formats, the following microinstruction sequence could be used to represent (in hexadecimal notation) the addition of the contents of Registers 4 and 5, with the result stored in Register 6.

0	0010	0020

Select Registers 4 and 5 as operands.

1	0040	0100

Add and store result in Register 6.

In the preceding example, involving the addition of 2 registers, the horizontal microinstruction format used 56 bits of memory, the vertical format used 72 bits, and the diagonal format used 66 bits. It would appear that the horizontal format is most memory-efficient. This, however, is due to the fact that *all* microoperation fields in the horizontal format are fully utilized for this particular case. This may not be the case for every micro-instruction sequence. The case where the sum of Registers 4 and 5 is to be stored in Registers 6 and 7 can now be considered.

The horizontal microinstruction sequence is (in hexadecimal notation) as follows.

| 01 | 0010 | 0020 | 0040 |

Register 6 ←— (Register 4) + (Register 5)

| 00 | 0000 | 0000 | 0080 |

Register 7 ←— (Register 4) + (Register 5)

This sequence requires 112 bits of control store, with 3 fields wasted in the second microinstruction. The vertical microinstruction sequence for the same example is

| 0 | 0010 |

Select Register 4 on A-bus.

| 1 | 0020 |

Select Register 5 on B-bus.

| 2 | 0001 |

Add Operation.

| 3 | 0040 |

Copy C-bus into Register 6.

| 3 | 0080 |

Copy C-bus into Register 7.

This sequence requires $5 \times 18 = 90$ bits of control store with no fields wasted, as only the required microcommands are specified. The diagonal microinstruction sequence with the format specified is

| 0 | 0010 | 0020 |

Select Registers 4 and 5.

| 1 | 0040 | 0100 |

Add and store in Register 6.

| 1 | 0080 | 0000 |

NOOP and store in Register 7.

and requires $3 \times 33 = 99$ bits of control memory with only one field wasted in the last microinstruction. For this example, the horizontal microinstruction sequence is the least memory efficient because of some unused microoperation fields. It should be clear that there is a need for a systematic analysis of trade-offs between the microinstruction formats. This aspect is discussed later in this chapter.

5.1.4. Encoding of Microinstruction Fields

In the preceding example, a single bit was associated with each possible function that could be performed using the data path of Fig. 5.1. For instance, the A-bus field was 16 bits wide, so that the gating of any one of the 16 registers to the A-bus could be specified. This, however, represents a very wasteful utilization of the A-bus field. At any given time, only *one* of the 16 bits in this field is 1; all others are 0 since only one of the 16 registers would be gated to the A-bus. Thus this 16-bit field represents 16 *mutually exclusive* microcommands, which can then be encoded into a field of 4 bits. As a matter of fact, an encoded field of 5 bits would be required in order to include the NOOP option specifying that no register is gated to the A-bus. Other fields can be encoded in a similar way, because they also represent mutually exclusive functions to be performed. This type of encoding reduces the size of a field from n bits to $\lceil \log_2 (n + 1) \rceil$ bits, where $\lceil \ \rceil$ is the ceiling operator. This saving in the number of bits is, however, achieved at the expense of the additional decoders required to decode the encoded fields when the microinstruction is processed.

Further economy in the number of bits in a microinstruction can be achieved by sharing the same bits between two mutually exclusive specifications. In this case, a small additional field is required to indicate which of the mutually exclusive specifications is represented by the common bits. As an example, if the output of ALU can be gated either to a bank of 16 registers or to 16 output ports but *not* to both at the same time, then a 4-bit field can be shared between these two microoperations (select register or select output port). An additional field of 1 bit is then required to specify which of these microoperations is to be performed, which results in a saving of 3 bits. Alternatively, this 1-bit field can be replaced by a machine flag set by a previous microinstruction. For example, if the machine is in I/O mode, then the aforementioned field would specify a *select output port* microoperation, whereas if the machine is in CPU mode, then the same field would specify a *select register* microoperation.

The encoding of microinstruction fields allows a logical grouping of related microoperations. These fields can consist of select operation and operands, condition codes, and immediate data. These fields can be logically combined to form a microinstruction that resembles a conventional assembler-type instruction. Some microinstruction formats may specify one or more next address fields, as discussed in the previous chapter.

In the examples of microinstruction formats given earlier, no encoding was specified. In the instruction *select A-bus*, Field A could, for example, be encoded in 5 bits because the 16 bits represent mutually exclusive fields (no two registers can be simultaneously gated to the A-bus). However, this may not be the case for the instruction *select C-bus*. In this case, care should be exercised: If, because of the particular hardware design, the C-bus can be gated to more than one register (storing an ALU operation result in several registers simultaneously), then encoding this field would remove this flexibility. If the C-bus can be gated to only one register, then encoding will not degrade performance.

5.2 MICROINSTRUCTION EXECUTION

5.2.1. Basic Microinstruction Cycle

As discussed in Sec. 4.1, the basic microinstruction cycle consists of two main steps: fetch and execute. The fetch step consists of fetching a microinstruction from control store and routing it to the MIR; the execute step consists of analyzing the various fields of a microinstruction, setting up of the data path, and moving data along this data path, with or without any modification performed on the data.

There are variations to this basic microinstruction cycle. These variations either are designed to improve the microinstruction throughput rate or they exist as a consequence of the hardware design. The variations in the fetch step essentially constitute the microinstruction sequencing problem, which was discussed in Sec. 4.1. The following paragraphs discuss the variations in the execute step.

1. Monophase Execution

In monophase execution, all control signals for the microoperations specified in a microinstruction are issued simultaneously [1]. This means all the specified microoperations are executed (in parallel) during the same time phase.

According to this concept, all three microinstruction types defined in Sec. 5.1 fall under the monophase execution category. A vertical microinstruction containing only one microoperation is obviously a monophase microinstruction. A horizontal microinstruction, consisting of microoperations that can be executed in parallel is also, by implication, a monophase microinstruction since the control signals for parallel microoperations must be issued simultaneously. Using the same argument, a diagonal microinstruction is also a monophase instruction, because it specifies a subset of possible parallel microoperations. The execution step timing diagram for monophase execution is shown in Fig. 5.2.

2. Polyphase Execution

Even though horizontal and diagonal microinstructions are defined to contain parallel microoperations, in practice these terms are used rather loosely. As a result, microinstructions often contain microoperations that are not executed strictly in parallel. This means the execution cycle of the

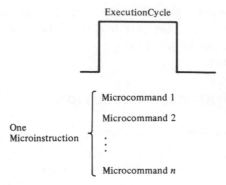

Figure 5.2 Monophase Instruction Execution Cycle

microinstruction is divided into several phases for sequential execution of nonparallel microoperations. During any given phase, however, a subset of the microoperations specified is executed concurrently. Such microinstructions are known as **polyphase microinstructions** [1]. A timing diagram for polyphase execution is shown in Fig. 5.3. It should be noted that the sequential nature of polyphase execution is of no direct concern to the microprogrammer.

Polyphase microinstructions can be further classified as one of two types [2].

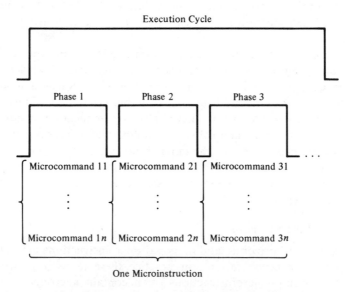

Figure 5.3 Polyphase Microinstruction Execution

1. Synchronous Polyphase

For these microinstructions, the execution cycle is divided into a fixed number of phases and all microinstructions require the same amount of execution time. The timing logic for these microinstructions is fairly simple since the execution starts at the same point in the timing cycle for all microinstructions.

2. Asynchronous Polyphase

For these microinstructions, the number of phases in the execution cycle depends on (a) microinstruction complexity, the number of microoperations to be performed; (b) characteristics of the data path, for example, specifying a bus with availability delayed due to a previous microcommand; and (c) execution time data, whether a jump is to be taken as a result of a flag or not. At the end of the execution of a microinstruction, a signal has to be generated to start execution of the next one. The timing logic for asynchronous polyphase microinstructions is more complex than that for synchronous polyphase microinstructions.

Despite a more complex timing logic compared to that for the monophase case, polyphase microinstructions provide a greater degree of (*conceptual*) parallelism. Consequently, the microprogrammer can work with instructions providing more parallelism than is actually supported by the hardware.

For example, with an ALU connected to a single bus, a polyphase microinstruction of the type

ALU Operation	Operand Register 1	Operand Register 2	Operand Register 3

will have to be implemented in 4 phases:

—Select Register 1 and move into Operand Latch 1.
—Select Register 2 and move into Operand Latch 2.
—Perform ALU operation.
—Select Register 3 and move result from ALU.

This microinstruction, however, provides the programmer with a conceptual multiple-bus ALU.

As a consequence of this type of conceptual parallelism, a hardware resource controlled by a microcommand is tied up during only one phase rather than for the whole execution cycle. This allows the resource to be reallocated for another phase in the same microinstruction or to be reallocated to a phase of another microinstruction, thereby facilitating parallel execution of microinstructions.

A polyphase microinstruction can (and should) be viewed as a sequence or concatenation of monophase microinstructions, where the microoperations performed during any given phase can be considered to constitute a monophase instruction [3, 4]. Consequently, the only *real* advantage of polyphase microinstructions is to minimize the number of control memory accesses that would otherwise be required for successive monophase instructions. Figure 5.4 graphically represents the various microinstruction characteristics. Note that the vertical axis parameter *n* is assumed to be constant for a given machine, that is, the various subsets of parallel microoperations are all of cardinality *n*.

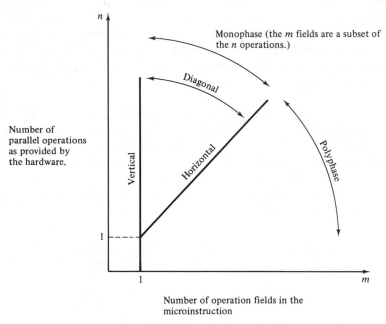

Figure 5.4 Graphical Representation of Microinstructions

5.2.2. Vertical Microinstruction Execution Example

A vertical microinstruction is a monophase instruction, because only one microcommand can be specified, requiring only one phase during the execution cycle. For example, a timing diagram for the vertical microinstruction sequence of Sec. 5.1.2 is shown in Fig. 5.5, where Fig. 5.5a represents the case of sequential microinstruction fetch and execution and Fig. 5.5b represents overlapped fetch and execution. The timing of the execution phase is the same as that shown in Fig. 5.2.

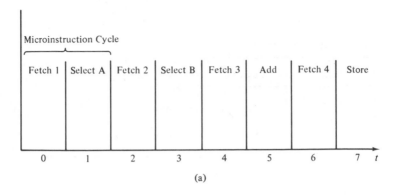

(a)

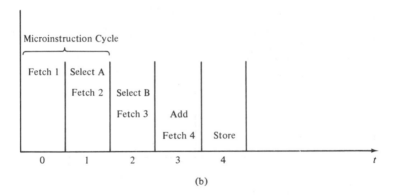

(b)

Figure 5.5 Vertical Microinstruction Timing Diagrams

5.2.3. Horizontal Microinstruction Execution Example

A monophase implementation of the horizontal microinstruction discussed in Sec. 5.1.1 would result in the timing diagram shown in Fig. 5.6a. On the other hand, a polyphase implementation would result in the timing diagram shown in Fig. 5.6b.

Figure 5.6b shows that after Phase 1 in the execution cycle, the A-bus is free and can be utilized by another microinstruction if necessary. Therefore the execution cycle of the next microinstruction (using the same format) can start at the end of this phase.

5.2.4. Diagonal Microinstruction Execution Example

A monophase implementation of the diagonal microinstruction sequence of Sec. 5.1.3 would result in the timing diagram shown in Fig. 5.7a. This diagram can be easily modified for fetch and execution cycle overlap. Figure 5.7b shows a timing diagram for polyphase implementation of this sequence. Note that in the latter case, the execution cycle of the second microinstruction

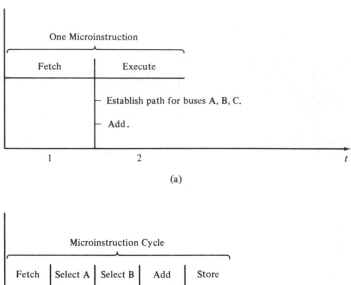

Figure 5.6 Horizontal Microinstruction Timing Diagrams

cannot start until the execution cycle of the first one is finished, because otherwise the operands for the second microinstruction would not be ready.

5.3 MICROINSTRUCTION DESIGN: SOME CONSIDERATIONS

This section outlines some of the factors that can influence the choice of the microinstruction format in a machine. These factors help determine, for example, whether the designer should choose a vertical or nonvertical (diagonal or horizontal) format, whether the number of bits per microinstruction should be minimized, or whether little or no encoding of microinstruction fields should be attempted.

5.3.1. Vertical versus Nonvertical Format

This choice is to be made when the microcode is to be memory-efficient; that is, when the control memory space required for the microprograms is to be minimized. In this context, Ramamoorthy and Tsuchiya [5] have

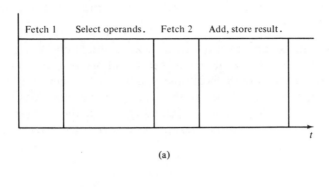

(a)

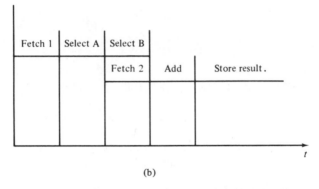

(b)

Figure 5.7 Diagonal Microinstruction Timing Diagrams

formulated a very simple analytical model, which is described in the following paragraph.

Suppose a microprogram consists of W_v vertical microinstructions where each microinstruction contains N_v bits. Suppose another microprogram, performing the same function, consists of W_{nv} nonvertical (horizontal or diagonal) microinstructions, with each microinstruction containing N_{nv} bits. Then the total number of bits required in the vertical case is $W_v \times N_v$, whereas the number of bits required in the nonvertical case is $W_{nv} \times N_{nv}$. Theoretically, two microprograms performing the same function would require the same number of microoperations regardless of the microinstruction formats. If, in the nonvertical format, an average of Q microoperations can be executed in parallel, then $W_{nv} \times Q = W_v$, or $W_{nv} = W_v/Q$. Therefore the number of bits in the nonvertical case, $W_{nv} \times N_{nv} = W_v \times N_{nv}/Q$. Hence:

1. If $Q = N_{nv}/N_v$, then $W_{nv} \times N_{nv} = W_v \times N_v$, which means either format is equally memory-efficient.
2. If Q is greater than the ratio N_{nv}/N_v then $W_{nv} \times N_{nv} < W_v \times N_v$, which means that the nonvertical format requires fewer bits.

3. If Q is less than N_{nv}/N_v, then obviously the vertical microprogram requires fewer bits.

This analysis can be easily extended to the trade-off between diagonal and horizontal formats. Let W_d be the number of diagonal microinstructions in a microprogram, with N_d being the number of bits per diagonal microinstruction. Let W_h and N_h denote the corresponding quantities in an equivalent horizontal microprogram. If Q_d and Q_h denote the average number of parallel microoperations in the diagonal and horizontal cases, respectively, then

$$W_d \times Q_d = W_h \times Q_h$$

or

$$W_h = W_d \times \frac{Q_d}{Q_h}$$

An analysis similar to the preceding one shows that if:

1. $Q_d/Q_h = N_d/N_h$, then both microprograms require the same amount of memory.
2. $Q_d/Q_h < N_d/N_h$, then the horizontal microprogram requires less memory;
3. $Q_d/Q_h > N_d/N_h$, then the diagonal microprogram requires less memory.

5.3.2. Minimization of Microinstruction Size

Once the choice of the microinstruction format has been made, the designer may be interested in minimizing or optimizing the number of bits per microinstruction. Such minimized or optimized microinstruction size obviously minimizes the control memory requirements in a processor. The minimization procedure is carried out only for the microoperation fields of a microinstruction; fields that are used to set or test for condition codes, next address field, and so on are fixed and no minimization is performed on these.

Basically, the method consists of finding *distinct* sets of mutually exclusive microcommands and then encoding these sets minimally. It should, however, be pointed out that this minimization restricts the flexibility for microprogramming; maximum flexibility is attained when the microinstruction contains a bit for each possible microoperation since in this case any parallelism in the microoperations can be fully utilized.

This problem was initially studied by Schwartz [6], and, subsequently, it has been the subject of investigation by many others. While Schwartz is credited with the first attempt to solve this problem, his method does not guarantee a minimal solution in all cases. Grasselli and Montanari [7], however, have reformulated the Schwartz model in the framework of switching theory and, in the process, have converted it to a prime implicant covering problem so that standard, well-known methods for solving cover tables can be applied in this case.

Let N denote the number of bits required for specifying the various microoperation fields in a microinstruction. Suppose $M_1, M_2, \ldots, M_k$ constitute a set of microinstructions that would occupy the control memory. Each of these microinstructions contains single or multiple microcommands that control the microoperations in the processor; fields other than the microoperation fields are not relevant to the analysis and, therefore, not considered here. The minimization procedure is based on the notion of compatibility, which is defined as follows. Two microcommands m_i and m_j are said to be **compatible** if $m_i \in M_h$ implies that $m_j \notin M_h$; that is, m_i and m_j are never specified together in a microinstruction. A **compatibility class** (CC) of microcommands is a set C_i with members (microcommands) that are all pairwise compatible. A **maximal compatibility class** (MCC) is a compatibility class to which no further microcommands can be added without violating the requirement of pairwise compatibility. The bit-dimension minimization problem can then be stated as follows. A set of compatibility classes $C = \{C_1, C_2, \ldots, C_n\}$ must be determined such that

1. Every microcommand m_i is contained in at least one element of C;
2. The quantity $N = \sum\limits_{i=1}^{n} \lceil \log_2 (|C_i| + 1) \rceil$ is minimal, where $|C_i|$ denotes the cardinality of the set C_i and $\lceil \ \rceil$ is the ceiling operator.

Note that 1 is added to $|C_i|$ in order to include the NOOP microcommand in each microoperation field. It should be obvious that $\lceil \log_2 (|C_i| + 1) \rceil$ is the minimum number of bits required to encode the elements of class C_i.

The approach taken by Grasselli and Montanari [7] was to first define a **prime compatibility class**. A compatibility class C_i is a *prime CC* if either of the following conditions hold.

1. C_i is nonmaximal and $|C_i| = 2^p - 1$, $p = 1, 2, \ldots$.
2. C_i is maximal and $|C_i| \neq 2^q$, $q = 1, 2, \ldots$.

The authors then go on to show that a minimal-N solution can be obtained from the set of prime compatibility classes by solving a cover table that lists all the prime CCs and the microcommands each of them covers. At this stage, any switching theory technique to solve a cover table can be employed to obtain a minimal solution.

Although Grasselli and Montanari succeeded in transforming the problem of minimizing control memory bit-dimension into a well-known problem of switching theory, their method potentially requires a large amount of computation. The main reason for this is that the number of *prime* CCs can be quite large, resulting in a correspondingly large cover table. To overcome this drawback, several techniques have been proposed [8–11]; an excellent survey of these methods has been provided by Agerwala [12]. The first modification to the Grasselli and Montanari method was proposed by Das, Banerji, and Chattopadhyay [8].

They essentially start with the same formulation as that of Grasselli and Montanari. However, in order to reduce the computational requirements, they do not form a cover table containing prime CCs. Instead, they use the set of MCCs to arrive at a solution. Since the number of MCCs is usually much smaller than the number of prime CCs, the amount of computation, in general, is reduced.

The algorithm by Das et al. can be summarized as follows.

Step 1. Determine all MCCs from the given control memory contents and form a control memory (CM) cover table.

Step 2. Select the *essential* MCCs from this table (those appearing alone in a column).

Step 3. Delete those columns of the CM cover table containing the essential MCCs, all but one of the columns with identical sets of MCCs, and dominated columns, if any.

Step 4. Form a reduced cover table consisting of the remaining columns, if any.

Step 5. Find all the solutions from the reduced cover table; that is; determine all sets of MCCs such that each column header of the reduced cover table is covered. Combine these sets of MCCs with the essential MCCs to obtain complete solutions of the CM cover table,

Step 6. Select a solution α_1 (set of MCCs) of the CM cover table as obtained in Step 5 and form a set-specific cover table corresponding to α_1.

Step 7. Identify all those columns containing more than one MCC, and determine all possible sets of MCCs for covering these columns. If $m_1, m_2, \ldots, m_i$ are such columns, and $M_1, M_2, \ldots, M_j$ is a set of MCCs covering these columns, then $m_1, m_2, \ldots, m_i$ are retained only in these MCCs and are deleted from the rest of the MCCs. This yields a set of MCCs and CCs such that each microcommand is contained in only one MCC or CC. Compute N from the resulting set of MCCs and CCs. Repeat this procedure for *each* set of MCCs covering the columns $m_1, m_2, \ldots, m_i$.

Step 8. Select another solution α_2 from Step 5 and proceed.

Step 9. Choose minimum N from all the solutions.

Agerwala [12] has rightly pointed out that the essence of this algorithm is to solve a number of small tables rather than one large table, as in the case of the Grasselli and Montarari procedure. This approach is expected to reduce the overall computational and storage requirements, although Das,

Banerji, and Chattopadhyay (hereafter referred to only as Das) have not shown that this is indeed the case.

The main drawback of the Das algorithm is that once the CM cover table has been solved, the rest of the procedure for obtaining a minimal solution consists essentially of exhaustive enumeration. To overcome this problem, Das has proposed two theorems that help reduce the computational requirements to some degree. Because of their limited utility, these theorems are not discussed here; the interested reader is encouraged to see Reference 8 for this purpose and for the details of the algorithm. As a final comment on this algorithm, it should be noted that an acceptable "engineering solution" can be obtained by starting with any solution of the CM cover table and following the rest of the procedure. This would always yield a "near minimal" value of N, which may be acceptable for all practical purposes.

Using an entirely novel approach to bit-dimension minimization, Jayasri and Basu [10] have formulated this problem as a linear programming problem, which is then solved using the well-known simplex method [17]. The authors [10] have made a very significant contribution in proving that there exists a lower bound for the bit-dimension N, and they have derived expressions for this bound under different conditions. This method always yields an "optimal" partition on the set of microcommands such that N meets the lower bound. It is possible, however, that such a partition does not *actually* exist for a given control memory specification.

In an attempt to improve on the Das algorithm, Srimani, Sinha, and Choudhury [11] have proved a number of interesting theorems. Their procedure for obtaining a minimal solution is essentially based on the Das method, with some modifications. Although their stated aim is to reduce the amount of computation by avoiding the calculation of *all* the solutions of the CM cover table, their method for determining a suitable partition yielding the feasible minimum value of N may require a considerable amount of trial and error. It is neither proved nor is it obvious from their paper that the amount of computation is indeed reduced.

All the minimization methods referred to so far [6–11] are based on the implicit assumption that all the microcommands constituting a microinstruction are issued simultaneously; that is the associated microoperations are executed in parallel within a given control memory clock cycle. In other words, these methods are applicable only in the case of *monophase* microinstructions. In the case of *polyphase* microinstructions, two microcommands m_i and m_j may appear to be compatible, yet they cannot be grouped together in the same field because they are issued during two different time phases of the control memory clock cycle. The minimization problem in the case of polyphase microinstructions has been considered by Dasgupta and Tartar [18]. They have shown that Das' method can be generalized to handle this problem. In their generalization approach, Dasgupta and Tartar assume a microprogram to be specified as a sequence of microcommands rather than as a sequence of microinstructions. A microprogram is represented as a directed graph G with nodes that correspond to distinct microcommands and edges that correspond to the flow of control from one microcommand to another. A straight line microprogram—SLM for short—is defined as a subgraph S of G ($S \subseteq G$) such that the final node of S is a branch, S does not contain any other branch nodes, and the only entry to S (from another SLM) is at the starting node. Here G can be partitioned into a set of such SLMs; thus a given microprogram can be broken down into a set of segments, each of which consists of a linearly ordered sequence of microcommands. A SLM, therefore, can be represented as an ordered set of microcommands

$$S = \{m_1, m_2, \ldots, m_t\}$$

where, for any two indices i and j, m_i **precedes** m_j if $i < j$.

Let us now suppose that a set of n SLMs $S_1, S_2, \ldots, S_n$ constitutes a microprogram (control memory contents). Let $\phi_1, \phi_2, \ldots, \phi_r$ denote the r different phases of the control memory cycle. Then the problem considered by Dasgupta and Tartar is to minimize the bit dimension N while ensuring that no two microcommands are grouped together in a field if they can be executed during two different phases. The approach taken by the authors is to partition each SLM into groups of *parallel* microoperations using an algorithm proposed by Jackson and Dasgupta [19] for this purpose. This exercise transforms the set of n SLMs into a set of groups of microcommands in which each group contains only those microcommands that may be executed in parallel. Let these groups be denoted as $P_1, P_2, \ldots, P_j$. It should be clear that, as far as the minimization problem is concerned, these groups are similar in nature to the microinstructions $M_1, M_2, \ldots, M_k$ considered earlier in the monophase case. In order to adapt the Das algorithm for the polyphase case, the authors [18] have modified the concept of compatibility as follows: Microcommands m_i and m_j are defined to be **compatible** if $m_i \in P_h$, $1 \leq h \leq j$, implies that $m_j \notin P_h$ *and* both are executed during the same phase ϕ_k. In this case, m_i and m_j can belong to the same field of a microinstruction; they are executed during the same phase ϕ_k of the control memory cycle in two different microinstructions. Once the modified concept of compatibility is established, the earlier definitions of compatability classes and maximal compatability classes can also be modified accordingly. For example, a compatibility class, in the polyphase case, can be defined as a set of pairwise compatible microcommands that belong to the same phase ϕ_k of the control memory clock cycle. An MCC in this case consists of a maximal set of pairwise compatible microcommands (which, therefore, cannot be executed simultaneously) such that all the microcommands in the MCC belong to the same clock phase. Once MCCs conforming to this definition are obtained for a given control memory specification, Das' method can then be used to minimize N.

As a final comment on the subject of bit-dimension minimization, Robertson [20] has claimed the problem to be **NP-hard,** although no proof for this assertion is provided in Reference 20. This means an algorithm for solving this problem in the general case would require exponential time for the solution. It is, therefore, important to realize that a realistic approach to this problem would be to concentrate on heuristic, rather than formal, methods to find near minimal solutions instead of insisting on absolute minimality [24].

5.3.3. Other Considerations

Apart from the two preceding factors affecting the design of microinstructions for a machine, there are several other considerations involved that the designer must evaluate. Some of these factors are discussed in the following paragraphs [13–16, 23].

The amount of encoding used in the various fields of a microinstruction has a direct bearing on its size. While the previous section was devoted to discussing the techniques for optimal or minimal encoding of the micro-command fields, it should be noted that such encoding may restrict the exploitation of any potential parallelism in the microoperations. In addition, this encoding necessitates decoders for the various fields before the microinstruction can be executed. The decoding process inevitably adds some delay to microinstruction execution; the designer must evaluate whether this delay is acceptable or not. The result of this evaluation will affect the microinstruction design accordingly. The choice in this case is clearly between control memory requirements and loss of flexibility along with some delay in microinstruction execution.

The number of microcommands per microinstruction is another factor to be considered by the designer. This factor was discussed in Sec. 5.3.1, but only from the point of view of conserving control memory. This, however, may not be a factor of prime importance in all designs. In order to utilize the capabilities of the hardware optimally, the number of micro-command fields per microinstruction should be consistent with the degree of parallelism existing within the hardware. Ideally, as Flynn [21] has suggested, each independent functional unit in the system should be controllable during the execution of a microinstruction. This would result in the design of the most powerful microinstructions that the hardware can support, providing maximum flexibility in the utilization of hardware resources during each microinstruction execution. Such microinstructions, however, necessarily increase the bit-dimension of the control memory regardless of whether the various microinstruction fields are encoded or not. At the same time, writing microcode with such microinstructions is relatively difficult, as was pointed out in Sec. 5.1. The fewer the number of control fields in a microinstruction, the easier it is to write microcode.

Another factor affecting microinstruction design is the choice of sequencing mechanism used. Obviously, an explicit addressing scheme requires longer microinstructions compared to implicit addressing. Generally speaking, explicit addressing fits better with microinstructions containing a large number of control fields. Implicit addressing in this case would require frequent unconditional branches after relatively short sequences of microinstructions required for interpreting the machine instructions.

The monophase or polyphase characteristic of microinstructions also affects their design. The polyphase microinstructions require a larger bit dimension because of the larger number of control fields required for different phases of the control memory cycle.

Finally, the system design goals also have an effect on microinstruction design. For a *specific* target architecture, the microinstructions can be designed to effectively support the architecture. However, for general-purpose emulation, microinstructions must provide a high degree of flexibility in the use of hardware resources, resulting in a large number of control fields. This flexibility may not be required by or be efficiently used in all target architectures but, nevertheless, it must exist to support the capability of general-purpose emulation.

REFERENCES

[1] REDFIELD, S. R., "A Study in Microprogrammed Processors: A Medium-Sized Microprogrammed Processor," *IEEE Transactions on Computers*, C–20, no. 7 (July 1971), 743–50.

[2] AGRAWALA, A. K., and T. RAUSCHER, *Foundations of Microprogramming: Architecture, Software, and Applications* (New York: Academic Press, Inc., 1976).

[3] SALISBURY, A. B., *Microprogrammable Computer Architectures* (New York: American Elsevier Publishing Company, Inc., 1976).

[4] RAMAMOORTHY, C. V., and M. TSUCHIYA, "A Study of User Microprogrammable Computers," *Proceedings of the AFIPS Conference 36 (SJCC)* (1970), pp. 165–81.

[5] RAMAMOORTHY, C. V., and M. TSUCHIYA, "Analysis of Microprogrammed Processor Design Trade-offs," *COMPCON 1972 Digest* (September 1972), pp. 111–14.

[6] SCHWARTZ, S. J., "An Algorithm for Minimizing Read-Only Memories for Machine Control," *1968 IEEE Tenth Annual Symposium on Switching and Automata Theory*, pp. 28–33.

[7] GRASSELLI, A., and U. MONTANARI, "On the Minimization of Read-Only Memories in Microprogrammed Digital Computers," *IEEE Transactions on Computers*, C–19 (November 1970), 1111–14.

[8] DAS, S. R., D. K. BANERJI, and A. CHATTOPADHYAY, "On Control Memory Minimization in Microprogrammed Digital Computers," *IEEE Transactions on Computers*, C–22, no. 9 (September 1973), 845–48.

[9] TSUCHIYA, M., and T. JACOBSON, "An Algorithm for Control Memory Minimization," *Proceedings of the Eighth Annual Workshop on Microprogramming* (September 1975), pp. 18–25.

[10] JAYASRI, T., and D. BASU, "An Approach to Organizing Microinstructions which Minimizes the Width of Control Storage Words," *IEEE Transactions on Computers*, C–25, no. 5 (May 1976), 514–21.

[11] SRIMANI, P. K., B. P. SINHA, and A. K. CHOUDHURY, "On Certain Investigations on Control Memory Minimization in Microprogrammed Digital Computers," *Proceedings of Second All India Symposium on Computer Architecture and System Design*, Indian Institute of Technology, New Delhi (November 1976), pp. 63–70.

[12] AGERWALA, T., "Microprogram Optimization: A Survey," *IEEE Transactions on Computers*, C–25, no. 10 (October 1976), 962–73.

[13] PAULL, M. C., and S. H. UNGER, "Minimizing the Number of States in Incompletely Specified Sequential Switching Functions," *IRE Transactions on Electronic Computers*, EC–8 (September 1959), 356–67.

[14] GRASSELLI, A., and F. LUCCIO, "A Method for Minimizing the Number of Internal States in Incompletely Specified Sequential Networks," *IEEE Transactions on Electronic Computers*, EC–14 (June 1965), 350–59.

[15] DAS, S. R., and C. L. SHENG, "On Finding Maximum Compatibles," *Proceedings of IEEE*, 57 (April 1969), 694–95.

[16] DAS, S. R., "An Approach for Simplifying Switching Functions by Using the Cover Table Representation," *IEEE Transactions On Computers*, C–20 (March 1971), 355–59.

[17] GASS, SAUL I., *Linear Programming: Methods and Applications* (New York: McGraw-Hill Book Company, 1969).

[18] DASGUPTA, S., and J. TARTAR, "On the Minimization of Control Memories," *Information Processing Letters*, 3, no. 3 (January 1975), 71–74.

[19] JACKSON, L. W., and S. DASGUPTA, "The Identification of Parallel Microoperations," *Information Processing Letters*, 2 (1974), 180–84.

[20] ROBERTSON, EDWARD L., "Microcode Bit Optimization is NP-Hard," *SIGMICRO Newsletter* (ACM), 8, no. 2 (June 1977), 40–43.

[21] FLYNN, M. J., "Control Through Microprogramming," *NATO International Advanced Summer Institute on Microprogramming*, Grenoble, August–September, 1971.

[22] JOHNSON, R., and R. E. MERWIN, "A Comparison of Microprogramming Minicomputer Control Words," *Digest of Papers, Compcon 74 Fall* (Washington, DC) pp. 161–66.

[23] MONTAGERO, C., "An Approach to the Optimal Specification of Read-Only Memories in Microprogrammed Digital Computers," *IEEE Trans. Comput.*, C–23, 4 (April 1974), 375–89.

[24] ROBERTSON, E. L., "Microcode Bit Optimization is NP-Complete," *IEEE Transactions on Computers*, C–28, no. 4 (April 1979), 316–19.

EXERCISES

5.1 Continue the discussion presented in Sec. 5.1.3 by proposing a program in which the diagonal format would yield the shortest microprogram (in total number of bits).

5.2 Use the three formats in Sec. 5.1 but encode the A, B, C fields and rework the examples provided. Did the conclusions change? Why?

5.3 Assuming a NOOP microcommand should be provided for all microcommand fields (select A, B, C, ALU operation), provide an encoded form of each of the horizontal, vertical, and diagonal formats. Note that a redesign of each format can be done minimizing the number of bits in the corresponding microinstructions. Which format is the least likely to be improved? Why?

5.4 If only one physical bus exists which can be connected to the A- or B-inputs or to the C-output, then the horizontal and diagonal microinstructions would have to be polyphased. Draw the timing diagram for the execution of each microprogram in Sec. 5.1 and determine the most time-efficient format.

5.5 Apply the model presented in Sec. 5.3.1 to the examples of Sec. 5.1. Verify the results.

5.6 The control memory contents of a machine are given as follows:

MICROINSTRUCTIONS	MICROCOMMANDS
M_1	a, b, c, d
M_2	a, c, e, g
M_3	b, d, f
M_4	a, c, f, h

Apply any minimization procedure to minimize the number of bits per microinstruction.

PART THREE

Microprogramming Practice

CHAPTER SIX

Developing
a Microprogram

This chapter concerns itself with the various steps that must be followed in order to implement a piece of firmware, from the actual coding of the microprogram to the final stage; that is, implementation in ROM. For each step, alternate ways are presented and discussed. Some or all of these steps must be undertaken, depending on the ultimate use of the firmware being implemented.

6.1 DIRECT MICROPROGRAMMING

6.1.1. Writing Absolute Code

Writing absolute code consists of writing a string of 1's and 0's necessary to form a given microinstruction. This process is similar to the one used in early days of programming, when machine language was the only tool available to the programmers. In general, this approach is not always desirable as it is very error prone and tedious. However, it has some uses in particular cases; for example, it is helpful when a microprogram is to be toggled directly into control storage using the console of the microprogrammable computer. In this case, absolute coding is obviously the only way available to the user. This kind of situation does arise more often than one might imagine, especially during the debugging phase of new firmware.

In order to write microcode this way, the programmer must have a thorough understanding of the microinstructions, including the structure and format of the microinstructions and size and significance of every field. With a little bit of familiarity and experience with the machine, it is relatively easy to write absolute microcode. This is particularly true for a vertical microinstruction format machine, because the microinstruction is relatively short. This experience is also useful in "reading" microprograms directly on the console lights, which is again a very common exercise when debugging a microprogram. However, for machines with horizontal microinstructions—where the size of a microinstruction can reach 64 or even 100 bits and where the number of fields is relatively high—it becomes much more difficult to write (or even read) absolute microcode. To add to this difficulty, horizontal microinstructions often have fields of varying sizes; this considerably increases the possibility of an error because of a misaligned or incomplete field. The total number of bits in the microinstruction does provide a check but, in general, writing absolute code remains prone to errors.

An improvement might be expected by grouping 3 or 4 bits together and using octal or hexadecimal notation for writing absolute code instead of using the binary notation, as it is commonly done in assembler language level programming. However, this is not of much help for the following reasons.

1. Absolute programming is used primarily when working at the console of a machine or when "patching" a given microprogram, and most computer consoles provide only binary switches and lights instead of octal or hexadecimal ones.
2. The fields of the microinstructions, especially for horizontal format instructions, are of varying sizes that are not always multiples of three or four. In this case, grouping bits in octal or hexadecimal digits actually complicates things because a single digit, for example, could very well contain the end portion of a register field, part of an opcode, and the beginning of some subsequent modifier field.

It might be fairly stated that absolute microprogramming suffers from the same disadvantages as the conventional machine-language programming. However it might be worthwhile to mention some positive aspects of this practice that are usually overlooked.

The first advantage is that by using abolute coding, the programmer does gain an insight into the program, although this usually is regarded as an eccentric practice.

The second advantage, already mentioned earlier, is that a knowledge of absolute coding is necessary when working at the console.

The third advantage is that absolute coding may help find logical errors in a source program. For example, a syntactically correct source microprogram may incorrectly modify a microinstruction at execution time. Such an error can be easily detected by examining the actual contents of the control store or microinstruction register.

In conclusion, writing microprograms in absolute form should be avoided in most situations. However, it is still a practical method with which one should be familiar, especially for writing short programs or for making corrections without having to resort to elaborate software aids such as a microassembler and a loader.

6.1.2. Testing a Microprogram

Once a microprogram has been written, whether in absolute code or via microassembler language or a high-level language, it must be thoroughly tested and debugged; this is because its final implementation is usually "frozen" in read-only memory, which makes it impossible to modify the firmware unless the whole ROM is remanufactured. Testing a microprogram involves using the object microcode to ensure that the defined machine architecture is functioning as specified. There are several techniques to carry out this testing; these are discussed in the following paragraphs:

1. Simulation

The use of a simulator provides the most flexible approach for testing a microprogram. A simulator is a program that interprets microinstructions and simulates their execution as if the microinstructions were executed by the real machine. Because it is a program, it is flexible enough to accommodate hardware design changes and it can even simulate the behavior of nonexistent machine hardware. The simulator runs on a host machine which can be the same as the one that is simulated or, more commonly, on a central installation and can be programmed in a high-level language such as FORTRAN or PL/1.

The input to a simulator consists of the object microprogram, which becomes the content of the simulated control storage. A secondary input specifies the various options that may or may not exist in a given hardware (for example, optional stacks, timers, sizes of simulated main memory and control store). Another input to the simulator is a program, written in the machine language of the target machine, that is to be interpreted by the new firmware.

The operation of the simulator consists of interpreting and simulating the execution of the microinstructions, which in turn simulate the execution of the target machine language program. This target machine program can be any program designed to run on the target machine, but most commonly it is a specially designed program with the purpose of checking the various aspects, functions, and operation of the target architecture.

In addition to producing any output that the simulated program is supposed to do, the simulator also prints out other information useful for debugging purposes. The functions most commonly performed by the simulator consist of the following.

Display of simulated control storage.
Display of simulated main memory.
Display of simulated hardware elements (such as registers and stacks).
Simulation of microinstruction execution one at a time.
Simulation of machine instruction execution one at a time.
Simulation of the execution of a complete program with a trace feature indicating the contents of the simulated elements, the cycle times used, and so on.

When the host machine has interactive computing facilities, some interactive features such as the following can be added to a simulator.

Modification of a simulated control storage location.
Modification of a simulated main memory location.
Modification of a simulated register.

After debugging the firmware, it might be helpful to output (for example, on punched cards or paper tape) the contents of the simulated control storage, as it now represents the final version of the operating firmware; this is a function which is provided by most simulators. Error messages provided by the simulator normally provide for detection of microprogram errors, machine program errors, hardware specification errors and operator errors (for example, referring to a nonexistent register during interactive debugging).

The main advantage of using a simulator comes from the fact that there is no need for the real machine during the firmware development phase. At this stage, even the hardware design can be modified to study the influence of a new hardware element on the performance of the machine. A simulator has certain drawbacks, also. It involves a considerable amount of software effort to build a simulator because microinstructions are usually complex and time dependencies have to be considered while simulating them. Furthermore, a simulator will simulate only one given machine. Often too, despite the claims of portability of high-level languages, a simulator running on one installation will require some changes, usually minor, to run on other installations. However, this is not a problem specific to simulators but is fairly common with most software packages.

2. EROM

Erasable read-only memory (EROM) provides another method of testing and debugging a microprogram. It is connected to the real machine with new firmware to be tested and behaves like the control storage for that machine. The firmware is entered into the EROM and remains frozen until a specific erase process is initiated that wipes out the contents of the EROM and makes it ready to store a new version of the firmware.

The main advantage of using an EROM consists of having a configuration which, with respect to hardware, is close to the final system. This provides an operational environment that is identical to the real one, but still allows for modifications in the firmware should errors be detected. Another advantage of EROM over a simulator is due, of course, to the fact that there is no need for a host installation to support the simulator or the need to make a sizeable investment in software should a simulator be unavailable. Other devices that perform similar functions but are known under different names, such as REPROM (reprogrammable read-only memory), FAMOS (floating gate avalanche injection MOS), or RMM (read most memory), can be used for the same purpose. Entering the microprogram is usually done electrically, although erasing the memory can be done via electric pulses or exposure to ultraviolet radiation. Further information on these devices and technologies can be found in the literature [1, 2].

The main disadvantage of EROMs is that additional equipment is needed for programming and erasing their contents. These devices generally prove useful as an intermediate step between testing and final implementation of firmware.

3. WCS

Writable control store (WCS) or alterable control memory (ACM) is a full read/write memory, which can be used for developing and testing microprograms. Although core memory can be used for this purpose, WCS is usually a semiconductor memory for reasons of speed. It provides a more dynamic test environment than EROMs since both the read and write operations are equally easy.

A common arrangement for using WCS consists of adding it to the machine hardware as a separate I/O unit; in this configuration, WCS can be read, written, and modified in the same way as, for example, a magnetic disk pack and can be used as such without any relation to microprogramming at all. It is in this mode that "dynamic" firmware is loaded into WCS from an external device (such as disk, cards, or main memory).

Another configuration, which coexists with the previous one, consists of connecting the WCS as the control memory of the computer; it then is used as the ROM, which contains the firmware. In this mode WCS can be used in two different ways.

1. The WCS can be addressed as a new entity, replacing the normal ROM of the computer.
2. It can be addressed as a continuation of the normal control memory, providing additional control store capacity.

For example, if the ROM of the computer extends from address 0_{16} to $3FF_{16}$ (1 K), another 1 K WCS module could be addressed from 0_{16} to $3FF_{16}$, replacing the ROM, or from 400_{16} to $7FF_{16}$, extending the capacity of the ROM. As an example of this configuration on the Microdata 1600 microprogramming systems [3], a console switch sets the WCS mode from an I/O unit to control store, and another switch sets the addressing system from ROM replacement to ROM extension.

Adding a WCS to given hardware might represent a sizeable cost. However, it provides for a very versatile tool to test microprograms because this testing is now done in the real environment, directly connected to the real computer console and I/O devices, yet it still allows for modification of the firmware in case of errors. In addition, WCS provides for a dynamically alterable firmware, allowing the development of "virtual control store" or even dynamic emulators for different machines. In machines with a reasonably good software support, entering microprograms in WCS is easily done via a small monitor when the WCS is in the I/O state. This monitor can usually pick up the output of a cross microassembler on cards or paper tape, the output of a microassembler on disk, or previously saved firmware from any I/O device supported by the system [4]. The monitor allows for display or modification of the WCS contents. Microprogram execution can be started when the WCS is placed in execute mode. Testing and debugging of microprograms is then carried out in the same way it is done for conventional programs; that is, using the console or reassembling and reloading the program. Due to its versatility, WCS is one of the most useful tools for microprogram development. There are some disadvantages of WCS, however.

1. Initial hardware cost.
2. The need for a monitor (although it is usually provided by the computer manufacturer).
3. Use is limited to a specific machine.

4. ROM simulator

A ROM simulator is simply a stand-alone read/write memory that is interfaced to:

1. An input device (for example, paper tape reader);
2. An output cable providing data (instructions) to the computer hardware for execution;
3. An operator console.

The testing of a given microprogram consists of loading it into the ROM simulator, verifying the correctness of the input operation by displaying the contents of the memory, plugging the interface cable into the computer control memory bus, and finally executing the microprogram. The ROM simulator then behaves like the computer control storage. Some obvious errors, such as invalid character or invalid address, can be detected directly at input or verification time.

6.1.3. Obtaining the Firmware

Once a microprogram or firmware has been developed and tested, it may be necessary or desirable to obtain a "hard" version of it. This is necessary if the firmware developed is to be part of a permanent system or a commercial product. The process consists of manufacturing a read-only memory from the binary pattern representing that firmware. There are several alternative ways of obtaining this firmware.

1. PROM

For low quantity production, the programmable read-only memory (PROM) is the usual choice. A diode array is programmed by burning out connections representing microcode bits. Although it is called a programmable memory, it can be programmed only once. This operation can be done at the factory or in the field and for a quantity of about 1 to 10, it provides a fixed version of the firmware at a reasonable price.

2. ROM

Once a firmware has been thoroughly debugged and field tested and if it is to be used in a high volume production machine, its implementation warrants the use of a ROM. The initial setup costs for ROM production are high, so high-volume production must occur to achieve a low cost per unit.

3. Other

Chapter 4 illustrated several types of technologies that can be used for a ROM; for each, a corresponding process is used to implement a microprogram.

6.2 ASSEMBLERS

6.2.1. Microassembler Language

The previous section showed that direct microprogramming is tedious and prone to errors and should be avoided for all but very small microprograms. Conventional assembler language programming provides most of the concepts for microassembler language programming: It is a first step towards a more user-oriented language, although an assembler language is still quite machine oriented.

The syntax of microassembler languages is very similar to the syntax of a normal assembler language in a vertical microinstruction machine. For horizontal microinstruction machines, especially the ones with a large number of bits (60–100), the structure of a standard assembler language might be less applicable. Indeed, sometimes it is difficult to distinguish an operation code in a horizontal microinstruction. The whole instruction can be viewed as one opcode with functional variations or as a set of operands with no distinguishable opcodes. In these cases, where it is difficult to distinguish between an action (opcode) and the elements to be acted upon (operands), a microassembler language with a structure that would reflect the structure of the horizontal microinstruction fields might still be defined. The remainder of this section considers the more common structure of an assembler or microassembler language, although the discussion might be applicable to machines with vertical microinstructions only.

The basic structure of an assembler language consists of the following fields in an instruction:

The label field;
The opcode field;
The operand fields;
Modifiers or condition fields.

For example, a typical microassembler instruction may have the following format.

TEST   TZ   I,#X′80′

THE LABEL FIELD

This field contains a label, chosen by the programmer, which refers to the corresponding instruction. The label field is usually the first field in an assembler instruction. It is an optional field that is separated from the next one by at least one space.

120

THE OPCODE FIELD

This is an operation mnemonic, belonging to the microcommand set of the machine, that specifies which of the commands must be executed. For some instructions, this field contains a code that does not refer to an actual machine microcommand but to a command instructing the assembler to take some action. In this case, the instruction is referred to as a **pseudo instruction.** For most pseudo instructions, no corresponding machine code is generated. The most commonly found pseudo instructions are the following.

1. *ORG* This instruction specifies the value of the microprogram location counter that indicates the address in control storage of the following assembled instructions.
2. *EQU* This instruction is used to assign a symbolic name to a value.
3. *DC* This instruction is used to generate a word in control storage and is in fact a pseudo instruction used for defining a constant value. In microprogramming practice, this instruction is not used to generate a data constant but could prove useful for generating special or new microinstructions that are not supported by the assembler.

It is worthwhile to note that a very common assembler pseudo instruction, DS (define storage), is not applicable in the context of microprogramming because control store contents are not modifiable when in execution mode. Hence there is no need to define variables, but only constants. Some of the other pseudo instructions are:

EJECT TITLE SKIP	Used for controlling the printout of the assembler listing.
END	Signals the end of a microprogram.

THE OPERAND FIELD

This field contains the various operands to be acted upon. The format of the field varies according to the instruction type. For example, it may contain data, register designations, or modifiers.

THE MODIFIERS

Modifiers and condition fields are sometimes concatenated to the opcode field in a way similar to the one used for denoting address modes at assembler level. They indicate that the action specified in the opcode is to be modified; that is, they specify a variation of that action.

Microassembler languages have a useful role to play in vertical format machines. For horizontal microinstruction machines, the use of micro-assembler language format is more complex and very dependent on the particular machine used. Specific assemblers for horizontal machines can be found in the literature [14].

The development of microprogrammable microprocessors has added a new momentum to microprogramming and some success has been achieved in the implementation of "flexible" microassemblers. These assemblers are designed for accomodating various field formats that seem well adapted to horizontal type machines. For details of these assemblers refer to the literature in the Further Readings [6, 33, 37].

6.2.2. The Assembly Process

A microprogram written in a microassembler language is processed by a program called an **assembler**; its main purpose is to translate the original program into an intermediate form called an **object code,** which can be read by a loader. The loader will load the actual binary representation of the microprogram in the control store. Some additional features are commonly added to microassemblers in order to aid the user.

1. An output listing is produced to help the programmer refer to or debug the programs. In addition, a listing is necessary for documentation and archival purposes.
2. Diagnostic messages are printed to point out syntax errors in the user program. Sometimes this may help to detect a logical error in a program.
3. A diode array map is produced when the microprogram is to be directly implemented in a read-only memory. This map can then be used to obtain a suitable read-only memory.

The actual assembly process consists of:

1. Reading and analyzing microinstructions;
2. Decoding opcodes and operand fields;
3. Replacing labels by their actual values;
4. Producing object code.

A complete description of the assembly process is outside the scope of this book; it will be sufficient here to give a brief summary of the various steps involved.

Pass 1

In the first pass, the microassembler reads the program from an external device and does partial assembly. This consists of building a symbol table consisting of entries that are the labels used in the program. Each label is assigned a value, which can be a control storage address, register address, or datum value. Most syntax errors are detected during this pass. It should be noted that it is worthwhile to copy the source program into a faster auxiliary memory (for example, disk) to speed up the operations since the source has to be reread in Pass 2.

Pass 2

The source program is reread, the opcodes are translated into their binary equivalents, and the operands decoded, whether they are self-defining terms, mnemonics, or labels from some other instruction. In the latter case, the operand address is obtained from the symbol table created in Pass 1. The symbol table is usually printed along with the output listing to provide a cross-reference, which is very useful in helping the programmer modify or debug the program.

In the preceding discussion, no mention was made of the machine that executes the assembler. If this machine is the same as the one used to run the assembled microprogram, then the assembler is called a **resident** micro-assembler, or simply a microassembler. However, if the microassembler is implemented to run on a different host machine, it is called a **cross** micro-assembler. In this case, the implementation of the cross microassembler is independent of the machine that will execute the assembled microprograms. Cross assemblers are commonly written in high-level languages (such as FORTRAN or PL/1) so that the packages are portable. Even with portable packages, some implementation problems are invariably encountered in a different installation.

It is perhaps worth mentioning here that, in theory, all microassemblers are, in fact, cross microassemblers. Even though it is a fine point, it should be noted that even a resident microassembler is executed by a virtual machine defined by an already existing firmware. This virtual machine is different from the microcode-level machine. In the strict sense of the term, a resident microassembler should be one written in the microassembler language itself.

6.2.3. Extra Features of Assemblers

This section discusses some additional features of assemblers that are intended to aid the user.

1. Pseudo Instructions

The concept of pseudo instructions was introduced in Sec. 6.2.1. The primary goal is to have the assembler take care of as many programming chores as possible. For example, the ORG pseudo instruction allows the programmer to define the storage locations for parts of the program, thus providing for relocation of program blocks. As another example, the pseudo instruction EQU allows the programmer to assign a symbolic name to a value that can make a program more readable. For instance, checking a register containing indicators for an I/O ready flag bit can be done by

> CP   2,X'80'   Compare contents of Reg. 2 with
>   hexadecimal value 80.

However the following sequence is more meaningful and is self-documenting.

> IOREADY   EQU   X'80'
>
>   ≡
>
>   CP   2,IOREADY

2. Macroinstructions

This feature of almost all assemblers is less commonly found and used in microassemblers. It allows one to refer to a group of instructions by a symbolic name. Once this has been done, the group of instructions need not be repeated when coding a program. Instead the associated name, called a *macroinstruction* or an open subroutine, can be used as a composite instruction. It allows the programmer to avoid repeating common sequences of instructions and also provides for better readability of programs. During assembly, each macroinstruction is expanded into its associated group of instructions. Therefore macroinstructions represent a coding convenience; they do not provide any help in optimizing memory requirements for a program.

Most assemblers provide a facility whereby parameters (operands) and generated instructions associated with a macroinstruction can be changed. This is referred to as **conditional assembly.**

As Chap. 8 will show, repeated sequences of microinstructions should be avoided because they waste control storage. Instead, it may be advisable to incorporate them in a microsubroutine. Macroinstructions are not commonly used in writing microprograms since the ease of coding they provide may well lead the programmer to forget that a simple macroinstruction may, in fact, generate quite a few object code words. Therefore microassemblers that provide such a macro facility are not commonly encountered.

3. Relocatability

Another feature of most assemblers that is not very common for microassemblers is the capability of producing relocatable object code. This simply consists of producing the object code in a format that can be processed by a program known as a **relocating loader** to produce the final object code. The output produced by the assembler is **relocatable,** which means that the object code can be loaded for execution in memory starting at any address. Once the program load address is given to the relocating loader, it takes care of all address modifications to load the program starting at that address. Microassemblers seldom have this feature because control store is usually not shared dynamically by several microprograms. Instead, microassemblers usually generate **absolute code,** which is loaded in predetermined control store locations. However, in some situations involving writable control store as a dynamic extension of an existing ROM, it might be necessary to provide relocatability of dynamic microsubroutines. The relocatability feature can also be used when, because of limited control storage, the firmware is paged to provide for a virtual control memory in a manner similar to that done in time-sharing or virtual operating systems.

6.3 HIGH LEVEL MICROPROGRAMMING LANGUAGES

6.3.1. Necessity and Advantages

As in the case of programming at higher levels, machine or assembler languages are difficult to use for coding relatively large and sophisticated microprograms. It was, therefore, unavoidable that high-level languages be developed to provide microprogrammers with the facilities already offered to programmers.

The advantages expected from a high-level microprogramming language are generally the same as those offered by high-level programming languages such as FORTRAN or PL/1. These advantages can be summarized as follows.

1. Writing programs is easier because algorithms rather than implementation details are described. This also makes reading and understanding the programs easier.
2. Writing and reading the programs is also facilitated by the fact that a more "human" syntax is used rather than machine-oriented syntax.
3. The ability to write machine-independent programs provides portability for those programs on any machine where a compiler for the same language is implemented. (This is a classical advantage of high-level languages that is not always provided in a real-life environment.)

Some high-level programming languages (PASCAL) provide the following additional aids to programmers that can also be applied to microprogramming.

1. The control structures available in such languages facilitate algorithm implementation. This, in turn, helps improve the reliability and maintainability of the programs.
2. More types of data structures that can be directly manipulated by the language are available, simplifying the programmer's task.

The nature of microprogramming, however, requires other features from a high-level language (and its compilers) that are not always to be found at the programming level.

1. The compiler should provide optimized code. (This is particularly relevant for compilers implemented to produce object microcode for a horizontal machine in order to take full advantage of the data path parallelism).

2. The language must be flexible so it can be compiled into a variety of micro-codes far exceeding the variety of machine languages. Machines at machine-language level provide numerous but rather standard and comparable instructions, consisting of opcode and a few operands. At microinstruction level, however, the format can vary considerably from one machine to another, ranging from a format (vertical) resembling machine-language instructions to a much more elaborate format (horizontal) containing several concurrent microoperation specifications.

6.3.2. Disadvantages and Trade-Offs

The disadvantages of high-level languages have hindered their development in the microprogramming area. The main drawback stems from the fact that high-level language programming and microprogramming are basically two very different activities. High-level language programming is concerned with implementing an algorithm with little or no concern about the internal details of the machine in which it is to be run, whereas microprogramming consists principally of establishing a specific machine architecture in order to better implement some class of algorithms. This necessitates a close under-standing of both the internal details of the machine and the implementation details of the algorithms. If, indeed, an algorithm is to be implemented with-out any concern about the object code, then it does not make any difference whether this code is microcode or not. Furthermore, as will be shown later, the inefficient code produced by compilers would soon overcome the speed advantage of microcoding an algorithm in a high-level language.

The investment necessary to produce a compiler for a high-level microprogramming language cannot be justified in most cases. The object code produced fits only one machine and the main use (so far) of micro-programming a machine is to define a machine architecture. This means that for a given machine, only a few microprograms are written and implemented. It is, therefore, much cheaper to write these microprograms directly in a low-level language than to produce a compiler and then write them in a high-level language. The development costs of a compiler would be acceptable only for a microprogrammable machine designed for general applications.

The relative inefficiency of object code produced by compilers is another disadvantage. As mentioned earlier, it defeats the purpose of defining an inner machine fast enough to be a base for further programming levels. The optimization techniques used in optimizing compilers can be applied for producing microcode as well; however, these techniques still do not match a good assembler programmer and, furthermore, they do not apply very well for horizontal machines where a new level of optimization (parallelism) can be put to work. Producing a reasonably optimized code requires a very complex and expensive compiler.

Another disadvantage of using a compiler comes from the fact that special machine features such as temporary hold registers, which are designed to allow the programmer to better utilize operating registers, may very well be overlooked by a compiler as such features might be absent from the language itself if it is to be machine independent. Using such a feature, if it is available in a high-level language, would require as much time and effort from a programmer as if the coding were done in assembler-level language.

For high-level microprogramming languages, machine independence is a goal to be attained rather than a reality. Microprogramming languages available so far are very tailored to a given machine or a given architecture.

Although the histories of programming and microprogramming are parallel, as Agrawala [5] notes, the development of high-level languages for microprogramming is far behind its counterpart for programming. In the authors' opinion, the reason for this is simple: Programming was a mass-production activity and has now reached the level of assembly-line production, where coding has become standardized and routine work (thanks to such concepts as structured and modular programming). Therefore efficient tools such as numerous languages and utility libraries could be developed at a fair price. On the other hand, microprogramming is still very much at a craftmanship level. Few microprograms (often only the native mode emulator) that are efficient in execution time, memory space, and services rendered are implemented on a given machine. Furthermore, because their size is limited, there is no need for a large programmer team. The current microprogramming trends may change this situation, one hopes with beneficial effects (see Part 4, Examples). However, concern has already been expressed about indiscriminate use of microprogramming [6]. In particular, Wilkes [7] notes that microprogramming should be considered mainly, if not only, as a way to design a control unit and not as an algorithm implementation tool.

6.3.3. Considerations in the Design of a Microprogramming Language

The goals to be achieved when designing a high-level language can be classified into two main categories.

1. Machine-related objectives

The language must be adapted or adaptable to a wide variety of machines, the compiler must provide for code optimization, and the language must be oriented towards its design application; that is, establishing data flow paths to implement a specific architecture.

2. User related objectives

A high-level language program expresses an algorithm symbolically in a readable and comprehensive way. This is provided by using devices such as symbolic names or clear control statements. The features commonly found in high-level languages must, therefore, be included in the design. For microprogramming purposes, a high-level language must also provide facilities for manipulating hardware features such as registers, flags, and stacks [8, 11, 13].

Because of the necessity of providing a language designed specifically for manipulating hardware items, existing languages such as FORTRAN or ALGOL cannot be used efficiently for microprogramming. It would be relatively easy to write a FORTRAN compiler, for example, that produces object code in the microlanguage of a vertical machine; however, for horizontal machines, there is little hope of providing a compiler producing optimized object code.

In order to provide a machine-independent language, the most common approach consists of providing a language and an associated compiler, which basically require the use of two different phases:

Phase 1   Definition of the machine structure.

Phase 2   Programming the algorithm.

During the first phase, the compiler builds dictionaries, tables, and so on, allowing the programmer to "enable" some language features particularly adapted to the target machine. These features can then be used during the second phase as part of the language. However due to the difficulty of taking into consideration all possible hardware details pertinent to various machines, the resulting languages have, for the most part, been developed for specific machines.

The remainder of this section presents some microprogramming languages, with no attempt to be exhaustive. It is restricted to the languages that can claim to be high-level and machine independent. Therefore we shall not mention numerous "higher-level languages tailored for given machines," despite their merits.

6.3.4. High Level Languages for Microprogramming

1. MPL

One of the first attempts to design a high-level microprogramming language was made by Eckhouse [10] in 1971. He chose to make extensions to an existing language (PL/1) in order to incorporate operations that are useful to microprogrammers. The purpose of microprogramming language (MPL) was to establish the relevance of a high-level language for microprogrammers and to demonstrate that such a language can also produce relatively efficient microcode.

The syntax of MPL resembles the syntax of its parent PL/1, with the necessary extensions to include the specifications of data items such as registers and memories, events such as carry and overflow, hexadecimal and binary constants, and so on. The executable statements have a very different syntax to allow the concatenation of data items such as registers (for double-length registers); operations include bit manipulation operations such as shifts and boolean operations.

The compilation is done by producing an intermediate language (SML) in the first phase and generating a dictionary containing specifications of real data items (machine dependent). The second phase translates SML into a virtual code; that is, into instructions using data items that may or may not exist on the machine (for example, multiple registers). The final phase maps the virtual code into real microinstructions, taking into account the dictionary describing actual hardware features.

2. A Language for Series 70

Another machine-independent microprogramming language was designed for the Univac Series 70 [8]. Its aim is to provide a basic programming tool for expressing an algorithm in a high-level language and still provide a reasonably efficient object microcode. The language defines DECLARE statements, which assign symbolic names, values, and conditions to machine-dependent resources. In addition, it defines command statements to:

Move and perform operations on data;
Provide conditional and unconditional transfers of control.

The operations provided are typical of bit-field manipulation (for example, set/reset, OR, and AND).

The compiler generates microcode output using several tables containing machine-dependent hardware descriptions. These tables are provided as part of the machine description to the compiler or built at execution time. The object output does not consist of microinstructions, but microcommands. The compiler optimization section processes the microcommands generated by the previous phase and tries to merge them into microinstructions.

3. SIMPL

Ramamoorthy and Tsuchiya [9] have developed a language called SIMPL and its compiler with the aim of highly optimizing the microcode for horizontal machines. The language is reasonably machine independent, although DeWitt [12] claims the language is best suited for the CDC 6600 machine.

The SIMPL language incorporates the single-assignment concept in its design. This concept forces a variable to be assigned a value only once during the execution of a program. In this context, it is used to detect statements that can be executed in parallel; that is, microoperations that can be combined in a horizontal microinstruction. The language itself resembles ALGOL, where complex control structures have been removed (together with the GO TO statement) and operators related to bit manipulation have been added; the READ/WRITE statements refer to transfer from or to main memory. The compilation proceeds in four basic steps: analysis of the syntax, generation of blocks of sequential microcode, analysis of timing and concurrency of microoperations, and optimization. The compile time is substantial, but the object code produced is claimed to be highly efficient (provided, of course, that the object machine offers parallelism via a horizontal format).

4. EMPL

The core approach in language design seems attractive in the context of microprogramming languages, because it allows the language designer to better fit the language to a given configuration by defining the desired hardware characteristics as extentions to the core language. This is the approach used by DeWitt [12] in the design of extensible microprogramming language (EMPL). The extension mechanisms are similar to the ones provided in ALGOL 68 or PASCAL and can be used to "define the machine" to the compiler. The extensions defined can then be used as part of the language.

The syntax of the language resembles that of languages such as PL/1 but with bit manipulation operators included. The control constructs available are IF-THEN-ELSE and DO-WHILE (with a surviving GO TO). The extension statements allow the definition of a new item (a hardware stack, for example), and the definition of the operations available on that item (PUSH, for example).

Although no compiler was designed together with the EMPL language, DeWitt explains the feasibility of writing such a compiler [12]. The problem of whether to compile an extension into one microinstruction (if the machine supports it) or into a microprogram (if the machine does not support this extension) is solved via a control language specifying to the compiler the existence or absence of hardware support for each declared extension. This would provide portability of the source microprogram.

6.4 MICROOPERATING SYSTEMS

6.4.1. Introduction

With the development of writable control memories attaining speeds comparable to ROMs, the static nature of firmware is bound to be replaced by a more dynamic environment. For example, in some models of the IBM Series 370, main memory is already shared by software and firmware, allowing firmware to be modified more easily. Another example of this trend consists of integrating modifications of the writable control store (that is, loading microprograms) in an existing operating system; control language then not only specifies which compiler is desired, for example, but also which emulator should be loaded for execution of the particular program.

In these dynamic environments, a microoperating system is necessary to take care of chores such as loading firmware and taking care of control memory management.

6.4.2. Components

The components of a microoperating system that are available on some systems [4] include, of course, the microassembler and any high-level microprogramming language compilers that may be used in a given installation. The control part of the operating system is much simpler, because control memory is not as widely shared as main memory is. On this system [4], the control program (written in software) basically consists of a monitor getting commands from an operator and an absolute loader that brings the object microcode into control store.

The commands available to the operator allow the display, change, or dumping of the contents of the control memory, controlled execution of a microprogram with breakpoints, tests, and so on.

The microobject input to the loader can be the output of a microassembler (on disk) or the output of a cross microassembler or a cross simulator (on cards).

The main operating system allows for control of the microoperating system via control cards or commands such as:

Load a given emulator;
Execute the microloader or microassembler;
Pass control to the microoperating system.

REFERENCES

[1] BURSKY, D., "Special Report: Memories Pace Systems Growth," *Electronics* (September 27, 1980), pp. 63–74.

[2] GREEN, R., and others, "The Biggest Erasable PROM Yet Puts 16,384 Bits on a Chip," *Electronics* (March 3, 1977), 108–11.

[3] *"Microprogramming Handbook,"* 2nd ed. (Irvine, Calif.: Microdata Corporation, 1972).

[4] RAYMOND, J., "Microoperating System for the Microdata 1600," Technical Report #76–06 (Ottawa, Ontario: Department of Computer Science, University of Ottawa, 1976).

[5] AGRAWALA, A. K., and T. G. RAUSCHER, *Foundations of Microprogramming* (New York: Academic Press, Inc., 1976), Chap. 7.

[6] LEHMAN, M.M., "Microprogramming Trend Considered Dangerous," *ACM-SIGMICRO Newsletter*, 6, no. 3 (September 1975), 37–39.

[7] WILKES, M. V., "Ten Years and More of Microprogramming," *ACM–SIGMICRO Newsletter*, 8, no. 4 (December 1977), 11–13.

[8] TIRREL, A. K., "A Study of the Application of Compiler Techniques to the Generation of Microcode," *Proceedings of ACM SIGPLAN–SIGMICRO Interface Meeting* (May 1973), pp. 67–84.

[9] RAMAMOORTHY, C.V., and M. TSUCHIYA, "A High-Level Language for Horizontal Microprogramming," *IEEETC*, C–23, no. 8 (August 1974), 791–807.

[10] ECKHOUSE, R. H., JR., "A High-Level Microprogramming Language (MPL)," *Proceedings of 1971 Spring Joint Computer Conference*, (Montvale, N.J.: AFIPS Press), pp. 169–77.

[11] HATTORI, M., M. YANO, and K. FUJINO, "MPGS: A High Level Language for Microprogram Generating System," *Proceedings of the ACM 1972 National Conference*, pp. 572–81.

[12] DEWITT, D. J., "Extensibility, A New Approach for Designing Machine-Independent Microprogramming Languages," *Proceedings of the Ninth Annual Workshop on Microprogramming*, also *SIGMICRO Newsletter*, 7, no. 3 (September 1976), pp. 33–41.

[13] MALLET, P. W., and T. G. LEWIS, "Considerations for Implementing a High-Level Microprogramming Language Translation System," *Computer*, 8, no. 8 (August 1975), 40–52.

[14] MARTIN, D., "An Eclipse Microassembler," *SIGMICRO Newsletter*, 8, no. 1 (March 1977), 13–23.

FURTHER READINGS

1. ALLRED, G. R., "System/370 Integrated Emulation Under OS and DOS," *AFIPS Conference Proceedings*, 38 (SJCC, 1971), 163–68.

2. ANCEAU, F., "Application of the Language CASSANDRE to Micropro-

gramming," *Preprints of the Workshop on Microprogramming*, Grenoble (June 1970).

3. ATKINS, J.D., "Paradigmatic Universal Microcode Assembler," *Preprints of the Workshop on Microprogramming*, Grenoble (June 1970).

4. BAGLEY, J.D., "Microprogrammable Virtual Machines," *Computer*, 9, no. 2 (February 1976), 38–42.

5. BAILLIU, G., and D. FERRARI, "A Method to Model Microprograms and Analyze their Behavior," *Proceedings of the Sixth IEEE Computer Society Conference*, San Francisco (September 1972).

6. BALPH, T., and W. BLOOD, "Assembler Streamlines Microprogramming," *Computer Design*, 18, no. 12 (December 1979), 79–89.

7. BANKOWSKI, J., and K. FIATKOWSKI, "Instruction Coding and Checking Problem for a Horizontally Microprogrammed Computer," *Bulletin de l'Académie Polonaise des sciences* (1965), pp. 119–22.

8. BERNDT, H., "A Microprogram Notation Resembling Statement of Higher-Level Languages," *Elektronishe Rechonanlagen*, 14 (October 1972), 220–28.

9. BERNDT, H., "Trends in Microprogramming Language Design," in *Microprogramming and Systems Architecture*, ed. C. Boon. Infotech State of the Art Report 23, Infotech Information Ltd., 1975, pp. 373–89.

10. BLAIN, G., and others, "Génération automatique de microprogrammes optimisés," *Revue Française de l'Afiro*, no. B-3 (1972), 61–90.

11. BORSCHEV, V. B., P. L. VASILEVSKY, and M. V. KHOMYAKOV, "A Programming Microlanguage for URAL-4," *Kibernetica*, no. 6 (1966), 47–49.

12. BOURICIUS, W. G., "Procedure for Testing Microprograms," *Preprints of the Seventh Annual Workshop on Microprogramming*, Palo Alto (October 1974), 235–40.

13. CHAPTAL DE CHATELOUP, V., "Problems of Microprogram Production," in *Microprogramming and Systems Architecture*, ed. C. Boon. Infotech State of the Art Report 23, Infotech Information Ltd., 1975, pp. 241–59.

14. CHU, V., "A Higher-Order Language for Describing Microprogrammed Computers," Technical Report 68–78, University of Maryland, Computer Science Center (September 1968).

15. CLARK, R. K., "Mirager, the 'Best Yet' Approach for Horizontal Microprogramming," *Proceedings of the 1972 ACM National Conference*, pp. 554–71.

16. DASGUPTA, S., "Towards a Microprogramming Language Schema," *Proceedings of the Eleventh Annual Microprogramming Workshop* (November 19–22, 1978), pp. 144–53.

17. DEWITT, D. J., M. S. SCHLANSKER, and D. E. ATKINS, "A Microprogramming Language for the B–1726," *Preprints of the Sixth Workshop on Microprogramming*, College Park, Maryland (September 1973), pp. 21–29.

18. ECKHOUSE, R. H., "An Investigation into the Use of a Higher-Level Machine Independent Language for Writing Microprograms," *Preprints of the Third Workshop on Microprogramming*, Buffalo, N.Y. (October 1970).

19. EVANS, R. H., L. H. MOFFETT, and R. E. MERWIN, "Design of Assembly

Level Language for Horizontal Encoded Microprogrammed Control Unit," *Preprints of the Seventh Annual Workshop on Microprogramming*, Palo Alto (October 1974), pp. 217–24.

20. GASSER, M., "An Interactive Debugger for Software and Firmware," *Preprints of the Sixth Workshop on Microprogramming*, College Park, Maryland (September 1973), pp. 113–19.

21. GERACE, G. B., and M. VANNESCHI, "Flowcharting, Microprogramming, and System Design," in *Microarchitecture of Computer Systems*, ed, R. W. Hartenstein and R. Zaks, pp. 225–32. North-Holland/American Elsevier, 1975.

22. GREEN, J., "Microprogramming, Emulators and Programming Languages," *Communications of the ACM*, 9, no. 3 (March 1966), 230–32.

23. GUYOT, A., P. MARTIN, and J. MARMET, "A Microprogram Metacompiler," *EUROMICRO Newsletter*, 1, no. 1 (October 1974), 35–43.

24. HAWK, D. R., and D. M. ROBINSON, "A Microinstruction Sequencer and Language Package for Structured Microprogramming," *Proceedings of the Eighth Annual Workshop on Microprogramming*, Chicago, Illinois (September 21–23, 1975) pp. 69–75.

25. HODGES, B. C., and A. J. EDWARDS, "Support Software for Microprogram Development," *SIGMICRO Newsletter*, no. 4 (January 1975), pp. 17–24.

26. HOPKINS, W. C., "A Multi-Emulator Operating System for a Microprogrammable Computer," *Preprints of the Third Workshop on Microprogramming*, Buffalo, N.Y. (October 1970).

27. KARCHER, G. W., and J. Y. HSU, "A Cross Assembler Implemented on IBM/360 for Variably Defined Microcode," *SIGMICRO Newsletter*, 5, no. 3 (October 1974), p. 89.

28. LAWSON, H. W., JR., and L. BLOMBERY, "The Datasaab FCPU Microprogramming Language," *Preprints of the SIGPLAN/SIGMICRO Interface Meeting*, New York (May 1973).

29. LEWIS, T.G., and C. HIBB, "AQL: A Meta Compiler for Microprogramming," *Computer Science Conference*, Columbus, Ohio (February 1973).

30. LLOYD, G. R., and A. VAN DAM, "Design Considerations for Microprogramming Languages," *AFIPS Conference Proceedings*, 43 (NCC 1973), 537–44.

31. MALIK, K., and T. LEWIS, "Design Objectives for High-Level Microprogramming Languages," *Proceedings of the Eleventh Annual Microprogramming Workshop* (November 19–22, 1978), pp. 154–60.

32. MALLETT, P. W., and T. G. LEWIS, "Approachs to Design of High-Level Languages for Microprogramming," *Preprints of the Seventh Annual Workshop on Microprogramming*, Palo Alto (October 1974), pp. 66–73.

33. "Microprogramming the Series 3000," Section 2: XMAS Language. Santa Clara, Ca.: Intel Corporation, 1975.

34. NOGUEZ, G. L. M., "Design of a Microprogramming Language," *Preprints of the Sixth Workshop on Microprogramming*, College Park, Maryland (September 1973), pp. 145–55.

35. OESTREICHER, D. R., "A Microprogramming Language for the MLP–900," *Preprints of the SIGPLAN/SIGMICRO Interface Meeting*, New York (May 1973).

36. PETZOLD, R., and H. P. ROHRS, "Flexible High-Level Microcode Generation," in *Microarchitecture of Computer Systems*, ed. R. W. Hartenstein and R. Zaks, pp. 45–52. North-Holland/American Elsevier, N.Y., 1975.

37. POWERS, V. M., and J. H. HERNANDEZ, "Microprogram Assemblers for Bit-Slice Microprocessors," *Computer*, 11, no. 7 (July 1978) pp. 108–19.

38. RAUSCHER, T. G., "Towards a Specification of Syntax and Semantics for Languages for Horizontally Microprogrammed Machines," *Preprints of the SIGPLAN/SIGMICRO Interface Meeting*, New York (May 1973).

39. RAUSCHER, T. G., and A. K. AGRAWALA, "On the Syntax and Semantics of Horizontal Microprogramming Languages," *Proceedings of the ACM 1973 Annual Conference*, pp. 52–56.

40. REIGEL, E. W., and H. W. LAWSON, "At the Programming Language–Microprogramming Interface," *Preprints of the SIGPLAN/SIGMICRO Interface Meeting*, New York (May 1973).

41. SCHREINER, E., "A Comparative Study of High-Level Microprogramming Languages," *SIGMICRO Newsletter*, 5 (April 1974), p. 4 (abstract).

42. TUCKER, A. B., and M. J. FLYNN, "Dynamic Microprogramming: Processor Organization and Programming," *Communications of the ACM*, 14 (April 1971), 240–50.

43. VICKERY, C., "Software Aids for Microprogram Development," *Preprints of the Seventh Annual Workshop on Microprogramming*, Palo Alto (October 1974), pp. 208–11.

44. WILLEN, D., "An Intel 3000 Cross Assembler," *SIGMICRO Newsletter*, 7, no. 4 (December 1976), 87–94.

45. YOUNG, S., "A Microprogram Simulator," *SIGMICRO Newsletter*, 2, no. 3 (October 1971), 43–56.

EXERCISES

6.1 Use the instruction set presented in Appendix B.
   a. Write a set of microinstructions in absolute form that copies a file register into another one.
   b. Write a set of microinstructions in absolute form that clears all file registers.
6.2 Use the instruction set and the assembler syntax presented in Appendix B to write the instructions outlined in Exercises 6.1, but in assembler language.
6.3 Write the machine code equivalent of the following microinstructions.

$$\begin{array}{ll} \text{CPY} & 4,\text{T} \\ \text{CPY} & 4,(\text{T}) \\ \text{CPY} & 4,\text{T}(\text{T}) \\ \text{LF} & 4,\text{X}'04' \\ \text{CPY*} & 4,\text{T}(\text{T}) \end{array}$$

6.4 Write the machine code equivalent of the following microprogram.

$$\begin{array}{ll} \text{ORG} & \text{X}'100' \\ \text{LF} & 2,\text{X}'00' \\ \text{JP} & *+2 \\ \text{DC} & \text{X}'AB' \\ \text{CPY} & 2,(\text{T}) \\ \text{HLT} \end{array}$$

6.5 Write the machine code equivalent of the ADD instruction example in Chap. 7; toggle this program in control memory, execute it, and verify the results on the console lights after stepping through each step of the microprogram.
6.6 Summarize the advantages and disadvantages of the various procedures of testing a microprogram.
6.7 For the following assembler language microprogram, detail the operations of the first pass, give the results of this first pass, then detail the operations of the second pass and give the final output of the assembler.

$$\begin{array}{lll} & \text{ORG} & \text{X}'100' \\ & \text{LF} & 2,\text{X}'00' \\ \text{X} & \text{LM} & \text{X}'00' \\ & \text{RMF*} & 2,\text{D}(\text{N}) \\ & \text{LM} & \text{X}'01' \\ & \text{WMF} & 2,\text{D}(\text{N}) \\ & \text{TZ} & 0,\text{X}'04' \\ & \text{JMP} & \text{X} \\ & \text{HLT} \end{array}$$

6.8 Write a FORTRAN or PL/1 program that performs a floating point ADD operation (using integer arithmetic). Compare it with the FADD program in Chap. 7.

CHAPTER SEVEN

Implementation
of Some Common
Machine Instructions
and Functions

7.1 INTRODUCTION

This chapter is concerned with the microprogrammed implementation of some common machine instructions and functions. Its purpose is to illustrate how the "inner" machine is microprogrammed to create a virtual machine at a higher level. The examples presented here are independent and self-contained. They were not designed as part of a machine, but rather to demonstrate the flexibility offered by microprogramming for implementing various functions. A complete machine-implementation example is discussed in Chap. 9 and Appendix C. "Standard operations" such as addition will be discussed first, then more specialized instructions such as the cyclic redundancy check instruction, third, some elaborate I/O operations (taking care of all the necessary I/O processing details), and finally some miscellaneous specialized instructions.

The examples have been written in Microdata 1600* microcode. It should be noted that the microprograms are not optimized in order to better detail the operations taking place. Before presenting these examples, a brief description of the Microdata 1600 is in order.

Microdata 1600 Computer†

The Microdata 1600 is a microprogrammable digital computer with an 8-bit word length in core memory. The standard CPU has capacity for up to 4 K words by 16 bits of control memory and, optionally can have an alterable control memory of up to 16 K words. Each 16-bit word in the control memory contains a single microinstruction. Most microinstructions are of the diagonal type, specifying from 1 to 6 microcommands. Appendix B gives a detailed list of the instructions used in the examples and is presented as reference for studying the examples. It might prove useful, however, to look at this instruction set first to get an idea of the microcommands involved. This material is not a substitute for the manufacturer's literature should this particular machine be used for actual implementation of other instructions and functions by the reader.

The architecture of the Microdata 1600 CPU is illustrated in Fig. 7.1. The major processing facility of the processor is the arithmetic logic unit (ALU). It performs addition, subtraction, data transfer, logical AND, OR, exclusive OR, and shifting. Inputs to the ALU are from the B-bus and from the selected file register, and output is via the A-bus to the selected destination register.

A status register consisting of File Register 0, common to both the primary and secondary files, is used for various internal flags such as overflow and negative or zero condition generated by the ALU.

All registers except the file registers have specific functions in the machine. A brief description of the processor registers follows.

T-REGISTER

The 8-bit T-register serves as the operand register for most operate-type commands as a buffer for data being written into or read from core memory, and for output on the byte I/O bus. It is the main work register.

M- AND N-REGISTERS

The 8-bit M- and N-registers hold the current 16-bit address of the location being accessed in core memory. The M-register holds the 8 high-order bits of the address, and the N-register holds the 8 low-order bits.

*Microdata Corporation, Irvine, Cal.

†This material is based on the *Microprogramming Handbook* and is reprinted with permission of Microdata Corporation, Irvine, Ca.

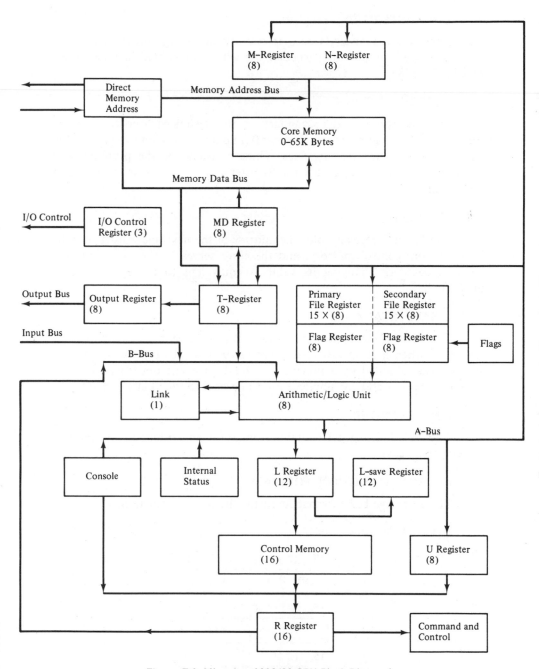

Figure 7.1 Microdata 1600/30 CPU Block Diagram*

*Reprinted with permission of Microdata Corporation, Irvine, California.

139

U-REGISTER*

The 8-bit U-register is used to modify the 8 high-order bits of the control memory output. Its particular use will be illustrated in some examples in Chap. 8.

FILE REGISTERS

Two files (primary and secondary) of 16 registers each provide storage for internal flags and user data. Register 0 (in both files) is not available to the user and is used for internal flags. These registers are the programmer's work storage space and, except for Register 0, have no preassigned use in the machine.

L-REGISTER

The 12-bit L-register holds the address of the next microinstruction to be read from control memory, and therefore serves as the microprogram location counter. Changing its value is equivalent to executing a jump instruction.

L-SAVE STACK

The 16 × 12-bit L-save stack saves the incremented contents of the L-register when a jump extended microinstruction (JE) is executed, unless storage was inhibited by a previous inhibit L-save microinstruction (ILS). This feature is useful for implementing microsubroutine calls and returns.

LINK REGISTER

The 2-bit link register contains storage for an arithmetic link bit and a memory link bit.

MICROINSTRUCTION FORMATS

There are five basic formats used for the microinstructions.

1. Literal commands.

```
 15   12 11   8 7          0
┌──────┬─────┬──────────────┐
│  OP  │  F  │     LIT      │
└──────┴─────┴──────────────┘

 15            8 7          0
┌──────────────┬────────────┐
│      OP      │    LIT     │
└──────────────┴────────────┘

 15   12 11                 0
┌──────┬────────────────────┐
│  OP  │        LIT         │
└──────┴────────────────────┘
```

*Reprinted with permission of Microdata Corporation, Irvine, California.

2. Operate commands.*

15 12 11	8 7	4	3	2	0
OP	F	C	*	r

3. Generic commands.

15	0
OP

The following symbols are used.

OP: Operation Code

F: File Register Designator

C: Control Field or Modifiers

LIT: Literal

*:   File Inhibit

r: Destination Register Designator

The Microdata 1600 microinstruction set is provided in Appendix B, and more details can be found in the *Microprogramming Handbook* [1]. The assembler language notation associated with these instructions is also summarized in Appendix B.

7.2 SOME COMMON MACHINE INSTRUCTIONS

1. The ADD Instruction

The fixed-point ADD instruction is one of the most common and basic instructions in a machine. It is used for the addition of two fixed-point (integer) operands with addresses that are specified either explicitly or implicitly as part of the instruction. The operands can be in one of several representations, such as sign-magnitude, 1's complement, or 2's complement, depending on the machine. A fairly common fixed-point representation is the 2's complement notation that will be used in the following examples. The ADD instruction considered in our example is of the format

ADD A,B

where A and B are two 16-bit registers available at the assembly-language level. The instruction adds the contents of Registers A and B and stores the

*Reprinted with permission of Microdata Corporation, Irvine, California.

sum in Register A. Furthermore, it sets the following values in a condition code register.

8	If sum is zero.
4	If sum is negative.
2	If sum is positive.
1	If an overflow occurs.

Some machines generate an internal interrupt in case of an arithmetic overflow; however, for purposes of simplicity, this feature will not be considered.

In the given example, the following Microdata 1600 file register assignments have been used:

Register A (low byte):	File Register 2
Register A (high byte):	File Register 1
Register B (low byte):	File Register 4
Register B (high byte):	File Register 3
Condition code register:	File Register 5

A microprogram implementing this instruction is shown in Listing 7.1. The algorithm is very simple and consists of adding the two low bytes and the two high bytes, plus the possible carry from the previous step; the condition code is then set as necessary through a sequence of tests on the result.

```
LOCN CODE FLAGS LABELS OP *    OPERANDS     COMMENTS                        PAGE   1

                ***
                ***   ADD INSTRUCTION ROUTINE
                ***
                ***
0000 C401               MOV    4,(T)         COPY LOW BYTE OF B IN T REGISTER
0001 8220               ADD    2,T           ADD LOW BYTES.RESULT IN LOW BYTE OF A
0002 C301               MOV    3,(T)         COPY HIGH BYTE OF B IN T
0003 81B0               ADD    1,LTC         ADD HIGH BYTES PLUS CARRY FROM LOW
              *                              BYTE SUM. SET CONDITION FLAGS, AND
              *                              RESULT GOES IN HIGH BYTE OF A.
0004 2501               LF     5,X'01'       OVERFLOW CONDITION CODE.
0005 4001               TZ     0,X'01'       OVERFLOW OCCURED?
0006 1020               RTN                  YES RETURN.
0007 2504               LF     5,X'04'       NEGATIVE CONDITION CODE.
0008 4002               TZ     0,X'02'       NEGATIVE RESULT?
0009 1020               RTN                  YES RETURN.
000A 2502               LF     5,X'02'       POSITIVE CONDITION CODE.
000B 41FF               TZ     1,X'FF'       HIGH BYTE SUM ZERO?
000C 1020               RTN                  NO,RETURN.
000D 42FF               TZ     2,X'FF'       LOW BYTE SUM ZERO?
000E 1020               RTN                  NO,RETURN.
000F 2508               LF     5,X'08'       SET ZERO CONDITION CODE.
0010 1020               RTN                  RETURN
                END
```

Listing 7.1 Microprogram for Fixed Point ADD

2. *Conditional Branch (BC) Instruction*

The conditional branch (BC) instruction is used to alter the flow of control in a program according to the current value of the condition code register. The condition code register is set as a result of the execution of some other instruction (for example, see the ADD instruction discussed earlier). The format of the BC instruction used in this example is as follows:

BC MSK,ADR

This represents a 16-bit machine language instruction of the type

15 12	11 8	7 0
Opcode (BC)	Mask (MSK)	$\pm$Displacement (ADR)

Here ADR is an 8-bit signed displacement value in 2's complement form; when added to the program counter (which points to the next instruction), it gives the branch address. Also, MSK is a 4-bit mask field used to specify the conditions under which a branch is to be taken. The mask field is logically AND-ed with the condition code register; if the result of this operation is null, then the branch is not taken. On the contrary, if the result contains at least a 1 bit, the branch is taken. For example, if after an ADD instruction, a BC instruction contains a mask field of 1100, then a branch would be taken if the result of ADD was less than or equal to zero.

The Microdata 1600 file register assignments for this example are:

Condition code register:	File Register 5
Program counter (low byte):	File Register 7
Program counter (high byte):	File Register 6
Instruction register (opcode):	File Register 8

A microprogram for the BC instruction is shown in Listing 7.2: The condition code register is checked against the mask in order to determine if the conditions specified by the mask are met or not. The branch is taken by adding the displacement to the program counter (6 and 7).

3. *Convert to Binary (CVB) Instruction*

The convert to binary (CVB) instruction is a common instruction in computers and is used for converting a number in decimal representation to its equivalent binary representation. This example assumes the decimal number is in binary coded decimal (BCD) format. The instruction used in

```
          ***
          ***   WHEN THIS ROUTINE IS ENTERED THE PROGRAM COUNTER(FILES 6 & 7)
          ***   POINTS TO THE BYTE CONTAINING THE BC OPCODE.
          ***
          ***
0000 110F         LT    X*0F*         PREPA ~ TO EXTRACT MASK FIELD.
0001 E829         AND*  8.T(T)        GET MA. IN T.
0002 E539         AND*  5.TC(T)       AND MAS. WITH CONDITION CODE.
0003 4004         TZ    0.X*04*       CHECK FO. ZERO RESULT
0004 1020         RTN                 CONDITION NOT MET RETURN.
0005 8743         INC   7.(N)         MOVE ADDRESS POINTER TO NEXT BYTE.
0006 A682         RMF   6.L(M)        UPDATE 6 AND READ DISPLACEMENT FROM MEMORY.
0007 B230         CPY   2.CT          SAVE INTO FILE 2(SAVE NEGATIVE CONDITION)
0008 8720         ADD   7.T           ADD DISPLACEMENT TO PROGRAM COUNTER.
0009 8680         ADD   6.L           WITH POSSIBLE OVERFLOW.
000A 4002         TZ    0.X*02*       WAS DISPLACEMENT NEGATIVE?
000B 9640         DEC   6             YES ADJUST FILE 6.
000C 1020         RTN                 NO,RETURN.
          END
```

Listing 7.2 Microprogram for BC Instruction

this example is of the form

$$\text{CVB} \quad \text{A,B}$$

where A and B are the same registers as in the ADD instruction example. The instruction takes a number in the BCD code which is in B-register and converts it into its binary representation, storing the result in Register A. Furthermore, it sets the following values in a condition code register.

3   If the BCD number is invalid.

1   If valid conversion took place.

In this example, the BCD number has the following format: the 12 low-order bits of B correspond to 3 BCD digits, while the 4 high-order bits of B are 1111 if the number is negative and 0000 if the number is positive. Any other bit configuration in the 4 high-order positions is considered an invalid sign. The three digits are represented in binary with values ranging from 0000 (zero) to 1001 (9), with any other bit configuration 1010 (A) to 1111 (F) being invalid. The file register assignments used in the ADD instruction are used here also. The contents of B remain unchanged. For example, if the contents of the B-register are

$$1111 \quad 0000 \quad 0001 \quad 0000 \quad (-10)$$

that is, −010 is in BCD, then the A-register will contain

$$1111 \quad 1111 \quad 1111 \quad 0110$$

that is, −10 in 2's complement form. A microprogrammed implementation of this instruction is shown in Listing 7.3.

144

```
******************************************************************
*     THE CVB INSTRUCTION.                                       *
*                                                                *
******************************************************************
0000 2501              LF    5,X'1'      SET CONDITION CODE.
0001 110F              LT    X'0F'       MASK TO SELECT DIGIT.
0002 E329              AND*  3,T(T)
0003 0024              JE    CHECK       CHECK VALIDITY.
0004 001A              JE    M10         MULTIPLY BY 10, RESULT IN REGISTER 1 & 2.
0005 7429              SRF*  4,(T)       SHIFT 4 HIGH BITS INTO 4 LOW BITS OF T.
0006 280F              LF    8,X'0F'     THE SHIFT OPERATION PADS WITH ONES, SO
0007 E821              AND   8,T(T)      WE MUST MASK THEM OUT.
0008 0024              JE    CHECK       CHECK VALIDITY.
0009 8221              ADD   2,T(T)      ADD AND STORE RESULT IN T.
000A 001A              JE    M10         MULTIPLY BY 10, STORE RESULT IN REG 1 & 2.
000B 110F              LT    X'0F'       MASK TO SELECT NEXT BCD DIGIT.
000C E429              AND*  4,T(T)      UNITS IN T REGISTER.
000D 0024              JE    CHECK       CHECK VALIDITY.
000E 8220              ADD   2,T         ADD TO TOTAL IN REG 2.
000F 8180              ADD   1,L         ADD CARRY IF ANY.
0010 43F0              TZ    3,X'F0'     WAS NUMBER POSITIVE?
0011 1413              JP    NOP         NO.
0012 1020              RTN               YES, RETURN.
0013 53F0     NOP      TN    3,X'F0'     WAS SIGN VALID?
0014 1427              JP    SCC         NO.
0015 D160     NEG      XOR   1,FT        ONE'S COMPLEMENT FILE 1.
0016 D260              XOR   2,FT        ONE'S COMPLEMENT FILE 2.
0017 8240              INC   2           INCREMENT 2.
0018 8180              ADD   1,L         TAKE CARE OF CARRY.
0019 1020              RTN
                *                        ROUTINE TO MULTIPLY A NUMBER
                *                        N, IN (T) BY 10, RESULT STORED
                *                        IN FILES 1 AND 2.
                *
001A 2100     M10      LF    1,X'0'      CLEAR 1.
001B 8220              CPY   2,T         SAVE IN 2.
001C F201              SFL   2,(T)       N*2 IN (T) AND FILE 2.
001D F200              SFL   2           N*4 IN (2) WITH
001E F180              SFL   1,L         POSSIBLE OVERFLOW SAVED IN FILE 1.
001F F200              SFL   2           N*8 IN (2) WITH
0020 F180              SFL   1,L         POSSIBLE OVERFLOW.
0021 8220              ADD   2,T         RESULT IN FILE 2.
0022 8180              ADD   1,L         POSSIBLE OVERFLOW IN FILE 1.
0023 1020              RTN
                *
                *                        ROUTINE TO CHECK DIGIT VALIDITY.
                *
0024 8820     CHECK    CPY   8,T         COPY IN FILE 8.
0025 68F6              CP    8,X'F6'     GREATER THAN 9?
0026 1020              RTN               NO,RETURN.
0027 2503     SCC      LF    5,X'03'     SET CONDITION CODE.
0028 1020              RTN
                       END   0
```

Listing 7.3 Microprogram for CVB Instruction

In this microprogram two subroutines are used; the subroutine M10, which receives a binary number in Register T as input, multiplies it by 10, and stores the result as a 16-bit number in Registers 1 and 2; the subroutine CHECK checks for the validity of a digit in T and sets the condition code accordingly.

The main routine consists of converting the first digit to its binary form, multiplying it by 10, adding the second digit, multiplying the result by 10, and adding the last digit; then the sign is processed and the number complemented if necessary.

4. Floating Point Add (FAD) and Subtract (FSU) Instructions

The instructions floating point Add (FAD) and floating point Subtract (FSU) are used to add and subtract floating point numbers, respectively. The format used for representing the floating point numbers is as follows.

```
31  30      24 23                      0
  ┌───┬───────────┬──────────────────────┐
  │ S │     E     │          F           │
  └───┴───────────┴──────────────────────┘
  Sign    Exponent        Fraction
```

This representation corresponds to a number $S16^{E-64} \times F$, $0 \leq F < 1$, which is a fairly common floating point representation.

In this example the numbers are first compared in magnitude to determine if unnormalization is to take place and on which one of the numbers. During this phase, a significance error (loss of significant digits) can be encountered; if this occurs the least significant argument is simply ignored and the result is equal to the other argument (or its complement). When the two numbers have the same exponent, the operation specified (add or subtract) is performed in a second phase between the two fractional parts. Finally the result is normalized if necessary (third phase). The implementation presented in Listing 7.4 uses the 32-bit floating point representation, which makes the whole microprogram longer. Although flowcharts (especially unstructured ones) are less clear than structured pseudo code, one is included in Fig. 7.2 because it directly reflects the microcode in Listing 7.4. It is hoped that it will clarify this rather long microprogram.

7.3 SPECIALIZED INSTRUCTIONS

1. Cyclic Redundancy Check (CRC)

Cyclic redundancy check (CRC) codes are frequently used to detect errors that may be introduced during data transmission and for checking the integrity of data on tapes and disks. Before discussing the implementation of this checking scheme, a brief description of the CRC generation mechanism is provided. Details of basic theory and other features of CRC's are provided in the references [2, 3].

The basic procedure for generating the CRC consists of dividing the polynomial (over a Galois field of 2 elements, 0 and 1) representing the data bits by a "generator" polynomial of degree n. In general, the division will not be exact, and there will be a remainder of degree $n - 1$. The bit configuration corresponding to this remainder polynomial is then appended to the data bits, and together they form the actual transmitted message. Mathematically, this can be expressed as follows.

```
                    ****************************************************************
                    *                                                              *
                    * FAD FSU FLOATING POINT ADD AND SUBTRACT                       *
                    *                                                              *
                    ****************************************************************
                    * 1ST ARGUMENT IS IN REGISTERS 4.5.6.7                          *
                    * REG 5 (SE1) SIGN AND EXPONENT                                 *
                    * REG 4 (M11)  MANTISSA HIGH BYTE                               *
                    * REG 7 (M12)  MANTISSA MIDDLE BYTE                             *
                    * REG 6 (M13)  MANTISSA LOW BYTE                                *
                    *                                                              *
                    * 2ND ARGUMENT IS IN CORE AT ADDRESS CONTAINED IN:             *
                    *                                                              *
                    * REG 2 (E)  LOW BYTE                                           *
                    * REG 3 (F)  HIGH BYTE                                          *
                    *                                                              *
                    * IT IS READ AND PLACED INTO REGISTERS 11.12.13.14             *
                    *                                                              *
                    * REG 11 (SE2) SIGN AND EXPONENT                               *
                    * REG 12 (M21) MANTISSA HIGH BYTE                              *
                    * REG 13 (M22) MANTISSA MIDDLE BYTE                            *
                    * REG 14 (M23) MANTISSA LOWBYTE                                *
                    *                                                              *
                    * TEMPORARY REGISTERS ASSIGNMENT                               *
                    *                                                              *
                    * REG 2 (E1) EXPONENT 1ST ARGUMENT                             *
                    * REG 3 (E2) EXPONENT 2ND ARGUMENT                             *
                    * REG 15 (DEP) DISPLECMENT E1-E2                               *
                    * REG 10 (A) OVERFLOW                                           *
                    ****************************************************************
                    *                                                              
                    *                                                              
                    *                                                              
                    *                                                              
                    * ASSIGNMENT OF NAMES TO REGISTERS                             
                    *                                                              
                    *                                                              
                    *                                                              
        0002        E       EQU     2
        0003        F       EQU     3
        0005        SE1     EQU     5
        0004        M11     EQU     4
        0007        M12     EQU     7
        0006        M13     EQU     6
        000B        SE2     EQU     11
        000C        M21     EQU     12
        000D        M22     EQU     13
        000E        M23     EQU     14
        0002        E1      EQU     2
        0003        E2      EQU     3
        000F        DEP     EQU     15
        000A        A       EQU     10
                    *
                    *
                    *
                    *
                    *
                    *
```

```
                    *
                    * FLOATING POINT SUBTRACT. COMPLEMENT ARGUMENT2
                    *
0000 2B80           FSU     LF      SE2,X'80'
0001 1403                   JP      ADD
                    *
                    * FLOATING POINT ADD  KEEP SIGN
                    *
C002 BB00           FAD     ZOF     SE2
                    ****************************************************************
                    *                                                              *
                    * THIS SEGMENT READS THE 2ND ARGUMENT AND CHECKS               *
                    * DEP=E1-E2 FOR UNNORMALISATION                                *
                    * BRANCHES TO SOS IF E1=E2                                      *
                    *              TO D1  IF E1>E2                                  *
                    *              TO D2  IF E1<E2                                  *
                    *              TO FIN IF SIGNIFICANCE ERROR (+- DEP >=6)        *
                    *                                                              *
                    ****************************************************************
```

Listing 7.4 Microprogram for Floating Add and Subtract

```
0003 C203    ADD     MOV     E.(N)
0004 A302            RMF     F.(M)
0005 DB20            XOR     SB2.T           IF SE2=X'80' THE SIGN IS INVERTED.
0006 8243            INC     E.(N)
0007 A382            RMF     F.L.(M)
0008 BC20            CPY     M21.T
0009 8243            INC     E.(N)
000A A382            RMF     F.L.(M)
000B BD20            CPY     M22.T
000C 8243            INC     E.(N)
000D A382            RMF     F.L.(M)
000E BE20            CPY     M23.T
000F C501            MOV     SE1.(T)         MOVE SE1 TO E1
0010 B220            CPY     E1.T
0011 CB01            MOV     SE2.(T)         MCVE SE2 TO E2
0012 B320            CPY     E2.T
0013 F200            SFL     E1
0014 F220            SFR     E1
0015 F300            SFL     E2
0016 F320            SFR     E2
0017 C301            MOV     E2.(T)          DEP = E1 - E2
0018 9239            SBT*    E1.T.C.(T)
0019 BF20            CPY     DEP.T
001A 4004            TZ      0.X'04'         IS E1 DIFFERENT THAN E2?
001B 1447            JP      SOS
001C 4002            TZ      0.X'02'         E1 > E2?
001D 142D            JP      PP              NO. BRANCH.
001E 1106            LT      X'06'           TEST IF DEP < 6.
001F 9F38            SBT*    DEP.T.C
0020 5002            TN      0.X'02'
0021 149F            JP      FIN
            *
            * UNNORMALISE ARGUMENT2
            *
0022 2304    D1      LF      E2.X'04'
0023 FC20    DP1     SFR     M21
0024 FDA0            SFR     M22.L
0025 FEA0            SFR     M23.L
```

LOCN CODE FLAGS LABELS OP * OPERANDS COMMENTS PAGE 3

```
LOCN CODE FLAGS LABELS OP *  OPERANDS      COMMENTS                    PAGE   3

0026 9350            DEC     E2.C
0027 5004            TN      0.X'04'
0028 1423            JP      DP1
0029 9F50            DEC     DEP.C
002A 5004            TN      0.X'04'
002B 1422            JP      D1
002C 1447            JP      SCS
002D 1106    PP      LT      X'06'           TEST IF DEP > -6.
302E 8F38            ADD*    DEP.T.C
002F 4006            TZ      0.X'06'
0030 143E            JP      R2
            *
            * UNNORMALISE ARGUMENT1
            *
0031 2204    D2      LF      E1.X'04'
0032 F420    DP2     SFR     M11
0033 F7A0            SFR     M12.L
0034 F6A0            SFR     M13.L
0035 9250            DEC     E1.C
0036 5004            TN      0.X'04'
C037 1432            JP      DP2
0038 8F50            INC     DEP.C
0039 5004            TN      0.X'04'
003A 1431            JP      D2
003B C301            MOV     E2.(T)          MOV E2 TO E1.
003C B220            CPY     E1.T
003D 1447            JP      SOS
003E CB01    R2      MOV     SE2.(T)         MOVE SE2 TO SE1.
003F B520            CPY     SE1.T
0040 CC01            MOV     M21.(T)
0041 B420            CPY     M11.T
0042 CD01            MOV     M22.(T)
0043 B720            CPY     M12.T
0044 CE01            MOV     M23.(T)
0045 B620            CPY     MI3.T
0046 149F            JP      FIN
0047 C501    SOS     MOV     SE1.(T)         TO TEST IF SIGN1 = SIGN2.
0048 DB38            XOR*    SE2.T.C
```

Listing 7.4 (continued)

```
        ************************************************************************
        *  THIS SEGMENT ADDS ARGUMENT1 AND ARGUMENT2 AS                        *
        *    - ARGUMENT2 IS COMPLEMENTED IF SUBTRACT                            *
        *    - E1 IS EQUAL TO E2                                               *
        *  OVERFLOW IS RECORDED IN REG 10                                      *
        ************************************************************************
0049 4002           TZ      0,X'02'
004A 1467           JP      SDF                        BRANCH IF THE SIGNS ARE DIFFERENT.
004B CE01           MOV     M23,(T)                    M1 = M1 + M2
004C 8623           ADD     M13,T,(N)
004D CD01           MOV     M22,(T)
004E 87A3           ADD     M12,L,T,(N)
004F CC01           MOV     M21,(T)
0050 84A3           ADD     M11,L,T,(N)
0051 2300           LF      E2,X'00'                   TO TEST FOR OVERFLOW
0052 8383           ADD     E2,L,(N)
0053 5301           TN      E2,X'01'
0054 1483           JP      NRM
0055 F420           SFR     M11                        SHIFT M1 4 BITS RIGHT.

LOCN CODE FLAGS LABELS OP *   OPERANDS        COMMENTS                    PAGE   4

0056 F7A0           SFR     M12,L
0057 F6A0           SFR     M13,L
0058 1180           LT      X'80'
0059 C420           LOR     M11,T
005A 2303           LF      E2,X'03'
005B F420    DP3    SFR     M11
005C F7A0           SFR     M12,L
005D F6A0           SFR     M13,L
005E 9350           DEC     E2,C
005F 5004           TN      0,X'04'
0060 145B           JP      DP3
0061 8250           INC     E1,C                       E1 = E1 - 1
0062 5001           TN      0,X'01'                    TO TEST FOR OVERFLOW OF E1.
0063 1483           JP      NRM                        BRANCH TO NORMALIZE.
0064 1104           LT      X'04'                      TO INDICATE OVERFLOW.
0065 CA20           LOR     A,T
0066 1483           JP      NRM                        BRANCH TO NORMALIZE.
0067 CE01    SDF    MOV     M23,(T)                    M1 = M1 - M2 - 1
0068 9663           SBO     M13,T,(N)
0069 CD01           MOV     M22,(T)
006A 97E3           SBO     M12,L,T,(N)
006B CC01           MOV     M21,(T)
006C 94E3           SBO     M11,L,T,(N)
006D 2300           LF      3,X'00'                    SAVE THE OVERFLOW IN FILE 3.
006E 8383           ADD     3,L,(N)
006F 8643           INC     M13,(N)                    M1 = M1 + 1
0070 8783           ADD     M12,L,(N)
0071 8483           ADD     M11,L,(N)
0072 8383           ADD     3,L,(N)                    ADD OVERFLOW TO FILE 3.
0073 4303           TZ      3,X'03'                    TEST IF OVERFLOW IS ZERO.
0074 1483           JP      NRM                        JUMP TO NORMALIZE.
0075 C401           MOV     M11,(T)                    COMPLIMENT M1.
0076 2400           LF      M11,X'00'
0077 9460           SBO     M11,T
0078 C701           MOV     M12,(T)
0079 2700           LF      M12,X'00'
007A 9760           SBO     M12,T
007B C601           MOV     M13,(T)
007C 2600           LF      M13,X'00'
007D 9660           SBO     M13,T
007E 8643           INC     M13,(N)
007F 8783           ADD     M12,L,(N)
0080 8483           ADD     M11,L,(N)
0081 CB01           MOV     SE2,(T)
0082 B520           CPY     SE1,T
        ************************************************************************
        *  THIS SEGMENT NORMALISES THE RESULT IF NECESSARY                     *
        *  AND COPIES RESULT INTO ARGUMENT1.                                   *
        *  OVERFLOW OR UNDERFLOW CONDITION IS STORED IN (A)                    *
        ************************************************************************
0083 C410    NRM    LOR     M11,C                      TEST IF MANTISSA IS ZERO.
0084 C790           LOR     M12,L,C
0085 C690           LOR     M13,L,C
0086 5004           TN      0,X'04'
0087 148A           JP      NZ
0088 2540           LF      SE1,X'40'                  SE1 = 40 WHEN MANTISSA IS ZERO.
0089 149F           JP      FIN
```

Listing 7.4 (continued)

149

LOCN	CODE	FLAGS	LABELS	OP *	OPERANDS	COMMENTS
008A	44F0	NZ		TZ	M11,X'F0'	IS NORMALIZATION NESCESSARY?
008B	149A			JP	EXP	
008C	2304			LF	E2,X'04'	SHIFT M1 4 BITS LEFT.
008D	F600	DG		SFL	M13	
008E	F780			SFL	M12,L	
008F	F480			SFL	M11,L	
0090	9350			DEC	E2,C	
0091	5004			TN	0,X'04'	
0092	148D			JP	DG	
0093	42FF			TZ	E1,X'FF'	
0094	1498			JP	OK	
0095	1104			LT	X'04'	NOTE UNDERFLOW OF E1.
0096	CA20			LOR	A,T	
0097	149A			JP	EXP	
0098	92E0	OK		DEC	E1,C	E1 = E1 - 1
0099	148A			JP	NZ	BEGIN TO NORMALIZE.
009A	F500	EXP		SFL	SE1	MOVE E1 TO SE1.
009B	B500			ZUF	SE1	
009C	F5A1			SFR	SE1,L,(T)	
009D	8229			ADD*	E1,T,(T)	
009E	B520			CPY	SE1,T	
009F	1780	FIN		HLT		
				END		

Listing 7.4 (continued)

$$M(x) = x^n D(x) + R_{n-1}(x) \tag{7.1}$$

where $M(x)$ is the message polynomial, $D(x)$ is the data polynomial, and $R_{n-1}(x)$ is the remainder polynomial.

The polynomial $R_{n-1}(x)$ is obtained from the following relation:

$$\frac{x^n D(x)}{G_n(x)} = Q(x) + \frac{R_{n-1}(x)}{G_n(x)} \tag{7.2}$$

Where $G_n(x)$ is the generator polynomial and $Q(x)$ is the quotient polynomial. Therefore we have

$$x^n D(x) - R_{n-1}(x) = G_n(x)Q(x) \tag{7.3}$$

All operations are performed modulo 2 (equivalent to the exclusive OR operation), which makes the addition operation equivalent to subtraction. Hence Equation 7.3 becomes

$$x^n D(x) + R_{n-1}(x) = G_n(x)Q(x) = M(x) \tag{7.4}$$

This means the message polynomial is evenly divisible by the generator polynomial. At the receiving end, the message polynomial is divided by $G_n(x)$; if no detectable errors occurred during transmission, then the remainder obtained as a result of this division would be zero. A nonzero remainder indicates an error condition.

In the present example, the CRC generation instruction has the symbolic format

CRC   ADDR,N

which generates a 16-bit CRC on a data block of N bytes and stores it in Register A. The ADDR represents a 16-bit pointer to the data block and

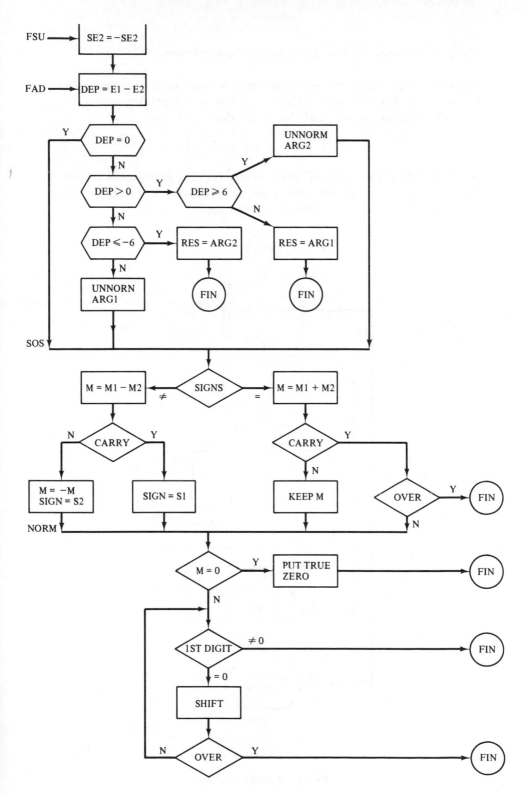

Figure 7.2 Floating Point Add and Subtract

occupies 2 bytes (high byte first) following the location of the opcode CRC. The value of N is contained in the byte following this pointer, so $0 \leq N \leq 255$. The generator polynomial chosen for the example is

$$G(x) = x^{16} + x^{15} + x^2 + 1$$

A top-level flowchart for CRC generation using this generator is shown in Fig. 7.3, and a corresponding microprogram is shown in Listing 7.5. The following file register assignments have been used:

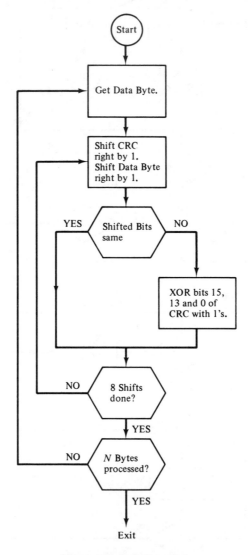

Figure 7.3 CRC Flowchart

```
                *************************************************************************
                *************************************************************************
                *                                                                       *
                *  CRC INSTRUCTION                                                       *
                *                                                                       *
                *  WHEN THIS ROUTINE IS ENTERED, THE PC(FILE 6&7) POINTS TO THE          *
                *  BYTE CONTAINING THE CRC OPCODE.                                       *
                *                                                                       *
                *                                                                       *
                *************************************************************************
                *************************************************************************
0000 B200    CRC      ZOF    2
0001 B100             ZOF    1               INITIALIZE CRC TO ZERO.
0002 0021             JE     RES
0003 B420             CPY    4,T             PUT HIGH BYTE OF DATA POINTER IN FILE 4.
0004 0021             JE     RES
0005 B520             CPY    5,T             PUT LOW BYTE OF DATA POINTER IN FILE 5.
0006 0021             JE     RES
0007 B820             CPY    8,T             PUT DATA BYTE COUNT IN FILE 8.
0008 C503             MOV    5,(N)           PUT LOW BYTE OF DATA POINTER IN N.
0009 2308    RPT      LF     3,X'08'         SET BIT COUNT TO 8.
000A A402             RMF    4,(M)           PUT HIGH BYTE OF DATA POINTER IN M AND READ
000B B920             CPY    9,T             SAVE DATA IN FILE 9.
000C F900    SR       SFL    9               SHIFT DATA LEFT BY 1.
000D FA80             SFL    10,L            SAVE SHIFTED BIT IN COMPARISON REGISTER
000E F200             SFL    2               SHIFT LOW BYTE OF CRC LEFT
000F F180             SFL    1,L             SHIFT HIGH BYTE OF CRC AND LINK BIT LEFT
             *                               SHIFTED OUT BIT GOES IN LINK.
0010 8A80             ADD    10,L            ADD LINK BIT TO COMPARISON REGISTER.
0011 5A01             TN     10,X'01'        SHIFTED BITS EQUAL?
0012 1417             JP     BYP             NO, BYPASS EXCLUSIVE OR OPERATION.
0013 1180             LT     X'80'           EX-OR MASK FOR HIGH BYTE OF CRC.
0014 D120             XOR    1,T             EX-OR WITH HIGH BYTE.
0015 1105             LT     X'05'           EX-OR MASK FOR LOW BYTE OF CRC.
0016 D220             XOR    2,T             EX-OR WITH LOW BYTE.
0017 9350    BYP      DEC    3,C             DECREMENT BIT COUNT AND SET CONDITION FLAG
             *                               IN FILE 0.
0018 5004             TN     0,X'04'         8 BITS SHIFTED?
0019 140C             JP     SR              NO, REPEAT.
001A F308             SFL*   3               CLEAR LINK BIT.
001B 8543             INC    5,(N)           PUT LOW BYTE OF DATA POINTER IN N
001C 8480             ADD    4,L             ADD OVERFLOW TO HIGH BYTE OF DATA POINTER.
001D 9850             DEC    8,C             DECREMENT BYTE COUNT AND SET
             *                               CONDITION FLAG.
001E 5004             TN     0,X'04'         DATA BLOCK PROCESSED?
001F 1409             JP     RPT             NO, GET NEXT BYTE.
0020 1020             RTN
             *
             *                               THE FOLLOWING BLOCK READS NEXT BYTE FROM
             *                               MEMORY AND CLEARS THE LINK BIT.
             *
0021 8743    RES      INC    7,(N)           INCREMENT LOW BYTE OF PC AND PUT IT IN N
0022 A682             RMF    6,L(M)          UPDATE HIGH BYTE OF PC, PUT IT IN M AND
             *                               READ A BYTE FROM MEMORY.
0023 F308             SFL*   3               CLEAR LINK BIT.
0024 1020             RTN                    RETURN.
                      END    0
```

Listing 7.5 Microprogram for CRC Instruction

Register A (low byte):	File Register 2
Register A (high byte):	File Register 1
Program counter (low byte):	File Register 7
Program counter (high byte):	File Register 6

2. The Translate and Test Instruction (TRT)

The translate and test instruction (TRT) is found in the IBM System 360/370 instruction set (among others) to help scan a line for various categories of characters (for example, digits, letters, or punctuation). This instruction has three parameters:

The address of the byte string to be scanned;

The length of the line (number of bytes);

The address of a translate table used to determine the scanning format.

This instruction is executed as follows.

The first byte of the line is utilized as an index (0 to 255) in the translate table to yield a function byte.

If the function byte is nonzero, the execution stops, the function byte is stored in the last byte of the General-Purpose Register 2, the address of the argument byte (in the scanned line) is stored in the General-Purpose Register 1, and the condition code is set to 1.

If this byte is zero, then this process is repeated for the next byte, and so on until all bytes of the line have been processed, in which case execution stops and the condition code is set to 8.

In the sample microprogram of Listing 7.6, the following assumptions have been made to simplify the emulation of the TRT instruction on the Microdata 1600.

1. The address of the string to be scanned is placed in File Registers 1 and 2.
2. The address of the translate table is placed in File Registers 3 and 4. This gives only 16-bit addresses instead of the 24-bit address of the IBM 360/370.
3. The condition code is placed in File Register 5 and the length is in File 6.

```
LOCN CODE FLAGS LABELS OP *    OPERANDS     COMMENTS                         PAGE   1

          ****************************************************************************
          *                                                                          *
          *   TRT   INSTRUCTION                                                       *
          *                                                                          *
          ****************************************************************************
0000 2501      TRT    LF    5,X'01'      SET CONDITION CODE TO 1.
0001 C102      TRI    MGV   1,(M)        COPY 1 INTO HIGH BYTE OF
               *                         MEMORY ADRESS REGISTER.
0002 A20B             RMF*  2,(N)        COPY 2 INTO LOW BYTE OF MAR AND READ
               *                         BYTE OF STRING TO BE SCANNED.
0003 842B             ADD*  4,T(N)       GET LOW BYTE OF FUNCTION BYTE ADDRESS
               *                         AND ADD INDEX INTO TABLE(FILE 4 UNCHANGED).
0004 A38A             RMF*  3,L(M)       COPY AND UPDATE HIGH BYTE INTO MAR AND
               *                         READ FUNCTION BYTE FROM TABLE.
0005 B720             CPY   7,T          SAVE FUNCTION BYTE INTO 7.
0006 47FF             TZ    7,X'FF'      IS FUNCTION BYTE ZERO?
0007 140F             JP    NO           NO.
0008 8240             INC   2            YES. INCREMENT ADDRESS OF BYTE IN STRING
0009 8180             ADD   1,L          IN 1 AND 2.
000A 9650             DEC   6,C          DECREMENT LENGTH, SET CONDITION CODES.
000B 5004             TN    0,X'04'      IS THE LENGTH ZERO?
000C 1401             JP    TRI          NO, CHECK NEXT BYTE IN STRING.
000D 2508             LF    5,X'08'      YES. SET CONDITION CODE TO 8.
000E 1020             RTN                RETURN.
000F 134B      NO     LN    X'4B'        GET ADDRESS OF REG 2 (LAST BYTE).
0010 A711             WMF   7,(T)        MOVE FUNCTION BYTE TO T REGISTER.
               *                         WRITE INTO EMULATED REGISTER 1 (LAST BYTE).
0011 1346             LN    X'46'        ADDRESS OF EMULATED REGISTER 2 (THIRD BYTE)
0012 A111             WMF   1,(T)        WRITE HIGH BYTE OF ADDRESS INTO THE THIRD
               *                         BYTE OF THE EMULATED REGISTER.
0013 1347             LN    X'47'        ADDRESS OF LAST BYTE OF REGISTER 2.
0014 A211             WMF   2,(T)        WRITE LOW BYTE OF ADDRESS INTO THE FOURTH
               *                         BYTE OF THE EMULATED REGISTER.
               END   0
```

Listing 7.6 Microprogram for TRT Instruction

4. The emulated general-purpose registers are placed in dedicated memory locations starting at address X'0040'.

Therefore GPR 1 is at address X'0044' to X'0047' and GPR 2 is at address X'0048' to X'004B'.

For the reader thoroughly familiar with the operation of the TRT instruction on IBM machines, it should be noted that in this example, the address stored in Register 1 is a 16-bit address and the upper half of that register is left unchanged, while on the IBM 360, it is set to all zeros. In addition, while on an IBM 360/370 the number of bytes minus one is specified in the instruction, in this example the number of bytes as specified is utilized and assumed to be nonzero. Note also that a condition code of 2 is not used in this example.

A flowchart for this instruction is shown in Fig. 7.4.

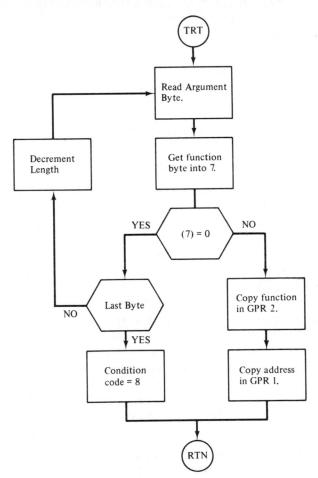

Figure 7.4 TRT Instruction Flowchart

7.4 EXAMPLES OF I/O INSTRUCTIONS

The factors involved in the implementation of I/O instructions vary depending on the I/O devices and the machine I/O structure. A microprogram implementing an I/O instruction can range from a simple routine that starts a channel operation to an elaborate routine that performs I/O transfers, synchronization, and control of the I/O device.

7.4.1. Microdata 1600 Input/Output System*

The Microdata 1600 system provides an extremely fast elementary input/output capability. The data paths and control functions are simple elements that can be sequenced from the control memory. Microprograms in the control memory can implement facilities with a high degree of versatility in timing, data paths and I/O capabilities.

The I/O facility consists of:

1. A 3-bit I/O control register;
2. A byte input bus and input control lines;
3. A byte output bus and output control lines.

A brief description of these facilities follows.

1. Input Output Control Register

The I/O control register can be loaded or cleared by the I/O control microinstructions; the contents of the I/O control register define an I/O bus mode. The byte I/O control instructions and control modes are shown in Table 7.1.

During the execution of I/O control microinstructions, the 3 low-order bits of the C-field are placed in the I/O control register. The I/O control register output may be decoded to form individual control signals defining the type of transfer to be performed on the byte I/O bus (for example, CIO or DIX) and the state of the serial interface output (for example, SOX). Of the eight possible states of the I/O control register, one represents no activity on the I/O bus (CIO), three are output modes (COX, DOX, SOX) and four are input modes (CAK, IAK, DIX, and SIX).

Whenever the value in the I/O control register is set to 4, 5, 6, or 7, the input bus is substituted for the T-register in any command (for example, ADD) that selects the T-register or its complement.

---

*This material is adapted from the *Microprogramming Handbook* and is reproduced with the permission of Microdata Corporation, Irvine, Ca.

TABLE 7.1

I/O CONTROL MICROINSTRUCTIONS AND CONTROL MODES*

COMMAND FORMAT

15 14 13 12	11 10 9 8	7 6 5 4	3 2	1 0
Opcode = 7	f	c	*	r

Mnemonic	Operand Field	C Field (in Hex.)	Mode or Contents of I/O Control Register	Control Activity
CIO	f,(r)	8	0	Clear I/O Mode
COX	f,(r)	9	1	Control Output
DOX	f,(r)	A	2	Data Output
SOX	f,(r)	B	3	Spare Output
CAK	f,(r)	C	4	Concurrent Acknowledge
IAK	f,(r)	D	5	Interrupt Acknowledge
DIX	f,(r)	E	6	Data Input
SIX	f,(r)	F	7	Stack Input

*Reprinted with permission of Microdata Corporation, Irvine, California.

2. Input Lines

The input data lines (byte input bus) are input to the B-bus (refer to Fig. 7.1) to transfer data from a peripheral device to the CPU under firmware (microprogram) control. The input control lines are input to the bits of File Register 0 to reflect the service request by an external device. The flag bits of File Register 0 are defined as shown in Table 7.2.

TABLE 7.2

MICRODATA 1600 FILE REGISTER 0 FLAGS

BIT NUMBER	DESCRIPTION
0	Overflow Condition
1	Negative Condition
2	Zero Condition
3	Concurrent I/O Request (or Spare)
4	Internal Interrupt
5	I/O Reply* (or Spare)
6	Stack Overflow (or Serial TTY)
7	External Interrupt

*This flag is normally not used in Microdata 1600 I/O units.

3. Output Lines

The output data lines (byte output bus) originate with the output register (OD Register, Fig. 7.1) to carry data from the CPU to an addressed peripheral, operated under firmware control. The output control lines originate with the I/O control register to generate the relevant signals (such as concurrent acknowledge or data output) for the external device.

INPUT/OUTPUT MICROINSTRUCTIONS*

Before giving any detailed description of the I/O microinstructions, we examine the control byte that directs the basic function of the Microdata 1600 I/O system. The control byte consists of a 3-bit device order and a 5-bit device address as follows.

7	6	5	4	3	2	1	0
Device Order (f)			Device Address (DA)				

DEVICE ADDRESS

Each device on the byte I/O bus is assigned a unique 5-bit number or address. The numbers are assigned by means of selectively placed jumper wires on the printed circuit board of the device controller. The assigned device address is used by the device controller to compare against the device address of the control byte to determine if it is being addressed and for identifying the device to the processor when requesting an interrupt or concurrent I/O transfer.

DEVICE ORDER

The 3-bit device order specifies the type of I/O operation to be performed. Standard device orders designate the operations shown in Table 7.3. Order codes are shown with their standard assignments, but they may be changed depending on the individual interface requirements. The device order accompanies the device address and is sent prior to each data transfer.

STATUS BYTE

The 8-bit status byte input as the result of a status order (refer to Table 7.3, order code = 1) has four bits with functions that are common to most devices; the 4 high-order bits have device-dependent functions. The functional meaning of the status bits is given in Table 7.4.

7.4.2. Examples

1. Output Data (OD) Instruction

The output data (OD) instruction in this example outputs a byte from main memory to a device with address zero. This device is assumed to be a teletypewriter or compatible terminal that requires only an output order followed by the actual data.

The output operation is initialized by sending out a control byte, as

*Reprinted with permission of Microdata Corporation, Irvine, California.

TABLE 7.3

DEVICE ORDERS*

ORDER CODE	OPERATION	DESCRIPTION†
0	Data Transfer	A data byte will be transferred between the addressed device and the processor. Direction of the transfer will depend on whether the instruction is an input or an output.
1	Status/Function	A status byte will be input from the addressed device or a function byte will be output to the addressed device, depending on whether the instruction is an input or an output.
2	Block Input/INT	The addressed device will start a concurrent block input to memory and will generate an external interrupt at the conclusion of the transfer unless the interrupt has been subsequently disarmed. This order is normally sent by an output instruction.
3	Arm Interrupt	Permits the addressed device to make an external interrupt request upon the satisfaction of an interrupt condition. This order is normally sent by an output instruction.
4	Disconnect	The block transfer in progress by the addressed device is stopped and end of block interrupt will occur unless the interrupt has been disarmed. This order is normally sent by an output instruction.
5	Disarm Interrupt	Inhibits the addressed device from making an external interrupt request under any condition. This order is normally sent by an output instruction.
6	Block Output/INT	The addressed device will start a concurrent block output from memory and will generate an external interrupt at the conclusion of the transfer unless the interrupt has been subsequently disarmed. This order is normally sent by an output instruction.
7	Unassigned	This order, if assigned, may perform any required function as interpreted by the individual interface. If a byte transfer is desired the order may be sent by an input or an output instruction.

*This table should be used only as a general source of information. Documentation of specific controllers should be consulted before programming for that controller and related I/O device is attempted.
†Reprinted with permission of Microdata Corporation, Irvine, California.

TABLE 7.4

STATUS BYTE DEFINITION*

BIT NUMBER	STATUS	DESCRIPTION†
0	Ready	This bit is 1 when the external device is in a ready state.
1	Input Flag	This bit is 1 when the external device has a byte ready for input to the computer.
2	Output Flag	This bit is 1 when the external device is ready to receive a byte from the computer.
3	Error	This bit is 1 when an error has occurred during a transfer. Errors may be timing or device malfunction. This bit is cleared when the status byte is input.
4–7		Device dependent.

*This table represents typical controllers only.
†Reprinted with permission of Microdata Corporation, Irvine, California.

shown in the previous section. In this particular case, the device order is 000_2 and the device address is 00000_2, yielding a control byte X'00'. The control byte is then followed by the data byte. The symbolic format for the instruction is

$$OD \quad ADDR$$

where ADDR is a 16-bit field containing the address of the data byte to be output. The program counter (PC) is assumed to consist of File Registers 11 (high byte) and 12 (low byte) and points to the opcode OD when the routine is entered. Listing 7.7 shows a microprogram implementation of this instruction.

This microprogram works as follows. The first two microinstructions send the control byte X'00' out, thereby selecting the I/O device with address zero and presenting the device code zero (write data) to that device. The next seven microinstructions simply fetch the data byte to be written. The next two instructions make this data available to the device and are followed by a delay to ensure the signal is present on the output bus for three microcycles (this is required by I/O devices on this machine). Finally, the control lines are cleared and the microprogram terminated.

2. Read and Echo Character (REC) Instruction

The read and echo character (REC) instruction is designed to read a character from a teletypewriter keyboard (or an equivalent device) and echo it back to the device for display. The device address is again assumed to be

```
                    ***
                    ***   THE OD INSTRUCTION ROUTINE
                    ***
                    ***
0000 1100           LT    X'00'         LOAD CONTROL BYTE.
0001 7090           COX   0             OUTPUT CONTROL BYTE.
0002 8C43           INC   12,(N)        ADDRESS OF NEXT BYTE
0003 AB82           RMF   11,L(M)       READ ADDRESS HIGH BYTE
0004 8C43           INC   12,(N)        ADDRESS OF NEXT BYTE.
0005 B720           CPY   7,T           SAVE
0006 AB82           RMF   11,L(M)       READ ADDRESS LOW BYTE
0007 B72B           CPY*  7,T(N)        SAVE LOW BYTE IN N.
0008 A702           RMF   7,(M)         READ DATA BYTE.
0009 7080           CIO   0             CLEAR I/O CONTROL REGISTER.
000A 70A0           DOX   0             OUTPUT BYTE.
000B 140C           JP    XX            DELAY FOR I/O.
000C 1000     XX    NOP
000D 7080           CIO   0             CLEAR I/O CONTROL REG.
000E 1020           RTN                 RETURN.
                    END   0
```

Listing 7.7 Microprogram for OD Instruction

00000_2 and the symbolic format for the instruction is

REC

which causes the character read-in to be stored in the low byte of Register A (File Register 2). The microprogram implementation of this instruction consists of checking the status of the device to see if a character has been typed, in which case the character is routed to File 2. It is then echoed back and the REC instruction execution is terminated. If no character is ready for input, the instruction enters a loop for status checking. Note that there is no need for checking the device ready status bit for output as, in this case, the input rate is much slower than the output rate capability. Listing 7.8 shows an implementation of this instruction.

3. Print a Line (PAL) Instruction

The print a line (PAL) instruction causes a complete line of characters to be sent to the line printer with an address assumed to be X'08'. The symbolic format for this instruction is

PAL   ADDR

where ADDR specifies the 16-bit absolute address of the first byte of the record to be printed. As in the OD instruction, the PC (Files 11 and 12) points to the opcode. We assume that a maximum of 132 characters are printed per line, and that a line shorter than 132 characters is terminated by the ASCII control character ETX (X'03'). The characters sent to the printer are supposed to be either printable characters or control characters valid for the line printer. Listing 7.9 shows a microprogram to implement this instruction. It uses a microsubroutine that sends out one character after checking the printer's ready status. The device address is 08 and the data

```
                    ***
                    ***    TERMINAL KEYBOARD INPUT AND ECHO PROGRAM.
                    ***
                    ***
                    ***
                    ***    THE FOLLOWING GROUP OF INSTRUCTION GETS STATUS BYTE FROM
                    ***    TERMINAL INTERFACE AND STORES IT IN FILE REG.2
                    ***
0000 1120    REC    LT    X'20'             READ STATUS OF DEVICE 0.
0001 7090           COX   0                 OUTPUT CONTROL BYTE.
0002 1000           NOP
0003 1000           NOP                     DELAY.
0004 7080           CIO   0                 CLEAR I/O CONTROL REGISTER.
0005 70E0           DIX   0                 READ STATUS IN.
0006 1000           NOP
0007 1000           NOP                     DELAY.
0008 B220           CPY   2,T               SAVE IN REGISTER 2.
0009 7080           CIO   0                 CLEAR I/O CONTROL REGISTER.
             ***    END STATUS INPUT.
             ***
             ***
             ***
             ***    FOLLOWING GROUP OF INST. CHECKS WHEATHER READY
             ***    IF NO,JUMPS BACK TO MAIN ROUTINE AND CONTINUES TO CHECK
             ***    IF YES,INPUTS DATA FROM KEYBOARD AND STORES DATA IN FILE REGISTER 2.
             ***
000A 5202           TN    2,X'02'           CHECK FOR CHARACTER READY.
000B 1400           JP    REC               NO,LOOP.
000C 1100           LT    X'00'             CONTROL BYTE FOR DATA TRANFER.
000D 7090           COX   0                 OUTPUT CCNTROL BYTE.
000E 1000           NOP
000F 1000           NOP                     DELAY.
0010 7080           CIO   0                 CLEAR I/O CONTROL REGISTER.
0011 70E0           DIX   0                 READ DATA.
0012 1000           NOP
0013 1000           NOP                     DELAY.
0014 B220           CPY   2,T               SAVE INTO REGISTAR 2(LOWBYTE OF A REG)
0015 7080           CIO   0                 CLEAR I/O REGISTER.
             ***    END DATA INPUT.
             ***
             ***
             ***
             ***    FOLLOWING CODE ECHOES THE DATA TO THE TERMINAL.
             ***
0016 1100           LT    X'00'             CONTROL BYTE FOR DATA TRANSFER.
0017 7090           COX   0                 OUTPUT CONTROL BYTE.
0018 1000           NOP
0019 1000           NOP                     DELAY.
001A 7080           CIO   0                 CLEAR I/O CONTROL REGISTER.
001B C201           MOV   2,(T)             COPY BYTE INTO T.
001C 70A0           DOX   0                 OUTPUT DATA.
001D 1000           NOP
001E 1000           NOP                     DELAY.
001F 7080           CIO   0                 CLEAR I/O REGISTER.
             ***    END DATA ECHO.
             ***    REGI
0020 1020           RTN                     RETURN.
```

Listing 7.8 Microprogram for REC Instruction

transfer device code is 3, yielding a control byte of X'68'. Each character of the line is sent out until X'03' is encountered or 132 characters have been processed. Then a carriage return and a line feed are sent out to cause printing.

7.5 INTERRUPT HANDLING

Microprogramming provides a very flexible tool for handling interrupts in a computer system. This section presents some examples of interrupt handling using a specific machine, Microdata 1600. However, before discussing any

```
                           ***
                           ***    THE PAL INSTRUCTION ROUTINE
                           ***
                           ***
                           ***
   0000 2884        LF      8,132              132 CHARACTER MAXIMUM.
   0001 8C43        INC     12,(N)             GET NEXT BYTE.
   0002 AB82        RMF     11,L(M)            READ HIGH BYTE OF ADDRESS.
   0003 B920        CPY     9,T                SAVE INTO FILE 9.
   0004 8C43        INC     12,(N)             GET NEXT BYTE.
   0005 AB82        RMF     11,L(M)            READ LOW BYTE OF ADDRESS.
   0006 B623        CPY     6,T(N)             SAVE INTO FILE 6 AND N
   0007 A902        RMF     9,(M)              READ DATA BYTE.
   0008 B720  COPY  CPY     7,T                SAVE BYTE IN FILE 7.
   0009 37FD        AF      7,X'FD'            CHECK FOR END OF LINE
   000A 47FF        TZ      7,X'FF'            WAS IT X'03'?
   000B 1411        JP      NEXT               NO.
   000C 110A  CRF   LT      X'0A'              LINEFEED CHARACTER.
   000D 0018        JE      SEND               SEND OUT.
   000E 110D        LT      X'0D'              CARRIAGE RETURN CHARACTER.
   000F 0018        JE      SEND               SEND OUT.
   0010 1020        RTN                        RETURN.
   0011 0018  NEXT  JE      SEND               SEND CHARACTER.
   0012 9850        DEC     8,C                DECREMENT CHARACTER COUNTER.
   0013 4004        TZ      0,X'04'            IS IT ZERO?
   0014 140C        JP      CRF                YES.
   0015 8643        INC     6,(N)              GET NEXT ADDRESS
   0016 A982        RMF     9,L(M)             READ IT.
   0017 1408        JP      COPY               AND CONTINUE.
                           ***
                           ***
                           ***    THE SEND SUB-ROUTINE
                           ***
   0018 B720  SEND  CPY     7,T                SAVE INTO 7.
   0019 1168  STAT  LT      X'68'              CONTROL BYTE FOR DATA TRANSFER.
   001A 7090        COX     0                  OUTPUT CONTROL BYTE.
   001B 1000        NOP
   001C 141D        JP      *+1                DELAY
   001D 7080        CIO     0                  CLEAR I/O REGISTER.
   001E 70E0        DIX     0                  READ STATUS BYTE.
   001F 1420        JP      *+1                DELAY
   0020 BA20        CPY     10,T               SURE STATUS IN FILE 10.
   0021 5A80        TN      10,X'80'           CHECK FOR PRINTER READY.
   0022 1419        JP      STAT               NOT READY.
   0023 7080        CIO     0                  CLEAR I/O REGISTER.
   0024 1168        LT      X'68'              CONTROL BYTE FOR DATA TRANSFER.
   0025 7090        COX     0                  OUTPUT CONTROL BYTE.
   0026 1000        NOP
   0027 1428        JP      *+1                DELAY.
   0028 7080        CIO     0                  CLEAR I/O REGISTER
   0029 C701        MOV     7,(T)              RESTORE T REGISTER.
   002A 70A0        DOX     0                  OUTPUT DATA BYTE.
   002B 142C        JP      *+1                DELAY.
   002C 1020        RTN                        RETURN.
                           END
```

Listing 7.9 Microprogram for PAL Instruction

examples, it is appropriate to describe the interrupt structure of the Microdata 1600.

7.5.1. Microdata 1600 Interrupt System*

The interrupt mechanism of the Microdata 1600 consists of the following.

1. Internal interrupts.
2. External interrupts and concurrent interrupt.

*This material is adapted from the *Microprogramming Handbook* and is reproduced with the permission of Microdata Corporation, Irvine, Ca.

The following are the interrupt control microinstructions.*

1. DEI: Disable External Interrupts

This command causes the external interrupt system to be disabled. Interrupts are not lost when the interrupt system is disabled, but they cannot be recognized by the processor.

2. EEI: Enable External Interrupts

The external interrupt system is enabled, allowing the processor to recognize external interrupts.

3. DRT: Disable Real-Time Clock

The real-time clock and its interrupt are disabled.

4. ERT: Enable Real-Time Clock

The real-time clock and its interrupt are enabled. The first interrupt will occur after a full interrupt interval.

THE CONTROL BYTE

Sending the control byte (arm/disarm for external interrupt, block-input/block-output for concurrent interrupt) via COX instruction directs the individual external device controller to respond to the interrupt system.

As soon as an external device requests service or an internal interrupt is generated, it sets the pertinent bit in File Register 0 and the internal status byte to gain attention of the processor.

The internal status byte reflects the status of the internal interrupts. When an internal interrupt is present, Bit 4 of File Register 0 is set. The firmware normally responds by executing an enter internal status (EIS) microcommand, which places the internal status byte on the A-bus. The panel, real-time clock, and power-fail interrupts are reset when the EIS command is executed. After sensing this flag bit ON, the corresponding internal interrupt routine should be initiated to handle the interrupt. The format of the internal status byte is given in Table 7.5.

External interrupts are associated with peripheral devices and are used to indicate such conditions as data ready, error, or end of operation condition for a device. Individual interrupts may be handled by an external interrupt module which provides for arming/disarming individual interrupts and enabling/disabling recognition of interrupts.

The external interrupt system contains a *single* interrupt line, a priority line, and a select line. A device may initiate an interrupt request when service is required only if it has the highest priority or priority has been received from higher-level interrupts on the priority chain. Devices not requiring interrupt service will propagate priority to the next device in line.

*Reprinted with permission of Microdata Corporation, Irvine, California.

TABLE 7.5

INTERNAL STATUS BYTE*

BIT NUMBER	STATUS MEANING
0	Panel Interrupt
1	DMA Termination (or Spare)
2	Real-Time Clock Interrupt
3	Spare
4	Spare
5	Spare
6	Panel Step Switch
7	Power-Fail/Restart Interrupt

*Reprinted with permission of Microdata Corporation, Irvine, California.

As an external interrupt occurs, it will automatically set Bit 7 of File Register 0 to signal the CPU accordingly. When the processor recognizes the interrupt signal, it enables the select line for the interrupt system. An IAK (interrupt acknowledge) microinstruction should be sent to respond to the interrupt.

By executing the IAK instruction, a value of 5 is placed in the IC register, which enables the interrupt acknowledge signal; device polling is started. Each device in order will interrogate the select line and, if not requesting, will propagate this signal to the next device in line. When the select signal is received by the requesting device, it will input its address on the I/O bus. This externally supplied address (ESA) has the following format.

```
7   6 5 4 3 2 1 0
┌─────────────────────────┐
│ 0   0 Device Number  0  │
└─────────────────────────┘
```

The interrupt acknowledge signal is not removed until a clear I/O command is executed. Upon removal of this signal, the requesting device interface controller will reset the external interrupt request flag bit in File Register 0.

CONCURRENT INPUT/OUTPUT

The concurrent I/O allows for block transfers (for example, transfer of 80 columns of data from a card reader) between an external device on the byte I/O bus and memory. Once started, it proceeds without program intervention until the whole block is transferred.

Concurrent I/O operations are started by executing the instruction COX with the proper control byte (device order code and address) in the T-register; for the standard controller, order code 2 is used for concurrent block input; order code 6 is used for concurrent block output. After a concurrent I/O operation is initiated, as the data (for example, a column of data from the card reader) are ready for transfer to or from the memory from or to the specified peripheral, Bit 3 of File Register 0 is set to gain the attention of the processor. After sensing the concurrent interrupt flag, the CPU should then respond to the request by executing the CAK (concurrent acknowledge) microinstruction.*

During execution of the CAK command, a value of 4 is placed in the IC register, which enables the concurrent interrupt acknowledge signal; polling of external devices starts in order to identify the requesting peripheral. When the requesting device is reached, it inputs an externally supplied address (ESA) on the byte I/O bus. The ESA is used by the processor to define the type of concurrent I/O operation request and to identify the requesting device. The format of this ESA (different from the ESA of the external interrupt) is shown as follows.

7	6	5	4	3	2	1	0	
I/O	0		Device No. (DN)				0	ESA

Bit 7 = 0   Signifies an input transfer.
Bit 7 = 1   Signifies an output transfer.

The concurrent acknowledge signal is not removed until a CIO command is executed. Upon removal of this signal, the requesting controller will reset the concurrent request flag bit in File Register 0.

7.5.2. Examples of Interrupt Handling

1. Variable Rate Real-Time Clock Interrupt

Most machines provide a real-time clock for timing and synchronization purposes. These clocks usually have a fixed rate, requiring the programmer to compute the number of cycles needed to generate a given delay. Through the facility of microprogramming, it is a relatively simple task to provide a more flexible, variable rate clock at the user level, thus allowing the programmer to specify the most convenient rate for the particular application at hand.

The basic mechanism for implementing a user-level clock consists of using the real-time clock-interrupt features of the microlevel machine. The hardware real-time clock sets a flag at its predetermined rate, which is checked at an appropriate time by the firmware. If this flag is set, the firmware branches to a clock-handling routine. This routine uses the programmer-supplied rate to decrement the programmer-supplied delay; when the value of this delay becomes zero, a branch is made to a specific user routine in main memory. This means the normal flow of control in the user program is

*Reprinted with permission of Microdata Corporation, Irvine, California.

interrupted after the user-specified delay has elapsed (this delay is specified in the user's units and not in hardware real-time clock units).

In the example considered here, the following assignments have been made for specific memory locations and file registers.

Locations 10 and 11: Delay in user units.

Location 12: Contains the rate as a divisor of the hardware clock rate.

Location 13: Used by firmware clock handler.

Locations 14 and 15: Pointer to user's clock-interrupt handling routine.

File Register 6: Program counter (high byte).

File Register 7: Program counter (low byte).

As an example, if the contents of main memory locations 10, 11, 12, 14 and 15 are 00_{16}, 64_{16}, 04_{16}, 10_{16} and 00_{16}, respectively, then an interrupt will be generated after 100_{10} user time units have elapsed, causing a branch to address 1000_{16}, which is the beginning of the user's clock interrupt handling routine. If the hardware real-time clock rate is 1 KHz, then the user-specified rate would be 250 Hz (4 ms interval), generating an interrupt in $100 \times 4 =$ 400 ms. Before branching to the user's clock-handling routine, the return address of the interrupted program (that is, the value in the program counter) is stored in Locations 10 and 11. A microprogrammed implementation of this feature is shown in Listing 7.10. The range of possible time units that can be specified in this implementation is 1 ms to 127 ms.

2. *Program Interrupt Handling*

In the process of decoding and executing target instructions, abnormal conditions can arise requiring transfer of control to an error-handling routine. These conditions could be invalid opcode or data, division by zero, floating point overflow, and so on. In the example considered here, the firmware routine for generating program interrupts sets an error code in a fixed memory location (20_{16}), stores the program counter (the address of the instruction following the erroneous instruction) in memory locations 21_{16} and 22_{16}, and branches to the user error handling routine, which has an address assumed to be in locations 23_{16} and 24_{16}. The file-register assignments used are as follows.

Program Counter (high byte): File Register 6

Program Counter (low byte): File Register 7

Error code register set by firmware decoding and execution routines: File Register 4

```
                    ***********************************************************************
                    *                                                                     *
                    *    REAL TIME CLOCK INTERRUPT CHECK AND HANDLING.                     *
                    *                                                                     *
                    *         CORE LOCATIONS 10 AND 11 CONTAIN THE DELAY.                  *
                    *                                                                     *
                    *         CORE LOCATION 12 CONTAINS THE RATE. (THE FIRST BIT IS        *
                    *              IS USED AS A SWITCH BY THE FIRMWARE.  THE RATE IS        *
                    *              COPIED INTO LOCATION 13, DECREMENTED AND THE SWITCH*
                    *              IS SET.  AT SUCCESSIVE INTERRUPTS LOCATION 13 IS         *
                    *              DECREMENTED.  WHEN IT BECOMES ZERO, THE SWITCH IS        *
                    *              RESET TO ZERO AND THE DELAY IS DECREMENTED.  THIS        *
                    *              PROCESS IS REPEATED UNTIL THE DELAY IS ZERO.             *
                    *                                                                     *
                    *         CORE LOCATIONS 14 AND 15 CONTAIN THE ADDRESS OF THE          *
                    *              USERS HANDLING ROUTINE                                  *
                    *                                                                     *
                    ***********************************************************************
0000 5010                       TN      0,X'10'           INTERNAL INTERRUPT?
0001 1020                       RTN                       NO.
0002 7140                       EIS     1                 ENTER STATUS IN 1.
0003 5104                       TN      1,X'04'           IS IT REAL TIME CLOCK?
0004 1020                       RTN                       NO.
0005 1312                       LN      X'12'             RATE ADDRESS.
0006 A020                       RMH     0                 READ SWITCH BIT.
0007 B130                       CPY     1,TC              SET CONDITION CODE.
0008 5002                       TN      0,X'02'           WAS SWITCH BIT 1?
0009 1421                       JP      ZER               NO.
000A A030                       WMH     0                 YES,RESTORE BYTE.
000B 1313                       LN      X'13'             SCRATCH AREA ADDRESS.
000C A020                       RMH     0                 READ
000D B120                       CPY     1,T               AND
000E 9151                       DEC     1,C(T)            DECREMENT COUNTER IN SCRATCH AREA.
000F 5004                       TN      0,X'04'           REACH 0?
0010 1427                       JP      NYE               NOT YET.
0011 1312            HER        LN      X'12'             RATE ADDRESS.
0012 A020                       RMH     0                 READ RATE SWITCH
0013 217F                       LF      1,X'7F'           TO RESET BIT.
0014 E121                       AND     1,T(T)            RESET SWITCH.
0015 A030                       WMH     0                 RESTORE.
0016 1311                       LN      X'11'             READ LOW
0017 A020                       RMH     0                 BYTE OF DELAY.
0018 B120                       CPY     1,T               SAVE AND
0019 A171                       WMH     1,D(T)            WRITE DECREMENTED BYTE.
001A 6101                       CP      1,X'01'           WAS IT X'FF' ?
001B 1429                       JP      CHK               NO (CHECK FOR ZERO).
001C 1310                       LN      X'10'             HIGH BYTE ADDRESS.
001D A020                       RMH     0                 READ.
001E B120                       CPY     1,T               SAVE IN 1
001F A171                       WMH     1,D(T)            DECREMENT AND WRITE BACK.
0020 1020                       RTN                       RETURN.
0021 3180            ZER        AF      1,X'80'           SET SWITCH BIT TO 1.
0022 A131                       WMH     1,(T)             WRITE IT BACK.
0023 317F                       AF      1,X'7F'           DECREMENT COUNTER AND CLEAR LEFT BIT.
0024 61FF                       CP      1,X'FF'           IS IT ZERO?
```

```
0025 1411                       JP      HER               YES.
0026 1313            FL         LN      X'13'             ADDRESS OF COUNTER.
0027 A111            NYE        WMF     1,(T)             INITIALIZE COUNTER.
0028 1020                       RTN
                    *
                    *
                    *                                     CHECK IF THE COUNTER IS ZERO.
                    *
0029 41FF           CHK        TZ      1,X'FF'           WAS IT X'00' ?
002A 1020                       RTN                       NO.
002B 1310                       LN      X'10'             HIGH BYTE ADDRESS.
002C A000                       RMF     0                 READ IT.
002D B120                       CPY     1,T               SAVE.
002E 41FF                       TZ      1,X'FF'           IS IT ZERO?
002F 1020                       RTN                       NO, RETURN
                    *  YES GENERATE INTERRUPT
0030 A611           INT        WMF     6,(T)             SAVE PC (HIGH BYTE) IN DELAY LOCATION.
0031 1311                       LN      X'11'
0032 A711                       WMF     7,(T)             SAVE PC (LOW BYTE) IN DELAY LOCATION .
0033 1314                       LN      X'14'             HIGH BYTE OF ROUTINE ADDRESS.
0034 A000                       RMF     0                 READ IT.
0035 B620                       CPY     6,T               NEW LOCATION COUNTER (HIGH).
0036 1315                       LN      X'15'             LOW BYTE.
0037 A000                       RMF     0                 READ IT.
0038 B720                       CPY     7,T               NEW LOCATION COUNTER (LOW).
0039 1020                       RTN                       RETURN.
                                END     0
```

Listing 7.10 Microprogram for a Real-Time Clock

A microprogram implementation of this facility is shown in Listing 7.11.

```
LOCN CODE FLAGS LABELS OP *   OPERANDS      COMMENTS                        PAGE   1

                         ****************************************************************************
                         ***    PROGRAM INTERRUPT CHECK AND HANDLING                            ***
                         ****************************************************************************
0000 54FF                    TN    4,X'FF'       ANY ERRORS?
0001 1020                    RTN                 NO. RETURN.
0002 1200                    LM    X'00'         CLEAR M.
0003 2120                    LF    1,X'20'       SET MEMORY ADDRESS IN FILE 1.
0004 C401                    MOV   4,(T)         COPY ERROR CODE IN T.
0005 A113                    WMF   1,(N)         WRITE IT.
0006 2400                    LF    4,X'00'       RESET FILE 4 TO ZERO.
0007 C601                    MOV   6,(T)         MOVE HIGH BYTE OF PC IN T.
0008 A1D3                    WMF   1,I(N)        WRITE IT IN MEMORY ADDRESS '21'.
0009 1000                    NOP                 WAIT FOR COMPLETION OF WRITE.
000A C701                    MOV   7,(T)         MOVE LOW BYTE OF PC IN T.
000B A1D3                    WMF   1,I(N)        WRITE IT IN MEMRY ADDRESS '22'.
000C 1000                    NOP                 WAIT FOR COMPLETION OF WRITE.
000D A1C3                    RMF   1,I(N)        READ FROM MEMORY ADDRESS '23'.
000E B620                    CPY   6,T           SET NEW PC IN FILE 6(HIGH BYTE).
000F A1C3                    RMF   1,I(N)        READ FROM MEMORY ADDRESS '24'.
0010 B720                    CPY   7,T           SET NEW PC IN FILE 7(LOW BYTE).
0011 1020                    RTN                 DONE. RETURN
                             END   0
```

Listing 7.11 Microprogram for Program-Interrupt Processing

3. I/O Interrupt Handling

In this example, a vectored interrupt mechanism is implemented when an I/O interrupt is present. The interrupt is acknowledged and the device address is read in; the address is then mapped to a dedicated memory location containing the user routine for handling the particular device. The device address is mapped to a memory location using the following mapping rule:

$$\text{Device Address } X \longrightarrow \text{Memory Address } (80 + 2X)_{16}$$
$$\text{and } (80 + 2X + 1)_{16}$$

For example, Device Address 2 is mapped into memory locations 84_{16} and 85_{16}. Before branching to the user device handling routine the PC is saved in locations 23 and 24, as in the previous example. A sample microprogram implementing this mechanism is shown in Listing 7.12.

7.6 STACK PROCESSING

The very common use of stacks in computer programming makes it attractive to have machine-level instructions that process one or more "hardware" stacks. This section presents a microprogrammed implementation of some stack-processing instructions. The various mechanisms implemented here at machine level work as follows.

1. The Stack

The stack is a set of 255 bytes of dedicated main memory locations from address X'0101' to X'01FF'. The location X'0100' is a pointer to the

```
        ************************************************************************
        *                                                                      *
        *         I/O  INTERRUPT CHECK AND HANDELING.                          *
        *                                                                      *
        ************************************************************************
0000 5080              TN      0,X'80'          ANY I/O INTERRUPT?
0001 1020              RTN                      NO.RETURN.
0002 1323              LN      X'23'            SAVE PC ADDRESS.
0003 A611              WMF     6,(T)            SAVE HIGH BYTE.
0004 1324              LN      X'24'
0005 A711              WMF     7,(T)            SAVE LOW BYTE.
0006 1000              NOP                      WAIT FOR COMPLETION OF WRITE.
0007 70D0              IAK     0                ACKNOWLEDGE INTERRUPT.
0008 21FF              LF      1,X'FF'          MASK TO GET ADDRESS OF DEVICE REQUESTING
      *                                         SERVICE.
0009 7180              CIO     1                READ ADDRESS AND CLEAR I/O.
000A 3180              AF      1,X'80'          MAP TO MEMORY ADDRESS.
000B A103              RMF     1,(N)            GET HIGH BYTE OF USER I/O ROUTINE ADDRESS.
000C 8620              CPY     6,T              NEW PC (HIGH).
000D A1C3              RMF     1,I(N)           GET LOW BYTE OF USER I/O ROUTINE ADDRESS.
000E 8720              CPY     7,T              NEW PC (LOW).
000F 1020              RTN                      RETURN.
                       END     0
```

Listing 7.12 Microprogram for I/O Interrupt Processing

next empty cell of the stack. The top of the stack is the high address X'01FF'.

2. Stack Overflow or Underflow Interrupts

If, as a result of a stack operation, the pointer has to be incremented above X'01FF' or decremented below X'0101', an interrupt is generated, causing a branch to a user routine with address stored in dedicated memory locations X'00FE' and X'00FF' (the cause of the interrupt is not recorded but the current value of the pointer can be used for that purpose; that is, X'01' will indicate an overflow and X'00' will indicate an underflow).

3. The PUSH and PULL Instructions

The PUSH instruction causes the machine-language level 16-bit accumulator to be stored in the next 2 free stack positions and the stack pointer to be incremented by 2. If an overflow occurs, nothing is stored or half (high byte) of the accumulator is stored, depending on the value of the current pointer, and an interrupt is generated.

The PULL instruction causes the 2 top stack entries to be stored in the accumulator and the pointer to be decremented by 2. If an underflow occurs, the accumulator is left unchanged or only the low byte is fetched, depending on the value of the current pointer, and an interrupt is generated.

4. The CALL and RETURN Instructions

The CALL instruction causes the accumulator and the program counter to be stored in the stack and the pointer to be incremented by 4. Then the address specified in the instruction becomes the new value of the program counter unless an overflow occurs.

170

The RETURN instruction causes the accumulator and the program counter to be fetched from the stack and the pointer to be decremented by 4. The program counter may be changed to the user's error-routine address if an underflow occurs.

The program counter is mapped to File Registers 6 (high byte) and 7 (low byte) and the accumulator is mapped to File Registers 14 (high byte) and 15 (low byte). When an instruction processing microroutine is entered, the program counter contains the address of the opcode of the instruction to be executed.

The implementaton of stack processing instructions is shown in Listing 7.13.

```
LOCN CODE FLAGS LABELS OP *  OPERANDS     COMMENTS                              PAGE   1
                **************************************************************************
                *                                                                        *
                *   STACK PROCESSING INSTRUCTIONS.                                        *
                *                                                                        *
                **************************************************************************
                *
                *
                *   RETURN INSTRUCTION.
                *
0000 0035       RTN      JE     FET         GET LOW BYTE OF PC FROM STACK
0001 B720                CPY    7,T         ASSIGN IT TO FILE 7.
0002 0035                JE     FET         GET HIGH BYTE OF PC FROM STACK
0003 B620                CPY    6,T         ASSIGN IT TO FILE 6.
                *
                *
                *   PULL INSTRUCTION.
                *
0004 0035       PUL      JE     FET         GET LOW BYTE OF ACCUMULATOR FROM STACK
0005 BF20                CPY    15,T        ASSIGN IT TO FILE 15.
0006 0035                JE     FET         GET HIGH BYTE OF ACCUMULATOR FROM STACK
0007 BE20                CPY    14,T        ASSIGN IT TO FILE 14.
0008 1020                RTN                RETURN.
                *
                *
                *   PUSH INSTRUCTION.
                *
0009 CE01       PUS      MLV    14,(T)      PUT HIGH BYTE OF ACCUMULATOR INTO THE STACK
000A 0021                JE     STO
000B CF01                MUV    15,(T)      PUT LOW BYTE OF ACCUMULATOR INTO THE STACK.
000C 0021                JE     STO
000D 1020                RTN                RETURN.
                *
                *
                *   CALL INSTRUCTION.
                *
000E 0009       CAL      JE     PUS         PUSH ACCUMULATOR INTO STACK.
000F 8741                INC    7,(T)       ACCESS NEXT BYTE OF INSTRUCTION.
0010 B120                CPY    1,T         ADDRESS SAVED IN 1.
0011 8681                ADD    6,L(T)      SAME FOR
0012 B220                CPY    2,T         HIGHBYTE IN 2.
0013 8740                INC    7           DO IT
0014 8680                ADD    6,L         AGAIN
0015 8740                INC    7           AND AGAIN TO POINT
0016 8681                ADD    6,L(T)      TO NEXT INSTRUCTION.
0017 0021                JE     STO         STORE HIGH BYTE OF PC IN STACK.
0018 C701                MUV    7,(T)       STORE LOW BYTE OF PC
0019 0021                JE     STO         INTO STACK.
001A C103                MUV    1,(N)       RESTORE N
001B A202                RMF    2,(M)       AND M AND READ NEW PC.
001C B620                CPY    6,T         HIGHBYTE AND
001D 8143                INC    1,(N)       ALSO
001E A282                RMF    2,L(M)      LOW BYTE OF
001F B720                CPY    7,T         PC.
0020 1020                RTN                RETURN.
```

Listing 7.13 Microprograms for Stack Processing

```
          *     THE STORE ROUTINE STORES A BYTE IN THE STACK,
          *     UPDATES THE POINTER,
          *     HANDLES POSSIBLE OVERFLOW
          *
0021 B320    STO   CPY   3,T              SAVE T.
0022 1300          LN    X'00'            SET N.
0023 1201          LM    X'01'            SET M.
0024 A000          RMF   0                STACK POINTER IS READ
0025 B420          CPY   4,T              AND MOVED INTO FILE 4.
0026 A4D9          WMF*  4,I(T)           UPDATE STACK POINTER.
0027 C403          MOV   4,(N)            COPY IN N.
0028 54FF          TN    4,X'FF'          WAS IT ZERO?
0029 142C          JP    OFL              YES, OVERFLOW
002A A311          WMF   3,(T)            WRITE BYTE IN STACK.
002B 1020          RTN
002C 1200    OFL   LM    X'00'            SET M.
002D 13FE          LN    X'FE'            SET N.
002E A000          RMF   0                READ HIGHER BYTE OF ADDRESS
002F B620          CPY   6,T              OF USER'S ROUTINE INTO PC.
0030 13FF          LN    X'FF'            SET N
0031 A000          RMF   0                FOR LOW BYTE
0032 B720          CPY   7,T              OF PC.
0033 1B02          DSP                    DECREMENT STACK POINTER TO RETURN
0034 1020          RTN                    TO MAINSTREAM FIRMWARE.
          *
          *     THE FETCH ROUTINE READS A BYTE FROM THE STACK.
          *     UPDATES THE STACK POINTER.
          *     HANDLES POSSIBLE UNDERFLOW.
0035 1300    FET   LN    X'00'            SET M AND N TO
0036 1201          LM    X'01'            STACK POINTER.
0037 A000          RMF   0                READ IT.
0038 B420          CPY   4,T              SAVE THE BYTE IN FILE 4
0039 A451          WMF   4,D(T)           DECREMENT AND WRITE IT BACK.
003A 64FF          CP    4,X'FF'          IS IT ZERO?
003B 142C          JP    OFL              YES, UNDERFLOW.
003C A403          RMF   4,(N)            READ DATA.
003D 1020          RTN                    RETURN.
                   END   0
```

Listing 7.13 (continued)

REFERENCES

[1] *Microprogramming Handbook*, 2nd ed., (Irvine, Ca.: Microdata Corporation, 1972).

[2] SWANSON, R., "Understanding Cyclic Redundancy Codes," *Computer Design*, 14, no. 11 (November 1975), 93–99.

[3] PETERSON, W. W., *Error Correcting Codes* (Cambridge, Mass.: MIT Press, 1961).

FURTHER READINGS

1. BAUER, S. M., "Bell Labs Microcode for the IBM 360/67," *Proceedings of the Eighth Annual Workshop on Microprogramming*, Chicago, Illinois (September 21–23, 1975), pp. 40–44.

2. BERNDT, H., "Microprogram Controlled Input/Output," in *Microarchitecture of Computer Systems*, eds. R. W. Hartenstein and R. Zaks, pp. 177–80., Nice, France, North-Holland/American Elsevier, 1975.

3. BROWN, G. A., "A Microprogrammed Interrupt Service Routine Using the Eclipse Computer," *SIGMICRO Newsletter*, 9, no. 1 (March 1978). 18–22.

4. LUK, C., "Microprogrammed Significance Arithmetic with Tapered Floating Point Representation," *Proceedings of the Seventh Workshop on Microprogramming*, Palo Alto, Calif. (October 1974), 248–52.

5. LUTZ, M. J., "The Design and Implementation of a Small Scale Stack Processor System," *AFIPS Conference Proceedings* 42 (NCC 1973), 545–53.

6. MALCOLM, M. A., "On Accurate Floating Point Summation," *Communications of the ACM*, 14, no. 11 (November 1971), 731–36.

7. MEADE, R. M., "A Discussion of Machine Interpreted Macroinstructions," *Proceedings of the ACM National Conference* (September 1961), p. 601.

8. MEGGITT, J. E., "Pseudo Division and Pseudo Multiplication Processes," *IBM Jour. of Research and Development*, 6, no. 2 (April 1962), 210–26.

9. TAUSNER, M. R., "Teaching Basic Computer Organization through Microprogramming," *Proceedings of the Sixth Workshop on Microprogramming*, College Park, Maryland (September 1973), pp. 166–67.

EXERCISES

7.1 Write a microprogram for a 16-bit subtract instruction that uses the ADD microprogram in Listing 7.1.

7.2 Write a microprogram to multiply two 16-bit integers. This can be done by using the shift and add algorithm and the use of the ADD instruction in Listing 7.1 as a subroutine.

7.3 Write a microprogram implementing a convert to decimal (CVD) instruction, which does the reverse of the CVB instruction in Listing 7.3. For simplification purposes, the binary number to be converted can be assumed to have an absolute value not greater than 999 in decimal.

7.4 Assume that floating point multiplication (MUL) and division (DIV) microprograms are available.

    a. Write a microprogram implementing a factorial instruction (FAC N). (*Note.* N should be checked for an integer value.)

    b. Write a microprogram for a SIN or COS function (or any other trigonometric functions). (*Note.* Although not particularly efficient, the Taylor series can be used. The precision should be the maximum attainable by the floating point representation used; that is, 6 hexadecimal digits.)

7.5 Write a microprogram that computes a parity bit for a given byte as the argument.

7.6 Write a microprogram for scanning a string of characters (first argument) and detecting the presence (and position) of a given substring (second argument). If the substring does not exist in the input, its absence can be recorded as a position of zero; this is like the PL/1 INDEX function.

7.7 Write a microprogram that does each of the following.

    a. Picks a card from the card reader (assume a device order code of 1 and a device address of 4).

    b. Reads all columns into an 80-byte buffer (assume a device order code of zero for reading one column). *Note:* Each byte should be read whenever the card reader status indicates a "data in" condition (a device order code of 2 can be assumed to read a status byte and a status value of 1 can be assumed to indicate "data in.")

    c. Waits for the card to complete its movement through the reader. (Assume a status byte value of 2 for card reader "ready.")

7.8 Using the real-time clock example, write a microprogram that puts in File Registers 1, 2, 3, and 4 the time of the day in the form HH in Register 1, MM in Register 2, SS in Register 3, and 0T in Register 4. HH is the hour in a 24-hour format, MM is the minutes, SS is the seconds and 0T is the tenth of a second. Assume the clock has a 1 KHz frequency (the execution of this microprogram is started at 00000000 hour).

7.9 Write a microprogram that dumps the complete contents of the main memory on a line printer, in hexadecimal form.

CHAPTER EIGHT

Performance
and Optimization

8.1 INTRODUCTION

This chapter concerns itself with the problem of optimizing the performance of a microprogram. The factors affecting this performance should be considered carefully *before* writing the microprogram, although the considerations and techniques presented in this chapter can be used to improve the performance of an existing microprogram. The following are the main considerations in this regard.

1. Control Store Requirements

Economizing on the usage of control store is often a factor to be considered in writing a microprogram, because the size of control store is usually quite limited. However, it should be obvious that if a microprogram fits in an allotted space, there is no need for any further minimization, unless this effort can result in reduced implementation cost. For example, suppose that a set of microprograms has to fit within 1K of a control store consisting of 256 word modules, and the resulting microcode occupies only 780 words. In this case, it is worthwhile to try to reduce use of the control store so that the microprograms occupy 768 words or less; that is, they occupy 3 modules, decreasing the ROM requirement by 25 percent. While memories are relatively inexpensive, this consideration is, nonetheless, very important while writing microcode that is to be incorporated into a high-volume commercial product.

2. Execution Time

Reducing the execution time of a microprogram is almost always a prime consideration, as it directly affects the target function. As an example, a real-time application requiring a very fast response time will dictate the execution speed requirements of the firmware, possibly at the expense of some other factors. As a result, the execution time of the firmware must be optimized to meet the response time requirements.

However, in some instances—for example, when implementing a controller for low-speed devices—it may not be necessary to optimize the execution time of some functions; in this case, the operational speed of the system is governed by the device.

3. Cost

Another consideration in the design of a microprogram is the cost of its development. This cost can be reduced by the use of a high-level microprogramming language because it can cut down program development time. It also facilitates easier maintenance and modification of the microprograms. However, the use of high-level languages has all the disadvantages mentioned in Sec. 6.3, the main one being that they result in relatively inefficient object code both in terms of execution time and control-store requirements. Although optimizing compilers exist, a good assembly language programmer can still produce better code.

Note that on top of these considerations is the requirement that the microprogram should perform the intended task! It is of no value to try to optimize a program that does not work properly.

8.2 CONTROL STORE OPTIMIZATION

8.2.1. Use of Parallelism

Where the data path of a microprogrammed machine allows *several* microoperations to be specified within one microinstruction, maximum use of this feature should be made in order to reduce the number of microinstructions necessary to perform the required number of microoperations. This requires the microprogrammer or the analyst to determine the strictly sequential microoperations to be performed; one can then identify those microoperations that can be performed in parallel with some other microoperations. For a given microprogram, the percentage of utilization of various microoperation fields would provide an estimate of this kind of optimization.

Even in some machines with a "vertical" microinstruction format, there often exists a *latent* parallelism that should be fully exploited. As an example, the Microdata 1600* does provide such parallelism in most of its microinstructions. For purposes of illustration, consider the following microinstruction sequence which increments a memory pointer and reads the corresponding byte.

INC   3   Increment File Register 3 by 1 (File 3

contains a memory pointer).

MOV   3, (N)   copy File 3 into Register N (low byte of MAR).

RMF   0   Read memory.

The same function can be performed by the folloing microinstruction.

RMF   3, I(N)   Increment File 3 by 1 and store the
result in File 3 *and* in Register N. Then
read a byte.

In the latter version it is obvious that all fields of the microinstruction are utilized.

8.2.2. Dynamic Instruction Modification

Most machines have some facility for dynamic microinstruction modification. This means some microinstructions can be modified at execution time to generate other microinstructions. This modification is usually done by logically OR-ing some of the microinstruction fields with the contents of a special register. In this manner, a base microinstruction can be transformed in order to perform different functions. Note that the microinstruction itself is not modified in ROM; it is modified temporarily only during decoding.

Dynamic instruction modification helps reduce the control store requirements in judiciously designed microprograms and should be used wherever control store usage is to be reduced as much as possible. Following are two examples of usage of this technique, using the Microdata 1600* machine.

The first example consists of a microprogram to save the contents of 8 file registers (1 to 8) in 8 consecutive memory locations.

*Reprinted with permission of Microdata Corporation, Irvine, California.

	LM SAVE	Load high byte of save address.
	LF 9, X'FF'	Initialize low byte of save address.
	LF 10, X'A0'	Initialize file register index and set up base opcode.
LOOP	INC 10, (U)	Increment file index and store in U-register for modification.
	INC 9, (N)	Set up memory pointer.
STORE	EOT 0, C, (T)	Generate "write memory" instruction as specified by File 10.
	CP 10, X'58'	File Register 8 saved?
	JP LOOP	No, repeat sequence.

This microprogram dynamically modifies the instruction labeled STORE, allowing one to use a loop instead of a straight-line sequence of 8 "write memory" microinstructions; the latter approach would require 18 microinstructions, as opposed to 8 in this example.

The second example shows how the opcode field of a microinstruction can be modified so the same microroutine can be used to perform different functions. The routine labeled DECINC either increments or decrements the contents of a given memory location depending on the contents of a file register (assume 6); assume that the address is contained in File Registers 4 (low byte) and 5 (high byte).

DECINC	MOV 4, (N)	Copy low address byte into Register N.
	MOV 5, (M)	Copy high address byte into Register M.
	RMH 0	Read the byte.
	CPY 1, T	Move byte to File Register 1.
	MOV 6, (U)	Copy opcode into U.
	EOT 1, I, (T)	Modify File Register 1 as specified by U-register and copy into T.
	WMH 0	Write updated byte.
	RTN	Return.

This routine can be used to increment the contents of a specified memory location by using the following calling sequence.

LF 6, X'80'	Set up INC opcode.
JE DECINC	Branch to Subroutine.

To decrement, the following sequence is used.

LF 6, X'90'   Set up DEC opcode.

JE DECINC   Branch to subroutine.

The saving is achieved by using a common code segment for incrementing or decrementing a byte.

8.2.3. Use of Subroutines

The concept of using microsubroutines is basically the same as that of using subroutines in normal assembly or high-level languages. The idea is to save control memory by not repeating the same code sequence wherever it is needed. Instead, this sequence is set up as a separate code block that can be called for execution when it is needed; after the execution of the subroutine, control returns to the calling program at the location following the CALL instruction.

The linkage between the calling microprogram and a subroutine is usually facilitated by some special features, such as instructions for call and return functions and return address register or stack. If these special features are not available, then the microprogrammer must create the linkage using existing microinstructions.

The calling sequence typically consists of the following operations.

1. Save the return address.
2. If subroutine nesting is allowed, update the pointer for saving of the next return address. The save area "overflow" condition should be indicated when maximum number of nested levels is exceeded.
3. Branch to the microsubroutine address.

The return sequence consists of the following operations.

1. Restore return address in the control memory location counter.
2. In case of subroutine nesting, decrement the save area pointer. Indicate error condition if save area "underflow" occurs; that is, if more "returns" are executed than "calls."
3. Branch back to the return address.

The input to a subroutine consists of certain arguments or parameters provided by the calling program. The subroutine performs its algorithm on this supplied data and its output consists of results to be passed back to the calling microprogram. Several mechanisms can be used for this purpose.

1. Assigning specific registers for both input and output data.
2. Using a main memory area for input and output data and providing a pointer to this area in a specific register.
3. Using a *dedicated* main memory area that has an address known both to the calling program and the subroutine. This is similar to the concept of a COMMON block in higher level languages.

Note that various combinations of these techniques can be used in specific situations; furthermore, the last two methods of passing arguments involve two levels of memory (control memory and main memory), unlike their counterparts in conventional programming.

A typical example of the use of a microsubroutine is in an emulator, where it can be used to read or write a word from or into a memory location. In this case, the arguments would consist of the memory address, the data transferred, and a flag to indicate whether the operation is read or write. Such a subroutine can be used several times while processing a machine instruction. The use of microsubroutines has the same advantages as the use of subroutines in higher level languages; that is, clarity, modularity, ease of debugging, and ease of modification.

8.2.4. Common Segments

The use of common segments is another technique for saving on control store requirements. The basic idea here, as in subroutines, is to share microcode between two or more processes. The essential difference between this technique and the use of subroutines is that the code and the flow of control are shared between the various processes. Although a subroutine can be called at anytime, a common segment can be performed only at a predetermined point in the flow of control. This, in turn, necessitates a careful design of the algorithms. This concept is best illustrated graphically, as shown in Fig. 8.1. This example considers the flowchart of some microprogram where one of the two processes must be performed at any given time. Each process consists of three parts labeled $P_{11}, P_{12}, \ldots$, as shown.

If P_{11} and P_{21} or P_{13} and P_{23} are identical, they can then be written as common segments yielding flowcharts, as in Fig. 8.1b or Fig. 8.1c. If, however, P_{12} and P_{22} are common, then the subroutine approach should be chosen because the flow of control after the execution of the subroutine differs (Fig. 8.1d); the subroutine returns control to the proper place. Whenever possible, the use of common segments is preferable to the use of subroutines in so far as the minimization of control store is concerned because there is no need for special call, return, and argument passing instructions.

A typical example of use of common segments is the decoding and generation of effective memory addresses while processing memory reference instructions in a machine before executing the particular function as called for by the opcode.

8.2.5. Extending the Control Store

This subsection addresses itself to the problem of fitting a microprogram of a given size into a control memory of a smaller size, assuming that the microprogram cannot be further reduced in size. The basic concept here is to use part of the control store in a dynamic fashion; that is, this part of the control

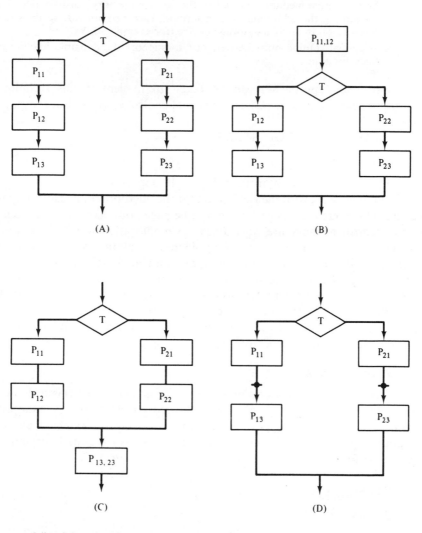

(A)

(B)

(C)

(D)

Call to Subroutine: $P_{12, 22}$

Figure 8.1 Common Segments and Subroutines

store contains microcode which, once executed, is replaced by other microcode when needed. In other words, several microroutines share the use of this part of control memory.

For implementing this feature, following requirements must be met.

1. The part of control memory to be used dynamically must be a WCS (writable control store).

2. Some storage medium external to the control memory must be available for storing the additional microroutines. This medium can be the main memory or an auxiliary storage device (for example, disk).
3. A special routine must be designed to support the dynamic loading of microprograms.

Two main approaches can be taken to implement this technique depending on the available resources; virtual control store, and overlays.

VIRTUAL CONTROL STORE

1. Concept

The concept of virtual memory [1] can be applied to control memory in much the same way, with the exception that the microprograms have only to be paged in; there is no need for them to be paged out because the contents of the control memory are not subject to modification during execution. However, the overhead associated with the implementation of virtual control store makes it unattractive in microprogramming applications as the system speed can be adversely affected. In an environment where flexibility rather than speed is a major consideration, virtual control store can be a viable alternative to acquiring additional control memory, at least in the experimental stages. This provides a virtual control store of size limited only by the address space of the control store.

2. Implementation

Dynamic address translation required for implementing this technique has to be done either by additional dedicated hardware or via nanoprogramming. However, the paging algorithms can be implemented at any programming level. Special control registers are also required for implementing virtual control store (such as page table pointer).

OVERLAYS

1. Concept

The concept of overlaying microprograms in control memory is similar to the concept of overlays employed with main memory [2]. To utilize this technique, the dynamically loadable microroutines must be organized in a tree structure; routines that are not interdependent will overlay each other in the same area of control store, thereby decreasing control store requirements. As in the case of virtual control store, there is a certain amount of overhead involved in implementing this technique for loading in microprograms from external storage, although in this case it is somewhat less involved. It should be noted that this technique is applicable only if the microroutines can be arranged in a tree structure.

An illustration of the savings of control store realized by this technique is shown in Fig. 8.2. Suppose a microprogram consists of the microroutines $M_0, M_1, \ldots, M_7$ (256 bytes each), organized in a tree structure as shown in the figure. The total control store requirement would be 8×256 (2048) bytes. If, however, the overlay technique is used, only 3×256 (768) bytes are required, which corresponds to the longest path in the tree. In addition to this requirement, the size of the overlay control routine must be taken into account.

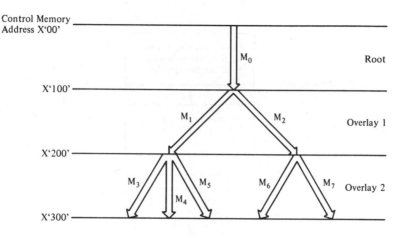

Figure 8.2 Overlays

2. Implementation

The implementation of overlays is reasonably straightforward as compared to virtual control store implementation. It requires an overlay control routine that is always resident in control store and may be software assisted. This routine gets control whenever a dynamic microroutine is invoked. It then loads the routine in a predetermined area of the WCS and transfers control to that routine.

In order to implement the structure shown in Fig. 8.2 with an overlay technique, for example, the following steps would have to be taken.

1. Before each call to subroutines M_1 and M_2, load in some register a code indicating the routine to be called, together with a code indicating the node level in the tree structure.
2. Change the calls to microsubroutines $M_1, M_2, \ldots$, into calls to the overlay control routine.
   As an example, the microinstruction

$$\text{CALL} \quad M_3$$

will be changed into

LOAD	R1, X'03'	Identifier of M_3 into Register 1.
LOAD	R2, X'02'	Node level indicator in Register 2.
CALL	OCR	Branch to Overlay Control Routine.

3. Write the overlay control routine with the functions shown in Fig. 8.3.

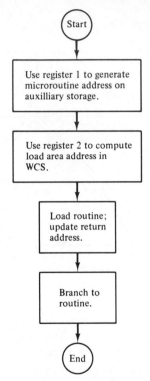

Figure 8.3 Overlay Control Routine

8.2.6. Formal Techniques

This section provides a brief overview of formal methods that have been developed for the optimization of control store requirements. Although important from a theoretical point of view, the applicability of these methods in a practical situation has yet to be proven. These techniques can be classified into two broad categories: (1) minimization of the number of steps (microoperations) in an algorithm; and (2) optimization of its implementation in a given environment (optimizing the number of microinstructions).

One of the earliest methods proposed for reducing the number of microoperations in an algorithm is due to Glushkov [4, 5]. The first step of

Glushkov's method consists of representing a microprogram algorithm in the form of a finite-state automaton. The equivalence between an abstract finite-state automaton shown in Fig. 8.4 and an abstract microprogram is shown in the following paragraph.

$$(S_{t+1}, O_t)$$

S_t	Input Variable			
	I_0	I_1	$I_2 \quad \cdots \quad I_p$	
S_0	(S_{00}, O_{00})	(S_{01}, O_{01})	(S_{02}, O_{02})	(S_{0p}, O_{0p})
S_1	(S_{10}, O_{10})	(S_{11}, O_{11})	(S_{12}, O_{12})	(S_{1p}, O_{1p})

Figure 8.4 State and Output Table of a Finite State Machine

$$S_0 \quad \text{IF } I = I_0 \quad \text{THEN } (O = O_{00}, S_{t+1} = S_{00})$$
$$\text{IF } I = I_1 \quad \text{THEN } (O = O_{01}, S_{t+1} = S_{01})$$
$$\cdot$$
$$\cdot$$
$$\cdot$$
$$\text{IF } I = I_p \quad \text{THEN } (O = O_{0p}, S_{t+1} = S_{0p})$$
$$S_1 \quad \text{IF } I = I_0 \quad \text{THEN } (O = O_{10}, S_{t+1} = S_{10})$$
$$\text{IF } I = I_1 \quad \text{THEN } (O = O_{11}, S_{t+1} = S_{11})$$
$$\cdot$$
$$\cdot$$
$$\cdot$$

where S_i is the ith state of the automaton (ith microinstruction), S_{t+1} is the next state (next microinstruction), I_i is the ith input value (flags or data in the microprogram), and O is the state output (flags set or data produced by microinstruction).

This shows that a microprogram can be represented as a finite automaton by associating a state with each microinstruction, with the various conditions in the processor acting as inputs.

The next step consists of applying any existing method for minimizing the number of states in this equivalent automaton. This reduced automaton then corresponds to a reduced microprogram. However, in case of a large microprogram, the number of states becomes unmanageably large, resulting in excessive computational requirements.

The formal techniques for optimizing the number of microinstructions have been developed by several researchers [6–9]. One of these methods, due to Kleir and Ramamoorthy [6], is briefly described here. Basically, the authors have applied the existing compiler code optimization techniques, such as removal of redundant and negated actions, code motion, etc., to microprograms. From a given microprogram an action table is generated, the entries of which specify input and output machine components used for a particular action (microinstruction). The action table also maintains two pointers for each action, designated as forward and backward pointers (FP and BP, respectively). The BP points to a previous action, where *input* to the current action is defined; the FP points to a following action, where the output of the current action is used. The table may contain additional identifiers for timing NO-OP actions.

Redundant actions are defined to be those whose outputs are predictable and available from preceding identical actions already executed. Similarly, negated actions are defined to be those whose results are not used in the microprogram under consideration. Kleir and Ramamoorthy have also given sufficient conditions for movement of an action either in the forward or backward direction from its current position. Suppose the action under condideration is in position i in the action table. It can be moved forward to position $i + k$ or backward to position $i - k$ if the following conditions hold.

1. Input to the action at location i is not redefined in the region of k microinstructions relative to location i.
2. a. For forward motion, the output of action at location i is not used as input to any of the k microinstructions following location i.
2. b. For backward motion, the output of action at location i is not redefined by any k preceding microinstructions.

The forward and backward pointers of the action table help identify the number of locations that a particular action can be moved either in the forward or backward direction. However, it should be noted that even though the conditions mentioned for the movement of an action are satisfied, the movement must not lead to a timing problem either in the old location or in the new location. This type of action movement may enable replacement of timing NO-OPs with productive actions.

Kleir and Ramamoorthy have also suggested the use of Tomasulo's algorithm [11] for merging actions that can be executed in parallel with the help of multiple hardware units. The following microprogram illustrates the application of the Kleir-Ramamoorthy optimization algorithm; the microprogram reads a byte from memory and outputs it for the Microdata 1600* machine.

*Reprinted with permission of Microdata Corporation, Irvine, California.

LT X'00'	Control byte in T-register.
MOV 3, (N)	Move File Register 3 to N.
COX 0	Output control byte.
NOP	Delay
NOP	required for
NOP	COX.
CIO	Clear I/O control register.
INC 2	Increment File Register 2.
MOV 2, (N)	Move Register 2 to N.
RMF 0	Read memory.
NOP	Wait for
NOP	memory data.
DOX 0	Output data to device.
NOP	Delay
NOP	required for
NOP	DOX.
CIO	Clear I/O control register.

The action table for this microprogram is shown in Table 8.1, where R denotes the microinstruction register of the Microdata 1600*, T is a temporary register, ICR denotes the I/O control register, and N is the lower byte of the memory address register. This table shows that the action

$$MOV \ 3, (N)$$

at Location 2 is a negated action, since the contents of Register N are redefined by the action

$$MOV \ 2, (N)$$

at Location 9, whereas N is not used as input to any action in Locations 3 through 8. Hence Action 2 can be removed from the microprogram under consideration.

As mentioned in Sec. 8.2.1, Actions 8, 9, and 10 can be merged into a single action (microinstruction)

$$RMF \ 2, I(N)$$

---

*Reprinted with permission of Microdata Corporation, Irvine, California.

TABLE 8.1

ACTION TABLE FOR THE MICROPROGRAM TO BE OPTIMIZED

NO.	INPUT PARTS USED	OPERATION	OUTPUT PARTS USED	FP	BP	COMMENTS
1	R	LT X'00'	T	3	0†	—
2	R, Register 3	MOV 3, (N)	N	0†	0	—
3	R, T	COX 0	ICR, D‡	7	1	—
4	R	NOP	Null	0	0⎫	
5	R	NOP	Null	0	0⎬ Timing NO-OPs.
6	R	NOP	Null	0	0⎭	
7	R, ICR	CIO	ICR	13	3	Even though BP = 3, the operation cannot be moved back due to time delay required for COX.
8	R, Register 2	INC 2	2	9	0	—
9	R, Register 2	MOV 2, (N)	N	10	8	—
10	R, N	RMF 0	T	13	9	—
11	R	NOP	Null	0	0⎫ Timing NO-OPs.
12	R	NOP	Null	0	0⎭
13	R, T, ICR	DOX 0	ICR, D	17	10	Cannot be moved back due to timing factors.
14	R	NOP	Null	0	0⎫	
15	R	NOP	Null	0	0⎬ Timing NO-OPs for DOX.
16	R	NOP	Null	0	0⎭	
17	R, ICR	CIO 0	ICR	0	13	Cannot be moved back due to timing factors.

†FP = 0 indicates that the output of the action is not used as input to any other action. BP = 0 indicates that the input to the action is not defined by any previous action in the table.
‡D is device.

This, in fact, represents an application of Tomasulo's algorithm. The reduced action table is now shown in Table 8.2. This table is further reduced by moving productive actions in place of timing NO-OPs without introducing any timing hazards.

With reference to Table 8.2, the microinstruction

$$RMF \quad 2, I(N)$$

at Location 7 can be moved to Location 3 without creating any timing problems. Then the NO-OP actions at Locations 4 and 5 will also satisfy the time delay required for the RMF action. Hence NO-OP actions at Locations 8 and 9 now become redundant and can be removed from the table. Therefore the optimized microprogram obtained is as follows:

TABLE 8.2

REDUCED ACTION TABLE

NO.	INPUT PARTS USED	OPERATION	OUTPUT PARTS USED	FP	BP	COMMENTS
1	R	LT X'00'	T	2	0	—
2	R, T	COX 0	ICR, D	6	1	—
3	R	NOP	Null	0	0	
4	R	NOP	Null	0	0	Timing NO-OPs.
5	R	NOP	Null	0	0	
6	R, ICR	CIO 0	ICR	10	2	Cannot be moved back due to time delay required for COX.
7	R, Register 2, N	RMF 2, I(N)	T	10	0	—
8	R	NOP	Null	0	0	
9	R	NOP	Null	0	0	Timing NO-OPs.
10	R, T, ICR	DOX 0	ICR, D	14	7	Cannot move back due to timing considerations.
11	R	NOP	Null	0	0	
12	R	NOP	Null	0	0	Timing NO-OPs.
13	R	NOP	Null	0	0	
14	R, ICR	CIO 0	ICR	0	10	Cannot move back due to delay required for DOX.

```
LT    X'00'
COX   0
RMF   2, I(N)
NOP
NOP
CIO   0
DOX   0
NOP
NOP
NOP
CIO   0
```

The number of microinstructions has been reduced from 17 to 11.

The Kleir-Ramamoorthy algorithm is applicable primarily to optimization of vertical microprograms. In general, it is not possible to generate an absolute minimal microprogram using this algorithm only. Moreover, the algorithm requires major modifications to deal with context-sensitive micro-operations, such as when a microinstruction is interpreted according to whether the machine is in I/O mode or in CPU mode. It is also difficult to use this algorithm to reduce microprograms by introducing subroutine structures. However, a heuristic approach for optimization using subroutines has been discussed in Sec. 8.2.3.

For optimization of microprograms using horizontal microinstructions, Ramamoorthy and Tsuchiya [12], and Tsuchiya and Gonzalez [13] have developed certain algorithms. Ramamoorthy and Tsuchiya designed a high-level language, SIMPL, and its compiler, which generates horizontal microinstructions from a given sequential microprogram. The code generated by the compiler is then optimized such that some microoperations can either be eliminated or can be merged together for execution in parallel. Tsuchiya and Gonzalez suggested a graph model for a microprogram in order to detect microoperations that can be executed in parallel.

A review of different optimization techniques has been presented by Agerwala [10]. All these algorithms require prohibitive amounts of overhead both in time and memory space, and even then an absolutely minimal micro-program is not guaranteed. These methods are mainly of pedagogical interest.

8.3 EXECUTION TIME OPTIMIZATION

8.3.1. Use of Parallelism

As in the case of control store optimization, use of parallelism in microopera-tions should be made to optimize the execution time as well. This means the various fields in a microinstruction should be used to the fullest extent for executing as many functions as possible within a microinstruction execution cycle. As in the case of control memory optimization, microoperations that are not strictly sequential must be identified in order to incorporate them into microinstructions whose fields are not fully utilized. The example given in Sec. 8.2.1 illustrates a saving in time as well as space; the second version for reading the contents of a memory location is obviously three times faster.

It is important to note that often *hidden* parallelism can be used to save on the execution time of a microroutine. This is due to the fact that some hardware components, when invoked by a microinstruction, invariably take longer to complete their function than a microinstruction execution cycle. In such a case, a "busy" flag is set; this delays the execution of any other microinstruction that wants to use the same hardware component, whereas microinstructions not using the busy component can be executed without being delayed. It is, therefore, advantageous in terms of execution time to do some other processing, if possible, whenever such a delay is encountered. A typical example of this situation arises with instructions for the main memory. The following example involving the Microdata 1600* machine shows the use of this technique. Consider the following sequence.

RMF	0	Read memory byte into T-register.
CPY	2, T	Store data in File Register 2.
INC	3	Increment File 3.
INC	4	Increment File 4.

This sequence uses four cycles for executing the microinstructions, *plus* a two-cycle delay following the memory read, which ensures that the data is in Register T. This sequence can be rewritten as follows.

RMF	0
INC	3
INC	4
CPY	2, T

This requires only four cycles for execution, as the delay due to memory read has been overlapped with the execution of two other microinstructions.

Sometimes the interfacing of input/output devices requires certain control signals from CPU to be ON for a period greater than the execution cycle of a microinstruction. In such cases, resetting a control signal has to be delayed for the required amount of time; this delay can be overlapped with some processing. The following example illustrates this concept using the Microdata 1600† microinstructions.

LOOP	LT X′00′	Control byte in T-register.
	COX 0	Output control byte.
	NOP	Delay required for
	NOP	COX.
	NOP	
	CIO 0	Clear I/O register.
	RMF 2,I(N)	Read a memory byte and increment pointer.
	NOP	Wait for memory
	NOP	data.

*Reprinted with permission of Microdata Corporation, Irvine, California.
†Ibid.

DOX 0	Output data to device.
NOP	Delay required for
NOP	DOX.
NOP	
CIO 0	Clear I/O register.
JP LOOP	Repeat.

This microroutine is part of a routine to output a message from memory onto an I/O device. It can be optimized in the following ways.

1. Do useful processing in place of NOP microinstructions if possible.
2. Overlap the required delays for memory reference and I/O related operations whenever possible.
3. Rearrange the microinstructions in a better sequence to reduce the number of cycles in the loop.

Using these optimizing techniques, the same routine can be written as follows.

	LT X'00'	Control byte in T-register.
LOOP	CIO 0	Clear I/O register.
	COX 0	Output control byte.
	RMF 2,I(N)	Read memory byte
	NOP	and increment pointer.
	NOP	Delay for read and COX.
	CIO 0	Clear I/O register.
	DOX 0	Output data to device.
	LT X'00'	Control byte in T-register and 1-cycle delay for DOX.
	JP LOOP	Repeat and 2-cycle delay for DOX.

It should be clear by now that optimization of execution time requires not only a thorough understanding of microoperation parallelism within a microinstruction but also requires a detailed knowledge of timing characteristics of each microinstruction.

8.3.2. Use of Suitable Programming Methodology

This section considers some of the commonly utilized techniques for optimizing the execution time of a given program; the same techniques can be adapted for microprogram execution time optimization as well.

1. Avoid excessive use of subroutines whenever possible, as the overhead involved increases the execution time. Although the use of subroutines optimizes control store usage and facilitates coding and comprehension, it tends to increase the execution time.

2. Use prespecified registers containing arguments for subroutine calls. This saves the overhead for fetching the arguments. This is similar to the use of COMMON statements in FORTRAN.

3. Remove all loop invariants from a loop. This eliminates redundant computations each time through the loop.

4. When a microprogram segment contains several tests in a sequence (for implementing a compound condition, for example), the order of tests should be arranged in a decreasing order of probability of exit from the sequence. This reduces to an optimum the number of tests performed. Compare, for example, the test sequences shown in Fig. 8.5a and b. Although both sequences perform the same function, Fig. 8.5b would result in a shorter execution time in all but the case where $A = B$.

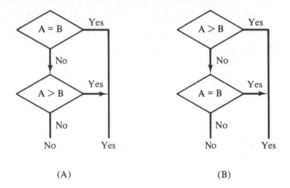

(A)   (B)

Figure 8.5 Condition $A \geq B$ with the Elementary Tests $A = B$ and $A > B$

5. Avoid storage of temporary variables in an external device (this includes the main memory in case of microprogramming). This requires an analysis of the usage of variables in order to provide an efficient utilization of existing internal registers.

6. Whenever possible, employ programming "tricks" to get the most out of a code sequence. Although this might raise some eyebrows, it is worth remembering that (a) microcode often resides in a ROM where it is not subject to user modifications and, therefore, it need not be self-documenting; and (b) efficiency is a major consideration in microcode execution. Therefore considerations of good style and clarity that apply to normal programming do not necessarily apply to microprogramming.

8.3.3. Algorithms

For a given algorithm, the techniques discussed in Sec. 8.3.1 and Sec. 8.3.2 can be used to optimize the execution time of a microprogram. However, if the microprogrammer has the option of designing or modifying an algorithm before actually coding it, then the question of efficiency of the algorithm itself should be examined. The benefits obtained by optimizing an algorithm or finding a better algorithm far outweigh those obtained by optimizing a program implementing an inefficient algorithm. Depending on the situation, a properly designed algorithm can typically save microseconds, whereas optimizing the implementation of a bad algorithm can save only nanoseconds while, at the same time, requiring much more effort on the part of the programmer. For example, the use of Chebyshev polynomials for approximating an elementary function like e^x provides a much faster convergence than the use of Taylor series expansion[3]. In this case, it is obviously a waste of effort trying to optimize the Taylor series implementation when far greater execution efficiency can be obtained by simply choosing a different algorithm. Further savings can then be obtained by applying the techniques of Sec. 8.3.1 and Sec. 8.3.2.

In normal programming practice, the usefulness of a general program is much greater than that of a specialized program. For example, a program to sort n numbers, where n is a variable, is obviously more useful than the one that sorts only k numbers for a fixed k. However, in microprogramming practice, *unneeded* generalization tends to increase execution time while the added flexibility is never utilized. For example, when implementing a microprogrammed circle generator for a graphics terminal, sine and cosine functions are needed. However, because the circle is approximated by a polygon, only the sine and cosine values corresponding to the vertices are needed. It is, therefore, not necessary to implement a complete sine or cosine function; in this case, a much faster circle generator can be obtained by using table look-up to get the required sine or cosine values.

REFERENCES

[1] SHAW, ALAN C., *The Logical Design of Operating Systems*, (Englewood Cliffs, N.J.: Prentice-Hall, Inc., 1974), pp. 112–16.

[2] DAVIS, WILLIAM S., *Operating Systems: A Systematic View*, (Reading, Mass.: Addison-Wesley Publishing Co., Inc., 1977), pp. 70–71.

[3] KUO, SHAN S., *Computer Applications of Numerical Methods*, (Reading, Mass.: Addison-Wesley Publishing Co., Inc., 1972).

[4] GLUSHKOV, V. M., "Automata Theory and Formal Microprogram Transformations," *Kibernetika*, 1, no. 1 (January/February 1965) 1–9.

[5] GLUSHKOV, V. M., "Minimization of Microprograms and Algorithm Schemes", *Kibernetika*, 2, no. 5 (September/October 1966) pp. 1–3.

[6] KLEIR, R. L., and C. V. RAMAMOORTHY, "Optimization Strategies for Microprograms," *IEEE Trans. on Computers*, C–20 (July 1971), 783–94.

[7] ASTOPAS, F., and K. I. PLUKAS, "Method of Minimizing Computer Microprograms," *Automatic Control*, 5, no. 4 (1971), 10–16.

[8] YAU, S. S., A. C. SCHOWE, and M. TSUCHIYA, "On Storage Optimization of Horizontal Microprograms," *Seventh Annual Workshop on Microprogramming*, Palo Alto, Calif. (October 1974) pp. 98–106.

[9] CHATELIN, P., and E. PICKAT, "Minimization of the Control Part of a Microprogrammed Memory," *Workshop on Microprogramming*, Grenoble, France (June 1970).

[10] AGERWALA, T., "Microprogram Optimization: A Survey," *IEEE Trans. on Computers*, C–25, no. 10, (October 1976), 962–73.

[11] TOMASULO, R. M., "An Efficient Algorithm for Exploiting Multiple Arithmetic Units," *IBM Journal of Research and Development*, 11, 1 (January 1967), pp. 25–33.

[12] RAMAMOORTHY, C. V., and M. TSUCHIYA, "A High-Level Language for Horizontal Microprogramming," *IEEE Transactions on Computers*, C–23 (August 1974), 791–801.

[13] TSUCHIYA, M., and M. J. GONZALEZ, "Toward Optimization of Horizontal Microprograms," *IEEE Transactions on Computers*, C–25, (October 1976), 992–99.

FURTHER READINGS

1. JACKSON L. W., and S. DASGUPTA, "The Identification of Parallel Micro-Operations," *Information Processing Letters*, 2, no. 6 (April 1974), 180–84.

2. TSUCHIYA, M., and M. J. GONZALEZ, JR., "An Approach to Optimization of Horizontal Microprograms," *Preprints of the Seventh Annual Workshop on Microprogramming*, Palo Alto, Calif. (October 1974), pp. 85–90.

3. TSUCHIYA, M., and T. JACOBSON, "An Algorithm for Control Memory Minimization," *Proceedings of the Eighth Annual Workshop on Microprogramming*, September 21–23, 1975, pp. 18–25.

4. VAN DAM, A., and G. R. LLOYD, "Optimization of Microcode for Horizontally Encoded Microprogrammable Computers," AD/A–006937/7 (October 1974), 61 pages.

EXERCISES

8.1 The examples given in Chap. 7 are not optimized in order to clarify their function. For each example, optimize the microprograms by each method.
   a. Using all possible parallelism in the microinstructions.
   b. Using dynamic instruction modification.

8.2 Write a microprogram implementing the functions in Fig. 8.3 and also providing a check for exclusive references from one microroutine to another.

8.3 Write an equivalent state and output table corresponding to the example in Sec. 8.2.1.

8.4 Write the action table for the example in Sec. 8.2.1.

8.5 Apply Tomasulo's method to the examples of Chap. 7.

8.6 Apply the "use of parallelism" method to the examples done in Exercise 8.5. More optimization can be achieved. Write an action table for these programs adding cycle time as an input resource (if the action has to wait for a given time) and as an output resource (if the action requires a delay to execute fully). Then rephrase the conditions for moving an instruction forward or backward.

PART FOUR

Microprogramming Applications

CHAPTER NINE

Microprogramming and Emulation

9.1 BASIC CONCEPTS

9.1.1. Introduction

This chapter discusses the concept of *emulation* and its applications. ***Emulation*** can be defined as the process of implementing one machine architecture on another machine via microprogramming. This definition, however, is not universally accepted. For example, Mallach[1] defines it as a combined hardware, software, and firmware implementation of a machine architecture. This chapter will not discuss the pros and cons of either definition; it will discuss emulation using microprogramming only. An ***emulator***, therefore, is a set of microprograms that implements the architecture of one machine on another. The machine executing the microprograms is called the ***host*** machine, while the machine defined by the emulator is called the ***target*** or ***virtual*** machine.

A machine with a given architecture can also be implemented in the following ways.

1. By hardwired logic

This implementation results in a real physical machine. It involves extensive hardware design and development, fabrication, testing, and so on. This approach has all the disadvantages of hardwired implementation discussed in Chap. 1.

2. By simulation

This process consists of writing software routines on the host that simulate the functional behavior of the target machine. The execution of a target machine instruction in this case requires many more host machine instruction executions, resulting in a large number of memory accesses which makes it relatively inefficient in terms of execution speed and utilization of the host hardware.

An emulator not only provides more flexibility than hardwired implementation, it also makes more efficient use of host facilities. As pointed out by Husson[2], it is the most desirable technique for implementing a virtual machine.

9.1.2. Characteristics of Host and Target Machines

It is necessary to examine and analyze the various characteristics of the host and the target machines in order to devise a proper strategy for the design of an emulator. This analysis will show the main incompatibilities between the two systems and point to potentially difficult areas in the emulator design. The following characteristics are to be examined.

1. Central Processing Unit (CPU) Characteristics

There are several features of the CPU organization to examine.

DATA PATH STRUCTURE

This is a comparison of the widths of the data paths of the host and the target systems in order to decide how one is mapped onto the other; this includes both instructions and data widths.

TARGET INSTRUCTION SET

This includes analyzing various types of instructions and their operation, various addressing modes, and handling of exceptional conditions such as wrong opcode or arithmetic overflow.

LOCAL STORAGE

This involves an analysis of how various operating and control registers in the target are to be mapped onto the host. In addition, other hardware features such as stacks and scratch-pad memory must also be considered.

MAIN MEMORY

Features such as word size, memory protection, and validity check must be examined to determine the proper mapping for the target memory operation.

2. Input/Output System Characteristics

I/O DEVICES

A very careful analysis of the objectives of the particular emulation must be carried out when considering I/O devices. This involves determining which of the target I/O devices must be emulated by host devices of similar characteristics and which ones can be emulated by other devices (see Sec. 9.3 for more details).

I/O DATA FORMAT

Even on two devices with similar characteristics (for example, two disk drives) the physical organization of the data may differ. Therefore, target I/O data format must be mapped properly onto the host device.

I/O OPERATIONS

A typical example of the problems that may be encountered in this category is the emulation of channel operation with programmed I/O on the host. Other considerations in this category are time-dependencies in I/O operations, I/O bus structure and width, and so on.

3. Interrupt Structures

Interrupt schemes vary widely from one machine to another. They range from simply setting an interrupt flag to an elaborate scheme that saves the internal registers and automatically causes a branch to various interrupt service routines. The following interrupt characteristics must be considered.

1. Number of interrupt lines.
2. Priority scheme amongst interrupts.
3. Types of interrupts.
4. Interrupt masking features.
5. Basic handling of the interrupts; that is, what has to be done between the detection of an interrupt and the branch to the service routine.

9.1.3. Strategy for Emulation

In designing an emulator for a target machine, the following steps may be taken.

1. Study of the Host Machine Characteristics

This involves being thoroughly familiar with the host machine operation and features as well as its microinstruction set, since these are the basic tools for the microprogrammer.

2. Study of the Target Machine Characteristics

The characteristics outlined in Sec. 9.1.2 should be analyzed at this stage in order to gain a complete understanding of the problem.

3. Determining Incompatibilities

As a result of following Steps 1 and 2, any incompatibilities between the host and the target systems can be identified.

4. Performance Goals

At this stage, it may be discovered that some target functions, although implementable, would have to be realized at the expense of some performance factors (for example, response time or a requirement for excessive control store). It may, therefore, be necessary to reexamine the goals in view of the performance factors.

5. Specifications for the Emulator

As a result of the previous steps, it should now be possible to write the specifications for the emulator. This would include (a) the specifications for the microprograms to be written; (b) software or hardware support (or both) that may be necessary for emulation; and (c) whether some target features would not be emulated.

6. Writing the Emulator Code

At this stage, normal programming practice should be followed. This includes writing the code (firmware and any software) and testing and debugging the code.

9.2 CPU EMULATION

This section discusses the process of emulating the CPU functions and instructions of the target machine. This is a relatively straightforward task since the CPU functions are similar in most machines.

9.2.1. Data Path Structure

Various components within the CPU, such as arithmetic registers, instruction register, location counter, memory address and data registers, and arithmetic circuits, communicate with each other via a data path. The widths of the various links and registers comprising the data path (the number of bits of information carried) are not normally the same. For example, the link between the instruction register and the memory address register may be 16 bits wide, whereas the link between the memory data register and arithmetic registers may be 32 bits wide. Each of these links and registers must be mapped onto the host system; in each case, the possible problem would be a mismatch between the widths of the host and target data paths. Another problem that may be encountered is that some target data path links or registers may not have corresponding counterparts in the host system.

In the case where a host data-path link (or register) is wider than the corresponding target link (or register), the latter can be mapped by selecting a subset of the bits from the corresponding host element and—depending on the circumstances—either masking out the unwanted bits or simply ignoring them. Note that in some cases this subset of host bits masked may not be contiguous and, therefore, some shifting and concatenation of bits may be necessary to properly map the target link or register.

Where a host and the corresponding target data path are of the same width, a one-to-one mapping of bits can be specified unless the meaning of the bit configurations differ. For example, the position of the most significant bit in the target link may be the reverse of that in the host link.

Finally, when a target link is wider than the corresponding host link, the operation of the target link must be emulated either by more than one operation cycle of the corresponding host link or by concatenating two or more appropriate host links or registers. For example, a 16-bit register from a target machine can be mapped on an 8-bit host either by successively processing the upper and lower bytes or by concatenating two host registers, if available.

In case where a target data path link has no direct counterpart in the host machine, a virtual link must be created in the host using an indirect route. For example, a direct link between two target machine registers may have to be emulated using an intermediate path (such as register to accumulator and then accumulator to register) in the host. In the worst case, register-to-memory and memory-to-register load operations may be the only choice to create such a virtual link.

9.2.2. Functional Processing Unit

This section discusses the fetching, analysis, and execution of target CPU instructions.

1. Fetching

The process of fetching a target machine instruction depends on its format. For a machine with an instruction set of fixed length, two approaches can be taken.

1. Fetch the entire instruction before starting any analysis.
2. Fetch a part of the instruction, process it, and then repeat this sequence for the rest of the instruction.

The choice between these two approaches may depend on the instruction register mapping, memory mapping, and whether it is possible to process the target instruction in parts. For example, while emulating an 8-bit instruction machine on a 16-bit host, the entire target instruction must be fetched. On the other hand, if a 16-bit instruction register is mapped onto an 8-bit host register, the second approach must be taken. Note that the selection of a suitable approach and the mapping of the instruction register are interdependent considerations. For instance, in the previous example, it may not be possible to break the target instruction into two parts, so the mapping of the instruction register has to be changed in order to use the first approach.

In the case where the choice is up to the microprogrammer, some advantages may be derived by using the second approach. First, as the memory cycle time is usually longer than the time for executing one microinstruction, some overlapping can be achieved between fetching the next part of the instruction and processing the previous part. Second, if an abnormal condition, such as an invalid opcode, is encountered while processing a part, the remaining parts of the instruction need not be fetched.

For a target machine with a variable instruction length, a part of the instruction must first be fetched and analyzed to determine the length of the instruction. Once this has been done, either of the two approaches mentioned before can be used to fetch the rest of the instruction.

2. Analysis

Once a target instruction has been fetched (in whole or in parts), its type must be determined in order to properly interpret the rest of the instruction. This information is usually contained in the opcode, although some additional information may have to be obtained from another field in the instruction. For example, the opcode may indicate a memory reference instruction—indicating the presence of a memory address field in the instruction—but it may not indicate how to compute the memory address; this latter information is then contained in another field (direct or indirect, indexed or nonindexed addressing, and so on).

At this stage, not only is the structure of the instruction known, but also the structure of the data, for example, whether the data are words or bytes, upon which the operation is done. Once the instruction structure is known, the various fields and subfields can be processed accordingly. The whole analysis should provide the following information.

1. The operation to be performed as specified by the target instruction.
2. How to get the operands.
3. The type of the operands (for example, integer or floating point).

3. Processing

Following the instruction analysis, the operands (if any) required for the instruction are fetched. Then the specific operation indicated by the opcode is performed by branching to the appropriate microroutine. The various microprograms for interpreting the target machine instructions should be designed using normal good programming techniques, such as sharing code for processing similar instructions.

Processing of an instruction also includes performing the following operations.

1. Incrementing the emulated instruction counter, unless it was modified as a result of the instruction execution (for example, a jump instruction).
2. Servicing any interrupts (to be discussed in more detail in Sec. 9.4).
3. Processing of exceptional conditions such as divide by zero or invalid opcode. This processing depends on how the target machine is supposed to handle these conditions.
4. Performing any concurrent operations specified by the target machine, such as concurrent I/O or updating emulated clock.

9.2.3. Mapping of Registers, Local Storage, and Main Memory

1. Registers and Local Storage

These consist of addressable registers, nonaddressable registers (for example, memory address register), scratch-pad areas and stacks. In general, these target components should be mapped onto the corresponding host facilities for speed considerations. If, however, not enough facilities are available on the host, then dedicated main memory locations in the host must be utilized for the mapping. This approach would inevitably result in some loss of operational speed because access to the main memory is usually slower than access to local storage or registers. These dedicated memory locations must not form a part of the "user area" in the memory. This can be achieved by simply excluding this area when mapping the target memory addressing system onto the host.

2. Main Memory

The first consideration in mapping the main memory is the word-size compatibility. For this problem, methods similar to those discussed in mapping data paths are applicable: masking some bits in the host word or iterating over multiple words. When multiple host memory words must be used for a target word, the emulator performance suffers in terms of speed. Note that the main-memory mapping dictates the mapping of target addresses in the host. For example, when mapping a 32-bit target memory word in an 8-bit host, the target address n would map to the host address $4n$.

Other considerations in memory mapping are the emulation of memory protection and checking features of the target. An example of the latter is the parity check on each target word that must be suitably emulated.

When the host does not have enough memory to allow large target programs to run, use of auxiliary storage may be necessary to emulate the required memory.

9.2.4. Example of CPU Emulation

At this point, it would be appropriate to discuss an example of emulation of an actual system (Data General Nova) on a Microdata 1600* microprogramming system. However, before giving any details of the emulator, a general introduction to these systems is necessary. (The complete emulator is listed in Appendix C.)

NOVA† SERIES COMPUTERS‡

Nova computers are general-purpose computers with a 16-bit word length. All machines are organized around four accumulators, which are used for temporary data storage and data manipulation in all instructions of arithmetic and logic class and also as part of the I/O system. The 15-bit address of the next instruction to be fetched is held in the PC. These five registers are accessible to programmers. Even though the internal organizations of various machines within the Nova family are different from each other, the same instruction set is used among them and the programming for all machines is completely compatible. A schematic of the arithmetic unit organization is shown in Fig. 9.1.

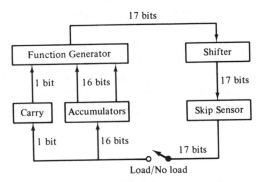

Figure 9.1 Organization of Nova Arithmetic Unit‡

*Reprinted with permission of Microdata Corporation, Irvine, California.
†Nova is a registered trademark of Data General Corporation, Southboro, Mass.
‡Reproduced by permission of Data General Corp. from their manual entitled *"How to use the Nova Computers."*

INSTRUCTION FORMATS

In the Nova-series machines, the bits of a word are numbered from left to right with 0 to 15; the same numbering scheme is used in the registers. By convention, all numbers representing instruction words, register contents, codes, addresses, and any data appearing in programs are octal unless otherwise specified. The whole word is partitioned as follows.

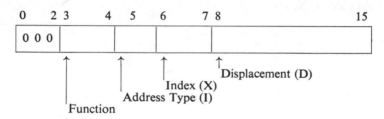

There are four basic types of instruction formats.

1. Jump and modify memory commands.

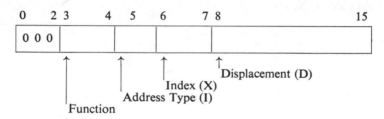

2. Move Data commands.

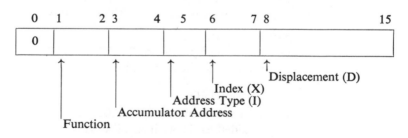

3. Input/output commands.

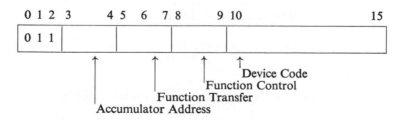

4. Arithmetic and logic commands.

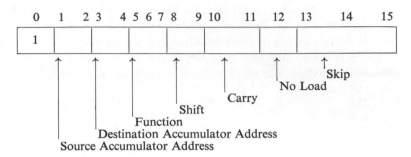

Addressing Mechanism

The effective address in the memory-reference instructions depends on the values of I, X, and D in

5	6	7 8		15
I	X		D	

where I is indirect bit, X is index bits and D is displacement.

X	Derivation of address
00	$\begin{cases}\text{Page zero addressing.} \\ \text{D is an address in the range } 00000_8 \text{ to } 00377_8.\end{cases}$
01	$\begin{cases}\text{Relative addressing.} \\ \text{D is a signed displacement } (-200_8 \text{ to } +177_8) \\ \text{that is added to the address in PC.}\end{cases}$
10	$\begin{cases}\text{Base Register addressing.} \\ \text{D is a signed displacement } (-200_8 \text{ to } +177_8) \\ \text{that is added to the address in AC2.}\end{cases}$
11	$\begin{cases}\text{Base Register addressing.} \\ \text{D is a signed displacement } (-200_8 \text{ to } +177_8) \\ \text{that is added to the address in AC3}\end{cases}$

The calculation of an operand address can be classified into three types.

1. Direct Addressing

If $1 = 0$, the effective address of the operand would be

Effective address = The contents of index register ± Displacement

or

Effective address = Displacement D if X = 00

2. Indirect Addressing

If I = 1, the processor retrieves another address from the location specified by the address already determined according to the information in the instruction. The 0-bit of the retrieved new word is the indirect address bit. If this bit is zero, bits 1 to 15 are the effective address; otherwise they specify a location for another level of address to be retrieved. The process continues until some referenced location is found with a zero in the 0-bit position. Then Bits 1 to 15 of the location are the effective address.

3. Auto Incrementing/Decrementing Addressing

If any memory location in the range 20_8 to 37_8 is accessed by indirect addressing, the processor will retrieve the contents of that specified memory location and increment or decrement the word retrieved, write the altered word back into the same location, and use the altered word as the new direct or indirect address.

—If the word is taken from locations 20_8 to 27_8, it is incremented by one.
—If the word is taken from locations 30_8 to 37_8, it is decremented by one.

The Microdata 1600 is described in Chap. 7. For more detailed information about both systems, the reader is referred to the literature supplied by the manufacturers [3, 4], and to Appendices A and B.

EMULATION OF THE NOVA* CPU
ON THE MICRODATA 1600†

In order to map the Nova machine onto the Microdata system, the following items should be considered.

1. Mapping of Nova Registers onto Microdata Registers

This step is shown in Table 9.1.

In the Nova computer, the PC register is automatically incremented by one after the execution of the current instruction or the effective address is loaded into the PC if a JMP or JSR instruction has been performed. Microdata primary File Registers 4 and 5 are assigned as the image of the Nova program counter and updated after execution of the current Nova instruction.

Bit 1 of primary File Register 1 is used to store the emulated carry bit to reflect the resulting state of the carry after execution of any arithmetic and logic instruction of the emulated system.

*NOVA is a registered trademark of Data General Corporation.
†Reprinted with permission of Microdata Corporation, Irvine, California.

TABLE 9.1

MICRODATA FILE REGISTER ASSIGNMENTS FOR NOVA SYSTEM

File Bank	File Register	Corresponding Nova Register
Primary	0	Microdata Condition Flags
	1 (bit 1)	Carry bit
	2, 3	Instruction Register
	4, 5	Program Counter
	6, 7	AC0
	8, 9	AC1
	A, B	AC2
	C, D	AC3
	E, F	Operand Register
Secondary	0	Microdata Condition Flags
	1, 2, 3	Temporary Storage
	4	RTC Counter
	5	Selected Clock Frequency (Initial RTC Counter Value)
	6	TTO Buffer
	7	TTI Buffer
	8	PTR Buffer
	9	Temporary Storage
	A	Low Byte of Mask Register
	B	PTR BUSY/DONE Byte*
	C	ID Byte**
	D	RTC BUSY/DONE Byte*
	E	TTI BUSY/DONE Byte*
	F	TTO BUSY/DONE Byte*

*Bit 7 indicates the BUSY flag condition; Bit 0 indicates the DONE flag condition.
**Bit 7 assigned as interrupt flag (IF bit); Bit 6 assigned as NI indicator.

2. Memory Mapping

Machines in the Nova* family are 16-bit machines, but the Microdata 1600† is an 8-bit, byte-oriented machine. Therefore, in order to represent a Nova word, two bytes of Microdata memory are used. During instruction

*NOVA is a registered trademark of Data General Corporation.
†Reprinted with permission of Microdata Corporation, Irvine, California.

fetch, two consecutive bytes are retrieved from the Microdata memory and stored in a pair of file registers corresponding to the Nova instruction register.

After the operand address calculation for a Nova instruction, the address is loaded in the operand register (Microdata File Registers 14 and 15). The contents of the operand register are multiplied by two and the address is then transferred to M- and N-registers if memory read/write is required; otherwise the contents of the operand register are transferred to the PC register if a JMP or JSR instruction is to be executed.

Before the emulator is activated, the virtual Nova machine must be initialized by placing initial values into the emulated PC and other registers. Once emulation mode is entered, the Microdata central processor behaves as it is were the emulated (Nova) central processor.

An instruction fetch microroutine gets the emulated PC and converts the PC-value to the address of the storage cell that contains the instruction to be interpreted; it then retrieves the Nova instruction from memory and places the subject instruction in the emulated instruction register (primary File registers 2 and 3). The Nova instruction is then interpreted by the emulator. After the Nova instruction is executed and the PC is updated, control passes to a microroutine that handles internal housekeeping, such as I/O data transfer and interrupt handling. If no I/O interrupt or other conditions requiring attention are detected, then the next Nova instruction is fetched and the whole cycle is repeated.

The instruction fetch and the housekeeping microroutines are the most significant routines in the emulator; they are used *once* for *each* Nova instruction. The basic flowchart and the memory-mapping diagram for the overall emulation process are shown in Fig. 9.2 and 9.3, respectively. A detailed flowchart for the Microdata emulation of Nova LDA and STA instructions is shown in Fig. 9.4.

Table 9.2 lists the execution times of the emulator for the Nova instruction set, along with the corresponding timings on a real Nova. The complete emulator is listed in Appendix C.

CONCLUSION

It is clear from Table 9.2 that a performance penalty must be paid for using the Microdata 1600 to emulate the Nova. This is somewhat inevitable, since the two systems employ different design philosophies. For every Nova instruction and operand, the Microdata must go through two cycles of memory addressing. In addition, the Nova instructions are implemented for optimum utilization of Nova hardware. But on the Microdata 1600, the highly condensed information contained in the Nova instructions has to be interpreted by a significant piece of microcode, so the decoding and execution of target instructions takes a great deal of time compared with the hardwired Nova 1200 system.

Apart from the difference in data-path widths, the processor functions

TABLE 9.2

EXECUTION TIMES FOR THE NOVA EMULATOR AND THE NOVA 1200 (in microseconds)

Instruction	Emulator	Nova 1200
1. Memory Reference Instructions (Direct Page Zero Addressing)		
JMP	5.0	1.35
JSR	6.0	1.35
ISZ	12.0	3.15
DSZ	12.0	3.15
LDA	9.0	2.55
STA	9.4	2.55
2. Arithmetic and Logic Instructions		
COM	16.8	1.35
NEG	18.0	1.35
MOV	16.8	1.35
INC	18.0	1.35
ADC	18.0	1.35
SUB	19.4	1.35
ADD	18.6	1.35
AND	18.4	1.35

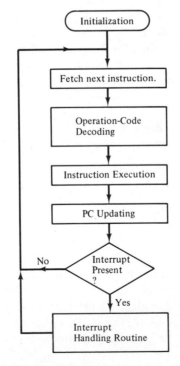

Figure 9.2 The Basic Flowchart of Nova Emulator

212

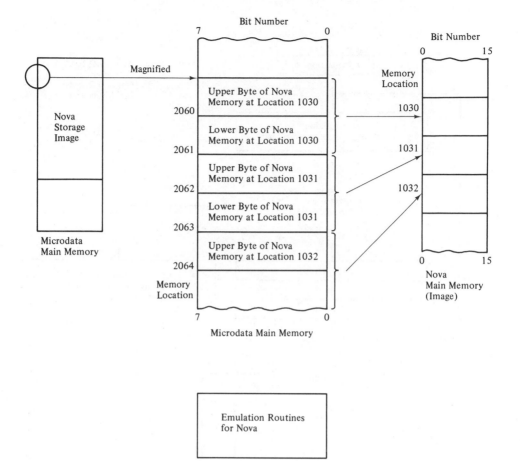

Figure 9.3 The Memory Mapping Diagram of Nova Emulator

of both the target and the host systems are similar. Some improvement in emulation speed would result if the Microdata 1600 were a 16-bit machine; that is, if its memory word size and data paths were 16 bits wide. For example, target instruction fetch would then require only one memory cycle instead of the present two. However, the process of interpreting the target machine instructions would essentially remain the same. Therefore the overall speed of the emulator would not necessarily be doubled; however, there would definitely be some improvement in speed.

9.3 EMULATION OF INPUT/OUTPUT SYSTEMS

This section is concerned with the problem of I/O system emulation. This problem, in general, requires more effort than CPU emulation primarily because of the following factors.

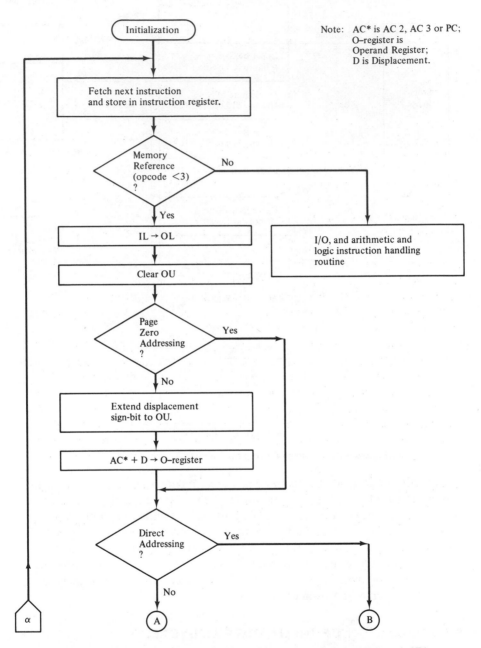

Figure 9.4 Flowchart for the Microdata Emulation of Nova LDA and STA Instructions

214

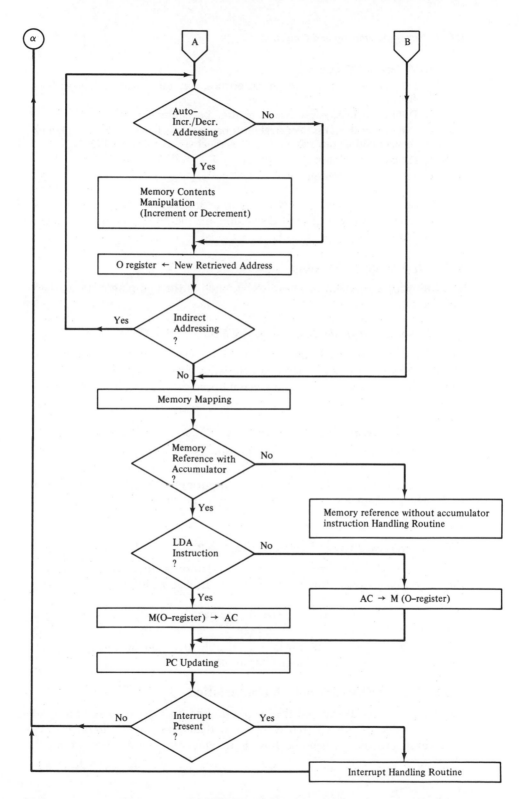

Figure 9.4 (continued)

1. Variety of I/O devices.
2. Differences in operational characteristics, even for similar devices (such as disks).
3. Differences in physical data formatting on similar devices.
4. Differences in I/O system structures between machines, such as single-bus versus multiple-bus I/O, or DMA channel versus I/O via CPU.
5. Differences in interrupt structures.
6. Timing considerations.

Because of the wide variety of differences between I/O systems of different machines, only a general discussion on the I/O emulation problem will be given.

9.3.1. I/O Device Mapping

The following considerations have to be made in the mapping of target I/O devices:

1. Sequential versus Direct Access Characteristics

While it is possible to map a sequential device to another sequential or direct access device (all other characteristics being similar), an extreme performance penalty must be paid when mapping a direct access device onto a sequential one.

2. Input versus Output Function

It should be obvious that an input-only device cannot be mapped onto an output-only device, and vice versa. However, an input/output device can be used to emulate an input-only or an output-only device. For example, a card reader cannot be emulated by a printer, but it can be emulated by a magnetic tape.

3. Interactive versus Noninteractive

An interactive device cannot be emulated on a noninteractive device; the reverse is possible, although it might result in some loss of performance.

It should be noted that a target device need not always be mapped onto the same device in the host. For example, if it is known that the target disk is used only sequentially, then it may be advisable to use the host magnetic tape to emulate it and save the host disk for another use.

9.3.2. Device Operational Characteristics

Although a target device and the corresponding host device may appear to be very similar, minor differences between their operational characteristics may cause problems when the host is in emulation mode. For example, mapping an operator's terminal with automatic line-feed and carriage-return features onto a similar host terminal without these features will require extra attention in the host in order to run the target software properly. In such situations, simply interpreting the target machine instructions will not be enough and additional processing has to be done. For the particular example mentioned, this would consist of keeping a character counter and generating a carriage return and line feed when the counter indicates the end of a line.

9.3.3. Data Formatting

Even with identical host and target devices, variations in data format on these devices must be considered when designing the emulator. A typical example of this is different record formatting on two different floppy disks. Once again, this requires additional processing in the host apart from the interpretation of target instructions. If the data format incompatibilities are such that they require extensive processing, then the necessity of achieving a true format mapping must be reassessed.

9.3.4. I/O Bus Structure

Input/output bus structures vary widely between machines (for example, single bus versus multiple bus and the number of buses in multibus systems). As a result, I/O bus access protocol varies from one system to another. In I/O system emulation, it is not necessary to duplicate the target bus access protocol exactly; what is needed, instead, is to emulate the target bus operation. Sometimes this may result in loss of performance while executing target programs. For example, if the target DMA bus has to be emulated by the host programmed I/O bus, the emulator performance would suffer. In such cases, additional hardware would be required for more efficient I/O emulation.

The width of I/O buses is another factor that must be taken into consideration. In this case, the techniques discussed in Sec. 9.2 for data path mapping apply as well.

9.3.5. I/O Interrupt Structures

Although interrupts are used frequently for input/output, within a machine there exist other types of interrupts as well. The emulation of the entire interrupt structure will be discussed in Sec. 9.4.

9.3.6. Timing Considerations

Some programs may use the fact that data transfer to or from an I/O device occurs at a given maximum rate determined by the device speed. If this device is mapped onto a host device of different speed, then the features of the program which depend on that rate may not function properly on the host unless some special action is taken by the emulator to resolve the problem.

For example, if a host input device operates faster than the corresponding target device, then intermediate buffering can be used by the firmware to reduce the apparent rate of arrival of data.

An example of I/O system emulation will be presented at the end of Sec. 9.4.

9.4 EMULATION OF INTERRUPT SYSTEMS

This section discusses the problem of emulating interrupts and interrupt handling. There are two fundamental classes of interrupts in a machine:

1. *Internal Interrupts* This includes interrupts generated by such factors as program errors (for example, divide by zero), machine malfunction (for example, wrong parity in a memory access), or an instruction designed for that purpose (for example, the TRAP instruction).
2. *External Interrupts* This includes interrupts caused by I/O devices or channels, console interrupts, power-fail/restart interrupt, real-time clock interrupts, and some others (for example, interrupts caused by other CPUs in a multiprocessor environment).

9.4.1. Mapping of Interrupt Systems

In a microprogrammed computer, the interrupt system is implemented primarily by firmware. The hardwired part of the interrupt system in these machines usually consists of a set of flags that signal the presence or absence of an interrupt. In addition, some associated information, such as the priority level of an interrupt, may be set in hardware registers. The firmware implementation provides for a flexible design of the interrupt handling mechanism.

The target interrupt features must be mapped onto the host, taking into account possible incompatibilities between the two systems. For example, a target console interrupt can be emulated via an I/O interrupt on the host by reserving a key for this purpose on the operator-console keyboard. Sometimes an interrupt system incompatibility can force a reevaluation of the design goals for the emulator. Consider, for example, a target with multiple interrupt lines and a host with all I/O devices connected to a single interrupt line. Furthermore, suppose that the host interrupt system is such that when two or more requests occur simultaneously on the interrupt line, only the interrupt from one device can be acknowledged while other requests are lost; usually the selected device is chosen on the basis of some priority scheme. In this case there are two options open for emulating the target interrupt-driven I/O operation.

1. Complete an I/O operation without overlapping it with any other operations. This means putting the processor in a "wait" state after starting the device and waiting until an interrupt is received, signaling the end of the

I/O operation, and then returning to the next instruction in the target program. With this solution, no I/O operation is started while another one is in progress and, therefore, two interrupts will never be allowed to occur simultaneously. However, the performance penalty paid might be prohibitive, and some target programs may not run properly.

2. Execute target interrupt-driven I/O operations as specified by the target program, ignoring the possibility of simultaneous interrupts, and use the single interrupt line to emulate the multi-interrupt target system. This will cause an error in the processing of a target program if two or more devices interrupt the processor simultaneously, as only one interrupt will be recognized. However, the designer of the emulator may prefer this solution to the preceding one if the probability of such a simultaneous occurrence is small enough.

9.4.2. Interrupt Handling

1. Recognition of an Interrupt

As stated earlier, the presence of an interrupt in a microprogrammed computer is usually indicated by the setting of a flag bit. It is the responsibility of the firmware to periodically check for the presence of an interrupt; this is usually done before a new machine instruction is processed.

2. Primary Level Handling

This consists of the actions to be performed as specified by the target interrupt handling procedure and generally includes the following.

1. Recognition of the type of interrupt and whether or not it should be serviced.
2. Saving the current status of the machine; that is, saving the contents of the location counter and other status bits. This is commonly referred to as saving the PSW (program status word).
3. Resetting the interrupt flag and branching to the corresponding interrupt handling routine (the branching is done by loading the target PSW with a new PSW associated with the type of interrupt).

3. Secondary Level Handling

Once the control has been passed to the appropriate interrupt service routine, the responsibility of the firmware for handling the interrupt is finished. The interrupt-service routine, consisting of target machine instructions, is then executed by the firmware like any other program.

Note that in some machines recognition of the type of interrupt is left to the secondary-level handling routine. On the other hand, in some other machines primary-level handling is more elaborate than previously mentioned and includes such functions as saving of the emulated operational registers and stacks.

9.4.3. Example: Emulation of Nova* I/O System on the Microdata† 1600

In this section, Nova I/O system emulation on the Microdata 1600 is described in detail; the purpose is to show the detailed mechanisms of a specific I/O emulation. However, before discussing this example any further, it is appropriate to introduce the Nova I/O system; the details of the Microdata 1600 I/O system are presented in Sec. 7.3.

1. Nova Input/Output System

The I/O system of the Nova computer consists of two main parts: input/output bus and device controllers.

1. Input/Output Bus

The I/O bus is the communication link between the CPU and input/output devices. It consists of the following parts.

1. Six device selection lines used to address the selected device. Only the selected device responds to control signals generated during an I/O instruction execution.
2. Sixteen bidirectional data lines. All data and addresses are transferred between the processor and the devices attached to the bus via these 16 lines.
3. Nineteen control lines from the processor to devices govern the synchronization of all transfers on the data lines, start and stop device operations, and control the program interrupt and data channel.
4. Six control lines from a device to the processor. Over these control lines a device can indicate the state of its BUSY and DONE flags and request a program interrupt or data channel access.

2. Device Control Unit

Every device connected to the I/O bus has certain fundamental circuit networks used to communicate with the processor to reveal its current status or to ensure the device will respond when it is selected.

Each device has a 6-bit device code that may be unique to it or be shared by more than one device. A device will respond when and only when it is addressed by the CPU over the I/O bus. There are BUSY and DONE flags associated with each peripheral device to denote the device state and interrupt request. When both BUSY and DONE are clear, the device is idle.

---

*Nova is a registered trademark of Data General Corp. This material contains excerpts reproduced by permission of Data General Corp. from their manual *How to Use the Nova Computers.*

†This material is based on the *Microprogramming Handbook* and is reprinted with the permission of Microdata Corp., Irvine, Calif.

As the program sets the BUSY flag, it places the device in operation. When the device has transferred a unit of data, it clears BUSY and sets the DONE flag to indicate that it is ready to receive new data for output or it has data ready for input. If the *interrupt disable* flag is clear and *interrupt on* is set, the setting of the DONE flag will signal the program by requesting an interrupt.

2. Input/Output Instruction Set

Instructions in the input/output class direct data transmission from and to the peripheral devices, and also perform various operations within the processor. The format of an I/O instruction is shown below.

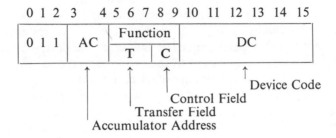

If the transfer field contents are zero or 7, there is no data transfer between a device and the CPU. In this case the control field specifies a control or skip function, respectively. If any number from 1 to 6 is assigned to the transfer field, it will select one of three buffers in the device and govern data transfer between the accumulator addressed by Bits 3 and 4 (AC field) and the device specified by the DC field. Device code 00 is not used and 77 is used for a number of special functions.

3. Interrupt Facility

The interrupt facility of Nova provides for enabling and disabling of devices from requesting service, establishing levels of priority interrupts, and servicing devices only when they request service. The interrupt system is enabled by the instruction INTEN, which sets the *interrupt on* flag to allow the processor to respond to interrupt requests; it is disabled by the instruction INTDS, which clears the *interrupt on* flag to prevent the processor from responding to further interrupt requests. An interrupt request by a device is governed by its DONE and *interrupt disable* flags. When a device completes an operation, it sets the DONE flag, and this action requests a program interrupt if *interrupt disable* is clear. The service request signal is a level signal, so once it is set, it will remain on the I/O bus until the program clears the DONE flag or sets *interrupt disable*. If the program does set the *interrupt disable* flag in a device by the instruction MSKO, that device cannot cause an interrupt when its DONE flag is set, and any request it may have already made is disabled; however, if the DONE flag is left set, clearing *interrupt disable* will restore the interrupt request.

At the beginning of every memory cycle, the processor tests for any interrupt request. If a request does exist, the processor clears the *interrupt on* flag, thus disabling any further interrupts; it then saves the contents of the program counter in memory location 0 and executes an indirect jump through location 1 (hardware function). Therefore location 1 should contain the address of the interrupt service routine or an indirect address that will get it there.

The interrupt service routine has to determine which device is requesting interrupt. This is done either by using a polling technique, which involves checking the DONE flag of every device in descending order of priority, or by a broadcasting technique which uses the INTA AC (interrupt acknowledge) instruction. When this latter command is issued, the device requesting an interrupt that is physically closest to the processor responds with its device code, which is deposited into the specified accumulator.

Once the interrupt service routine has determined the device to be served, it executes a jump to the specific device service program. Generally, a device service routine will save the contents of any accumulators, carry, or memory cells that may be destroyed by the service routine. The service program can simply leave the interrupt off while serving the device by leaving *interrupt on* clear, or it can enable interrupt and establish a priority structure that allows a higher priority device to interrupt the service routine of the current device. This priority is established by a new MSKO instruction that controls the states of the *interrupt disable* flags in the various devices. After serving a device, the service routine of the device should restore the processor to its original state prior to the interrupt, turn on the interrupt, and jump to the interrupted program to continue processing.

The device priority mechanism of the Nova system is very flexible. There are several ways in which priorities are determined for or assigned to a device on the I/O bus. The most significant method is by specifying which devices can interrupt a service routine currently in progress. This is done through the use of a MSKO AC command. The *interrupt disable* flag of each device is wired to a particular data line on the bus and is effectively connected to one of the 16-bit positions in the accumulator AC. If the bit position in the AC contains a 1, all *interrupt disable* flip-flops connected to it are set, thus disabling the devices from requesting interrupts. If, however, the bit position contains a zero, all *interrupt disable* flip-flops connected to it are reset. This enables the corresponding devices to request interrupts; consequently these devices are regarded by the program as being of higher priority. By means of the MSKO instruction, programs can establish any priority structure, and because accumulator AC has 16 bit positions, there are 16 possible levels of interrupt priorities.

For further information on this system, the reader is referred to the literature supplied by the manufacturer [3].

4. Emulation on the Microdata 1600

The I/O instruction set of Nova computers can be classified as two types.

1. Peripheral device-oriented instructions (device codes range from 01_8 to 76_8).
2. Special function instructions (device code $= 77_8$).

In the former class of instructions, the programmer can select the device buffers (named A-buffer, B-buffer, and C-buffer) for holding the information being transferred. The number of device buffers available to the programmer is device-dependent. Typically, all the simple data handling devices, such as a teletypewriter or paper tape reader, have only the A-buffer. In order to emulate this feature, local storage is used to map the device buffers for an individual device. For instance, the Microdata secondary File Register 6 is assigned as the teletypewriter output (TTO) A-buffer.

Similarly, the BUSY and DONE flags of an individual device are mapped into the host system to indicate the status of the emulated device. The major resources of Nova I/O system are mapped to most of the secondary file registers on the Microdata system. This mapping is shown in Table 9.1.

Besides these basic mappings, there is an additional virtual match created for the Nova real-time clock (RTC) instruction. The real-time clock rate of Microdata 1600 is fixed at 1000 Hz. However, in the Nova system it is possible to select one of four clock frequencies: AC line frequency 60 Hz, 10 Hz, 100 Hz and 1000 Hz. Therefore, for emulating Nova RTC frequencies other than 1000 Hz, a counter has to be set up in order to generate the RTC interrupt at the selected rate.

In Nova the special function instructions facilitate various operations within the processor, such as interrupt enable/disable or read switch. Instructions for testing interrupt on or off conditions (SKPBN CPU, CKPBZ CPU) are provided in the repertoire. The Nova interrupt flag (IF) is mapped onto Bit 7 of secondary File Register 12. The IF bit can be used to distinguish whether the emulated system (Nova) is actually in the interrupt mode or program mode in order to govern the emulator to take proper actions (whether to emulate Nova interrupt mode operation or not). More details on this aspect are provided later.

In the Nova system, the interrupt enable command cannot take effect until the next instruction has been executed, allowing the return jump to be made successfully after the interrupt service routine is finished. This feature should also be faithfully incorporated in the emulator. Bit 6 of secondary File Register 12 (NI, no interrupt) is used to indicate whether a Nova interrupt is to be serviced or not. (If NI = 0, then Nova interrupts are serviced; otherwise they are not serviced.)

In the present version of the emulator, a basic Nova system has been emulated. It includes the emulation of CPU and some fundamental I/O devices: teletypewriter input/output, high-speed paper tape reader and real-time clock. In Nova, reassignment of priority levels for these devices can be achieved by specifying a mask pattern in an accumulator, which is then transferred to the mask register by a MSKO instruction. The high-order byte of the mask register contains the mask priority bits for the disk pack and 16-line TTY multiplexor; the low-order byte contains the mask bits for other devices such as the teletypewriter or paper tape reader. Since the present version of the emulator does not emulate the Nova disk pack or TTY multiplexor, a Microdata file register (secondary File 10) is sufficient to map the low-order byte of the mask register.

Before the emulator is entered into the emulation mode, it is necessary to initialize the host (Microdata) I/O system. Establishing the character format for a device, baud rate control, and processor interrupt enable, place the host I/O system in its operating mode. Subsequent initialization of the virtual system (Nova) will clear the control flags (for example, the BUSY and DONE flags of all devices or the Nova interrupt flag). The Nova program counter is then initialized to the appropriate starting address by the operator, after which the emulator begins its major function by fetching a target instruction from the main memory and interpreting the instruction. A microroutine for interrupt checking is executed immediately after the execution of each Nova instruction. The major functions of this routine are to examine the status of the I/O devices, carry out any data transfer, and update the status flags of emulated I/O devices. If input data from a device is ready, this routine will issue I/O microinstructions to accept the data from the device and store it in the emulated device buffer. On the contrary, if data is to be output to a specified device, the actual output operations are also carried out by this microroutine when the device is ready to receive data. Flowcharts for this routine and Nova TTI instruction emulation are shown in Fig. 9.5 and Fig. 9.6, respectively, for illustrative purposes.

The configurations of the emulated (Nova) and the emulating (Microdata 1600) machines are shown in Table 9.3. The CRT display and keyboard are used instead of a teletypewriter as the operator's console in this system. A virtual match is created to simulate the teletypewriter functions on the operator's console—the keyboard simulates the TTI operations and the CRT display simulates the TTO functions. Another version of the Nova emulator provides the option of emulating the TTO functions either on the CRT display or on a hard-copy data terminal by setting or not setting sense switch

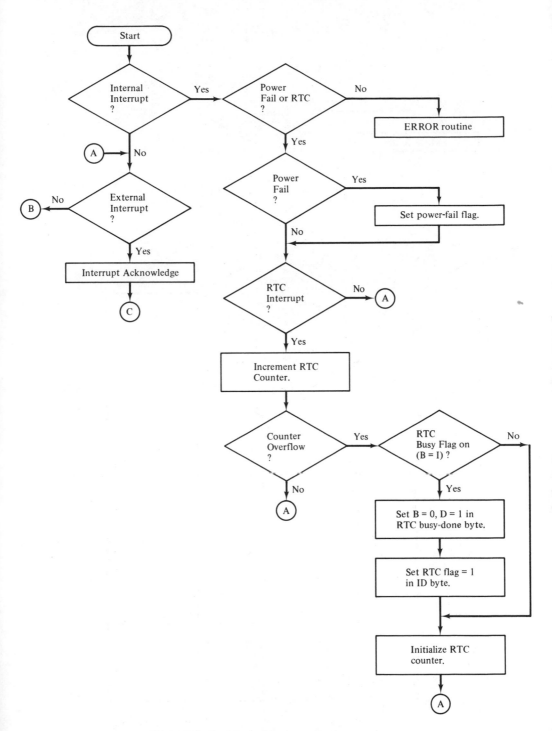

Figure 9.5 Flowchart of Interrupt Checking Routine

225

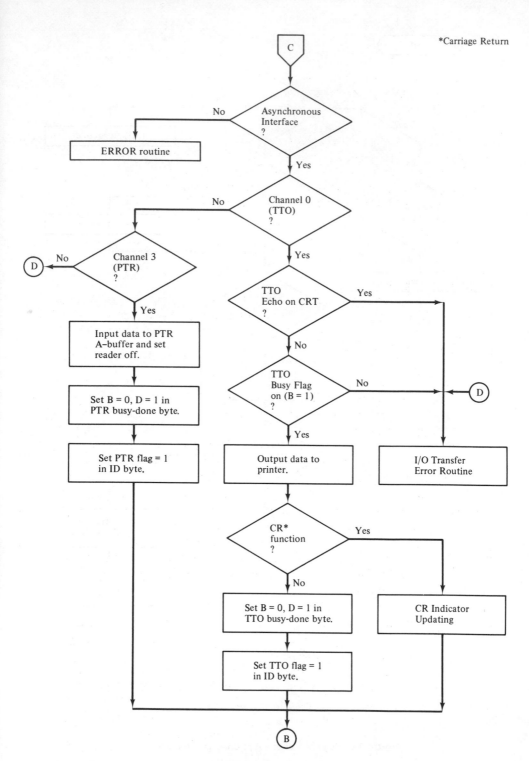

*Carriage Return

Figure 9.5 (continued)

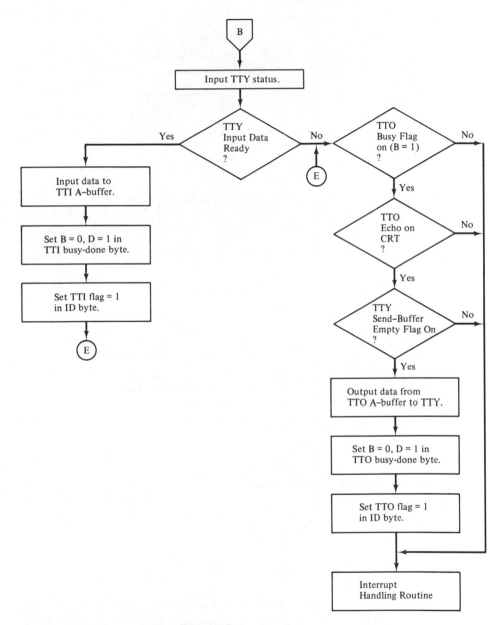

Figure 9.5 (continued)

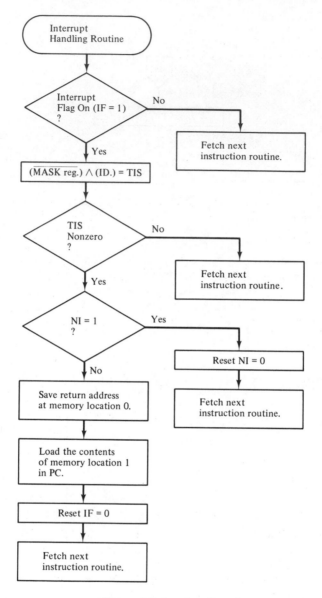

Figure 9.5 (continued)

1 on the Microdata console. The *read console switch* function of the Nova
has been emulated by the keyboard/display combination on the Microdata.
A prompt character (s) is output on CRT display when the emulator executes
the *read console switch* command. In response, the operator must enter the
values of the Nova console data switches in octal via the keyboard.

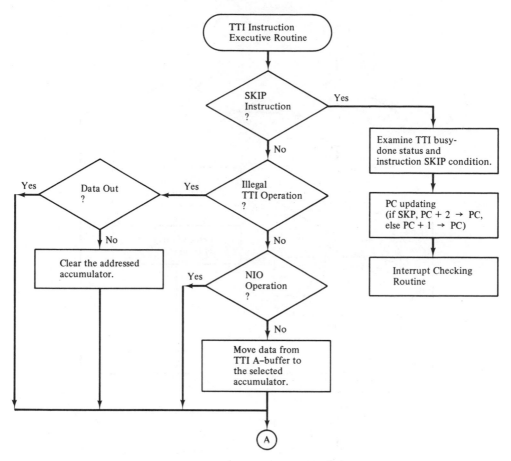

Figure 9.6 Flowchart of Nova TTI Instruction Executive Routine

The target I/O transfer operations, in general, can be handled either in program mode or in interrupt mode at the conventional machine level. Both modes may be implemented separately in the emulator in the form of separate modules. However, in the implementation of the Nova emulator, data transfer is always handled in the Microdata interrupt mode and the interrupt microroutines take care of all data transfers. The routines for emulating a device's I/O instructions only set or reset some flags (for instance, the BUSY and DONE flags) or perform test and skip functions (for instance, SKP instruction). This approach is based on the following factor.

In the emulation of program mode operation, the data-transfer routines have to examine the status flags of a device before issuing a data-transfer command. Similarly, in the emulation of the interrupt-mode operation, checking the status flags of all the devices is necessary between two Nova instructions. Therefore duplicated status checking operations will be per-

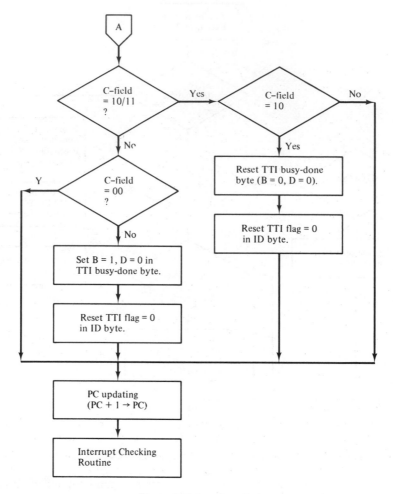

Figure 9.6 (continued)

formed if the two I/O modes are implemented in separate modules, resulting in unnecessary usage of control storage and redundant operations. For this reason, the interrupt microroutines handle both the interrupt and program-mode data transfers. In the emulator, a special flag—called the interrupt flag (IF)—has been used to indicate whether the target machine is in program mode or interrupt mode. If the target system is in program mode (IF = 0), then no interrupt functions are emulated, and the firmware only handles the data transfer functions. On the other hand, if the target system is set in interrupt mode (IF = 1), the firmware not only handles the data transfer functions but also emulates the interrupt strategy of the Nova computer.

TABLE 9.3

THE CONFIGURATIONS OF THE HOST
AND TARGET MACHINES

Target Computer	Host Computer
Nova 1200	Microdata 1600
Console Input	CRT Terminal Keyboard
TTY Input	CRT Terminal Keyboard
TTY Output	CRT Display or Data Terminal (on asynchronous line interface, Channel 0)
Paper Tape Reader (PTR)	Paper Tape Reader (on asynchronous line interface, Channel 3)
Real-Time Clock	Real-Time Clock

Table 9.4 lists the emulator execution times for the Nova I/O instructions, along with the corresponding timings on a real Nova 1200.

TABLE 9.4

EXECUTION TIMES FOR I/O INSTRUCTIONS
(microseconds)

Instruction		Emulator	Nova 1200
SKP__	TTI	8.4	2.55
NIOS	TTI	9.0	3.15
NIOC	TTI	9.6	3.15
DIAS	AC, TTI	10.8	2.55
DIAC	AC, TTI	11.4	2.55
SKP__	TTO	8.6	2.55
NIOS	TTO	15.2	3.15
NIOC	TTO	11.4	3.15
DOAS	AC, TTO	16.6	3.15
DOAC	AC, TTO	12.8	3.15
SKP__	PTR	8.6	2.55
NIOS	PTR	27.2	3.15
NIOC	PTR	11.4	3.15
DIAS	AC, PTR	29.4	2.55
DIAC	AC, PTR	13.6	2.55
SKP__	RTC	8.6	2.55
NIOS	RTC	9.0	3.15
NIOC	RTC	9.8	3.15
DOAS	AC, RTC	13.8	3.15
DOAC	AC, RTC	14.6	3.15

9.5 GENERAL REMARKS

9.5.1. Hardware, Firmware, and Software Trade-Offs in Emulation

While the main concern of this chapter is microprogramming and emulation, this section discusses the virtual machine implementation through a trade-off between hardware, software, and firmware. It is not always desirable to implement a virtual machine entirely by firmware because of various factors.

In implementing a virtual machine, it may turn out that some functions are better implemented via additional hardware added on to the host. For example, while it is theoretically possible to emulate the operation of a magnetic disk on a sequential access device on the host, it is obviously cumbersome. In this case, additional hardware, with direct access characteristics, is much preferable. As another example, implementing the dynamic address translation (for virtual memory operation of the target machine) may be more efficiently done via special hardware rather than firmware, due to the firmware overhead and the frequency of use of this function.

Similar considerations apply for implementing some functions of the target machine via software rather than firmware. For example, if some instructions of the target machine (such as code conversion) require a table look-up operation, it may be better to create this table in the main memory rather than in control memory, thus decreasing the requirements for control storage space. Furthermore, part of the processing for some instructions can be done by software should control store be limited.

As another example, the frequency of use of some target instructions might warrant their implementation in software rather than firmware. As a result, the execution times for these instructions will be increased, but if their use is sufficiently low, the overall effect on the execution time of a target program will be hardly noticeable. This would free the control store space for better utilization. Even if some instructions, such as programmed I/O, are frequently used, it may not be worthwhile to implement them via firmware because these instructions are usually encountered in a program with execution time governed by the speed of the I/O devices. Implementing such instructions via firmware would not improve the overall execution time of such a program. A typical example of this situation is a loop for checking the "ready" status of an I/O device. In such cases, the processor waits for the device to be ready, and it is not important to increase the execution speed of the instruction that reads in the status.

The performance of an emulated system depends, to a great extent, on the degree to which the incompatibilities between the host and target machines have been resolved in the implementation of the emulator.

Consider, for example, a target disk with a record size of 128 bytes, which is mapped onto a host disk with a record size of 256 bytes. The simplest approach in this case would be to map one target record onto one host record. This would result in a relatively simple firmware implementation (simply ignoring the incompatibility of the record sizes), but would waste 50 percent of the host disk capacity. A more complex firmware routine, which compresses two target records into one host record, utilizes the disk space more efficiently but at the expense of longer execution time and more control store space. In this case, a trade-off between efficient disk utilization and firmware complexity has, therefore, to be made; it becomes more critical as the incompatibility becomes harder to manage (for example, when a target record of 133 bytes is to be mapped onto the host record of 256 bytes). Note that the additional processing needed for a more efficient disk utilization need not be implemented in firmware. Depending on the design goals, additional hardware (incorporated into the disk controller) or software can be used for this purpose. Similar trade-off considerations apply to other factors in the design of an emulator. The following are some of these factors.

1. Implementation of a feature or function that cannot be implemented by firmware alone.
2. Size of control memory.
3. Size of dedicated main memory required for software implemented emulator functions.
4. Optimization of overall emulator performance. This includes speed of execution, percentage of target functions and features emulated, and development costs.
5. Expected amount of usage of the emulator. This includes the consideration of whether the emulator is to be used only on an interim basis while the software is being converted and the frequency of its use.

9.5.2. Universal Host Machine

Most commercially available user-microprogrammable machines have fixed characteristics such as a predefined data path, a given number of internal registers, and a fixed memory structure (word or byte organized). This makes it difficult to map any arbitrary target structure onto such a machine. However, if some of these characteristics could be dynamically specified, then the task of mapping an arbitrary structure would be simplified considerably. As an example, a host machine with a bit-addressable memory structure would obviously be capable of accommodating target memory words of arbitrary length. In addition, the ability to extract fields of arbitrary length from a target instruction would be a desirable feature for instruction analysis. Such a universal host machine would be an ideal tool for research purposes by virtue of its flexibility.

9.5.3. Emulation of Front Panel Operation

Some target software, especially for minicomputers or microcomputers, may use switch settings on the front panel of the target machine for communication with the operator. The functions usually provided by the front panel of a machine consist of:

1. Examining and modifying the contents of internal registers and memory locations;
2. Program interrupt and stepping;
3. Setting of data and sense switches;
4. Other specialized functions (such as channel status or CPU busy).

In designing an emulator, some of the target front-panel functions must be incorporated in order to properly execute those target programs that use these functions. For example, setting of some sense switches may be required by a program in order to select a particular I/O device or to specify an operating option. It is quite likely that incompatibilities will exist between the host and target panel functions or features. As a case in point, the host may have fewer sense or data switches than the target panel. In this case the emulator firmware will have to resolve this incompatibility. This can be achieved in several ways. One approach is for the firmware to read the host sense switches more than once and then create an image of target switches when a target *read sense switches* command is encountered. This approach has the disadvantage of being inconvenient for the operator if this type of dialogue with the target programs is quite extensive. In such a case, a better approach consists of mapping the target sense switches onto the operator's keyboard on the host and entering the switch settings directly in binary, octal, or hexadecimal notation. With this solution, it may be necessary to send a prompt character or message to the operator's console whenever the target switch settings are to be read.

Other target panel functions such as *examine* or *deposit* can be implemented either via the host panel or the operator's console.

REFERENCES

[1] MALLACH, EFREM G., "Emulator Architecture," *COMPUTER*, 8, no. 8 (August 1975), pp. 24–32.

[2] HUSSON, SAMIR S., *Microprogramming: Principles and Practices* (Englewood Cliffs, N.J.: Prentice-Hall, Inc., 1970.) pp. 87–98.

[3] "How to Use the Nova Computers," (Southboro, Mass.: Data General Corporation, 1972).

[4] *Microprogramming Handbook*, 2nd ed. (Irvine, Calif.: Microdata Corporation 1972).

FURTHER READINGS

1. ADAMS, J. M., and V. W. POOCH, "A General Purpose Microprogrammable Emulator," *Proceedings of the Southwestern IEEE Conference and Exhibition* (April 3–6, 1973), pp. 360–67.

2. BAKER, D. M., "Economic Considerations for Conversion," *Datamation*, 12, no. 6 (June 1966), pp. 30–34.

3. BENJAMIN, R. I. "The Spectra 70/45 Emulator for the RCA 301," *Communications of the ACM*, 8, no. 12 (December 1965), pp. 748–52.

4. BERNDT, H., "Input/Output Microprogramming: An Overview," *EUROMICRO Newsletter*, 2, no. 3 (April 1976), 3–8.

5. CHURCHILL, P., and F. ROY, "An Emulator for the IBM 360 on the Microdata 1600," *Internal Report*, Dept. of Computer Science, University of Ottawa (1975).

6. DEMCO, J. C., and T. A. MARSLAND, "PDP-11 Emulation: An Insight," *IEEE Computer Society Repository*, R75–302, 21 pages.

7. FRIEDER, G., "A Procedural Definition of Emulation," *SIGMICRO Newsletter*, 3 no. 4 (January 1973), 65–68.

8. FULLER, S. H., and others, "Microprogramming and its Relationship to Emulation and Technology," *Preprints of the Seventh Annual Workshop on Microprogramming*, Palo Alto (October 1974), pp. 151–58.

9. GREEN, J., "Microprogramming, Emulators and Programming Languages," *Communications of the ACM*, 9, no. 3, (March 1966), pp. 230–32.

10. HOEVEL, L.W., "Micro Emulation: When To Do It and When Not To Do It," *Preprints of the Sixth Workshop on Microprogramming*, College Park, Maryland (September 1973), pp. 176–183.

11. HOUSE, D., "Designing a Microprogrammed Minicomputer for Emulation," *SIGMICRO Newsletter* 5, no. 1 (April 1974), p. 3.

12. ILIFFE, J. K., and J. MAY, "Design of an Emulator for Computer Systems Research," in *Microprogramming* ed. G. Boulaye and J. Hermet, Paris, France: Hermann, 1972, pp. 281–305.

13. JONES, L. M., "An Experimental Seminar on Microprogramming and Emulation," *SIGMICRO Newsletter* 5, no. 2, (July 1976), pp. 79–83.

14. MALLACH, E. G., "Emulation: A Survey," *Honeywell Computer Journal*, 6, no. 4 (1972), pp, 287–97.

15. MALLACH, E. G., "On the Relationship Between Virtual Machines and Emulators," *Proceedings of the Workshop on Virtual Computer Systems* (March 1973), pp. 117–26.

16. PETIT, J., "Design of a General Emulation Machine," in *Microarchitecture of Computer Systems*, ed. R.W. Hartenstein and R. Zaks, Elsevier North Holland, Amsterdam, 1975, pp. 25–33.

17. RAUSCHER, T. G., "On the Feasibility of Emulating the AN/UYK-7 Computer on the AADC Signal Processing Element," *NRL Memorandum Report* 2525 (November 1972).

18. ROSIN, R. F., "Contemporary Concepts of Microprogramming and Emulation," *Computing Surveys* (December 1969), pp. 197–212.

19. ROSIN, R. F., G. FRIEDER, and R. H. ECKHOUSE, "An Environment for Research in Microprogramming and Emulation," *Communications of the ACM*, 15, no. 8 (August 1972), 748–60.

20. SALISBURY, A. B., "The Evaluation of Microprogram Implemented Emulators," *IEEE Computer Society Repository*, R76–109, 123 pp.

21. TRIMBLE, G. R., JR., "Emulation of the IBM System/360 on a Microprogrammable Computer," *Preprints of the Seventh Annual Workshop on Microprogramming*, Palo Alto, (October 1974), pp. 141–50.

22. TUCKER, S. G., "Emulation of Large Systems," *Communications of the ACM*, 8, no. 12 (December 1965), pp. 753–61.

23. TUCKER, S. G., "Emulation Techniques," in *Microprogramming*, Paris, France: Hermann, 1972, ed. G. Boulaye and J. Hermet, pp. 397–417.

24. VANNESCHI, M., "On the Microprogrammed Implementation of Some Computer Architectures," *EUROMICRO Newsletter*, 2, no. 2 (April 1976), 14–20.

25. WHILBY-STEVENS, C., and A. M. CROXON, "Systemsware—A Technique for Digital Emulation and Interfacing," *Proceedings of the 1972 ACM National Conference*, p. 590, Boston, Mass.

EXERCISES

9.1 A 16 by 32-bit set of target registers is to be mapped in dedicated memory on a 12-bit word host starting at Address 0. Write the algorithm necessary to find the host memory address corresponding to a target register.

9.2 On some machines the memory protect feature is implemented by adding an extra bit indicating if a word is protected or not. Suppose a 16-bit word memory plus a 1-bit protect flag is to be emulated on a 16-bit word memory host. Find several ways to implement this feature.

9.3 A 4K by 12-bit word target memory is to be mapped into a 6K by 8-bit word host memory. Find an algorithm to convert a target address into the corresponding host address.

9.4 Suppose you are given a host with a general-purpose memory (that is, containing data and program instructions) and a target machine with a dedicated memory containing instructions only and another memory for data only; evaluate the processes necessary in the emulation of a target instruction in this case.

9.5 A target multiple-interrupt system with priorities is to be mapped on a host system with polling only. Assume, for example, there are 8 devices; Device 8 has the highest priority and Device 1 has the lowest priority. Write a polling algorithm that emulates the interrupt system.

9.6 Given a host line printer that is line oriented, write an algorithm to emulate the printer mechanism of a teletypewriter (character oriented). Assume a record is printed on the host printer whenever it receives a combination CR | LF or LF | CR; if only a carriage return (CR) or only a line feed (LF) is sent, then the appropriate function is performed.

CHAPTER TEN

Microprogramming Support for Operating Systems and High-Level Languages

Traditionally, machine language instructions have been implemented by hardwired logic or interpreted via firmware, thus providing a basic machine architecture upon which the software system is built. In particular, operating system functions are implemented using these machine instructions. In order to improve the performance of an operating system, direct implementation of operating system functions via firmware has been studied. In the area of high-level languages, these have, traditionally, been processed either interpretively (for example, APL or BASIC) or by compilation into machine language (for example, FORTRAN, PL/1, or COBOL). The purpose of this chapter is to present the various ways in which microprogramming can be applied to implement, support, or enhance operating system performance and high-level language processing.

10.1 OPERATING SYSTEM SUPPORT

10.1.1. Review of Operating System Concepts

This text will not present a lengthy description of operating systems and their principles. This material is available from numerous sources [1, 2, 3] and it is assumed that the reader has a general background on this subject. However, some operating system concepts will be briefly presented in order to facilitate an understanding of the material presented in this chapter.

An **operating system** (OS) is a set of routines that provides a means to share the resources of a computer installation among a community of users. In order to achieve this goal, numerous OS functions have to be implemented. These OS functions can be decomposed into several broad categories.

1. Resource Management Functions

This category includes functions that perform the task of allocating the computer system resources among various users or tasks. This includes, for example, functions to allocate main memory to a program, including memory allocation for another component of the operating system. It also includes allocation of I/O devices to a job step.

2. Scheduling Functions

Scheduling functions perform the task of deciding which process, program, or job is to be executed. The scheduling of jobs, which also depends on resource availability, is usually decided on a priority basis; in the case of task scheduling, however, other functions such as clock monitoring for time sharing systems, interrupt monitoring, or abend processing, may be involved.

3. Input/Output Functions

The I/O functions provide ease of I/O programming, file management, and overall control of the I/O system. The I/O modules relieve the programmers from the burden of coding their own I/O routines, thus making the details of I/O programming transparent. The file management facilities provide for security and protection of the user's data. They also allow the programmer to refer to files by name rather than by parameters related to a device. In addition, these functions provide a facility for generating and maintaining data sets (such as creating a backup or restructuring a file).

The I/O functions also exercise overall control on the I/O system. This includes scheduling I/O, allocating shared I/O device time, allocating channel time, and monitoring I/O interrupts.

4. Support and Diagnostic Functions

Some services such as timing services (clock, timer) or debugging services (dump, tracing, breakpoints) are examples of support that an operating system offers to the users. Another particularly important function provided by OS is error processing. This function is performed at various levels: hardware error, program error, and system error. For each of these error categories, the minimal service rendered is the notification of an error condition. Most operating systems, however, provide detailed diagnostics of the errors, including the type of error, location of the error, and status of the system at the time of the error. Some operating systems provide a further service consisting of error recovery and even error correction.

5. Utility Functions

These functions provide additional facilities to the users for easier utilization of the computer system. They include such items as relocating and overlay loaders, language processors (assemblers, compilers, interpreters), file I/O utilities, and sort/merge routines.

An operating system, therefore, makes a computer installation more manageable by sharing resources among its users. A schematic diagram of an OS is shown in Fig. 10.1.

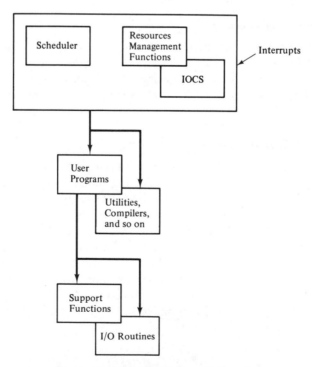

Figure 10.1 Operating Systems Schematic

10.1.2. OS Overhead

So far, operating systems have generally been implemented in software. An analysis of shortcomings of operating systems will underline the motivation for use of microprogramming in the design and implementation of such systems. Some of these shortcomings are now summarized.

1. Time Overhead

The great number of services and functions performed by an OS necessarily results in a large amount of CPU time being used up by the OS routines; this time is therefore not available to the users. This time overhead depends on the size and complexity of the OS and can be as much as 75 to 80 precent of CPU time. However, it is difficult to measure the actual time overhead because, for example, OS services such as I/O routines would take a comparable amount of time to execute had they been part of user's routines. In such a case, part of OS overhead should really be counted as part of the program-execution time of the user.

2. Space Overhead

Although most of an operating system resides in auxiliary storage, the resident functions of the main memory plus the internal tables do account for a large amount of memory space. This naturally limits the amount of real memory space available to the users. This problem can be especially acute in minicomputer systems with limited memory size.

3. Programming Overhead

General-purpose operating systems have reached gigantic proportions, involving thousands of lines of code and years of programming time. The time, effort, and cost to produce a functional operating system implemented in software has become quite large. Furthermore, the complexity and size of operating systems has hindered the reliability of such systems.

It is clear, therefore, that any approach that would help reduce the overhead associated with an OS is worth investigating. One such approach that has been investigated with considerable interest is the use of microprogramming.

10.1.3. Improvements Expected from Firmware Support

There are several reasons why firmware can help improve the performance of an operating system.

1. Speed of Execution

One of the main reasons for considering implementation of OS functions via firmware is increased operating speed. The increased speed is basically the result of three factors.

1. A microprogrammed function executes faster than its software counterpart.
2. Main memory fetch cycles are reduced as only data required by the function need be fetched, instead of both data and machine-level instructions.
3. In software implementation, the use of the existing instruction set may sometime cause the programmer to utilize instructions that are really general-purpose instructions and, hence, may be more powerful than required for the particular application at hand. The (necessary) use of such instructions would, therefore, add unnecessary overhead to the execution of a function. Microprogramming the function would eliminate this overhead by using only the required microinstructions.

2. Main Memory Requirements

Microprogramming can allow the creation of instructions and functions better suited to OS programming. This would, therefore, reduce the number of software level instructions, decreasing main memory requirements.

3. Development Cost

With the availability of instructions and functions suitable for OS, both the design and development costs for an OS can be reduced. Furthermore, as an OS becomes easier to program, its reliability can be expected to increase thereby reducing its maintenance costs.

In addition, firmware support of operating systems offers the following advantages as well.

1. Better security, as software security mechanisms can be easily bypassed.
2. Improved integrity, as it is much harder to accidentally modify a function implemented in firmware than a function implemented in software.

10.1.4. General Considerations in Firmware Support

1. Limitations

Despite the advantages expected from the introduction of firmware in the implementation of operating systems, there are limitations to be faced using such an approach. One such limitation is obviously the size of control memory required for the associated microprograms. Even though memories are relatively cheap, often the size of the control memory is limited even in large-scale computers; this limitation is more serious in the case of minicomputer systems. The problems associated with microprogram development also are limiting, because there are relatively few microprogrammers (as opposed to programmers) available and relatively few user-oriented development tools (as compared to tools available to programmers). A third limitation is the cost associated with this approach. It would be unrealistic to assume that an existing operating system can be completely or partially microcoded without a sizeable redesign of the system. This obviously represents a high cost. A further limiting factor is that not all OS functions gain by firmware implementation, either due to infrequent use of the function or due to the fact that the function execution time is determined by some external factors (such as the speed of an I/O device).

2. *Different Approaches*

Depending on the goals to be achieved and taking into consideration the constraints mentioned, there are different approaches that can be taken when considering firmware support for an operating system. These approaches can be broadly classified into two categories.

IMPLEMENTATION-ORIENTED APPROACHES

The main objective in these approaches is to improve the performance of an existing operating system. For an effective enhancement, frequently used modules or functions form the primary candidates for firmware support or implementation.

The first implementation-oriented approach consists simply of selecting a module or function (one at a time) and moving it from software into firmware. In this case, it is easy to experiment and to measure improvements by running benchmark programs in order to ensure that the desired improvements are indeed being achieved.

In the second approach, an analysis is made of the different modules in order to determine common basic operations. Once these operations have been identified, these are implemented in firmware as additions to the existing instruction set. Examples of these basic operations are search a list and update pointers. As in the previous approach, benchmarks are run to ensure that desired performance goals are met; that is, the basic operations were properly selected.

DESIGN-ORIENTED APPROACHES

In this class of approaches, firmware implementation is considered as a design objective, thereby affecting the total operating system architecture. There are several structural approaches to the design of an operating system [1–4]. One such approach consists of basing an operating system on a small nucleus while the rest of the system is visualized as a user or application program [2]. This approach is well-suited to firmware implementation, where the nucleus is microprogrammed and the rest of the system uses the nucleus as a set of additional, powerful machine instructions. Another structured approach consists of organizing an operating system as a series of hierarchical layers that are strictly separated [4]. This approach is also well-suited to firmware implementation. For example, the first few layers or layer-communication processes could be microprogrammed. The decision to use microprogramming when using these approaches will influence the content of the nucleus or the structure and contents of the layers, respectively.

10.2 IMPLEMENTATION

This section describes the various steps to be taken when implementing firmware support for operating systems. Due to the complexity of the problem, the discussion will be kept at a fairly general level encompassing the various approaches outlined in Sec. 10.1. The necessary steps are outlined as follows.

10.2.1. Identification of Primitives

The first step to be taken consists of structuring the operating system into hierarchical sets of processes. (See Fig. 10.2 for an example.) Processes at the

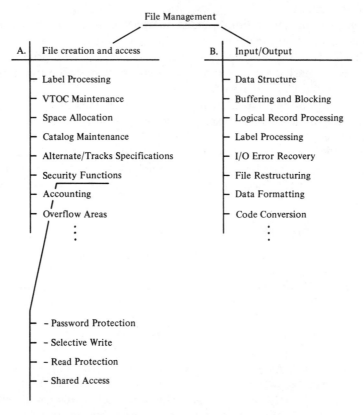

Figure 10.2 Example of Hierarchy of Processes

lowest level of this hierarchy are called **primitive processes** or, simply, **primitives**. Note, however, that this term is relative, as a process at any level can be considered as primitive in relation to the next level. The primitives are, therefore, processes that can be considered as basic building blocks for the next higher levels and that cannot be further subdivided into more primitive processes within the same level. Furthermore, for the purpose of simplifying firmware implementation, the primitive processes should not be interruptable. It is relatively difficult to precisely classify a process as a primitive. A very basic component of an operating system that might be a candidate for firmware implementation may not be a primitive in the strict sense of the definition and may be decomposible into primitives. For example, the GETMAIN function that allocates main memory to user programs, application programs, and OS functions can indeed be decomposed into more primitive processes such as list search and bit manipulation. However, it can be considered to be a (higher-order) primitive process for an operating system because of its very frequent use. For this reason, Werkheiser [5] has introduced the notion of levels of primitives, which are called **miniprimitives, midiprimitives,** and **maxiprimitives,** respectively. The miniprimitives are at the same level as conventional machine instructions. They can, in fact, be viewed as powerful machine language instructions that are useful for programming but not especially oriented towards operating system implementation. Examples of such miniprimitives are bit-field manipulation, table or list search, and subroutine linkage. It should be noted that some manufacturers have already included some of these miniprimitives in the instruction sets of their machines. For example, the CALL and RETURN instructions that perform a complete subroutine linkage, including saving and restoring of registers, argument passing, and recursion, are available on some machines.

As opposed to miniprimitives, the midiprimitives are oriented towards OS functions. For example, Werkheiser [5] has classified system macros as midiprimitives. This is true from a programmer's viewpoint because system macros do provide the next higher level of sophistication over machine-language instructions. However, it may not be true from the OS designer's point of view. The CALL macroinstruction used to invoke subroutines in OS/360 is really a miniprimitive as it is relatively simple to microcode. In the same OS/360, the macroinstruction ENQ that builds a request block for a given resource and puts the requesting task in the wait state until this resource is made available is a primitive function of OS/360, so it does qualify as a midiprimitive. Another OS/360 macroinstruction, ABEND, that terminates the processing of a task after an error detection, should not be considered as a primitive in the context of firmware implementation due to the amount of processing involved and the relatively infrequent use of such a function.

10.2.2. Criteria for Firmware Implementation

The first step helps establish a hierarchy among the OS functions, providing a set of primitives. The next step consists of establishment of criteria for selecting which of these functions should be implemented in firmware. These criteria can be summarized as follows.

1. In order to simplify the firmware implementation, the first criterion would be to select those primitives that are indivisible and noninterruptable and have a well-defined communication interface with the rest of the operating system [5]. Miniprimitives, for example, would satisfy this criterion.
2. In order to optimize the speed enhancement of an operating system, the next criterion for choosing a primitive should be its use of the CPU time. Thus, computation bound, rather than I/O bound, primitives should be chosen [6] since the speed of I/O bound primitives is governed by other (external) factors.
3. In order to both save execution time and provide additional programming convenience when coding the software part of the OS, the next criterion should be the relative frequency of use of a function by other functions. Basically, this process helps identify the most heavily used functions. Even if such functions use a small amount of CPU time by themselves, their frequent use by other functions makes them worthwhile for firmware implementation.

10.2.3. Selection of Primitives for Firmware Implementation

The next logical step consists of applying the criteria mentioned above to the set of primitives identified in the first step. This will yield a subset of primitives that are candidates suitable for firmware implementation. Although the criteria will help identify a suitable primitive, they do not guarantee that microprogramming this primitive will result in a significant gain in the overall performance of the operating system. A necessary intermediate step is to evaluate which of the selected primitives are likely to be vital to improving OS performance. This analysis has been carried through in some instances using a statistical package indicating the number of times each of the primitives is executed. To complete the analysis, each of these (selected) primitives is clocked to determine the amount of CPU time spent on each of them. This measurement is done while running a typical stream of jobs. For the purpose of evaluating the performance gain, the results of this analysis will be much more valuable than simply counting the number of times a primitive is executed. Once a total execution time is obtained for each of these primitives, it provides a better understanding of which primitives are the most likely candidates for firmware implementation.

In the process of designing a new operating system, these measurements must, of course, be obtained from a comparable existing operating system. Creating a statistical package to provide this kind of information may prove to be costly and time-consuming unless the primitive monitored is uninterruptable and nondivisible and has a clean interface with other processes; in this case it is relatively easy to add the clocking feature to the firmware that processes the CALL and RETURN instructions. This avoids the tedious task of inserting the clocking feature in each of the routines to be monitored.

Normally most, if not all, of the primitives to be monitored are interruptable; usually only the machine-language instructions are uninterruptable. Interruptions can occur anywhere within a routine and eventually, after an unknown amount of time, control returns to the interrupted point, thereby making the clock measurements useless. In this case, the clocking mechanism must also monitor interrupts to determine the actual time spent on a primitive. This complicates the design of a package to produce timing statistics.

Another approach for evaluating the performance enhancement achieved through firmware consists of using analytical models for performance prediction [7]. With these models, the effect of improving the execution times of selected primitives on the overall performance of an operating system can be predicted. These figures can then be used to select the primitives offering the best performance gain.

10.2.4. Firmware Implementation

Once a number of primitives have been selected for firmware implementation, they should be microprogrammed and OS performance measurements should be carried out to determine if significant gains are actually achieved. The only result of system overhead reduction in terms of CPU time will be to increase the availability of CPU time for other purposes. This freed time should, however, be put to proper use because otherwise the CPU will simply spend more time in a wait state (this is particularly true in I/O bound systems). This necessitates some reorganization of the operating system, which may then accept more users or provide better turnaround to heavily CPU-bound programs.

Although the previous step helps identify those primitives that are most important in terms of saving CPU time, the main memory freed as a result of microcoding these primitives may not be sufficient to accommodate additional jobs in the system. In this case it is worthwhile to consider microcoding less vital primitives or functions, resulting in reduced savings of CPU time but providing greater memory savings, which gives a better overall gain. It should be clear, therefore, that firmware implementation of OS primitives is essentially a process of "tuning" the system until acceptable performance is obtained.

10.2.5. Firmware Support

In the case of those OS functions that are not suitable for direct firmware implementation, either because of their relatively infrequent use or because they interface with numerous other functions, substantial improvement can still be obtained by microprogramming selected parts of those functions. This process, in turn, consists of two steps.

1. Determining the type of operations that are useful to most of these functions. This, in fact, consists of identifying the miniprimitives that were not explicitly identified in the system hierarchy.
2. Making these operations general enough to be used by the various modules in which they are required [8]. An attempt should be made not to sacrifice efficiency for the sake of generality.

An example of such operation is data structure manipulation (for example, list, stack, and table manipulation). Once again, OS performance measurements should be carried out to ensure that desired improvements are achieved.

10.3 EXAMPLES

This section presents some examples of microprogramming support for OS functions, which either have been implemented or proposed for implementation.

10.3.1. Microprogramming of a Scheduler

Microprogrammed implementation of a scheduler illustrates the first implementation-oriented approach given in Sec. 10.1.4. In this case, a particularly important part of an operating system, the scheduler, is simply moved from software to firmware.

1. Scheduler

In a multiprogramming operating system, user and system programs continuously switch between "states." As far as scheduling is concerned, a process can be in one of the following states:

—RUN state;
—WAIT state;
—READY state.

When in the RUN state, if a process request for a computer system resource is made and this resource is not available, then the process switches to the WAIT state and another process is run. The resource requested can be a hardware resource such as an I/O device or a software resource such as shared data in main memory.

When a process is in the WAIT state, the eventual freeing of the resource (or resources) requested will cause this process to switch to the READY state; that is, the process can be scheduled for execution.

A process in the READY state is placed in the RUN state whenever this process is selected for execution. From this state, it can either go to the WAIT state as mentioned earlier or to the READY state should an interrupt occur that causes control to be passed to a higher priority routine. In the latter case, the interrupted process is not waiting for any resource but processor time; that is, the READY state is equivalent to the WAIT state when the resource being requested is only CPU time. Figure 10.3 gives an overview of the process states.

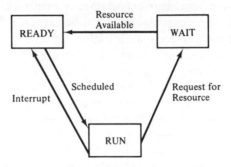

Figure 10.3 Task State Transitions

This transition between the two basic states RUN and WAIT is controlled by the operating system scheduler whose functions are:

—Management of the WAIT and READY queues;
—Management of the RUN queue (in the case of multiprocessor systems);
—Deciding which READY process must be run (scheduling algorithm);
—Interfacing with the interrupt handler;
—Passing control to the selected process.

The following points should be noted.

1. In some systems the management of the queues (inserting, deleting, or transferring a process) is done by the various resource allocators and the scheduler simply worries about the READY queue.
2. The scheduler has to have access to CPU time and, therefore, is itself a process. When the READY queue is empty, either the scheduler places the CPU in the wait state (with at least one interrupt source enabled) and when an interrupt occurs, the scheduler is the first process to gain control, or the scheduler continuously loops, scanning the READY queue for an entry.

The scheduling algorithms allow one to decide which process from the READY queue is to be run. These algorithms apply certain criteria in order to make this decision. Numerous scheduling algorithms have been devised and implemented, depending on the requirements of the particular computer installation [11]. However, except for the most simple type of algorithms (for example, a first-in, first-out algorithm), these scheduling algorithms require a fair amount of computation involving parameters that are dynamically changing.

2. Microprogrammed Implementation

It can be seen from the preceding discussion that a scheduler is not a simple program. It involves several functions and, therefore, could be classified as a midiprimitive. However, due to the importance of a scheduler as an OS function, it is reasonable to expect improvements when microprogramming this function. Time improvements can be expected by microprogramming scheduler primitives such as inserting, removing, and transferring processes to and from a queue. These primitives are well defined and can be implemented fairly easily. The processes of interfacing with the interrupt handler and passing control to the selected process can also be implemented easily in firmware since these functions are simple enough and very close to the hardware. However, due to the reasons mentioned earlier, microprogramming of scheduling algorithms presents more challenging problems. Selecting a scheduling algorithm is heavily influenced by the environment; that is, by such factors as resources already allocated or current requirements of the processes to be scheduled [10]. In order to accommodate this evolutionary environment, it might not be advisable to implement this function in firmware.

3. Example

The implementation of a microprogrammed scheduler has been described by Chattergy [9]. On a multiprocessor facility, one of the processors has been dedicated to the scheduling function. This specific processor is microprogrammed to emulate a virtual machine and to implement the schedule enforcement functions such as queue maintenance. The virtual machine is then used to implement, in software, the scheduling algorithm. It should be noted that in this configuration, the scheduler is complicated by the fact that a READY process can be assigned to one of several processors. The microscheduler described also assists in the paging of processes, which would tend to increase its complexity.

10.3.2. Microprogramming Some Basic Operations

This example illustrates the transition of some basic functions of an existing operating system from software to firmware; it corresponds to the second implementation-oriented approach mentioned in Sec. 10.1.4.

1. The problem

The problem described here arose because of insufficient main memory on the Microdata 1600 microprogramming system acquired by the University of Ottawa several years ago. The operating system TOS provided with this machine was initially used for running jobs. After system generation, the version of TOS providing support for various I/O devices required approximately 3K bytes of memory. Furthermore, the use of the relocating loader required an additional 6K bytes plus the size of the external symbol table, making it difficult to develop and debug programs of size greater than 6K since the main memory size in the system was only 16K bytes. For financial reasons, it was not possible to acquire additional memory and this provided the motivation to support TOS with firmware.

2. Analysis and Solution

In order to reduce the development time, it was decided to simply microprogram some of the existing routines of TOS rather than designing and implementing a new operating system.

The TOS is organized around a small nucleus consisting of subroutines performing common basic operations and a set of independent routines performing various processing functions. Other OS components such as assemblers or loaders are run as independent utilities. The nucleus functions can be classified by three categories.

1. The operator's command input processor.
2. Input/output drivers for the devices used by TOS.
3. A few simple utilities, such as code conversion.

The microprogrammed version of TOS (MTOS), which was designed to reduce the memory requirements to a minimum, is organized in much the same way as TOS; that is, the basic functions form a nucleus that controls and supports the processing functions. The nucleus resides in control memory and, in addition to the basic functions mentioned, contains a paging mechanism to overlay processing functions in a transient area of memory consisting of one page (256 bytes). This organization is shown in Fig. 10.4.

3. Performance

The following improvements have been achieved as a result of implementing MTOS in firmware.

1. The main improvement, in terms of the university's requirements, has been the savings in main memory, because MTOS requires only 512 bytes of memory (256 bytes transient area and 256 bytes I/O buffer area). Note that the savings are caused by the following two factors.

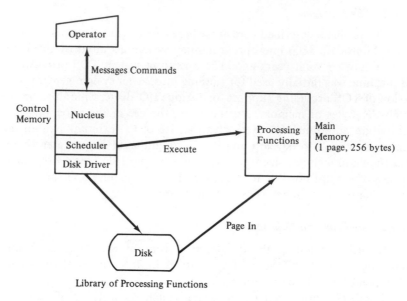

Figure 10.4 MTOS Organization

—Moving the nucleus to control memory which frees approximately 1K of main memory.
—Moving the processing functions to disk storage and paging them into memory one at a time.

2. As a result of microprogramming the nucleus, substantial savings in main memory can be achieved by user programs, because almost all I/O functions are now provided at machine-language level. This also increases programming convenience.

A side effect of implementing MTOS has been the integration of other OS components. For example, the relocating loader was later reorganized using the MTOS nucleus functions. This reduced the size of the relocating loader in such a way that the rest of the loader functions were small enough to fit as a MTOS processing function resident on disk. This approach reduced the core-memory requirements of the loader to the size of the external symbol table. (*Note.* In this particular example, time was not a factor to be considered since most nucleus functions perform I/O services.)

10.3.3. Other Examples

1. The Venus Operating System

The Venus operating system has been described by Barbara Liskov [12]. It is a multiprogramming system designed to test OS implementation relationships with machine architecture. The Venus operating system can be

252

viewed as a software-implemented operating system using a machine architecture specifically designed to support complex software; this specific architecture is defined by a set of microprograms.

The architecture provided consists of several OS-oriented features on top of a standard instruction set. These features are segmentation of the memory, paging, scheduling of 16 virtual machines, procedure linkage, and a virtual I/O channel.

The Venus operating system based on this architecture is designed to support several users, where a virtual machine is dedicated to asynchronous system tasks such as input/output. The organization of the system is based on Dijkstra's hierarchy of levels.

The facilities offered by the microprogrammed architecture reportedly simplified considerably the design of the Venus operating system. In the authors' view, the Venus system is an excellent example of how microprogramming can be used to define an application-oriented architecture to assist the user in developing complex software systems, in this case an operating system.

2. TSS Enhancement

Another example of operating system enhancement through microprogramming is found in the paper by S. M. Bauer [13]. This enhancement consists of using microcode to replace two routines for storage management in IBM's time sharing system (TSS), which runs on the 360/67. These routines (quickcell) manipulate a stack of addresses pointing to available pages. Two new machine instructions, GETQC and GIVEQC, were added to replace the two storage management routines.

Due to the small amount of change in the system, it is not surprising that the overall improvement in performance was hardly noticeable despite the fact that the microprogrammed instructions execute an average of five times faster than the previous quickcell routines. Using a count of function usage, as mentioned in Sec. 10.2.3, Bauer has claimed a 2 percent saving in CPU time. However, the conclusions drawn from the experience are particularly interesting.

1. The execution time of a microprogrammed routine might not be significantly reduced compared to that for a corresponding software routine for complex routines. This is due to the fact that the 360/67 microinstruction set is tuned for efficient emulation of S/360 instruction set rather than for general algorithm implementation. This is probably true in general for most microprogrammed computers, as opposed to microprogrammable ones, although a few exceptions can be found.
2. For large-scale processors, user microprogramming is not advisable unless even a small improvement, but in a critical area, makes the effort worthwhile in terms of performance.

3. *Channel Enhancement*

Input/output programming support and monitoring are operating system functions that are used indirectly by the programmer. This indirect use makes the programmer's job simpler and hides a tremendous amount of processing. This processing consists of reserving I/O devices, monitoring the use of shared devices, optimizing device operation, performing error-recovery functions, performing the actual I/O, buffering and formatting data, and synchronization. This set of operations is performed by the operating system, the channel, and the devices. However, most of the functions performed by the operating system (for example, optimization of the arm movement in a disk drive) could, in fact, be done by the channel, thus relieving the CPU from these tasks.

It has been suggested that through microprogramming, a channel may be able to perform more functions [14]. The additional functions suggested are those for which the channel already has the data available. These are the device-dependent functions such as I/O programs, command and data chaining, access optimization, error processing, and code conversion. Some operating system-oriented functions such as task status-change operations could also be included as part of microprogrammed channel operation. An example of how performance would be improved by removing unnecessary double work and simplifying coordination between the CPU and its channels has been developed [14].

10.4 FIRMWARE SUPPORT FOR HIGH-LEVEL LANGUAGES

10.4.1. The Problem

Traditionally, high-level languages have been processed either interpretively, as in the case of APL and BASIC, or by being compiled into the host computer's machine language and then executing the machine-language program, as in the case of FORTRAN, PL/1, or COBOL. Figure 10.5 shows a simplified view of these two approaches. The process of compilation consists of analyzing the high-level language (source) program and then producing an equivalent sequence of machine-language statements. The resulting program can be referred to as a **surrogate** for the original source program, and it can be executed repeatedly without going through the analysis phase again. The process of interpretation consists of examining and analyzing each statement of the source program and executing the operation(s) specified by the statement. In reality, however, most interpreters translate the source program into an intermediate code and then execute this code.

In the past, the compile-and-execute process has been preferred, in general, over interpretation because of higher overhead involved in the interpretive process. This is due to the fact that no object program surrogate is

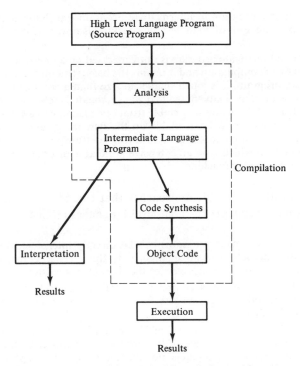

Figure 10.5 Simplified View of Compilation and Interpretation

generated in the interpretive process and, as a result, the analysis phase is repeated each time the original (source) program is to be executed. Furthermore, interpreters were generally implemented in software, and these two factors made them very slow compared to the compile and execute process. As a result, interpreters were generally not used for processing high-level languages except in certain interactive environments, such as in the case of APL and BASIC. However, microprogramming has opened up new and exciting areas of exploration as far as the processing of high-level languages is concerned. This is not because the interpretive overhead can be done away with when using microprogramming, but because a part or whole of the interpreter can be executed out of the control store, which is usually several times faster than main store. Thus microprogramming has, once again, made the interpretive process a viable alternative to the compile and execute process. In addition the interpretive process has the following advantages.

1. The intermediate program (surrogate) bears a close resemblance to the source program and hence, it is easier to "fix" for diagnostic purposes. This is not so in the case of compiled programs, which bear little or no resemblance to the source program.

2. The source program to intermediate program translator is greatly simplified because a lot of compile-time checking is now performed at execution time.

3. Since the surrogate program is not generated on a one-to-many basis as in the case of compilation and it retains the basic structural information of the source program, it is much smaller in size than a compiled program. This has the additional advantage that the surrogate is relatively machine independent, which makes it portable from one machine to another. Of course, an interpreter must be available on the new machine to execute the surrogate. This is much easier than trying to transport a compiled (object) program, in which case an extensive simulator or emulator must be provided in the new machine.

There are three possible approaches that can be taken in considering microprogramming support for high-level languages (HLL).

1. High-level language programs can be directly interpreted by microcode. In this approach, the source language to the internal representation translator as well as the interpreter for the surrogate is written in microcode.

2. The HLL source can be compiled into microcode. In this case, the equivalent microcode is the surrogate for the source program and it is executed by the hardware.

3. The HLL source can be compiled into an intermediate language that is not the machine language of the processor. In this case, the surrogate is neither the machine language nor the microcode for the processor, but an intermediate language program which should be directly and efficiently interpretable by microcode executed by the host machine.

Figure 10.6 provides a pictorial representation of these approaches. The relative merits of these approaches will be examined next. In this context, the work done by Hoevel [15], who has analyzed these approaches in terms of

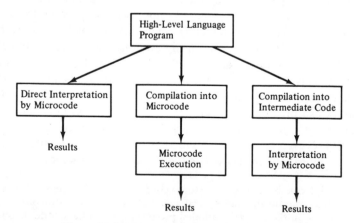

Figure 10.6 Microprogramming Support for HLLs

time and space requirements, is cited. Hoevel has defined the concept of an *ideal* directly executable language (DEL) and has shown that such an ideal DEL is neither the source language nor the machine language of the host processor. He views a computer system that processes a high-level language as a two-phase processing system: the translation processes are defined to constitute the compiler component, whereas interpretive processes (including interpretation of microcode by hardware or interpretation of intermediate code by microcode) are defined to constitute the emulator component. A **directly executable language** (DEL) is defined as the lowest level language into which HLL programs are translated before being interpreted. Hoevel points out that for a given source language and host machine, a suitably designed DEL results in significant savings both in terms of time and space required for processing a user (source) program. An *ideal* **DEL** is defined as one that results in minimal overall space and time while processing a typical user program.

Hoevel first examines the source language and the host machine language as potentially ideal DELs. The source language is not an ideal DEL; the amount of memory space required can be reduced by generating a surrogate in which the source program symbolic names are properly encoded and arithmetic expressions appear without parentheses, such as in the Polish notation. The time required for interpretation can also be reduced because it is easier and faster to evaluate a linear expression such as a Polish string with no operator priority, as compared to the evaluation of an equivalent expression in infix notation with operator priorities. It is, therefore, clear that the source language is not an ideal DEL. It can also be argued that the machine language of the host is not an ideal DEL since the time required to generate the machine-language surrogate and the space required for storing the surrogate are relatively large. The first factor arises because it requires a nontrivial amount of time and program space to generate an efficient surrogate that utilizes the host resources and parallelism in an effective manner. The second factor arises because it is always possible to replace a given sequence of instructions in the surrogate by a single (higher-level) instruction which is expanded into the given sequence dynamically; that is, during the interpretation phase. It is, therefore, reasonable to expect that an ideal DEL, for a given source language and host machine, occupies a level between the source language and the machine language of the host. With this in mind, the work done so far in the area of microprogramming support for high-level languages is now summarized.

10.4.2. An Overview of the Work Done

Perhaps the best-known early work in this area is the one reported by Weber [16], in which he described the implementation of the high-level language EULER on a System 360/30. In this implementation, he used the System

360/30 microcode to write the compiler, which translates EULER source code to a reverse Polish string surrogate; the interpreter for the surrogate is also written in 360/30 microcode. Finally an I/O control program has been written in the machine language of the 360. This control program provides a link between the System/360 operating system and the translator and interpreter; it takes care of all the I/O requests of the translator and interpreter by passing control to the appropriate routines in the operating system.

Weber has pointed out that his processing system for EULER is experimental and does not include all the features of EULER. Furthermore, to keep the implementation simple, the storage areas for stacks, compiled programs, and so on, have fixed rather than relocatable addresses. Weber has also raised the question of whether the reverse Polish string represents an ideal DEL for EULER source and Model 30 host, but he has left it as an open question. The interpreter in this implementation occupies 2500 words of control store, where each word is 60 bits wide. Although the translation from EULER source to reverse Polish string surrogate is performed by microcode, the translator does make use of main memory for such things as storage of compiled code, translation tables for delimiters, and compile-time stack. The translator occupies approximately 500 words of control store, whereas the main memory space used by the translator is approximately 1200 bytes. The speed enhancement obtained as a result of microprogrammed support for EULER is quite impressive. It is pointed out that for those functions of EULER that do not have simple System/360 machine-language equivalents, the interpreter is about ten times as fast as the execution of an equivalent machine-language surrogate. However, where simple machine-language equivalents do exist for EULER functions, the speed enhancement is not so dramatic, although the interpreter is still faster.

Wulf [17] describes a novel approach to processing of high-level language *programs*. Wulf's approach is different from that of others in the sense that instead of worrying about the general question of processing high-level language programs efficiently, he worries about how to execute a *given* HLL program efficiently. In this context he presents the concept of *adaptive optimization*, which will be discussed shortly.

In discussing the general problem of executing HLL programs efficiently, Wulf makes certain suggestions, some of which ought to be obvious to anyone concerned with this problem. The first suggestion is to improve compiling methods in order to produce highly optimized code, which would increase the execution speed of object programs considerably. However, the main problem encountered in trying to design suitable compiling techniques is that the generality of certain constructs in a given high-level language causes a compiler to produce inefficient code. These are called **locally inefficient constructs,** and according to Wulf, these are of two kinds:

1. Constructs that are inefficient on a given machine;
2. Constructs that are inefficient on any machine.

Another factor that can help programs run faster is **functional specialization**. This means a machine should be capable of handling certain programming practices efficiently. The example used in this context is that most programmers perform vector operations using linear ordering. Therefore the machine ought to have a built-in facility that makes the linear search of vector elements an efficient operation.

These efforts help the compilation phase so that an efficient object program surrogate is generated. In trying to improve the performance of the execution phase of a program, Wulf's **adaptive optimization** strategy is examined. This strategy is based on the observation that programs tend to spend most of their time executing only a small part of the code. Based on actual measurements, Wulf mentions that in a given (random) program, one usually finds that about 5 percent of the code consumes 50 percent of the program execution time, and 10 to 15 percent of the code consumes about 90 percent of the execution time. However, this kind of data about a program can be obtained only after the program is actually executed. Therefore, for one-time programs, production of this data is not going to help the execution speed at all. If, on the other hand, the program (surrogate) is to be executed repeatedly, then the process of adaptive optimization can be used to improve execution speed.

The strategy for adaptive optimization consists of using an *adaptive compiler*. The source language for the compiler is FORTRAN, on which a fairly simple translation is performed to generate code that is interpreted. During interpretation the surrogate is monitored to see where it is spending most of its time. Once the section of code consuming most of the execution time is identified, the interpretation is stopped and a translator is used to translate that part of the surrogate into machine language. This first translation is done without much regard for producing efficient machine code. This new surrogate is then executed and the monitoring is repeated. If another part of the interpretive code is found to consume most of the execution time, then it is also translated into a relatively inefficient machine code. If a part of the machine-language segment of the surrogate is executed very frequently, then that part is optimized. This process is continued until the core (5 to 15 percent) of the surrogate consumes about 90 percent of the execution time. This core can exist either in the form of highly optimized machine code or, for a more effective optimization of execution time, in the form of microcode. It is suggested that, in fact, this core *should* exist as microcode. This approach is to be preferred over compiling an entire high-level language program into microcode since the microcode surrogate may require large amounts of control memory.

The results obtained by using this adaptive optimization technique are quite impressive. The adaptive compiler can be tuned to behave like the WATFIV, FORTRAN G, or FORTRAN H compilers in terms of the kind of optimization it performs. This helps in comparing the *total* execution time (compile time plus object code execution time) of a FORTRAN program run under these compilers as well as under the adaptive compiler. Wulf also reports [17] that the adaptive compiler not only provides very fast compilation (better than WATFIV) but also provides object-code execution speed exceeding that provided by the other three compilers. This kind of performance is directly attributed to the fact that information about program behavior is fully utilized in this approach. It is emphasized once again that this method is oriented towards the *specific* problem of executing a given HLL program efficiently via microprogram support; it does not concern itself with the more general problem of microprogramming support for HLL processing. It is important to remember that the adaptive optimization technique ultimately produces a surrogate for the source program that is not in the same uniform representation; parts of the surrogate consist of interpretive code, while other parts consist of machine code and microcode. This is in contrast to the standard practice of generating a surrogate in a uniform representation (for example, Polish string or machine language). This approach, in a very real sense, does away with the problem of looking for an ideal DEL since the most critical part of the surrogate ultimately ends up in microcode.

Another interesting work has been reported by Flynn and others [18] from Stanford University. This work has been done using a universal host machine called EMMY designed to support efficient emulation for a wide spectrum of target machine architectures.

Flynn reported the design and implementation of a DEL that is specifically tailored to FORTRAN II as the source language and EMMY as the host machine. The name given to this DEL is DELtran, and an attempt has been made to design it as an ideal DEL so that both space and time are optimized during execution. The process of compilation of FORTRAN II source into DELtran has the following noteworthy features.

1. The compiler requires at most two passes over the source. During the first pass, a symbol table is generated; during the second pass, a DELtran surrogate is produced.
2. The time required to generate the DELtran surrogate is linearly proportional to the number of operators in the source.
3. There exists a simple correspondence between the DELtran operators and FORTRAN II operators.
4. There exists a simple correspondence between explicitly named items such as variables, labels, and constants in the source program and explicitly referenced items in the surrogate.

In the implementation reported, not all I/O and floating point features of FORTRAN II are included. The program and data-space requirement for DELtran is restricted to 64K bytes of main memory; the source can contain a maximum of 2000 distinct, named items. The emulator for interpreting DELtran requires approximately 2K words by 32 bits of control store.

DELtran programs consist of linear arrays of instruction units. The size of the instruction units varies from 8 bits to more than 32 bits. Each instruction unit is divided into one or more fields called **syllables**, which are ordered according to their use in the emulation process. These syllables are decoded during the emulation process to affect transfer of control to appropriate microroutines.

The preliminary results obtained by Flynn are extremely encouraging and they confirm that DELtran is indeed a *very good* DEL for the combination of FORTRAN II source and EMMY host. In terms of raw execution speed, the EMMY processor executes DELtran code at a rate of 60 to 80 thousand instruction units per second. Compared to S/360 machine code generated by an optimizing FORTRAN compiler, the DELtran surrogate requires one-fourth to one-tenth the storage space. However, for arithmetic expressions, this reduction in code space is of the order of one-half to one-fifth. It is reported that an average of 3.5 to 4.5 instructions of the S/360 are needed to perform the function of a DELtran instruction unit.

DELtran execution speed has been compared with machine code of the S/360 using the common denominator of emulating both the surrogates on the same host, EMMY. The following results were obtained.

1. The S/360 RR instructions require approximately 20 percent less time than the equivalent instruction units of DELtran.
2. Register-to-memory instructions require comparable amounts of time.
3. Program control instructions require 20 to 500 percent more time in 360 code.
4. References to built-in functions may require several thousand percent more time in 360 code.

For simple FORTRAN II programs, the DELtran surrogate executes 4 to 12 times faster; for programs using functions such as logarithms, the speed enhancement factor using DELtran can be as high as 30. At the time of writing the report (1976), the authors anticipated that their compiler (with DELtran as target language) would execute 20 to 100 times as fast as the S/360 optimizing compiler.

Finally, in another noteworthy work reported by Hassitt and Lyon [19], the interpretation of the high-level language APL is supported by microcode. The implementation has been done on an S 370/145 which directly executes S/370 instructions as well as APL statements. Interpretation of APL is supported by a microprogram named *APL Assist*. The installation of this microprogram in S 370/145 requires approximately 20,000 bytes of control store.* A new microprogrammed instruction called APLEC, for APL emulator call, is added to the S/370 instruction repertoire, and 50 additional microroutines are incorporated in the control store for emulation of APL. The machine transfers control to the APL emulator on executing the APLEC instruction and switches back to S/370 emulation when the APLEC execution is finished. It should be noted that when APL Assist is used, microprograms interpret APL statements; without the APL Assist, microprograms emulate S/370 instructions and the latter are used to interpret APL statements. The time required for executing APLEC depends on the APL functions to be performed. However, in the multiprogramming environment of the S/370 operating system, it is *essential* that the system be capable of interrupting APLEC execution. It should be remembered in this context that normally the execution of a machine instruction is not interruptable and any interrupt that occurs during the execution of an instruction is examined only after the instruction execution is finished. The APL emulator periodically checks an interrupt flag, and if the flag is set, the emulator stores all the required status information in the workspace and then allows a normal S/370 interrupt to occur. The APL emulator does not use microcode for all APL functions; frequently used functions are optimally microcoded, whereas those functions that do not benefit from microprogramming are provided in software. The linkage to these software routines is provided by the emulator. A majority of these software routines have been implemented in machine language, although a few have been implemented in APL.

Most of the APL operations and functions are executed by the emulator, in addition to scanning and syntax analysis of APL statements and such tasks as call or return to or from functions and getting and freeing blocks of memory in the data area. Software routines are used for translation of APL source to an internal representation (on a one-to-one basis) and for operations such as encode, decode, grade, scan, format, and matrix inversion. Hassitt and Lyon [19] point out that the decision not to use microcode for an operation is based on several factors. For example, an operation requiring a large number of floating point computations does not benefit significantly from being microcoded. Therefore Hassitt and Lyon chose to perform matrix inversion entirely by software routines.

In evaluating the performance of the emulator, Hassitt and Lyon have measured the CPU time for executing 19 test problems. These problems were run on a dedicated machine, both with the emulator and without it; they cover a broad spectrum of application areas such as numerical analysis, statistics, linear programming, text processing, and compilation. The per-

---

*Control store and program store in S 370/145 are physically the same units but are logically separated by a boundary.

formances of following three APL implementations on a S 370/145 were compared:

1. APL/CMS with APL Assist microprogram;
2. APL 360;
3. APL/CMS using a software interpreter.

For the selected test problems, APL/CMS with APL Assist was found to be 2 to 20 times as fast as APL 360. The same problems executed 1.5 to 2.5 times faster on APL/CMS without APL Assist than APL 360. It is to be noted that the execution times were measured on a single-user system, since otherwise the timings would be dominated by OS functions relating to a multi-user interactive system. It is claimed by Hassitt and Lyon that, in most cases, an APL program performing a lot of operations would execute much faster with APL Assist. It is further estimated that with APL Assist installed, the CPU time for an APL program is cut by one-half (on an average) due to good implementation techniques, and by one-fifth due to microcode.

In addition to the four examples discussed so far, other researchers have also reported on performance enhancements due to microprogram support for HLL processing [20–24]. Most of this effort has been directed towards compilation of a high-level language source into an intermediate language and then execution of the intermediate language surrogate. Of the four examples discussed in this section, the first and third follow this approach; the second is unique in the sense that the process of adaptive optimization ultimately results in a mixed representation surrogate—part interpretive code, part machine code, and part microcode. The last example corresponds to direct execution of high-level language programs by microcode, although the interpreter does use some software routines. The authors believe that the compilation of HLL source into microcode is not likely to yield any encouraging results since the size of the compiled program, for a source of reasonable size, will exceed the size of the control store in most cases. In such a case, part of the surrogate will have to reside in main memory. As a result, page faults during execution would degrade the performance appreciably.

REFERENCES

[1] KURZBAN, S. A., T. S. HEINES, and A. P. SAYERS, *Operating Systems Principles* (New York: Petrocelli/Charter, 1975).

[2] BRINCH HANSEN, P., *Operating System Principles* (Englewood Cliffs, N.J.: Prentice-Hall, Inc., 1973).

[3] SHAW, A. C., *The Logical Design of Operating Systems*, (Englewood Cliffs, N.J.: Prentice-Hall, Inc., 1974).

[4] DIJKSTRA, E., "The Structure of THE Multiprogramming System," *CACM*, 11, no. 5 (May 1968).

[5] WERKHEISER, A., "Microprogrammed Operating Systems," *Preprints of the Third Annual Workshop on Microprogramming*, Buffalo, N.Y., October, 1970.

[6] SOCKUT, G. H., "Firmware-Hardware Support for Operating Systems: Principles and Selected History," *ACM SIGMICRO Newsletter*, 6, no. 4, (December, 1975), pp. 17–26.

[7] BROWN, B. E., R. H. ECKHOUSE, and J. ESTABROOK, "Operating Systems Enhancement Through Firmware," *Proceedings of the Tenth Annual Workshop on Microprogramming*, Niagara Falls, N.Y., October 1977.

[8] BURKHARDT, W. and R. RANDEL, "Design of Operating Systems with Microprogrammed Implementation," NTIS Report PP 224484, September 1973.

[9] CHATTERGY, R., "Microprogrammed Implementation of a Scheduler," *Proceedings of the Ninth Annual Workshop on Microprogramming*, New Orleans, La., September 1976.

[10] LAMPSON, B. W., "A Scheduling Philosophy for Multiprocessing systems," *CACM*, 11, no. 5 (May 1968), pp. 347–60.

[11] CONWAY, R. W., W. L. MAXWELL, and L. W. MILLER, *Theory of Scheduling* (Reading, Mass.: Addison-Wesley Publishing Co., Inc., 1967).

[12] LISKOV, B. H., "The Design of the Venus Operating System," *CACM*, 15, no. 3 (March, 1972), 144–49.

[13] BAUER, S. M., "Bell Labs Microcode for the IBM 360/67," *Proceedings of the Eighth Annual Workshop on Microprogramming*, Chicago, Ill., September 1975.

[14] FRIEDER, G., "Microprogramming an Operating System," *Microprogramming and Systems Architecture:* Infotech State-of-the Art Report 23, Infotech Information Ltd., 1975.

[15] HOEVEL, LEE W., "Ideal Directly Executable Languages: An Analytical Argument for Emulation," *IEEE Trans. on Computers*, C–23, no. 8 (August 1974), 759–67.

[16] WEBER, HELMUT, "A Microprogrammed Implementation of EULER on IBM System/360 Model 30," *Communications of the ACM*, 10, no. 9, (September 1967), 549–58.

[17] WULF, W. A., "The Influence of High Level Languages on Microprocessor Design," *Microprogramming and System Architecture*, Infotech State-of-the Art Report 23, Infotech Information, Ltd, 1975, pp. 225–40.

[18] FLYNN, MICHAEL J., L. W. HOEVEL, and C. J. NEUHAUSER, "The Stanford Emulation Laboratory," *Technical Report 118*, Stanford Electronics Laboratories, Stanford University (June 1976).

[19] HASSITT, A., and L. E. LYON, "An APL Emulator on System/370," *IBM Systems Journal*, 15, no. 4 (1976), pp. 358–78.

[20] DOUCETTE, D. R., "Performance Enhancement by Special Instructions on the System/360 Models 40 and 50," *Preprints of the Third Workshop on Microprogramming*, Buffalo, N.Y., 1970.

[21] PARK, H., "FORTRAN Enhancement," *Proceedings of the Sixth Workshop on Microprogramming*, College Park, Md., 1973.

[22] BROCA, F. R., and R. E. MERWIN, "Direct Microprogrammed Execution of the Intermediate Text from a High Level Language Compiler," *Proceedings of ACM SIGPLAN/SIGMICRO Interface Meeting*, Harriman, N.Y., May 1973.

[23] LUTZ, M. J., and M. J. MANTHEY, "A Microprogrammed Implementation of a Block Structured Architecture," *Proceedings of the Fifth Workshop on Microprogramming*, Urbana, Illinois, September 1972.

[24] NISSEN, S. M., and S. J. WALLACH, "An APL Microprogramming Structure," *Proceedings of the Sixth Workshop on Microprogramming*, College Park, Md., September 1973.

FURTHER READINGS

1. BRIDGES, CHARLES W., "Direct Execution of C-String Compiler Texts," *Proceedings of the Twelfth Annual Microprogramming Workshop*, Hershey, Penn., November 18–21, 1979, pp. 84–92.

2. BROADBENT, J. K., "High Level Language Implementation through Microprogramming," in *Microprogramming and System Architecture*, Infotech State-of-the-Art Report 23: Infotech Information, Ltd., 1975, pp. 337–357.

3. BROWN, G. E., R. H. ECKHOUSE, JR., and R. P. GOLDBERG, "Operating System Enhancement through Microprogramming," *SIGMICRO Newsletter*, 7, no. 1 (March 1976), 28–33.

4. COURTOIS, B., and G. SAUCIER, "Microprogramming as a Means of Evaluation of a Computer's Performance and Reliability," in *Microarchitecture of Computer Systems*, ed. R. W. Hartenstein and R. Zaks, (North-Holland/American Elsevier, 1975). pp. 53–61.

5. COX, C. W., and V. B. SCHNEIDER, "On Improving Operating Systems Efficiency through Use of a Microprogrammed, Low-level Environment," *Preprints of the Seventh Annual Workshop on Microprogramming*, Palo Alto, Ca. (October 1974), pp. 297–98.

6. DEMARTEAU, J., "Microcontrol Hardware and High Level Languages Interpretor—An Attempt of Macro Supported by Firmware," *Preprints of the Seventh Annual Workshop on Microprogramming*, Palo Alto, Ca. (October 1974), pp. 52–58.

7. FRIEDER, GIDEON, "The FORTRAN Project—A Multifaceted Approach to Software," *Proceedings of the Ninth Annual Workshop on Microprogramming*, New Orleans, La. (September 1976), pp. 47–50.

8. GOLDSTEIN, B. C., and T. W. SCRUTCHIN, "A Machine-Oriented Resource

Management Architecture," *Proceedings of the Second Annual Symposium on Computer Architecture*, January 20–22, 1975, pp. 214–219.

9. HABIB, S., "Microprogrammed Enhancements to Higher Level Languages— An Overview," *Preprints of the Seventh Annual Workshop on Microprogramming*, Palo Alto, Ca. (October 1974), pp. 80–84.

10. ————, "Microprogrammed Enhancements to the Interpretive Translation Process," *IEEE Computer Society Repository*, R75–271, 32 pages.

11. HOEVEL, LEE W., "Languages for Direct Execution," *Preprints of Seventh Annual Workshop on Microprogramming*, Palo Alto, Ca. (October 1974), pp. 307–16.

12. LEW, A., "A Basic Operating System and Interpreter for Diagnostic and Pedagogic Purposes," in *Microarchitecture of Computer Systems*, ed. R. W. Hartenstein and R. Zaks. North-Holland/American Elsevier, pp. 85–91.

13. MACRES, P., and G. F. COULOURIS, "On the Use of 'Top Stack Sets' for the Storage Management of a Paged Stack Machine," *EUROMICRO Newsletter*, 1, no. 1 (October 1974), 45–52.

14. MOULTON, P., "Microprogrammed Subprocessors for Compilation and Execution of High-Level Languages," *Preprints of the Seventh Annual Workshop on Microprogramming*, Palo Alto, Ca. (October 1974), pp. 74–79.

15. PETIT, J., and others, "A Microprogramming Strategy for HLL Interpretation," *SIGMICRO Newsletter*, 7, no. 4 (December 1976), 46–69.

16. SAAL, H. J., and L. J. SKUSTEK, "On Measuring Computer Systems by Microprogramming," in *Microprogramming and Systems Architecture*, Infotech State-of-the-Art Report 23, ed. C. Boon. Infotech Information Ltd., 1975, pp. 473–89.

17. SPREEN, H., "Partially Integrated Input/Output Channels," *EUROMICRO Newsletter*, 2, no. 3 (April 1976), 41–46.

18. SUFRIN, B., "Microprogram Design for High Level Languages," in *Microprogramming and System Architecture*, Infotech State-of-the-Art Report 23, Infotech Information, Ltd., 1975, pp. 315–35.

19. SVOBODOVA, L., "Computer System Performance Measurement: Instruction Set Processor Level and Microcode Level," *Technical Report 66*, Stanford Electronics Laboratories, Stanford University (June 1974), 84 pp.

20. TAFVELIN, S., and A. WIKSTROM, "Aspects of Compact Programs and Directly Executed Languages," *BIT*, 15 (1975), 203–214.

21. TALLMAN, P. H., "Virtual Machine Assist Feature Microcode Implementation," in *Microprogramming and Systems Architecture*, Infotech State-of-the-Art Report 23, ed. C. Boon. Infotech Information Ltd., 1975, pp. 527–40.

22. TUO, W. Y. Y., "A Firmware Data Compression Unit," *IEEE Computer Society Repository*, R74-262, 58 pages.

23. WADE, J. F., and P. D. STIGALL, "Instruction Design to Minimize Program Size," *Proceedings of the Second Annual Symposium on Computer Architecture*, January 20–22, 1975, pp. 41–44.

24. WILKES, J. L. "Application of Microprogramming to Medium Scale Computer Design," *Preprints of the Seventh Annual Workshop on Microprogramming*, Palo Alto, Ca. (October 1974), pp. 135–40.

EXERCISES

10.1 Write the algorithms for a CALL subroutine function (and the associated RETURN) that perform the branch to the subroutine, saving of the return address, and restoration of the return address upon return from the subroutine.

10.2 Rewrite Exercise 10.1 assuming the subroutines are to be recursively called.

10.3 Rewrite Exercise 10.1 assuming the CALL performs the branch, the saving of the return address, and the saving of the register contents.

10.4 Repeat Exercise 10.3 for the case of recursive subroutines.

10.5 Using Exercises 10.3 and 10.4, find the primitive operations composing both algorithms. Rewrite Exercises 10.3 and 10.4 assuming the stack management functions have been microprogrammed. Evaluate the improvements in coding convenience, memory requirement, and execution time.

10.6 Using a microprogrammable machine, microcode the complete algorithm of Exercise 10.4. Evaluate the cost in control memory. Evaluate the differences in execution time between this version of the CALL instruction, the version done in Exercise 10.4 and the version in Exercise 10.5.

10.7 Write a microprogram to execute an arithmetic expression represented as a Polish string, where all operands are designated by their absolute addresses. Compare the memory requirements (control and main) and the execution time with a machine-language implementation.

10.8 Design and microcode a "loop" machine-language instruction such as the following example.

Loop	Initial value	Final value	Step size	Address of Loop Body

The execution of the loop body can be done by software and ends with an instruction "end of body." (*Note*: This microprogram should provide for nested loops.)

10.9 Repeat Exercise 10.8 with a DO-WHILE construct (see Chap. 12).

PART FIVE

Examples

CHAPTER ELEVEN

Microprogrammable Microprocessors: An Example

11.1 INTRODUCTION

It was mentioned earlier in the book that a user-microprogrammable machine can be used very effectively to suit specific application requirements of the user. This feature of microprogrammable machines is elaborated upon in other chapters, where some of the application areas and the role of microprogramming have been discussed. This discussion was based on the underlying assumption that a microprogrammable machine, as supplied by the manufacturer, is available to the user. However, the user as a designer can sometimes be faced with a problem where the use of a minicomputer or large computer would amount to computational overkill, even though the problem at hand can be solved. An example of such problems is the design of a limited-function dedicated processor for process control applications or the design of a peripheral controller for a computer system. Of course, such designs can be carried out by using MSI chips; however, this approach has the usual disadvantage of hardwired logic—it is not flexible. For this reason, microprocessors have generally come to replace the MSI chips in such applications because they provide the flexibility of programmed logic and a lower package count in the design. For lower-speed applications, MOS microprocessors have been used quite effectively as a replacement for hardwired logic. However, MOS microprocessors do not have the speed to be utilized in high-speed applications. For example, they are unsuitable for use in the design of a disk controller to handle data transfer rates of 1M bytes or more. Such high-speed applications require the speed of bipolar technology.

A number of microprocessors fabricated with Schottky bipolar LSI technology are available in the market. They typically contain 2- or 4-bit slices of a CPU and are microprogrammed by the user (designer) for performing the desired processing functions. For this reason, they are also known as **bit-slice microprocessors** or **microprogrammable microprocessors**. Designs based on these microprocessors have the following advantages over those based on conventional TTL elements.

1. They are physically much smaller since the package count is considerably reduced.
2. They are cheaper.
3. Their power requirements are lower.
4. They are more reliable due to lower package count and fewer interconnections.

In terms of speed, bit-slice microprocessors are much faster than their MOS counterparts. As an example, a 16-bit processor designed with bit-slice components can perform a register-to-register addition in approximately 125 ns, which is about 15 times as fast as the fastest MOS microprocessors. Furthermore, a wide variety of word sizes and instruction sets can be implemented with bit-slice microprocessors, unlike their MOS counterparts.

A number of manufacturers offer a variety of bit-slice microprocessors and support chips, which can be used in different configurations to suit specific design requirements. Some of these microprocessor families are Intel 3000, Motorola 2900 and 10800, Advanced Micro Devices AM 2900, and Texas Instruments SBP 0400.

It is not possible within this chapter to discuss the details of all the available bit-slice microprocessor families. Rather, the purpose of this chapter is to acquaint the reader with one typical bit-slice microprocessor family that can be microprogrammed to suit user requirements.

There are two essential components of any design using bit-slice microprocessors.

1. *Control section.* This consists of a microprogram memory, a microprogram control unit (MCU) or sequencer and some support logic. Figure

11.1 shows the typical configuration of a microprogram control unit. The MCU basically determines the sequencing of microinstructions controlling the processor functions. The following are the main components of the MCU.

a. *Address generation logic.* Typically, the inputs to this unit are the macroinstruction opcode, address-control information from the previous microinstruction, and system status flags (for conditional branching). This information is utilized for generating the address of the next microinstruction to be fetched from microprogram memory.

b. *Microprogram address register.* This holds the address of the next microinstruction as generated by the address generation logic.

c. *Address stack and stack control.* The optional LIFO stack is used for storing microprogram addresses during microsubroutine calls. The stack control, on a subroutine call, increments the present address and pushes it onto the stack; similarly, on a return from a subroutine, it controls the popping-up operation.

2. *Processor Section.* This typically contains the ALU, registers, microfunction decoder, and processor status flags. The central processing element, or the bit-slice processor, is functionally complete in itself. A number of

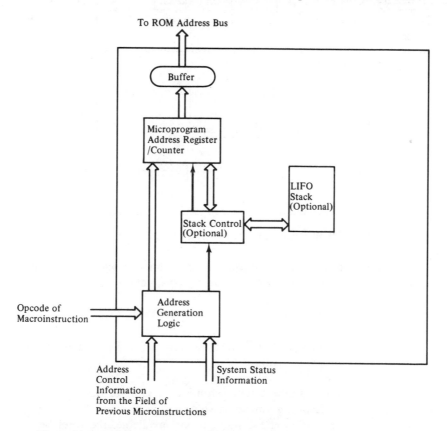

Figure 11.1 Block Diagram of a Typical Microprogram Control Unit

these elements may be cascaded to form a processor of desired word length. Such cascading requires all the similar control lines to be connected in parallel and the carry-out of one stage to be connected to the carry-in of next stage. Figure 11.2 shows a typical schematic of a bit-slice processor. The processor gets its directives from the microfunction fields of a micro-instruction. For an n-bit slice processor, the data bus, address bus, registers, ALU, and so on, are all n-bits wide. It should be noted that we have presented only a general schematic of the control and processor sections. The internal details of these vary from manufacturer to manufacturer.

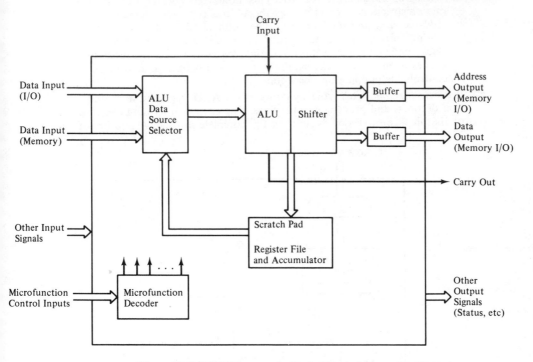

Figure 11.2 Block Diagram of a Typical Central Processing Element

The approach to a design problem using microprogrammable (bit-slice) microprocessors consists essentially of two distinct steps:

1. Organization of the members of a bit-slice family to meet the design objectives.
2. Design of microprograms to direct the activities of the configuration to meet the desired objectives.

The following sections describe a representative example of design support available for such a microprogrammed design.

As an example of the logic design support available, the Intel Series

3000 microprogrammable microprocessor* family will be considered [1, 2]. The software support for development of microprograms will be presented by a description of the CROMIS system for Intel 3000 Series.

11.2 INTEL SERIES 3000

The Intel Series 3000 is a Schottky bipolar microcomputer set of high performance compatible LSI components. These components serve as basic building blocks for user microprogrammable processors or controllers. A list of the members of this family of LSI components follows.

1. 3001   Microprogram Control Unit (MCU)
2. 3002   Central Processing Element (CPE)
3. 3003   Look-Ahead-Carry Generator
4. 3212   Multimode Latch Buffer
5. 3214   Priority Interrupt Unit
6. 3216   Noninverting Bidirectional Bus Driver
7. 3226   Inverting Bidirectional Bus Driver
8. 3601   256 × 4 bit Programmable Read-Only Memory
9. 3604   512 × 8 bit Programmable Read-Only Memory
10. 3301 A   256 × 4 bit Read-Only Memory
11. 3304 A   512 × 8 bit Read-Only Memory

The following section describes the two major components of this family; namely, 3001 MCU and 3002 CPE. The other components enhance the performance and capabilities of these two components. Before going into the description of the MCU and CPE, it is worthwhile to consider a typical Series 3000 configuration (see Fig. 11.3) for a processor-controller application. The discussion of the figure will identify the role played by the microprogram memory, the MCU and the CPE, which are the essential components of the architecture of any Series 3000 configuration.

The microprogram memory may be viewed as an addressable array of locations. Each location, identified by a unique address, stores a microinstruction word. All the control information for a particular microinstruction cycle is stored in the corresponding microinstruction word, which determines the state of the control lines. A set of related control lines is called a **function bus**. Each field of a microinstruction is related to one function bus. The behavior of each functional unit in the system is controlled by a function bus, the state of which is determined by the corresponding field of the microin-

---

*Excerpts and diagrams in this and the following sections have been reprinted by permission of Intel Corporation, copyright 1975 and 1976.

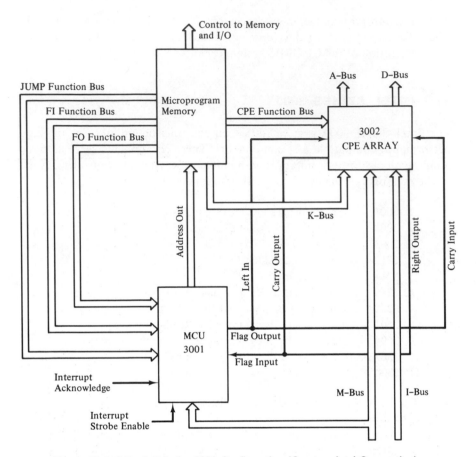

Figure 11.3 A Typical Series 3000 Configuration (Courtesy Intel Corporation)

struction. In other words, the microinstruction word consists of a fixed group of commands that are executed in parallel by corresponding functional units when the microinstruction is selected from the microprogram memory. A typical Series 3000 microinstruction word format is shown in Fig. 11.4.

The 3002 CPE is a 2-bit data processing module. It may be considered as vertically complete but horizontally expandable to any desired word width. Thus N CPEs may be cascaded to produce a $2N$-bit processor array. Each module includes a 2-bit slice of a number of general and special-purpose registers, arithmetic and logic circuits, and several buses for data input and output. A CPE array has the capability of performing more than 40 functions, such as 2's complement arithmetic, logical functions (AND, OR, NOT, EX-NOR), shift right or left, incrementing or decrementing, bit testing, and zero detection. The CPE array function (7 bits), along with the mask field of the microinstruction word, controls the primary internal actions of the CPE

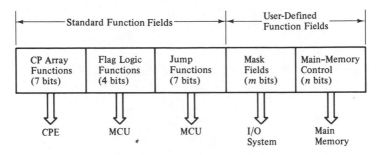

Figure 11.4 A Typical Microinstruction Format

array by selecting the operands and operations to be performed during a machine (microinstruction) cycle.

The 3001 Microprogram Control Unit (MCU) controls the sequence in which microinstructions are fetched from the microprogram memory. For this purpose, the MCU has a microprogram address register along with associated logic for generating the next address. The other important control function performed by the MCU is control of two flag flip-flops for interaction with carry input and carry output of the CP logic array.

The characteristics of a particular implementation with microprogrammable hardware are dictated by the set of microprograms written to meet the desired objectives. In order to write an effective and efficient microprogram, the microprogrammer must have a thorough understanding of the microprogrammable processor configuration. He or she must understand the functions that each group of logic in the configuration is capable of performing and how these functions relate to each other and to the microinstruction word format. The next two subsections provide a logical and functional description of the MCU and CPE from a microprogrammer's point of view.

11.2.1. 3001 Microprogram Control Unit

The organization of the 3001 MCU is shown in Fig. 11.5. A brief description of the organization, as a supplement to Fig. 11.5 follows.

PX4–PX7 : Primary instruction bus input

This bus is fed by the data bus of the main memory. Usually this is used to facilitate macroinstruction decoding. In such a case, this bus contains the 4 high-order bits of the operation code. Data on this bus is tested by the JPX function for branching to the proper microprogram address.

SX0–SX3 : Secondary instruction bus input

This is also fed by the data bus of the main memory. Data on this bus is synchronously loaded into the PR-latch while the data on the PX-bus is

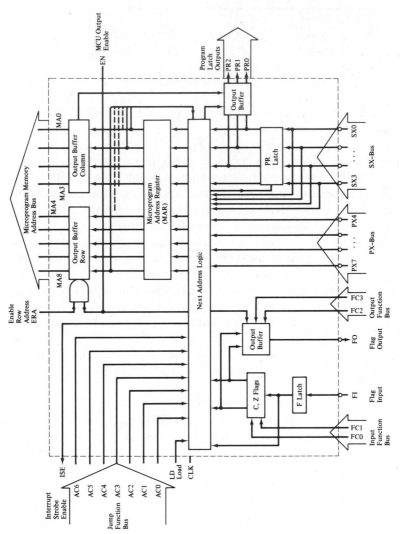

Figure 11.5 MCU Organization (Courtesy Intel Corporation)

being tested by the JPX function. In a subsequent cycle, the contents of PR-latch may be tested by JPR, JLL, or JRL functions for branching to the proper microprogram segment.

FC0–FC3 : Flag logic control inputs

These inputs are derived from the *flag logic function* field of the micro-instruction. The data on this bus is used to cross switch the flags (C and Z) with flag logic input (FI) and the flag logic output (FO). FC0 and FC1 control flag input logic, while FC2 and FC3 control the output logic.

FI : Flag logic input

The flag logic input is controlled by FC0 and FC1 to be applied to the inputs of either of the flags C or Z. The flag input data is saved in the F-latch. Typically, FI is connected to the carry output and shift output (tied together) of CP-array.

FO : Flag logic output

The outputs of the flags (C and Z) are multiplexed internally to form the common flag logic output. This output is typically connected to the carry input and the shift input of the CP-array.

C- AND Z-FLAGS

The C-and Z-flags provide the capability to save the status of a parti-cular result over several microinstruction cycles.

MA0–MA3

This is the column address output for the microprogram memory.

MA4–MA8

This is the row address output for the microprogram memory.

AC0–AC6

This constitutes the next address control function input. Often this is referred to as the **jump function bus**. The next address generation logic is primarily controlled by the information on this bus.

EN : Enable input

This input (when high) enables the microprogram memory address, PR-latch, and flag outputs.

PR-LATCH : Program latch

This latch stores the information on the secondary instruction bus. Some conditional address control functions (JPR, JRL, and JLL) make use of this stored information for generation of the next microinstruction address.

ISE : Interrupt strobe enable output

This provides the strobe signal required by the priority interrupt control unit or other interrupt handling circuitry (for a detailed explanation, see functional description).

LD : Microprogram memory address load input

When active, LD input inhibits all jump functions and synchronously loads the data on the instruction buses into the microprogram address register.

11.2.2. Functional Description of the MCU

The 3001 MCU provides the microprogrammer with three functional facilities that are independently controlled.

1. Address-control functions: unconditional and conditional jump functions.
2. Flag control functions: Flag input-control functions and flag output-control functions.
3. Load and interrupt strobe functions.

1. Address Control Functions

The address-control function or jump function logic determines the sequence in which microinstructions are accessed from the microprogram memory. The next address logic, under the control of the jump function field of the current microinstruction (that is, current status of jump function bus AC0–AC6), formulates the address that is loaded into the address register at the end of the current microinstruction cycle. There is a comprehensive set of 11 jump functions that the MCU can perform. Four of these are unconditional jumps and 7 are conditional.

To understand the MCU jump functions, the microprogram memory must be thought of as a 2-dimensional matrix consisting of 32 rows and 16 columns, providing 512 unique microinstruction locations as shown in Fig. 11.6. The address of the microprogram memory is delivered via the output lines MA0–MA8. The 5 high-order bits of the MAR (MA8–MA4) specify the row address (Row_0–Row_{31}) and the 4 low-order bits (MA3–MA0) represent the column address (Col_0–Col_{15}), respectively. The basic addressing capability supported by the MCU is 512 words; however, extension of the addressing capability is possible and is discussed later.

The unconditional jump functions specify a jump to a specific location. The formulation of the target address is based on the current microinstruction address and the information on the jump function bus.

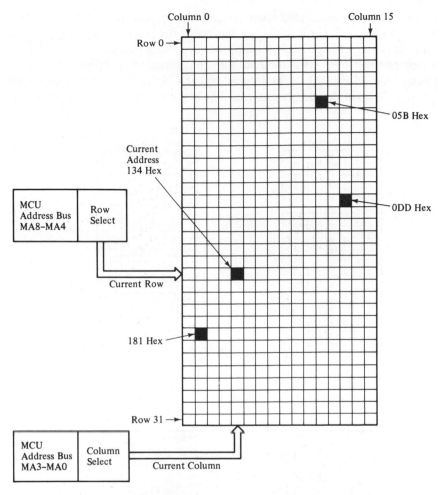

Figure 11.6 Microprogram Memory Addressing

A conditional jump function specifies a jump to a group of locations, depending on the data in the latch or bus being tested. The number of possible target addresses for a conditional jump depends on the number of possible states of the latch or bus being tested. In this case the jump address is formulated on the basis of the information in AC0–AC6, the current microinstruction address and current state of data being tested. The two types of conditional jump functions, depending on the latch or bus being tested, are (a) flag conditional jump/test functions (testing conditions of F-latch, C-flag or Z-flag), and (b) PX-bus or PR-latch conditional jump functions.

Using a particular jump function, it is not possible to jump from a given location in the matrix to any arbitrarily desired location. A specific jump set is associated with each jump function. The jump set diagram is given in Fig. 11.7. From a given location in the matrix, using a particular jump function, it is possible to jump only to those subsets of locations belonging to the jump set associated with that function. The figure illustrates the set of locations that can be reached by each of the 11 jump functions from (Row_{16}, Col_8) of the memory matrix. The black square indicates the location

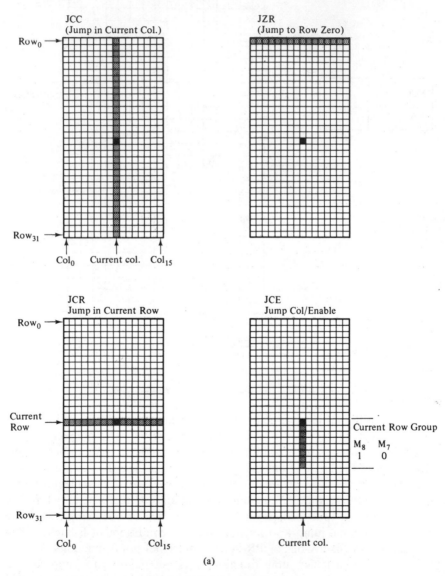

(a)

Figure 11.7 Jump Set Diagram

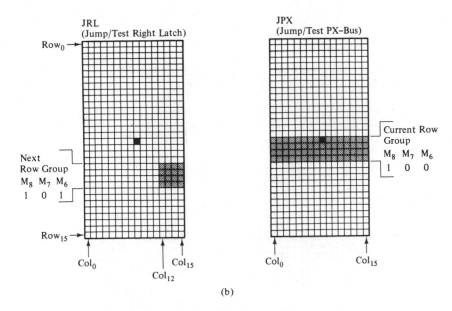

Figure 11.7 Continued

of the current microinstruction (address 264_{10}). The grey squares indicate the subset of locations that may be chosen as the next address corresponding to the particular jump function used.

A summary of all the address-control functions is given in Table 11.1. Four of these address-control functions will be described so that the reader may easily interpret all the other functions from the table.

JCE (Jump in Column/Enable)

This is one of the unconditional jump functions. This function allows a jump in the current column within the specified row group (refer to jump set for JCE). As shown in the table, the next column address (MA0–MA3) remains unaltered and the next row address is specified by the bits AC0–AC2 on the jump function bus. Note that the row group is specified by the current microinstruction address (MA7–MA8); AC0–AC2 select 1 out of 8 locations in the current row group as the jump target location. Moreover, the PR-latch outputs are asynchronously enabled.

JFL (Jump/test F-latch)

This is one of the conditional jump functions that tests the condition of F-latch in selecting the target location. In this case, the jump is limited within the current row and column groups specified by MA8 and MA3, respectively. Here AC0–AC3 are used to select 1 out of 16 rows as the next row address

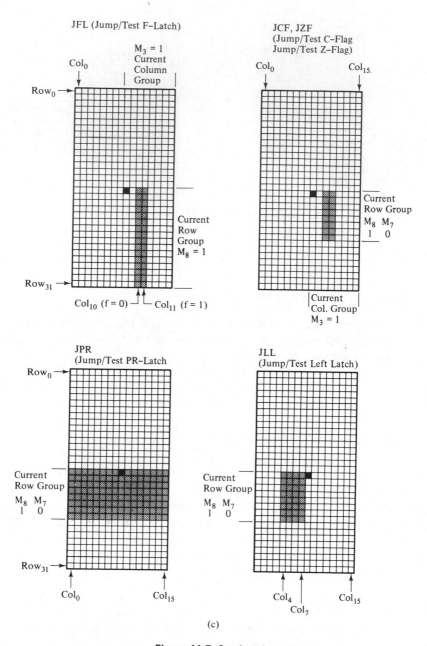

(c)

Figure 11.7 Continued

TABLE 11.1
ADDRESS CONTROL FUNCTION SUMMARY*

MNEMONIC	DESCRIPTION	FUNCTION AC6	5	4	3	2	1	0	NEXT ROW MA8	7	6	5	4	NEXT COLUMN MA3	2	1	0
JCC	Jump in current column	0	0	d_4	d_3	d_2	d_1	d_0	d_4	d_3	d_2	d_1	d_0	m_3	m_2	m_1	m_0
JZR	Jump to zero row	0	1	0	d_3	d_2	d_1	d_0	0	0	0	0	0	d_3	d_2	d_1	d_0
JCR	Jump in current row	0	1	1	d_3	d_2	d_1	d_0	m_8	m_7	m_6	m_5	m_4	d_3	d_2	d_1	d_0
JCE	Jump in column/enable	1	1	1	0	d_2	d_1	d_0	m_8	m_7	d_2	d_1	d_0	m_3	m_2	m_1	m_0
JFL	Jump/test F-latch	1	0	0	d_3	d_2	d_1	d_0	m_8	d_3	d_2	d_1	d_0	m_3	0	1	f
JCF	Jump/test C-flag	1	0	1	0	d_2	d_1	d_0	m_8	m_7	d_2	d_1	d_0	m_3	0	1	c
JZF	Jump/test Z-flag	1	0	1	1	d_2	d_1	d_0	m_8	m_7	d_2	d_1	d_0	m_3	0	1	z
JPR	Jump/test PR-latches	1	1	0	0	d_2	d_1	d_0	m_8	m_7	d_2	d_1	d_0	p_3	p_2	p_1	p_0
JLL	Jump/test left PR bits	1	1	0	1	d_2	d_1	d_0	m_8	m_7	d_2	d_1	d_0	0	1	p_3	p_2
JRL	Jump/test right PR bits	1	1	1	1	1	d_1	d_0	m_8	m_7	1	d_1	d_0	1	1	p_1	p_0
JPX	Jump/test PX-bus	1	1	1	1	0	d_1	d_0	m_8	m_7	m_6	d_1	d_0	x_7	x_6	x_5	x_4

SYMBOL	MEANING
d_n	Data on address control line n
m_n	Data in microprogram address register bit n
p_n	Data in PR-latch bit n
x_n	Data on PX-bus line n (active LOW)
f, c, z	Contents of F-latch, C-flag, or Z-flag, respectively

*(Courtesy Intel Corporation)

in the current row group. The corresponding next column address component in the current column group is specified by the F-latch. If the current column group is col_0-col_7 (that is, MA3 $= 0$), then the state of F-latch selects col_2 or col_3 as the next column address. If MA3 $= 1$ (that is, column group col_8-col_{15}), the state of the F-latch selects col_{10} or col_{11} as the next column address (refer to jump set for JFL).

JPR (Jump/test PR-latch)

This is one of the conditional jump functions that uses the data held in the PR-latch to select the next address. In this case, the jump address is restricted to one of the four current row groups (specified by current MA7–MA8). Here AC0–AC2 select 1 of 8 rows in the current row group as the next row address component; the corresponding column address is decided by the contents of the 4 bits of the PR-latch.

2. *Flag Control Functions*

Flag control functions are controlled by the 4 bits of the "flag logic function" field of the microinstruction word (see Fig. 11.4). These bits are available on the input-function bus (FC0–FC1) and the output-function bus (FC2–FC3) of the MCU. Table 11.2 gives a summary of the flag-control functions.

TABLE 11.2

SUMMARY OF FLAG CONTROL FUNCTIONS*

TYPE	MNEMONIC	DESCRIPTION	FC1	0
Flag Input	SCZ	Set C-flag and Z-flag to f	0	0
	STZ	Set Z-flag to f	0	1
	STC	Set C-flag to f	1	0
	HCZ	Hold C-flag and Z-flag	1	1

TYPE	MNEMONIC	DESCRIPTION	FC3	2
Flag Output	FF0	Force FO to 0	0	0
	FFC	Force FO to C-flag	0	1
	FFZ	Force FO to Z-flag	1	0
	FF1	Force FO to 1	1	1

*(Courtesy Intel Corporation)

FLAG INPUT FUNCTIONS

Basically these functions assign the destination for the storage of the flag input line (FI) of the MCU. These functions provide a mechanism for storing the status of selected CPE array operations (the result of every CPE array operation is reflected on the carry output or shift output line of the array). Typically the carry output and shift output lines of the CPE array are tied together and connected to the FI line. During every microinstruction cycle, the data on the FI line is stored in the F-latch (when clock is low). The destination of the contents of F-latch to C and/or Z-flag register is controlled by the flag input function. The C- and Z-registers are loaded at the rising edge of the clock.

FLAG OUTPUT FUNCTIONS

The flag-output function bus controls the state of the FO line of the MCU. Depending on the contents of this field, FO line is either forced to the zero state, the 1-state, the state of the C-flag, or the state of the Z-flag. The FO line is typically connected to the carry input and shift input of the CPE array, and thus affects any arithmetic or shift-right operation of the array.

3. Load and interrupt strobe functions

The load function is used to load the data on the primary and secondary instruction buses, PX4–PX7 and SX0–SX3, into microprogram address register bits MA0–MA3 and MA4–MA7, respectively. The high order bit MA8 is set to zero. So the contents of PX-bus and SX-bus select 1 out of 16 column addresses and row addresses, respectively. The load function is controlled by the input line LD. It is important to note that the load function always overrides the address control function on AC0–AC6. However, it does not override the latch enable or load subfunctions of the JCE or JPX instructions, respectively. Moreover, it does not inhibit the strobe enable or any of the flag-control functions.

To support the interrupt facility, the interrupt strobe enable of the MCU is available on the output line ISE. Normally an interrupt condition is stored in the 3214 interrupt-control unit during processing of a macroinstruction. For servicing such pending interrupt conditions, a JZR jump function is executed by the MCU at the start of a new fetch/execute cycle. The JZR function should specify col_{15} (row_0 is implied). When MCU executes JZR to col_{15}, it activates the ISE line, which in turn allows the interrupt-control unit to disable the MCUs row-address output (via MCUs row address enable line) and forces an alternate row address on the row-address lines of the microprogram memory. The alternate location is typically the start of the interrupt service microroutine. It is important to note that the alternate row address does not alter the contents of the microprogram address register.

11.2.3. Extended Addressing

The MCU supports a basic microprogram memory-addressing capability of 512 words; however, a larger addressing capability may be implemented. To extend the addressing capability, latches may be added to the MCUs standard address register. The microprogram memory may then be visualized as a three-dimensional configuration. The extra bits represent the particular plane to be selected. At the end of each microinstruction cycle, these latches are loaded directly from an address-extension field in the currently executing microinstruction word. A 2-bit latch can extend the addressing to 2K words.

11.2.4. 3002 Central Processing Element (CPE)

The organization of 3002 CPE is as shown in Fig. 11.8. A brief logical description of 3002 follows as a supplement to Fig. 11.8.

I0–I1 : External bus inputs

This is an input port for external input devices.

M0–M1 : Memory data bus inputs

This is a separate input port for incoming data from main memory.

F0–F6 : Microfunction bus inputs

This input is decoded internally to select the arithmetic or logic functions, register address generation, and to control the A and B-multiplexers. The bus is fed by the 7-bit CPE function field of the microinstruction (see Fig. 11.4).

D0–D1 : Memory data bus outputs

These are the buffered output lines from the accumulator register and serve as data inputs of the main memory or external output devices.

A0–A1 : Memory-address bus output

These are the buffered outputs of the main-memory address register. These form the A-bus of CP array.

A AND B MULTIPLEXERS

These two multiplexers select the two inputs to the arithmetic/logic section (ALS) under the control of microfunction bus decoder. The inputs to the A-multiplexer are the M-bus, the accumulator, and the scratch pad. The inputs to the B-multiplexer are the accumulator, the I-bus, and the K-bus. It is important to note that the selected B-multiplexer input is *always* logically ANDed with the data on the K-bus.

ALS : The arithmetic/logic section

The ALS performs a variety of arithmetic and logic operations, including 2's complement addition, incrementing and decrementing, logical AND, logical OR, logical complement, and exclusive NOR. It can also

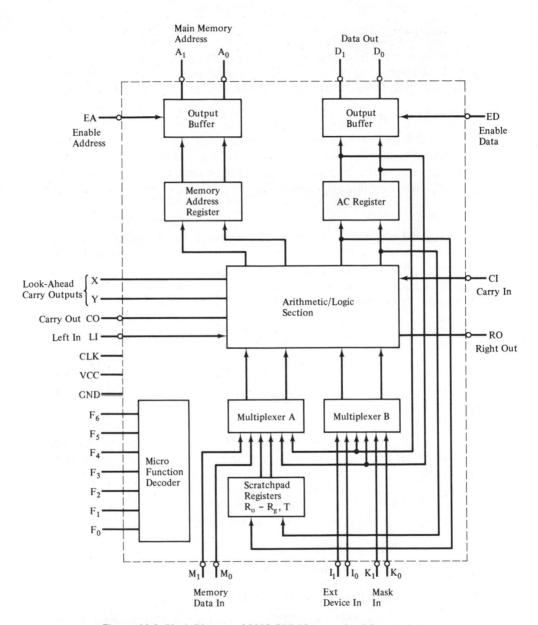

Figure 11.8 Block Diagram of 3002 CPE (Courtesy Intel Corporation)

perform the right-shift operation where LI and RO are the shift input and output, respectively. The result of an ALS operation may be stored in the AC-register or in one of the scratch-pad registers.

SCRATCH PAD

This contains 11 registers (2 bits wide) designated by R0 through R9 and T. The output of the scratch pad is multiplexed internally for input to ALS. The ALS output is returned for input into the scratch pad.

AC-REGISTER

An independent register called the accumulator (AC) is available for storing the result of the ALS operations. The output of the AC is multiplexed internally to act as an input to ALS. At the same time, the output is available on the D-bus via a three-state buffer.

K0–K1 : Mask bus inputs

The K-bus is fed by the mask field of the microinstruction word. The data on this bus is used to mask the inputs to the ALS. During nonarithmetic operations, the K-bus provides the CPE with a flexible bit testing capability (described later). Moreover, the K-bus is used to supply constants to the CPE from the microprogram.

LI

This is the shift-right input.

CI

This is the carry input (for ripple carry configuration).

X, Y

These are carry-look-ahead cascade outputs, and are used in conjunction with Intel 3003 look-ahead-carry generator for high-speed arithmetic operations.

CO : Ripple-carry output

This output is disabled during the shift-right operation.

RO : Shift-right output

This is enabled only during the shift-right operation.

11.2.5. Functional Description of 3002 CPE

The functions performed by the 3002 CPE are controlled by the 7 bits of the "CPE array function" field of the microinstruction word (shown in Fig. 11.4). During a microcycle, the microfunction is decoded, the operands are selected by the multiplexers, and the specified operation is performed by the ALS.

The 7-bit function field basically consists of a function group (F-group, bits F4–F6) and a register group (R-group, bits F0–F3). The microfunction to be performed by the CPE is determined by the particular F-group and R-group selected by the data on the F-bus.

The F-groups zero through 3 are arithmetic functions (with the exception of F-group zero, R-group III) and F-groups 4 through 7 are Boolean functions. R-group I involves R0–R9, T and AC; any of these registers is denoted by the symbol R_n. R-group II and R-group III include only T and AC, denoted by the symbol AT. The function and register-group formats are shown in Tables 11.2a and 11.2b.

As stated before, the K-bus plays an important role in determining the exact operands in the CPE functions. The data selected by the B-multiplexer (that is, data from either I-bus or AC) is always ANDed with the data on K-bus. In most cases, the effect of placing the K-bus in an all-one or all-zero state is either to select or to deselect the accumulator in operation, respectively.

A summary of all the possible microfunctions the CPE may perform is given in Table 11.3a. This section discusses three of these microfunctions in detail, so that the remaining functions will be clear from the summary given in Table 11.3a. A general functional description for each of these operations is followed by an additional description of the effective microfunction with all-zero and all-one K-bus states. All such microfunctions, along with their mnemonics, are shown in Table 11.3b. The microfunction mnemonics are introduced here to assist the reader in following the next section of this chapter.

1. F-group zero, R-group II

The contents of AC are logically ANDed with the data on K-bus. The result is added to the data on the M-bus and the carry input (CI). The resultant sum is stored in AC if bit F0 of the function field is high, otherwise the result is stored in register T (refer to Table 11.2b).

TABLE 11.2a

FUNCTION GROUP FORMAT*

FUNCTION GROUP	F6	F5	F4
0	0	0	0
1	0	0	1
2	0	1	0
3	0	1	1
4	1	0	0
5	1	0	1
6	1	1	0
7	1	1	1

*Courtesy Intel Corporation.

TABLE 11.2b

REGISTER GROUP FORMAT*

REGISTER GROUP	REGISTER	F3	F2	F1	F0
	R0	0	0	0	0
	R1	0	0	0	1
	R2	0	0	1	0
	R3	0	0	1	1
	R4	0	1	0	0
I	R5	0	1	0	1
	R6	0	1	1	0
	R7	0	1	1	1
	R8	1	0	0	0
	R9	1	0	0	1
	T	1	1	0	0
	AC	1	1	0	1
II	T	1	0	1	0
	AC	1	0	1	1
III	T	1	1	1	0
	AC	1	1	1	1

*Courtesy Intel Corporation.

K-Bus = 00; Mnemonic: ACM

The CI is added to the data on the M-bus. The result is stored in AC or T as specified by F0. The specific purpose of this function is to load the specified register with data from memory or with the incremented memory data.

K-Bus = 11; Mnemonic: AMA

The data on the M-bus is added to the contents of AC and also CI. The result is stored in AC or T as specified. This function is used to add memory data or incremented memory data to AC and store the sum in AC or T.

2. F-group 3, R-group III

The data on the I-bus is logically ANDed with the data on the K-bus. The contents of AC or T (as specified by F0), along with the carry input are added to the result. The resultant sum is stored in AC or T (as specified).

K-Bus = 00; Mnemonic: INA

If CI is present, the contents of AC or T (as specified) are incremented. This function is used for conditional increment of AC or T.

TABLE 11.3a

MICROFUNCTION SUMMARY*

F-GROUP	R-GROUP	MICROFUNCTION	
0	I	$R_n - (AC \wedge K) + CI \rightarrow R_n, AC$	
	II	$M + (AC \wedge K) + CI \rightarrow AT$	
	III	$AT_L \wedge (\overline{I_L \wedge K_L}) \rightarrow RO$ $\quad$ $LI \vee [(I_H \wedge K_H) \wedge AT_H] \rightarrow AT_H$ $[AT_L \wedge (I_L \wedge K_L)] \vee [AT_H \vee (I_H \wedge K_H)] \rightarrow AT_L$	
1	I	$K \vee R_n \rightarrow MAR$	$R_n + K + CI \rightarrow R_n$
	II	$K \vee M \rightarrow MAR$	$M + K + CI \rightarrow AT$
	III	$(\overline{AT} \vee K) + (AT \wedge K) + CI \rightarrow AT$	
2	I	$(AC \wedge K) - 1 + CI \rightarrow R_n$	
	II	$(AC \wedge K) - 1 + CI \rightarrow AT$ $\Big\}$ (see Note 1)	
	III	$(I \wedge K) - 1 + CI \rightarrow AT$	
3	I	$R_n - (AC \wedge K) + CI \rightarrow R_n$	$R_n \wedge (AC \wedge K) \rightarrow R_n$
	II	$M + (AC \wedge K) + CI \rightarrow AT$	$M \wedge (AC \wedge K) \rightarrow AT$
	III	$AT + (I \wedge K) + CI \rightarrow AT$	$AT \wedge (I \wedge K) \rightarrow AT$
4	I	$CI \vee (R_n \wedge AC \wedge K) \rightarrow CO$	
	II	$CI \vee (M \wedge AC \wedge K) \rightarrow CO$	
	III	$CI \vee (AT \wedge I \wedge K) \rightarrow CO$	
5	I	$CI \vee (R_n \wedge K) \rightarrow CO$	$K \wedge R_n \rightarrow R_n$
	II	$CI \vee (M \wedge K) \rightarrow CO$	$K \wedge M \rightarrow AT$
	III	$CI \vee (AT \wedge K) \rightarrow CO$	$K \wedge AT \rightarrow AT$

TABLE 11.3a Cont.

F-GROUP	R-GROUP	MICROFUNCTION	
6	I	$CI \lor (AC \land K) \to CO$	$R_n \lor (AC \land K) \to R_n$
	II	$CI \lor (AC \land K) \to CO$	$M \lor (AC \land K) \to AT$
	III	$CI \lor (I \land K) \to CO$	$AT \lor (I \land K) \to AT$
7	I	$CI \lor (R_n \land AC \land K) \to CO$	$R_n \overline{\oplus} (AC \land K) \to R_n$
	II	$CI \lor (M \land AC \land K) \to CO$	$M \overline{\oplus} (AC \land K) \to AT$
	III	$CI \lor (AT \land I \land K) \to CO$	$AT \overline{\oplus} (I \land K) \to AT$

*Courtesy Intel Corporation.

NOTES:
1. 2's complement arithmetic adds 111 ... 11 to perform subtraction of 000 ... 01.
2. R_n includes T and AC as source and destination registers in R-group 1 microfunctions.
3. Standard arithmetic carry output values are generated in F-group 0, 1, 2 and 3 instructions.

SYMBOL	MEANING
I, K, M	Data on the I-, K-, and M-busses, respectively
CI, LI	Data on the carry input and left input, respectively
CO, RO	Data on the carry output and right output, respectively
R_n	Contents of register n including T and AC (R-Group I)
AC	Contents of the accumulator
AT	Contents of AC or T, as specified
MAR	Contents of the memory-address register
L, H	As subscripts, designate low- and high-order bit, respectively
+	2's complement addition
−	2's complement subtraction
$\land$	Logical AND
$\lor$	Logical OR
$\oplus$	Exclusive NOR
$\to$	Deposit into

TABLE 11.3b

ALL-ZERO AND ALL-ONE K-BUS MICROFUNCTIONS*

K-BUS = 00 MICROFUNCTION	MNEMONIC	K-BUS = 11 MICROFUNCTION	MNEMONIC
$R_n + CI \rightarrow R_n$, AC	ILR	$AC + R_n + CI \rightarrow R_n$, AC	ALR
$M + CI \rightarrow AT$	ACM	$M + AC + CI \rightarrow AT$	AMA
$AT_L \rightarrow RO$ $AT_H \rightarrow AT_L$ $LI \rightarrow AT_H$	SRA	—	—
$R_n \rightarrow MAR$ $R_n + CI \rightarrow R_n$	LMI	$11 \rightarrow MAR$ $R_n - 1 + CI \rightarrow R_n$	DSM
$M \rightarrow MAR$ $M + CI \rightarrow AT$	LMM	$11 \rightarrow MAR$ $M - 1 + CI \rightarrow AT$	LDM
$\overline{AT} + CI \rightarrow AT$	CIA	$AT - 1 + CI \rightarrow AT$	DCA
$CI - 1 \rightarrow R_n$ (See Note 1)	CSR	$AC - 1 + CI \rightarrow R_n$ (See Note 1)	SDR
$CI - 1 \rightarrow AT$ (See Notes 1,4)	CSA	$AC - 1 + CI \rightarrow AT$ (See Notes 1,4)	SDA
(See CSA above)	—	$I - 1 + CI \rightarrow AT$	LDI
$R_n + CI \rightarrow R_n$	INR	$AC + R_n + CI \rightarrow R_n$ (See AMA above)	ADR
(See ACM above)	—		—
$AT + CI \rightarrow AT$	INA	$I + AT + CI \rightarrow AT$	AIA

TABLE 11.3b Cont.

K-BUS = 00 MICROFUNCTION	MNEMONIC	K-BUS = 11 MICROFUNCTION		MNEMONIC
$CI \to CO$ $0 \to R_n$	CLR	$CI \vee (R_n \wedge AC) \to CO$	$R_n \wedge AC \to R_n$	ANR
$CI \to CO$ $0 \to AT$	CLA	$CI \vee (M \wedge AC) \to CO$	$M \wedge AC \to AT$	ANM
(See CLA above)	—	$CI \vee (AT \wedge I) \to CO$	$AT \wedge I \to AT$	ANI
(See CLR above)	—	$CI \vee R_n \to CO$	$R_n \to R_n$	TZR
(See CLA above)	—	$CI \vee M \to CO$	$M \to AT$	LTM
(See CLA above)	—	$CI \vee AT \to CO$	$AT \to AT$	TZA
$CI \to CO$ $R_n \to R_n$	NOP	$CI \vee AC \to CO$	$R_n \vee AC \to R_n$	ORR
$CI \to CO$ $M \to AT$	LMF	$CI \vee AC \to CO$	$M \vee AC \to AT$	ORM
(See NOP above)	—	$CI \vee I \to CO$	$I \vee AT \to AT$	ORI
$CI \to CO$ $\overline{R_n} \to R_n$	CMR	$CI \vee (R_n \wedge AC) \to CO$	$R_n \overline{\oplus} AC \to R_n$	XNR
$CI \to CO$ $\overline{M} \to AT$	LCM	$CI \vee (M \wedge AC) \to CO$	$M \overline{\oplus} AC \to AT$	XNM
$CI \to CO$ $\overline{AT} \to AT$	CMA	$CI \vee (AT \wedge I) \to CO$	$I \overline{\oplus} AT \to AT$	XNI

*Courtesy Intel Corporation.

4. The more general operations, CSR and SDR, should be used in place of the CSA and SDA operations, respectively.

K-Bus = 11 ; Mnemonic : AIA

The data on I-bus is added to the contents of AC or T, as specified. Also, CI is added to the result and the sum is stored in the specified register. This is used to add input data or incremented input data to AC or T.

3. F-group 5, R-group 1

The data on the K-bus is logically ANDed with the contents of R_n (as specified by bits F0–F3; see Table 11.2b). The final result is stored in R_n. The bits of the final result are wordwise ORed and then logically ORed with CI. The result of the last OR operation is placed on CO.

K-Bus = 00; Mnemonic : CLR

The specified register R_n is cleared to all zeros and the carry output of CPE (CO) is forced to CI.

K-Bus 11 ; Mnemonic : TZR

If R_n is nonzero, CO is forced to 1. This is used to test a register for zeros. This function may also be used to logically AND the K-bus data with a register for masking, as stated earlier, and, optionally, testing for a zero result.

11.3 CROSS MICROPROGRAMMING SYSTEM (CROMIS)

Intel's cross-microprogramming system provides the software support for the development of microprograms for the Series 3000. It consists of two FORTRAN source programs, cross microassembler (XMAS) and ROM programming file generator (XMAP).

The XMAS language is an extensible microassembly language used to write microprograms for user-designed Series 3000 configurations. It has a complete set of mnemonics to represent the various CPE and MCU functions and allows symbolic addressing to simplify microprogram sequencing. One of the unique features of the XMAS language is its extensibility. A wide variety of configurations is possible with the Series 3000 computing elements. The detailed format of the microinstruction word with all the possible variations cannot be built into the XMAS language, so XMAS provides a mechanism for describing extensions to the microinstruction word in the form of user-defined fields. All the important features of the XMAS language are described in Sec. 11.3.1.

The fundamental function of the cross-microprogramming system is to convert an XMAS language program into a format suitable for programming the physical microprogram memory. This function is performed in two steps: the assembly of the XMAS language program, and the generation of a ROM programming file. It is necessary to provide this functional division because a microprogram will be assembled many times before the microcode is mapped onto the ROMS or PROMS during the development process. Consequently, two separate programs, XMAS and XMAP, are provided. The functional relation between XMAS and XMAP is shown in Fig. 11.9.

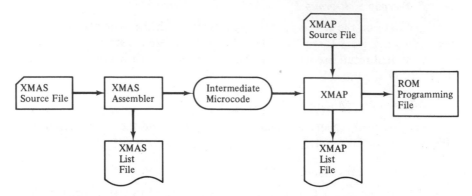

Figure 11.9 Relation Between XMAS and XMAP (Courtesy Intel Corporation)

The records in the XMAS source file are control language statements and XMAS language statements. The control language statements specify I/O formats, select files, and establish other parameters. The XMAS language statements symbolically represent the microprogram. During assembly, two files are generated by the XMAS assembler: (a) list file, and (b) microcode file. The list file may contain the source file statements, the bit patterns generated for those statements that specify microinstructions, error messages, a cross-reference directory, and a graphic representation of the microprogram memory image generated by the assembly. The microcode file is an intermediate binary file of the bit patterns generated by the assembly. The XMAP source file contains control language statements and ROM-mapping language statements. These statements specify the mapping of the intermediate microcode file generated during XMAS assembly into the bit locations of the physical ROM or PROM that will be used for microprogram memory. The XMAP language and its capabilities will be discussed in Sec. 11.3.2.

11.3.1. XMAS Language

The first part of this subsection formally introduces the XMAS language through a description of the syntax of the language. The second part contains the description of the language. This latter half relies heavily on examples to illustrate the function of the XMAS language constructs, though the formal description of the first half is used as the skeleton for the development of this second part.

1. Syntax Summary for the XMAS Language

The syntax of the XMAS language will be presented by means of a meta notation, which is a modified version of the standard BNF notation. Before going into the description of the syntax, a few examples are presented to illustrate the modifications done on the standard BNF notation. It is assumed that the reader is familiar with the standard BNF notation.

As a first example of the modification, consider the simplification used in the modified notation to describe a recursively expandable rule.

In the standard BNF notation a production rule is given as

$$\langle \text{identifier} \rangle ::= \langle \text{letter} \rangle \,|\, \langle \text{identifier} \rangle \,\langle \text{letter} \rangle$$

In the modified BNF notation, the same rule will be represented by

$$\langle \text{identifier} \rangle ::= \langle \text{letter} \rangle \ldots$$

where . . . represents an arbitrary number (greater than zero) of occurences of the entity preceding it.

Another useful addition to the BNF notation is a bracketing tool: braces—{ }—may be used to bracket syntactic entities and constructs to form a single entity. The braces are used to indicate that what is enclosed in them is both a requirement when using the rule and a single compound entity. For example, the rules

$$\langle \text{a} \rangle ::= \{ \langle \text{b} \rangle \,\langle \text{c} \rangle \} \ldots$$
$$\langle \text{b} \rangle ::= B$$
$$\langle \text{c} \rangle ::= C$$

say that an $\langle \text{a} \rangle$ can be an arbitrary number of repetitions of BC, such as BC, BCBC, or BCBCBC. In addition, if entities are stacked vertically within the braces, it indicates that one and only one of these stacked alternatives should be chosen. If the rule in standard BNF is given as $\langle \text{a} \rangle ::= AB\,|\,AC$, in the modified form it is represented as

$$\langle \text{a} \rangle ::= A \begin{Bmatrix} B \\ C \end{Bmatrix}$$

Similarly, a recursive rule represented in standard BNF as:

$$\langle \text{a} \rangle ::= A \langle \text{b or c} \rangle$$
$$\langle \text{b or c} \rangle ::= B\,|\,C\,|\,\langle \text{b or c} \rangle B\,|\,\langle \text{b or c} \rangle C$$

may be represented in the modified version as

$$\langle a\rangle ::= A\begin{Bmatrix}B\\C\end{Bmatrix}\cdots$$

which is much easier to understand. The final addition to BNF, which allows more abbreviated and less obscure notation, is the brackets that indicate an optional entity. A syntactic entity or construct enclosed in brackets [ ] may be chosen as an option when the rule is used. For example, the rules

$$\langle a\rangle ::= A[B]\quad\text{and}\quad\langle a\rangle ::= A\,|\,AB$$

are the same. The brackets have a property similar to braces, in that items enclosed in the brackets become a single entity.

When items are stacked vertically between [ ], this indicates that one and only one of the items may be chosen. The rule

$$\langle a\rangle ::= A\begin{bmatrix}B\\C\end{bmatrix}$$

is equivalent to

$$\langle a\rangle ::= A\,|\,AB\,|\,AC$$

The following paragraph contains a summary of the syntax of the XMAS language. The descriptive meta notation used is that described in the preceding paragraph.

$\langle$program$\rangle$ ::= [$\langle$declaration part$\rangle$]$\langle$specification part$\rangle$EOF

$\langle$declaration part$\rangle$ ::= {$\langle$declaration statement$\rangle$}; . . . .

$\langle$declaration statement$\rangle$ ::= $\langle$string statement$\rangle$|$\langle$value statement$\rangle$|
$\qquad\qquad$ $\langle$field statement$\rangle$|$\langle$imply statement$\rangle$|
$\qquad\qquad$ $\langle$K-bus statement$\rangle$|$\langle$address statement$\rangle$

$\langle$specification part$\rangle$ ::= {$\langle$specification statement$\rangle$} ; . . .

$\langle$string statement$\rangle$ ::= $\langle$string identifier$\rangle$STRING{$\langle$character string$\rangle$} . . .

$\langle$string identifier$\rangle$ ::= $\langle$identifier$\rangle$

$\langle$value statement$\rangle$ ::= $\langle$value identifier$\rangle$VALUE$\langle$expression$\rangle$

$\langle$value identifier$\rangle$ ::= $\langle$identifier$\rangle$

$\langle$field statement$\rangle$ ::= $\langle$field name$\rangle$FIELD$\langle$field spec$\rangle$ . . .

$\langle$field name$\rangle$ ::= $\langle$identifier$\rangle$

$\langle$field spec$\rangle$ ::= LENGTH = $\langle$integer$\rangle$|DEFAULT = $\langle$expression$\rangle$|
$\qquad\qquad$ MICROPS({$\langle$microp$\rangle$ = $\langle$expression$\rangle$} . . .)

$\langle$imply statement$\rangle$ ::= $\langle$microp$\rangle$IMPLY$\langle$imply list$\rangle$

⟨imply list⟩ ::= {⟨field name⟩ = ⟨expression⟩} . . .

⟨K-bus statement⟩ ::= ⟨field name⟩K-BUS

⟨address statement⟩ ::= ⟨field name⟩ADDRESS

⟨specification statement⟩:: = ⟨label part⟩{⟨fields part⟩} . . .

⟨label part⟩ ::= [*]⟨integer⟩ : [⟨address identifier⟩ :] . . .

⟨address identifier⟩ ::= ⟨identifier⟩

$$\langle\text{fields part}\rangle ::= \begin{Bmatrix} \langle\text{field name}\rangle = \langle\text{expression}\rangle \\ \langle\text{microp}\rangle \\ \langle\text{CPE microp}\rangle(\langle\text{register name}\rangle) \\ \langle\text{JUMP microp}\rangle(\{\langle\text{expression}\rangle\}) \end{Bmatrix} \dots$$

⟨comment⟩ ::= /*⟨character string excluding*/⟩*/

$$\langle\text{expression}\rangle ::= \langle\text{term}\rangle \left[\begin{Bmatrix} + \\ \text{OR} \\ \text{XOR} \end{Bmatrix} \langle\text{term}\rangle \right] \dots$$

⟨term⟩ ::= ⟨subterm⟩[AND⟨subterm⟩] . . .

$$\langle\text{subterm}\rangle:: = \langle\text{factor}\rangle \left[\begin{Bmatrix} \text{SHL} \\ \text{SHR} \end{Bmatrix} \langle\text{factor}\rangle \right] \dots$$

⟨factor⟩ ::= [NOT]⟨primary⟩

⟨primary⟩ ::= ⟨value identifier⟩ ⟨address identifier⟩
            ⟨integer⟩|(⟨expression⟩)

⟨integer⟩ ::= ⟨decimal integer⟩|⟨binary integer⟩|
            ⟨octal integer⟩|⟨hexadecimal integer⟩

⟨decimal integer⟩ ::= {⟨decimal digit⟩} . . . [D]

⟨binary integer⟩ ::= {⟨binary digit⟩} . . . B

⟨octal integer⟩ ::= {⟨octal digit⟩} . . . Q

⟨hexadecimal integer⟩ ::= ⟨decimal digit⟩[⟨hexadecimal digit⟩] . . . H

⟨decimal digit⟩ ::= 0|1|2|3|4|5|6|7|8|9

⟨binary digit⟩ ::= 0|1

⟨octal digit⟩ ::= 0|1|2|3|4|5|6|7

⟨hexadecimal digit⟩ ::= 0|1|2|3|4|5|6|7|8|9|A|B|C|D|E|F

$$\langle\text{identifier}\rangle ::= \text{letter} \left[\begin{matrix} \langle\text{letter}\rangle \\ \langle\text{digit}\rangle \end{matrix} \right] \dots$$

⟨letter⟩ ::= A|B|C|D|E|F|G|H|I|J|K|L|M|N|O|P|Q|R|S|T|U|V|
            W|X|Y|Z

⟨digit⟩ ::= 0|1|2|3|4|5|6|7|8|9.

2. Description of the XMAS Language

The XMAS language statements are free-format; physical record boundaries and character positions within a record are not significant. There are no restrictions about where a statement begins or ends or how long it is. A statement may span several records, or more than one statement may be wholly or partly contained in a single record. Commas and spaces may be used freely and interchangeably to enhance readability. The semicolon, when it appears outside a comment, marks the end of a statement. A comment may appear anywhere a space is allowed, with its proper delimiters. The XMAS language **character set**, along with its uses, is shown in Table 11.4. All characters not given in this table are treated as spaces by XMAS.

Table 11.5 lists the **reserved words**. Reserved words constitute a permanent vocabulary of the XMAS language and their definitions are intrinsic to the language. In a XMAS language program, the microprogram-

TABLE 11.4

XMAS CHARACTER SET SUMMARY*

CHARACTER	USED
A through Z (alphabetics) 0 through 9 (numerics)	To compose reserved words, user-defined identifiers and integers.
; (semicolon)	Separates statements within program.
: (colon)	Delimits the microprogram memory address and statement labels in a specification statement.
= (equals)	Assignment operator.
+ (plus)	Arithmetic addition operator.
( ) (parentheses)	Used to indicate precedence in an expression. Used to enclose operands of CPE and JUMP microps.
' (single quote)	To enclose a character string.
$ (dollar sign)	To introduce a control language statement.
* (asterisk)	Used in certain contexts to inhibit XMAS addressing checking.
/* (slash-asterisk) */ (asterisk-slash)	To mark the beginning (/*) and end (*/) of a comment.
. (period)	Interpreted as a null character, used only to punctuate integers and identifiers.
, (comma)	Used to delimit identifiers and integers where no other delimiter appears.
(space)	Used to enhance readibility of statements.

*Courtesy Intel Corporation.

TABLE 11.5
XMAS RESERVED WORDS*

	DECLARATIONS			MICROPS					
				Field				CPE	
Program Terminator	Statement Type	Field Statement Keywords	Intrinsic Field Names	JUMP	FI	FO	CPE	Register Names	Operators
EOF	FIELD	LENGTH	JUMP	JCC	HCZ	FFC	ACM INR	AC	AND
	IMPLY	DEFAULT	FI	JCE	SCZ	FFZ	ADR LCM	R0	NOT
	KBUS	MICROPS	FO	JCF	STC	FF0	AIA LDI	R1	OR
	ADDRESS		CPE	JCR	STZ	FF1	ALR LDM	R2	XOR
	VALUE			JFL			AMA LMF	R3	SHL
	STRING			JLL			ANI LMI	R4	SHR
				JMP			ANM LMM	R5	
				JPR			ANR LTM	R6	
				JPX			CIA NOP	R7	
				JRL			CLA ORM	R8	
				JZF			CLR ORR	R9	
				JZR			CMA SDA	T	
							CMR SDR		
							CSA SRA		
							CSR TZA		
							DCA TZR		
							DSM XNI		
							ILR XNM		
							INA XNR		

*Courtesy Intel Corporation.

mer may define his or her symbolic names, called **identifiers**. Identifiers may be used to define new fields, specify statement labels, assign mnemonics for user-defined functions, and so on. But it is important to note that both the reserved words and the user-defined identifier can have only one definition in a particular XMAS program. A formal syntactic definition of an identifier is as described in the preceding subsection.

As suggested by the syntactic description in the preceding subsection, an XMAS language program is expressed as a series of optional declaration statements followed by a set of specification statements. A semicolon marks the end of a statement and the reserved word EOF marks the end of a program. The declaration statements are optional because intrinsic fields, if used in the specification statements, require no field declaration.

Declaration statements, as in any other assembly language, build the framework for writing the specification statements. The declaration statements may be used to declare and describe new fields and also associate new mnemonics with these fields. Establishment of a hierarchy of default bit-pattern assignments for different fields is also done by means of declaration statements. Some other functions of these statements include designation of K-bus, definition of address-extension field, and so on. The details of these different types of declaration statements are given later in this subsection.

The **specification statements** are the active elements in an XMAS program. They are solely responsible for providing the XMAS microassembler with sufficient information to generate bit patterns for every field in a single microinstruction word and to assign that word to a particular location in the microprogram memory.

The architecture of the Series 3000 configuration requires a minimum set of fields in the basic microinstruction word. Consequently, XMAS initially assumes a basic microinstruction word of the following form.

6 5 4 3 2 1 0	1 0	1 0	6 5 4 3 2 1 0
CPE	FI	FO	JUMP

The reserved words CPE, FI, FO, and JUMP are called **intrinsic field names**. They may be used in XMAS language programs to refer to their respective fields. In most cases, the format shown is not adequate, as additional fields are necessary to control other resources in the configuration. For example, additional fields might be required to control an external main memory or K-bus inputs to the CPE array. A typical complete microinstruction word might have the following format:

6 5 4 3 2 1 0	1 0	1 0	6 5 4 3 2 1 0	2 1 0	7 6 5 4 3 2 1 0	4 3 2 1 0
CPE	FI	FO	JUMP	MEM	KB	X1

The fields MEM, KB and X1 as shown are user-defined fields. There may be functional relationships between fields (for example, the CPE field, FI field and the K-bus field all together play an important role in determining the functions performed by the CPE array), but this does not imply any positional relationship between these fields within the microinstruction word.

In XMAS language, the additional fields are declared by FIELD statements. For example the new fields MEM, KB and X1 are declared by the following field statements.

$$
\begin{array}{lll}
\text{MEM} & \text{FIELD} & \text{LENGTH} = 3; \\
\text{KB} & \text{FIELD} & \text{LENGTH} = 8; \\
\text{X1} & \text{FIELD} & \text{LENGTH} = 5;
\end{array}
$$

The numbers 3, 8, and 5 specify the number of bits allocated to the new fields MEM, KB and X1 respectively. After proper declaration, the user-defined field names may be used in other statements to refer to their respective fields.

3. Specification Statements

Once the programmer has described all extensions of the microinstruction word via FIELD statements, the framework for writing the specification statements is established. Each specification statement must provide XMAS with sufficient information to assign bit patterns to every field and to fix the location of the word in the microprogram memory. A typical specification statement could take the following form:

$$
\begin{array}{llll}
65\text{: CPE} = 15 & \text{FI} = 3 & \text{FO} = 0 & \text{JUMP} = 12 \\
\text{MEM} = 0 & \text{KB} = 0 & \text{X1} = 2;
\end{array}
$$

Here 65 is the memory location for the microinstruction word representing the statement. The values following the assignment operator ($=$) specify the bit patterns for the respective fields.

The order in which field bit pattern assignments occur in a specification statement is arbitrary. The preceding statement could just as well be written as:

$$
\begin{array}{l}
65\text{: CPE} = 15, \quad \text{KB} = 0, \quad \text{FO} = 0 \\
\text{FI} = 3 \\
\text{X1} = 2, \quad \text{MEM} = 0 \\
\text{JUMP} = 12;
\end{array}
$$

This example also illustrates the free-format nature of the XMAS language. Commas, which are equivalent to spaces in the XMAS language, may be used to separate statement entities. A statement may be continued to any number of lines and a semicolon is required to mark the end of each statement. Since every specification statement is linked with a specific microprogram memory address, they might appear in any order the programmer desires.

In the preceding example, all the values are represented by decimal integers. As shown in the syntax description, XMAS language allows other representations (hexadecimal (H), octal (O or Q) and binary (B) integers) as well. So the preceding specification statement may be written as:

$$41H: JUMP = 0001100B, \quad MEM = 0, \quad X1 = 2$$
$$CPE = 17Q \quad FI = 3, \quad FO = 0 \quad KB = 0;$$

A hexadecimal number should begin with a decimal digit so that it may be distinguished from an XMAS identifier; a leading zero is sufficient.

The value of the microprogram memory locations must be represented by integers, but the values for field assignments may be represented by expressions. For example, the CPE field could have been specified by CPE = 7 + (010B SHL2), where + is the addition operator and SHL is the shift-left operator. Other operators might also be used. The formal rules governing the expressions and operators are presented later.

The field assignment in a specification statement may be done in two ways:

1. Keyword assignment form;
2. Using microps.

The form of field assignment shown so far is called **keyword assignment**. Although a keyword assignment may always be used, it is not necessarily the best way of specifying a field. A keyword assignment emphasizes the bit pattern itself rather than the function the bit pattern designates. While writing a microprogram, a programmer is more concerned with specifying a particular function a microinstruction is going to perform than the encoding of the fields in the microinstruction.

Keeping the basic objective of the programmer in mind, XMAS language includes a set of mnemonics called **microps**. The microps are defined in the language for each of the four intrinsic fields CPE, FI, FO, and JUMP. Each microp is a mnemonic for one of the functions controlled by the respective fields. Microps are listed in Table 11.5. They are considered as reserved words of the XMAS language. The mnemonics used for the microps have a direct equivalence with the functional mnemonics as given in Sec. 11.2.2 and 11.2.4. The bit-pattern assignment corresponding to a microp may be directly obtained from Tables 11.1, 11.2, 11.2a and 11.2b. The CPE field, JUMP field, and FI and FO fields serve directly as input to the CPE function bus, jump-function bus, flag input-control bus, and flag output-control bus, respectively. Corresponding to the different control function mnemonics described earlier, microps are of four types: (1) CPE microps, (2) JUMP microps, (3) FI microps, and (4) FO microps. Using the microps, the assignment statement discussed earlier may be represented as

$$65: SRA(AC), \quad KB = 0, \quad MEM = 0, \quad X1 = 2$$
$$JCC(0CH), \quad FF0, \quad HCZ;$$

In a specification statement, a CPE microp must always be followed by a register name enclosed in parentheses. For example, SRA(AC) means that the function represented by the CPE microp SRA will be performed using register AC. Similarly a JUMP microp must always be followed by one or more operands enclosed in a single set of parentheses. The operand of a JUMP microp helps in specifying the target location of the JUMP function. For example, JCC(0CH) specifies that the next microinstruction in the microprogram sequence is to be taken from the twelfth row of the current column in the microprogram memory. In the case of a two-way conditional branch, the specification statement could be JFL(12H, 13H), where 12_{16} is the branch destination address if the F-latch is reset and 13_{16} is the branch destination address if the F-latch is set. A specification statement may include one or more symbolic statement labels. These symbols are called **address identifiers**, because they represent a particular location in the microprogram memory. Using symbolic statement labels, the previous specification statement may be written as:

$$65: ENTRY: CONT: SRA(AC), \quad KB = 0, \quad MEM = 0, \quad X1 = 2$$
$$JCC(0CH), \quad FF0, \quad HCZ;$$

Address identifiers may be used as operands for JUMP microps, allowing the programmer to represent program sequencing symbolically. For example a typical sequence may be:

$$44H: ENTRY: \ldots JZR(TOP) \ldots ;$$
$$07H: TOP \quad : \ldots JCR(EXM) \ldots ;$$
$$02H: EXM \quad : \ldots JCC(TYP) \ldots ;$$
$$32H: TYP \quad : \ldots JFL(ONE, TWO) \ldots ;$$
$$\vdots$$

As XMAS assembles specification statements, it performs jump function checking. If a specification statement references another specification statement that is not within the range of the JUMP function, then XMAS will output an error message.

There is a special JUMP microp, JMP, which represents all the unconditional jump functions (JCC, JCR, and JZR). The JMP microp may be used in place of any of these unconditional jump microps. For each occurrence of the microp JMP, XMAS will attempt to select the appropriate jump function. If this is not possible, XMAS will report an addressing error.

In cases where specification statements appear in the order in which they are to be unconditionally executed, an explicit specification for the JUMP field is not required. For example, the preceding sequence of specification statements may be written as:

$$44H: ENTRY: \ldots \qquad \ldots;$$
$$07H: TOP \quad : \ldots \qquad \ldots;$$
$$02H: EXM \quad : \ldots \qquad \ldots;$$
$$32H: TYP \quad : \ldots \qquad JFL(ONE, TWO) \ldots;$$
$$\cdot$$
$$\cdot$$
$$\cdot$$

When none is specified, XMAS will attempt to supply the appropriate unconditional jump function.

With XMAS, the users can define those microps that they would like to define for the fields other than the intrinsic fields. Microps for a new field are defined in the FIELD statement that creates that field. The FIELD statement

$$MEM \ FIELD \ LENGTH = 3 \qquad MICROPS(READ = 2$$
$$WRITE = 4);$$

defines the two microps READ and WRITE and assigns bit patterns 010_2 and 100_2, respectively, to them. In a specification statement, where the programmer would have written MEM = 4, WRITE might be specified instead.

XMAS provides default bit-pattern assignments for the FI and FO fields if these fields are not otherwise specified in a specification statement. The default for FI field is 11_2(HCZ) and the default for the FO field is 00_2(FF0). XMAS also permits the declaration of a default bit pattern assignment for a newly created field via the FIELD statement. For example the FIELD statement

$$X1 \ FIELD \ LENGTH = 2 \qquad DEFAULT = 3;$$

defines the field X1 and declares a default bit pattern assignment of 11_2 for this field. The default bit pattern assignment for the K-bus field is dictated by the CPE microps, which are mnemonics for CPE functions (described in detail in Sec. 11.2.5).

4. Declaration Statements

In the XMAS language, there are six types of declaration statements altogether. Out of these six types, the FIELD statement has already been discussed. In the following paragraphs, the K-bus statement, IMPLY statement, ADDRESS statement, VALUE statement and STRING statement will be discussed.

K-BUS STATEMENT

The K-bus statement allows the programmer to identify which of the fields that were defined will be treated as the K-bus field. For example, the statements

$$\text{KB FIELD LENGTH} = 6;$$

$$\text{KB KBUS};$$

serve to define KB and to identify that field as the K-bus field. After the KB field is identified as the K-bus field, the default bit pattern assignment for this field will be automatically implied by the CPE microps. The defaults provided by the CPE microps can always be overridden by specifying the KB field explicitly.

In the specification statement

$$65: \text{SRA(AC)}, \quad \text{MEM} = 0, \quad \text{X1} = 2, \quad \text{JCC(0CH)}, \quad \text{FF0}, \quad \text{HCZ}$$

the default bit pattern to be assigned to the KB field (or, equivalently, to the K-bus field) is implied by the CPE microp SRA. Recalling the discussion on CPE functions, it may be found that the mnemonic SRA is classified in F-Group 0 and R-Group III, which implies K-Bus $= 00_2$.

IMPLY STATEMENT

A microp carries an explicit bit-pattern assignment only for the field for which the microp is defined. However, a microp can also carry default bit pattern assignments for the fields other than the one for which the microp is defined. The IMPLY statement is used to declare the defaults in such cases. Consider the following statements.

$$\text{GO FIELD LENGTH} = 2 \ \text{MICROPS (PUT} = 3, \text{STOP} = 1, \text{RDY} = 2);$$

$$\text{PUT IMPLY FI} = 2, \quad \text{MEM} = 0, \quad \text{KB} = 07\text{H};$$

The field statement defines the field GO and the microps PUT, STOP, and RDY. The first IMPLY statement declares the default that the microp PUT carries for the FI, MEM, and KB fields. Considering the statements

MEM FIELD LENGTH = 3, MICROPS (READ = 2);

50 : CSR(R2) JZR(LAST) FF0, PUT, READ;

it may be noted that the default for the FI field, which the PUT microp carries, serves to specify the FI field since this field is not otherwise specified in the specification statement. Both CSR and PUT carry defaults for the K-bus field KB; however, PUT's default for KB overrides CSR's default for KB. Here PUT also specifies a default for the MEM field; however, the microp READ is an explicit assignment for the MEM field and so it overrides PUT's default for the MEM field.

ADDRESS STATEMENT

The extension of the standard addressing capability of the MCU was discussed in Sec. 11.2.3. For increasing the addressing capability, extra address information is typically provided by an address extension field in the microinstruction word. The microprogrammer declares the address extension field by an ADDRESS statement in the following way.

XA FIELD LENGTH = 2;

XA ADDRESS;

Including the address extension field in the previous microinstruction word, which was discussed earlier, the format becomes

6543210	10	10	6543210	210	76543210	43210	10
CPE	FI	FO	JUMP	MEM	KB	X1	XA

In this case, the microinstruction words are identified by an 11-bit address (instead of a 9-bit address). The first 2 bits represent the address of the plane of the microprogram memory.

Once the address extension field is declared by an ADDRESS statement, the microprogrammer is completely relieved of the responsibility of making bit pattern assignments for this field in a specification statement.

VALUE STATEMENT

It is often desirable to use a symbol to represent a frequently used constant. The VALUE statement allows the programmer to define a symbol and associate a numerical value with it. For example the VALUE statement

CONST1 VALUE 1FH;

defines the symbol CONST1 and assigns the value $1F_{16}$ to it. The defined symbol is called a **value identifier**. The identifier may be used anywhere in a specification statement where expression is allowed. For example

60H: ... KB = CONST1, ... ;

supplies the bit pattern for the KB field.

STRING STATEMENT

A microprogrammer may often find that a particular group of symbols occurs quite frequently in a XMAS program. For example

JZR(LAST) PUT READ

might often appear together in specification statements for a particular program. The STRING statement allows the programmer to define a symbol and associate it with a string of characters. For example, the STRING statement

LOOP STRING' JZR(LAST) PUT READ'

associates the symbol LOOP with the character string included within the quotes. So the specification statements

50: CSR(R2) JZR(LAST) FF0 PUT READ;

and

50: CSR(R2) LOOP FF0;

are functionally equivalent.

Every specification statement must provide either an explicit or implicit assignment for every field in the microinstruction word, except the JUMP field, as discussed before. The ways in which a given field can be specified, in decreasing order of effectiveness, are as follows.

1. An explicit keyword or microp assignment.
2. A default assignent from a microp bound to another field, as declared in the IMPLY statement,
3. In the unique case of K-bus field, a default assignment from the CPE microp.
4. The field's default assignment, as declared in the FIELD statement or as supplied by XMAS for FI and FO fields.

An important thing to note is that XMAS is capable of supporting a microinstruction word of up to 64 bit positions. As the intrinsic fields require 18 bit positions, the combined user-defined fields cannot exceed 46 bit positions.

11.3.2. XMAP Language and Control Language

1. XMAP

A microcode file is generated after the assembly of the microprogram by the XMAS assembler. The XMAP language statements direct XMAP to operate on this microcode file to produce a ROM programming file. This ROM programming file is suitable for programming the physical memory devices—ROM or PROM.

The microcode file generated by XMAS contains a complete logical description of each microinstruction word. The description includes a logical address for each instruction, as well as the logical bit pattern for every field of that microinstruction. The physical microprogram memory is available in various organizations, such as 512 words by 4 bits or 256 words by 4 bits. To construct a microprogram memory of 512 words by 32 bits, 4 memory chips of 512 words by 8 bits can be used. In such an organization, each physical ROM will contain an 8-bit slice of the microinstruction word. The role of the XMAP is to map the bit patterns in the microcode file into the desired ROM or PROM bit locations. The XMAP language is used to describe the memory organization and the detailed mapping procedure.

The details of the XMAP language or the control language are not presented in this chapter; only a brief overview is presented here. Interested readers may consult the *Intel Series 3000 Microprogramming Manual* [1].

The XMAP language is a free-format language. An XMAP program consists of a series of XMAP statements. There are only two types of statements in the XMAP language: ROM specifications and mapping specifications. A ROM specification statement describes the organization of a ROM or PROM. The mapping specification statement describes the relationship between microprogram addresses and physical ROM/PROM addresses.

2. Control Language

The control language is used to specify various operating parameters for XMAS and XMAP. The control language provides the facilities for designating files, specifying I/O data record format, and selecting listing options. All control language statements should precede the XMAS or XMAP language statements. Both XMAS and XMAP packages include a control language interpreter.

Every control language record (statement) must begin with a dollar sign ($) in the first active character position. The control language operates on some control variables. A number of control variables are common to both XMAS and XMAP, while the others are specifically associated with XMAS or XMAP only. The functions that the control language performs on these control variables are display of the current values of the control variables and assignment of new values. The two functions are the DISPLAY function and the SET function. The interested reader may consult the *Intel Series 3000 Microprogramming Manual* [1] for details on the control language.

11.3.3. Microprogramming Techniques for Series 3000

The use of XMAS declaration statements to define the characteristics of a particular Series 3000 configuration and specification statements to represent the operations to be performed in the defined environment have been discussed. Once the hardware configuration and microinstruction fields are properly declared, a microprogram is nothing but a sequence of specification statements. As far as techniques for writing microprograms for Series 3000 are concerned, the two major concepts of writing declaration and specification statements have been discussed in detail. A very important technique that still remains undiscussed is the technique of efficient assignment of each microinstruction to ROM locations. This subsection is devoted to the development of such an assignment technique; it also includes example microprograms.

1. Microprogram Memory Assignment

As described earlier, the microprogrammer visualizes the microprogram memory as an array of 32 rows and 16 columns (provided no address extension field is declared). It is the job of the programmer to assign each of the specification statements to unique locations in this array. For example, the specification statement

5AH : YES : KZERO, FF1, INR(R8), JFL(ZERO, ONE)

includes an assignment of this statement to memory location $5A_{16}$ (that is, row_5 and col_{10}). Of course, within the XMAS program, this particular specification statement may be referenced by the identifier *YES*.

Initially, a microprogram should be written in the logical sequence in which it will be executed. For such a sequence, minimal consideration should be given to memory assignment. As discussed before, if the order in which the statements appear in the source file is the same as the order of execution, then the specification of the JUMP field is not necessary. When unconditional program branching is required, the general JMP microp should be used (unless it requires enabling of ISE line or PR latch outputs). When a conditional branch in the program sequence is required, the programmer will use one of the conditional jump microps and should also note the number of possible targets for each such jump. Initially, it is always useful to assign an address identifier instead of exact memory-location values to each of these target locations. These identifiers should be used in the expression portion of the conditional JUMP microps. An example will illustrate the point:

CHAR: AIA(R6) FF0 JFL(GO, STOP);

         .

         .

         .

GO   : ANR(R6) SCZ;

STOP : . . . . . . ;

Having written the microprogram with all sequencing represented symbolically or implied by statement order, the actual assignment to microprogram memory locations must be indicated. To assist in this task, a complete microinstruction state sequence chart should be prepared. In such a chart, each microinstruction is represented by a node in the diagram. Conditional jumps should be labeled by type and condition corresponding to each possible destination. The address identifiers associated with each microinstruction may also be shown. To illustrate the point, an example microprogram is shown with its state sequence chart in Fig. 11.10.

    .

    .

    .

MEM FIELD LENGTH = 3 DEFAULT = 0

    MICROPS (RMW = 010B, RRM = 110B, RWM = 111B

     ROT = 100B);

    MRF: ILR(R4);

       ALR(R9), JRL(MX1, MX2, MAD, TPG);

       .

       .

    MX1 :LMI(AC), RRM;

       ACM(AC), JLL(NDA, ODA, XDA, ADA);

    MX2 : LMI(AC), RRM

       ACM(AC), JLL(ALD, XLD, PDS, XAD);

       .

       .

       .

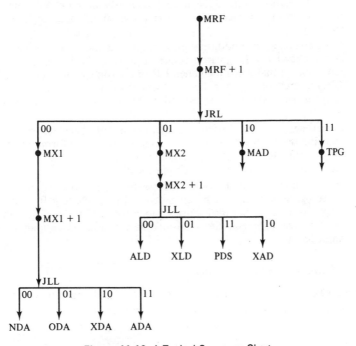

Figure 11.10 A Typical Sequence Chart

Once the sequence chart is ready, it is advisable to use a grid diagram of the microprogram memory showing 32 rows and 16 columns. As each microinstruction is assigned a location, the grid diagram is marked to show occupancy of that word and the flowchart is marked to show assignment of the microinstruction. Using the flowchart and the memory grid diagram, memory assignment can be easily accomplished if the following sequence is used.

1. Those microinstructions with memory locations dictated by purely hardware considerations are assigned first. For example, the hardware might require the first microinstruction in the system initialization routine to have location 00.
2. For the best possible assignment, most restricted microinstructions should be assigned first. In general, clusters of conditional jump targets that must be located within a limited range constitute the most restricted set of microinstructions. All the targets for each conditional jump instruction should be assigned before assigning the jump instruction itself. In a 512-word microprogram memory, there are 64 possible destination pairs for each of JCF, JZF, and JFL conditional jump functions. It is, therefore, important to ensure that enough destination pairs are available for such functions. Also it must be kept in mind that the JPX and JPR conditional jump functions can require one entire row each time they are used.

3. Row 0 locations should be used judiciously because only they can be reached from anywhere else in the program using a single JZR jump function.

4. Long chains of unconditional jump sequences should be considered at the end as they have the greatest range of possible destinations. It should be remembered that when the general JMP microp (in place of JCC, JCR, or JZR) is used or no jump field is explicitly specified, the next executable microinstruction should be located in the current row, current column, or Row 0.

5. Sometimes it is quite useful to include state-linkage information while marking the control memory grid diagram; that is, information regarding the memory location(s) that reference the current location and memory location(s) referenced by the current location.

6. When reassignment becomes necessary, sequences of unconditional microinstructions should be considered first, excluding those which are targets of conditional instructions, since they are the easiest to move. In cases of reassignment, the state-linkage information simplifies the task appreciably.

2. *Microprogramming Examples*

Two sample microroutines for the 8-bit processing unit configuration shown in Fig 11.11a will be given next. The interconnections of the different lines of the 4 CPE elements to form the 8-bit CPE array are as shown in Fig. 11.11b.

EXAMPLE 1

This example considers the macrooperation "POP stack to memory (PSM)." The example will not go into the details of macroinstruction decoding and address formation (which might vary from one design to the other). Assume that before beginning this segment (PSM), the accumulator (AC) contains the destination address of the main memory where the popped data from the stack has to be stored.

```
/* SEGMENT SHOWS PSM OPERATION
    A   STANDS FOR ACCUMULATOR(AC)
    S   STANDS FOR STACK POINTER(R4)
THE FIELD MCF REPRESENTS MEMORY CONTROL FUNCTIONS*/
MCF   FIELD LENGTH = 2      DEFAULT = 0
    MICROPS (NBO = 00B, RRM = 01B, RWM = 10B,
        RMW = 11B);
    A   STRING 'AC';/* ACCUMULATOR*/
    S   STRING 'R4';/* STACK POINTER*/
```

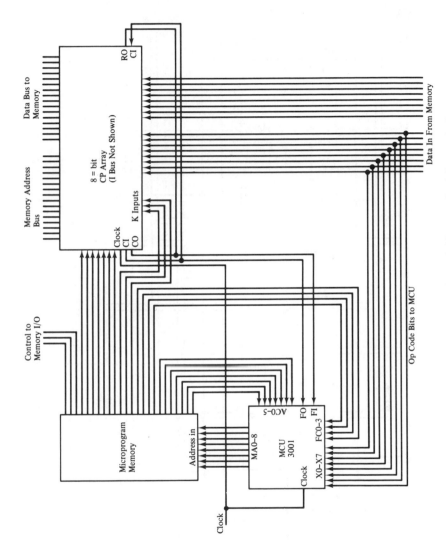

Figure 11.11a An 8-bit Processing Unit (Courtesy Intel Corporation)

317

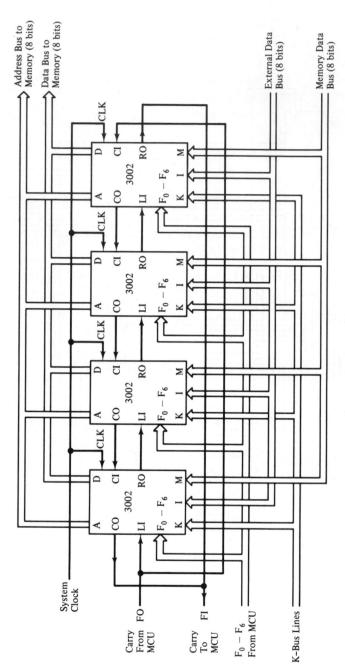

Figure 11.11b 8-bit CPE Array

318

SDR   IMPLY FO = 11B;
.
.
.

0AH: FETCH : . . .
              .
              .
              .

56H: PSM   : SDR(T); /*MICROINSTRUCTION 1*/
58H: LMI(S) FF1 RRM; /*MICROINSTRUCTION 2*/
88H: ACM(AC) FF0;   /*MICROINSTRUCTION 3*/
89H: LMI(T) RWM JZR(FETCH);
                                  /*MICROINSTRUCTION 4*/

This example does not illustrate the technique for memory assignment, but it shows how a sequence of microinstructions may be written to represent a macroinstruction. In the first three microinstructions, no explicit specification of the JUMP field is made, so these instructions are assigned to control memory locations in the current row or current column. It is assumed that the destination memory address is available in the accumulator (AC) before the execution of the first microinstruction (labeled PSM). The operations performed by these four microinstructions are as follows.

First Microinstruction (PSM): The memory address is stored in T, as the CI input is 1 (IMPLY statement).

Second Microinstruction (PSM + 1): The stack pointer contents are loaded into the MAR, the stack pointer is incremented to show the top of the stack, and memory read is requested.

Third Microinstruction (PSM + 2): The data from the stack is loaded into AC.

Fourth Microinstruction (PSM + 3): MAR is loaded with contents of T, memory-write operation is requested, and a jump is executed to the FETCH routine.

EXAMPLE 2

This example illustrates the technique of writing a microroutine for an 8-bit unsigned multiplication. As in the previous example, the opcode decoding and address formation phases are not shown. Also, it is assumed that the multiplier is already available in T and the multiplicand is buffered and available on the M-bus.

/*UNSIGNED 8-BIT MULTIPLY*/
/*K-BUS DEFINITION*/
  KB FIELD LENGTH = 8
        MICROPS (KZ = 00, K1 = FFH, K8 = F8H);
  KB KBUS;
/*STRING DEFINITIONS*/
  TEST STRING' K1, FF0, TZR';
  SET STRING' K0, FF0, CSR';
  INCR STRING' K0, FF1, INR';
  COUNT STRING 'R6';
    /*INITIALIZATION*/
40H: BEGIN: SET(COUNT); /*SET COUNT REG TO ALL ONES*/
41H: FF0, TZR(COUNT), K8; /*COUNT IS SET TO -16 IN
                    2's COMPLEMENT*/
44H: K0, CLR(AC), STZ; /*CLEAR AC AND Z-FLAG*/
    /*MULTIPLICATION LOOP*/
54H: LOOP: TEST(COUNT), STC; /*COUNTER IS TESTED FOR
                    ZERO, C-FLAG SHOWS COUNT
                    STATUS*/
51H: K0, SRA(T), FFZ, STZ, JCF (CONT, OUT);
        /*LSB OF MULTIPLIER SHIFTED TO Z, LSB OF
          PARTIAL PRODUCT IS SHIFTED INTO MSB OF T*/
43H: CONT: INCR(COUNT), JZF(ZERO, ONE);
        /*COUNTER INCREMENTED, JUMP ACCORDING TO
          LSB OF MULTIPLIER*/
53H: ONE: FF0, AMA(AC); /*MULTIPLICAND IS ADDED TO
                    PARTIAL PRODUCT*/
52H: ZERO: K0, SRA(AC), STZ, JMP(LOOP);
        /*LSB OF PARTIAL PRODUCT SHIFTED INTO
          Z-FLAG*/
42H: OUT: . . . JZR(FETCH); /*PRODUCT IN T*/.

Figure 11.12 illustrates the flowchart for this example. Initially the flowchart is prepared with the help of statement labels. The microprogram memory

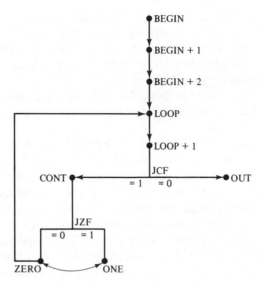

Figure 11.12 Flowchart Example

assignment is shown with the grid diagram in Fig. 11.13. Initially the targets
for the conditional jumps are assigned. The possible targets for the conditional jump JCF(51H) are CONT and OUT; they are assigned to 43H and
42H respectively. Similarly the assignments for the JZF jump targets are done.
It should be noted that the targets for unconditional jumps, whether or not
they are explicitly specified, are in the same row.

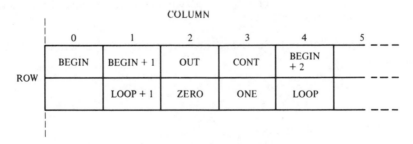

	COLUMN					
	0	1	2	3	4	5
	BEGIN	BEGIN + 1	OUT	CONT	BEGIN + 2	
ROW		LOOP + 1	ZERO	ONE	LOOP	

Figure 11.13 Grid Diagram Example

11.4 ADDITIONAL SUPPORT: IN-CIRCUIT EMULATION

The CROMIS support described in Sec. 11.3 facilitates the user-development
and debugging of microprograms for the Intel 3000 family. However, this
software support does not allow the user to verify the functional correctness
of the microprograms and the associated logic. To aid the process of overall
verification of the total design, Intel Corporation offers a combined hard-

ware-software package known as an **incircuit emulator** for Series 3000 (ICE–30) [3]. This package resides in the Intellec® MDS (microcomputer development system) and interfaces directly to the user's prototype via an external cable. By plugging the ICE–30 cable into the prototype's 3001 MCU socket, the debugging capabilities of the ICE module are made directly available to the user's system. Basically, ICE–30 emulates the 3001 MCU, controls carry or shift data to and from the 3002 CPE array, and controls microprogram interrupts.

The operation of the ICE–30 hardware is controlled by the host Intellec® MDS CPU. The software driver of ICE–30 is a RAM resident program that recognizes and translates a set of high-level language commands entered from the MDS console keyboard and issues control commands to the ICE–30 hardware or accepts messages from the hardware for displaying status on the console. In this manner, the user communicates with the ICE–30 hardware and can monitor, control, or alter the ICE–30 operations. A ROM-simulator module is also available which, if used with the MDS system, allows the ICE–30 software driver to interrogate and alter the microprograms. Some of the features of ICE–30 that assist the user in verifying the proper functioning of the microprograms are as follows.

1. Specifying a microprogram starting address.
2. Specifying of breakpoints.
3. Halting microprogram execution to display or alter the contents of the internal registers and external pin signals of the MCU.
4. Tracing and displaying of the current microprogram address along with some preceding addresses.
5. Generating a series of single steps without operator intervention and stopping single stepping at desired breakpoints.

The details of ICE–30 usage and operation are described in the literature [3].

REFERENCES

[1] *Intel Series 3000 Microprogramming Manual*, (Santa Clara, Ca.: Intel Corporation, 1976).

[2] *Intel Series 3000 Reference Manual* (Santa Clara, Ca.: Intel Corporation, 1976).

[3] *ICE-30 In-Circuit Emulator Reference Manual* (Santa Clara, Ca.: Intel Corporation, 1975).

[4] ALEXANDRIDIS, N. A., "Bit-sliced Microprocessors, PLAs and Microprogramming in Replacing Hardwired Logic," *Proceedings of International Symposium on Wired Logic Versus Programmed Logic*, Lausanne, March 1977.

[5] ALEXANDRIDIS, N. A., "Bit-sliced Microprocessor Architecture," *COMPUTER*, June 1978.

[6] ADAMS, PHILLIP M., "Microprogrammable Microprocessor Survey," *SIGMICRO Newsletter*, 9, no. 1 (March 1978).

CHAPTER TWELVE

A Firmware Implementation of Block-Structured Programming

The purpose of this chapter is to give an example to illustrate the use of microprogramming to implement a powerful new feature on an existing machine. Many details have been included (short of the whole microprogram and its associated software) so that the curious reader can appreciate all the power and flexibility of the microprogramming approach for designing a specific machine architecture. This example has been implemented on a Microdata 1600 [3] and represents the work of several undergraduate projects at the University of Ottawa.

This chapter describes the structure and operation of a microprogram which, when added to a microprogram-controlled computer, provides basic machine instructions for top-down structured programming. The concept of hierarchical black boxes is used to build the proposed architecture via firmware. All control statements are programmed using procedure calls and the three common instructions (DO-END, DO-WHILE, and IF-THEN-ELSE). Existing processing routines on a given installation can continue to be executed at any level. The mechanisms necessary to pass parameters between functions and the evaluation of control variables are also discussed.

The purpose of this microprogram is to implement the basic concepts of top-down structured programming at the machine level. Some other examples exist in this area. In some cases [1], the result provides a set of macroinstructions which, while allowing a programmer to structure an assembler language program, would still generate nonstructured executable code. In other cases, the structures implemented support a high-level language and are not meant to be used at machine level [10].

In order to implement both a simple flow of control and block structuring in machine language, microprogramming is an obvious choice because it does not require any new hardware and provides a means to define a flexible machine architecture.

The first section of this chapter describes the concept of the hierarchical black box, and the three new machine instructions needed to implement it. The second section presents the organization of the firmware implementing these mechanisms.

12.1 TOP-DOWN STRUCTURED PROGRAMMING AT MACHINE LEVEL (TDSP)

12.1.1. Primitives and Control Programs

The purpose of this section is not to discuss the relative merits of TDSP [2]; the objective is simply to add it to an existing machine architecture. Rather, TDSP will be regarded as a programming tool which uses the following concepts.

1. An application-oriented function, process, or subroutine can be referred to, while the implementation details can be worked out later.
2. These functions (represented as black boxes) can be invoked only through the following three control instructions.
   a. DO function name (parameters).
   b. WHILE condition, function name (parameters).
   c. IF condition THEN function name 1 (parameters) ELSE function name 2 (parameters).
3. All processing (such as arithmetic operations, assignments, or I/O) is done as a function. Therefore a program will contain only the three control instructions mentioned and will not contain a mixture of control instructions and normal machine instructions.
4. As a corollary, processing functions, ultimately written in assembler language (or any programming language), will contain only existing machine instructions and not any of the three new control instructions.

In the remainder of this chapter a function written with the newly defined control instructions will be called a **control program** and one written with the normal existing machine instructions will be called a **primitive**.

Items 3 and 4 have been added to the accepted concept of TDSP for the purpose of this implementation; the main idea is to add on the three control instructions to an existing instruction set and not to design a new instruction set including structured control. A control program or a primitive will, therefore, be characterized only by its input, output, and the algorithms it implements; it can be stored on direct-access storage, be resident in memory, or even ultimately be implemented in hardware. In the implementation described here, the size of a control program or a primitive is limited to 256 bytes of main memory that is referred to as one page.

The computer resources will then be represented as shown in Fig. 12.1. In this organization, the existing instruction set of the machine is relevant only for the building of primitives (for example, I/O drivers, search and sort routines, or computations). For the programmer using the control instructions, the computer resources consist of a set of primitives that can be augmented at any time. At this point it might be worthwhile to note that the distinction between control programs and primitives can become obscure if a given function is viewed as a new, although complex, primitive. An example is given in Fig. 12.2. Of course in this example, it is always possible to program TAN entirely in machine language; this decision depends on the frequency of usage of the new primitive. A machine-language implementation would provide a more efficient primitive at execution time, but it would necessitate a greater programming effort.

(A) Elementary Resource

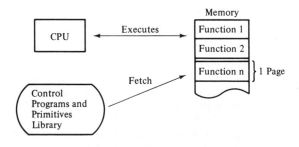

(B) Resources Organization

Figure 12.1 Computer Resources

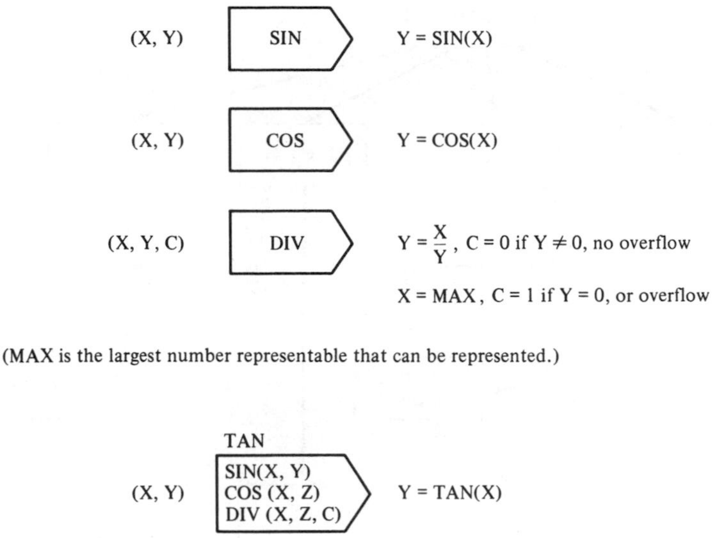

(X, Y) | SIN > Y = SIN(X)

(X, Y) | COS > Y = COS(X)

(X, Y, C) | DIV > $Y = \dfrac{X}{Y}$, C = 0 if Y ≠ 0, no overflow

X = MAX, C = 1 if Y = 0, or overflow

(MAX is the largest number representable that can be represented.)

TAN
(X, Y) | SIN(X, Y) COS (X, Z) DIV (X, Z, C) > Y = TAN(X)

Figure 12.2 Example of Control Program TAN

12.1.2. The Hierarchy of Control

Writing a program consists of writing control functions, which themselves make use of other control functions, and so on, until at a final stage, the bottom level consists of the primitives. As an elementary example, a simplified program for an assembler, using such control functions, would be:

DO INIT
DO PASS_ONE
DO PASS_TWO
DO OUTPUTS

An intermediate level program, for example HASH, could be:

HASH:　　DO HASHCODE
　　　　　IF CONFLICT THEN OVERFLOW ELSE INSERT
　　　　　DO UPDATE_TABLE

A final primitive could be:

READ a card, OPCODE search, ...

A schematic representation for this program is given in Fig. 12.3.

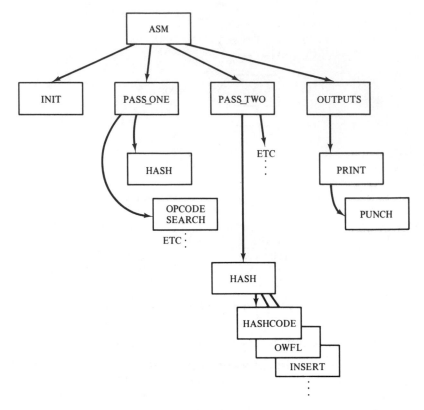

Figure 12.3 Control Hierarchy

12.1.3. Arguments

All arguments needed for a function are passed by a table of addresses in a way similar to a subroutine call in FORTRAN, for instance. They may refer to any type of data, including control blocs (for example, a data control bloc for an I/O primitive).

The only uses made of an argument by a control program are:

1. To pass its address to the lower-level functions or primitives (primitives do the actual work on the arguments to provide the required result);
2. To evaluate a Boolean expression in order to take a decision in the DO-WHILE and IF-THEN-ELSE cases.

A control program (or a primitive) may need additional intermediate storage locations. Such storage locations are called **local variables**; these are created when the function is initiated and the corresponding memory freed when the function is completed. When local storage is created for a function at level i, it becomes available to its subfunctions at level $(i + 1)$ if passed as arguments, but it is not available to the previous functions at level $(i - 1)$.

12.1.4. Machine Instructions for Control

The new instructions have been designed as follows:

DO		FUNCTION		Argument List	
WHILE		POINTER		FUNCTION		Argument List
IF		POINTER		FUNCTION		Argument List
				FUNCTION		Argument List
EOP					

The END-OF-PAGE (EOP) indicates the end of a function and is equivalent to a RETURN instruction. The following fields are used.

1. An 8-bit byte is assigned for the opcode. This is always the first byte of the instruction. The instruction has a varying length depending on the type.
2. *Function.* The function name is represented by a 16-bit field containing the sector address, if—as is the case in this example—the function is stored on disk. On the Microdata 1600, a disk sector is 256 bytes long, which corresponds to one page in the main memory. This field is filled by the machine language programmer or by a compiler with the help of a dictionary which contains function names and their addresses (up to 16K functions in this example, as one bit is used to indicate if the function is on disk or memory resident).
3. *Pointer.* This 8-bit field contains the indirect address, within the same page, of the machine-language representation of the Boolean expression specifying the test to be made. This representation, which is fully described in the next section, is written by the machine-language programmer (or generated by a compiler) in the form of a Polish stack. This expression is computed every time it is encountered; its final Boolean value determines the execution of the rest of the instruction.
4. *Argument List.* The table of addresses of the arguments to be passed to the function specified is stored in the same page (starting from the end) and the 8-bit field points to this parameter list. (See the next section for more details.)

12.1.5. Overview of the Execution of One Instruction

The operation of the firmware supporting the control instructions is described in detail later; however, a few preliminary comments will summarize the execution of one instruction in order to provide a general idea of the operation of this firmware.

1. *Decoding*. The opcode is decoded and the Boolean expression, if any, evaluated to decide if some function has to be initiated. If appropriate, the address of the function is selected (the function can be memory-resident or on auxiliary storage).

2. *Paging*. If necessary, the function is paged into memory following the current page (a page pointer is kept by the firmware in an internal register), together with a second page associated with the function, which contains the descriptors of the local variables needed by this function,

3. *Initiation*. The argument lists and the Boolean stacks used by this function when calling the functions at the next level are processed. This processing consists of establishing links between argument lists and the actual data. The local variable descriptors are scanned, the required storage is obtained from a memory bank (part of memory is reserved for this purpose), and the initial values established.

4. *Execution*. The first instruction of the newly selected function is decoded, which brings us back to Step 1.

5. *Returning*. When the instruction EOP is decoded, the memory allocated to the local variables is freed, the stack page pointer is decremented, and the execution resumes at the next instruction at the previous level (unless the instruction was a WHILE, in which case execution continues at the same instruction as long as the condition is satisfied). An example program is given in Fig. 12.4.

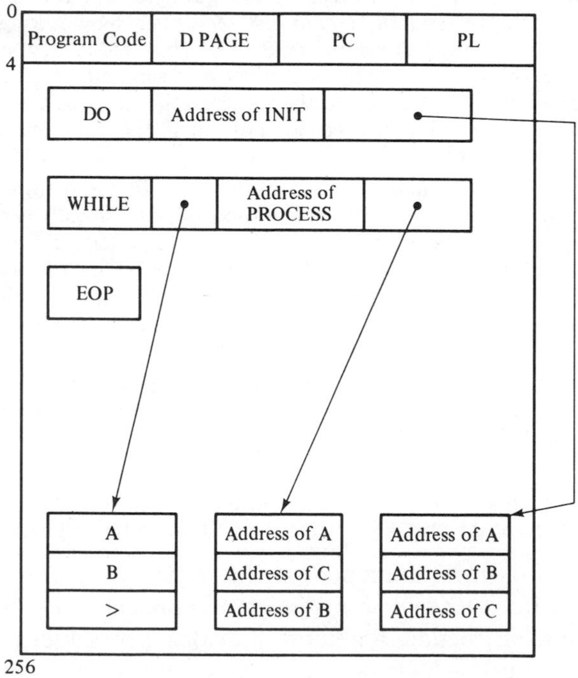

Figure 12.4 Example of Program

Note that the primitives, although written using the existing instruction set of the machine, must return control using the EOP instruction in order to be compatible with the rest of the processing. Therefore, the EOP instruction can be considered as a new control instruction as well as a part of the normal instruction set of the machine.

12.2 DESCRIPTION OF THE CONTROL PROGRAM INSTRUCTIONS

A control program, when the new instructions are available on a given machine, is written in four parts. It should be noted that such a program is to be written by a machine-language programmer (as no support software is available for these new instructions); however, the concepts presented here are applicable in the case of object programs produced by a compiler.

12.2.1. Writing a Control Program

A control program contains the following four parts:

1. The local variable descriptors;
2. The parameter lists;
3. The Boolean expressions;
4. The executable code.

Parts 1, 2, and 3 together are allocated one page (256 bytes) and Part 4 is also allocated a page; this second page is not resident in main memory during the execution of the program but is used only at the control program initialization stage. Fig. 12.5 shows the general memory configuration of a control program.

Note that the limit of 256 bytes has been set only for the purpose of this particular implementation in order to facilitate the management of the various pointers. A symbolic notation is used to describe the examples but, as no assembler has yet been defined, it should be kept in mind that the actual writing has to be done in machine language (using hexadecimal codes, for example). This notation is given in Fig. 12.6.

1. The Local Variable Descriptors (LVDs)

The LVDs, contained in a separate page associated with a function, describe the characteristics of the local variables needed by the function. An LVD must be written for each variable used in a function, except if the variable is passed as a parameter from a previous level (that is, a global variable for this level). When the function is initiated (called in via a control instruction), the LVDs are scanned by the firmware, the necessary memory is reserved, and the addresses of the variables are stored in appropriate pointers. The general format of an LVD is shown in Fig. 12.7. When all LVDs are

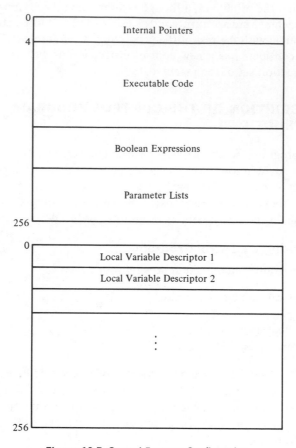

Figure 12.5 Control Program Configuration

processed, that is, when all local variables for the function have been created in a memory bank reserved for the local variables, the descriptor page is freed for other uses, namely, for the next lower-level page.

2. The Parameter Lists

For each function call in a control program, parameters are passed using a table containing the addresses of the parameters. One bit in the address is used to indicate the end of the parameter list. A pointer to this table is written as an operand in the function call instructions.

The elements of the table are written as parameter descriptors (see Fig. 12.8), indicating the type of variable being passed as a parameter. These descriptors also include the representation of Boolean operators (for the purpose of simplifying the microprogram implementation). Five types of

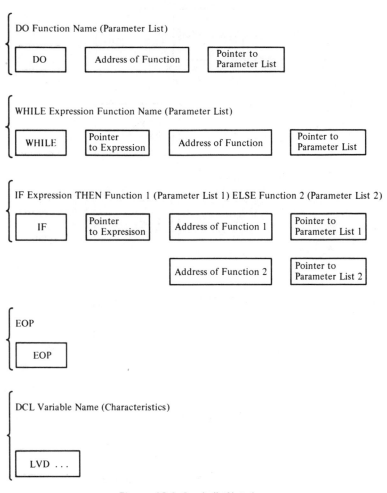

Figure 12.6 Symbolic Notation

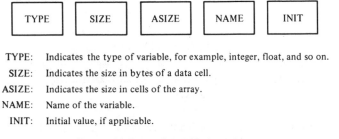

TYPE: Indicates the type of variable, for example, integer, float, and so on.

SIZE: Indicates the size in bytes of a data cell.

ASIZE: Indicates the size in cells of the array.

NAME: Name of the variable.

INIT: Initial value, if applicable.

Figure 12.7 Local Variable Descriptor

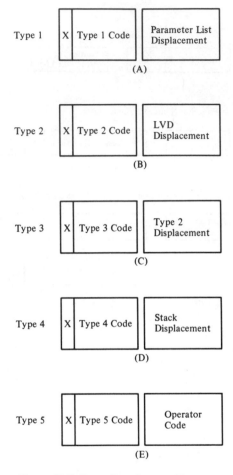

Figure 12.8 Data Descriptors (Parameter Lists and Boolean Stacks)

parameter descriptors are used (Fig. 12.8), to indicate whether a parameter is:

1. A variable passed from a previous function;
2. A local variable to be created (first occurrence of a variable);
3. A local variable already created (all other occurrences);
4. A Boolean expression address;

When a function is invoked, the firmware scans the parameter list and performs the following operations, depending on the descriptor type:

1. Type 1

This element (Fig. 12.8A) contains the displacement of the parameter address in the parameter list (for example, first, second, or third parameter).

By adding this displacement to the current pointer for the parameter list, the absolute address of the variable can be retrieved; it then replaces the Type 1 descriptor.

2. Type 2

This element (Fig. 12.8B) contains the displacement of the LVD in the next page. The firmware then reserves memory for this variable according to factors such as its type or size and stores its absolute address replacing the Type 2 descriptor.

3. Type 3

This element (Fig. 12.8C) contains a pointer to the Type 2 element representing the first occurrence of the same variable. The absolute address of the variable is then simply recopied.

4. Type 4

This element (Fig. 12.8D) contains a pointer to a Boolean expression and is updated to contain the absolute address of this expression.

5. Type 5

This element (Fig. 12.8E) is also processed by the firmware, by flagging it to distinguish an operator from an address.

When writing a program, the parameter lists will, therefore, contain data elements containing various relative pointers to the actual data. However, prior to execution and after the initiation phase, the lists will contain the absolute addresses of these data.

3. The Boolean Expression

The tests that direct the execution of the IF-THEN-ELSE and WHILE instructions are written in the form of stacks representing the expressions in Polish form. An example is given in Fig. 12.9. This form has been chosen to simplify the evaluation of an expression by the firmware. Such a stack contains elements that are either addresses of operands or operators. The operands are written using the same Type 1, 2, 3, or 4 data elements mentioned earlier and are scanned and processed by the same firmware routines. This is the reason why the operators are represented as Type 5 elements; although this wastes main memory, it simplifies the scanning routine that has to process only 16-bit (fixed length) fields. The Boolean stack is referred to by

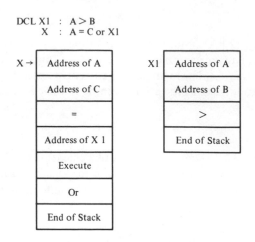

DCL X1 : A > B
  X : A = C or X1

Figure 12.9 Boolean Expressions

an instruction via an indirect address. The pointer field in the instruction points to a Type 4 element, which itself contains the absolute address of the stack; this seems to create an unnecessary intermediate step. However, the reason for this is to allow passing a Boolean expression as a parameter to a lower-level function. The indirect address allows one to use the same firmware routine to retrieve a Boolean expression passed as an argument, just as in the case of retrieving a parameter.

4. The Executable Instructions

Once variables have been defined, their uses in Boolean expressions or as parameters established, and the tests controlling the program written, the executable instructions can be coded to program the given algorithm.

5. Example

The actual representation of the example of Fig. 12.4 (in hexadecimal) in memory before execution (that is, when the program has just been paged in) is shown in Fig. 12.10. For this particular example the following assumptions are made.

1. The variables A and B are global; that is, they are passed as parameters when, for example, this particular control program is invoked by the following instruction:

DO EXAMPLE (A, B)

2. The variable C is a local variable, declared within the program EXAMPLE itself. Therefore a LVD describing this variable is written in a second page.
3. At the time the function EXAMPLE was invoked, the free area in the

memory bank was X'3000', absolute addresses of A and B were X'2F0(
and X'2F80', respectively, and the program was loaded at address X'1100.
Fig. 12.10 shows the program as written by the programmer, together wit!
comments explaining each instruction. Fig. 12.11 shows the same progra!
after being processed by the initialization firmware, just before its interpretation by the microprogram.

First page

0	3F 00 00 00	Control page indicator (see next section).
4	01 01 00 FA	DO opcode; the function INIT is on disk
		at address 0100,
		FA points to the address list.
8	02 E8 02 00 F4	DO–WHILE opcode; the function PROCESS is
		on disk at address 0200, F4 points to
		the address list;
		E8 points to the stack.
D	04	EOP opcode.
E6	0000	End of parameter area.
E8	04EA	Pointer to stack.
EA	0100	Global parameter, first entry (A).
EC	0101	Glocal parameter, second entry (B).
EE	0509	Stack operator, code >.
F0	FFFF	End of stack.
F2	FFFF	Code.
F4	0100	Global parameter, first entry (A).
F6	03FE	Second occurrence of C, points to first
		occurrence.
F8	8101	Global parameter (B), end of list.
FA	0100	Global parameter (A).
FC	0101	Global parameter (B).
FE	8200	Local variable, first entry in DLV's
		in second page.

Second page

0	01 01 01 C3 40 40 40

Figure 12.10 Example of Control Program

This processing during initialization updated the following fields.

Addresses

E8	Type 4 element: the stack indirect pointer now contains the absolute address of the stack.
EA, EC	Type 1 elements: global variable addresses.

0	3F XX XX XX	Changed by Initializer (See next section).
4	01 01 00 FA	
8	02 E8 02 00 F4	Unchanged
D	04	

E6	0000	
E8	11EA	Absolute Address of Stack
EA	2F00	Absolute Address of A
EC	2F80	Absolute Address of B
EE	8509	Flagged as Operator
F0	FFFF	Unchanged
F2	FFFF	
F4	2F00	Address of A
F6	3000	Address of C
F8	2F80	Address of B
FA	2F00	Address of A
FC	2F80	Address of B
FE	3000	Address of C

Figure 12.11 Initializations

F4, F8, FA, FC	Updated by using the corresponding entries from the parameter list of the calling program.
EE	Type 5 element: flagged to indicate an operator as address goes up to X'3FFF'.
F6, FE	Type 2 and Type 3 elements: the first occurrence of C (at address X'FE') was resolved when memory was assigned to C and the second occurrence (at address X'F6') gets a copy of this address.

12.2.2. Description of the Execution of a Control Instruction

1. Firmware Control of a Program

The first 4 bytes of the program (see Fig. 12.4 and Fig. 12.10) are used by the firmware to control the status of execution of the program.

1. The PTYPE is an 8-bit field containing a code specifying whether the program is a control program or a primitive. In this implementation, it is simply one of the unused opcodes of the machine instruction set for the Microdata 1600. Normally, program instructions are executed by the machine's instruction interpretation firmware (1600/30 firmware). When this unused opcode is encountered, control is passed to the new firmware, which then analyzes the rest of the page (where this opcode appears)

according to the new architecture. If no unused opcode is encountered, then the existing firmware executes the program (which is, therefore, a primitive) in the existing machine architecture.

2. The DPAGE contains the beginning of free memory (not yet allocated) in the memory bank. At initiation time, the firmware stores the address of the free memory in this field. A copy of this pointer is kept by the firmware and is updated whenever a variable is created. When a function is deleted from the memory after its completion, this field allows the firmware to reset its internal pointer to the value it had before the initiation of the function, thereby freeing the memory used for the local variables of this function.

3. The PC contains a pointer to the instruction to be executed next. It is updated for the DO and IF-THEN-ELSE instructions. In the case of the WHILE instruction, it is updated if the WHILE condition is false. When a control program terminates, the PC of the previous level function will indicate where to resume execution.

4. The PL field contains a pointer to the parameter list of the function to be invoked. When this function is initiated, Type 1 parameter addresses will be returned using this field from the previous level function. The PL is stored in one of the existing registers in case the invoked function is a primitive.

In addition to these fields, the firmware keeps a PSW consisting of the concatenation of the PC and the page level (0 to 16) in the internal registers, indicating, thereby, the instruction being executed and the function level being processed.

2. Execution of One Instruction

Decoding the opcode field allows the firmware to decide if a Boolean expression has to be evaluated. If so, this expression is evaluated as a normal Polish stack evaluation (see the next paragraph). Depending on the result (1 or 0), the function address field is decoded. This field indicates:

1. Whether the function is memory resident or on disk;
2. The address of the function.

If the function is on disk, it is paged in. The page pointer in the PSW is incremented and the PC part of the PSW reset to zero. If the function is resident, control is passed to the existing firmware together with the address of the function.* Fig. 12.12 shows the flowchart of the microprogram.

The decoding of the opcode field determines the microsubroutine to be executed.

---

*Note in this implementation the memory-resident functions are restricted to primitives only. This is done to simplify the microprogram because the page pointer in the PSW is also used for the page allocation microroutine when a function is paged in.

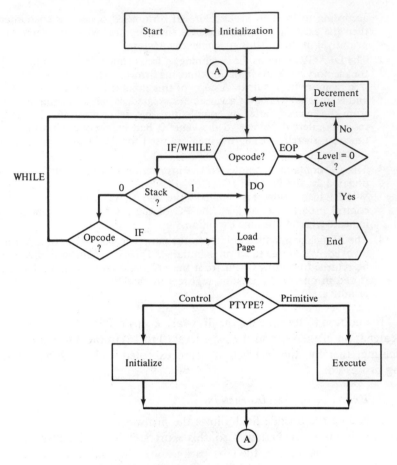

Figure 12.12 Flowchart of the Microprogram

EOP SUBROUTINE

This microprogram branches to END if the current level counter is zero when the last instruction of the first level is encountered. If this level count is not zero, then it is decremented, the free-memory pointer reset to the previous value (freeing the memory allocated to the local variables of that level), and the PC pointer reset, thereby pointing to the next instruction in the previous page.

DO SUBROUTINE

This microprogram decodes the page address of the function to be performed. If the function is resident (indicated by a flag in the address), control is passed to the native firmware. If not, the selected page is brought in memory, the level counter incremented, and the current PC saved in the corresponding field. The PTYPE field of the new page is decoded. If it indicates a primitive, control is passed to the native firmware as for a resident function. If it indicates a control program, initializations, including the memory allocation of local variables, occur and the process is repeated for the first opcode of this page.

IF-WHILE SUBROUTINE

This microprogram passes control to the software stack evaluator, which returns a result of zero or 1. For a result of 1, the function address is selected and the routine branches to the DO subroutine. For a result of zero, if the WHILE opcode was present, control is passed to the main program for decoding the next opcode. If the IF opcode was present, the ELSE function address is selected and control branches to the DO subroutine.

Although the implemented firmware was written according to the flow-chart in Fig. 12.12, another representation of this microprogram in structured pseudo language follows.

```
DO      INITIALIZATIONS;
DO-WHILE    level ≥ 0;
IF OPCODE = EOP THEN      level = level − 1;
IF OPCODE = IF THEN DO;
            IF STACK = 1    THEN address = Function 1
                            ELSE address = Function 2;
        END;
IF OPCODE = WHILE THEN DO;
            IF STACK = 1    THEN address = Function
                            ELSE address = NOOP;
        END;
IF OPCODE = DO THEN address = Function;
IF OPCODE ≠ EOP THEN DO;
        Load Page;
        IF PTYPE = 0    THEN execute native mode
                        ELSE DO; INITIALIZE;
                                level = level + 1;
        END;                    END;
END;
```

3. Evaluation of a Boolean Stack

This part is programmed in the machine language of the Microdata 1600/30 and not microprogrammed, because the size of control memory in the machine under discussion was too limited; the relative complexity of the task made a software implementation easier. Furthermore, the selection of the correct arithmetic mode according to the type of variables has not been implemented (only integer variables are supported). When a Boolean expression has to be evaluated, the pointer field in the instruction allows the program to have access to the corresponding Polish stack. This stack contains operand addresses and operators and is evaluated as a normal arithmetic or logical expression. For arithmetic variables, the address points to the actual memory location containing the data, which has been obtained at initiation time. When this memory was allocated, the LVD for the variable was also copied in the data area, together with the data value. It is, therefore, possible to determine whether the operation to be performed is of integer, floating, or some other type, if data conversion has to take place, or if the data is an array. If an operand of a Boolean expression is itself a Boolean expression, the operator EX must always be coded after such an operand; the entire expression is evaluated by the step-down levels of a tree structure of stacks, as illustrated in Fig. 12.13.

Each stack here represents a Boolean expression. The order of evaluation of the stacks as shown is done by the normal arithmetic method. If an

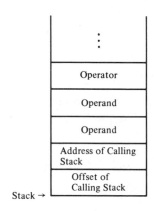

Stack:	Address of a stack.
Stack (1):	Contains the offset in the calling stack where evaluation was interrupted.
Stack (2):	Address of the calling stack.

Figure 12.13 Stack Structure

EX operator occurs during the evaluation of a stack then the computations on the current stack are momentarily halted while processing of the new stack continues at the indicated address. For the linkage of stacks, the necessary pointers and addresses are stored and updated by the program. When a stack evaluation is completed, the reverse process occurs and the address of the final value of the Boolean expression is returned to the previous stack, whose evaluation is resumed. This process is repeated until the root node is encountered and the final value can be returned to the IF or WHILE instruction that caused the expression evaluation. The structure of a Polish stack is shown in Fig. 12.13. Each item in this stack contains operators and addresses of operands and hence it is 2 bytes in length. The first 4 bytes of each stack are used by the program to save addresses and offsets for tree branching. Figure 12.14 lists the operators that are provided.

0	End of Stack
1	Or
2	And
3	Not
4	Add
5	Subtract
6	Divide
7	Multiply
8	Exponentiation
9	$>$
A	$\geq$
B	$=$
C	$\neq$
D	$<$
E	$\leq$
F	Execute

Figure 12.14 Type 5
Elements: Stack Operators

At execution time only, an associated stack is created in the main memory bank, corresponding to each Polish stack. This is a temporary stack and is used as a save area for the intermediate results. At the completion of the evaluation of a Boolean stack, its associated stack and contents are automatically deleted from the memory and, therefore, do not interfere with the allocation of local variables. The associated stack shown in Fig. 12.15 has 4 bytes reserved for the pairing of temporary pointers.

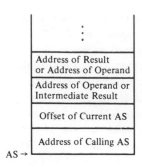

Figure 12.15 Associated Stack Structure

—AS is the associated stack.

—AS (1) is the offset to the AS address at the time when evaluation is continued at a lower level in the tree structure. This offset is required for resuming activities at the correct location in the stack yet to be completed.

—AS (2) is used mainly for linkage. It stores the address of the calling associated stack or the associated stack just above it logically in the tree hierarchy.

This firmware occupies the entire control store available on the Microdata 1600, and functions such as stack evaluation and function paging are done by software. The addition of this particular microprogram does provide the software programmer with a very simple and powerful facility to code structured programs. The restriction that a program can contain only control instructions or existing machine instructions was found in fact to be cumbersome because the fragmentation of a program can be extreme unless a very sizeable collection of primitives is first created; however, removing this restriction would have caused the firmware to be much more complicated as it would have to interact with the existing firmware. With this restriction, the interface between the existing microprograms and the add-on firmware is minimal, requiring only two new operation codes (one for control program processing and one for the EOP instruction). For this reason, the concepts presented in this example should be easily adaptable to any machine with microprogrammed control.

REFERENCES AND FURTHER READINGS

[1] KESSLER, N. N., *"Assembly Language Structured Programming Macros,"* (Gaithersburg, Md.: IBM Corp., 1972).

[2] MCGOWAN, C. L., and J. R. KELLY, *"Top Down Structured Programming Techniques,"* New York: Petrocelli/Charter, 1975.

[3] CHIENG, C., "A Firmware Implementation of Block Structured Programming," Internal Report 4200, Computer Science Department, University of Ottawa, 1978.

[4] WILNER, W. T., "Microprogramming Environment on the Burroughs B1700," *Proc. of the 6th Annual IEEE Computer Society International Conference*, San Francisco, Sept. 1972.

[5] TANENBAUM, A. S., "Implications of Structured Programming for Machine Architecture," *Communications of the ACM*, vol. 21, no. 3 (March 1978).

[6] JOHNSTON, J. B., "The Contour Model of Block Structured Processes," *Proceedings of the SIGPLAN Symposium on Data Structures in Programming Languages*, Gainesville, Fla. (Feb. 1971), pp. 55–82.

[7] WORTMAN, D. B., "A Study of Language Directed Computer Design," Ph.D. thesis, Stanford University, 1973).

[8] JONES, L. H., "The Role of Instruction Sequencing in Structured Programming," *SIGMICRO Newsletter*, 4, no. 3 (October 1973).

[9] RAYMOND, J., "A Firmware Implementation of Block Structured Programming," Technical Report TR78–04, Computer Science Department, University of Ottawa.

[10] LUTZ, M. J., and M. J. MANTHEY, "A Microprogram Implementation of a Block Structured Architecture," *Fifth Annual Workshop on Microprogramming*, University of Illinois, Urbana, Il., September 1972.

EXERCISES

12.1 Formulate and implement the microprogram described in (3) of 12.2.2 (Evaluation of a Boolean Stack) in the case where all types of variables (such as floating, integer, character, and so on) are considered. Assume that all relevant operations for implementation exist in the host.

12.2 Redefine the top level algorithm of instruction execution in the case where structured control instructions can be mixed with native mode instructions (Fig. 12.12).

12.3 In order to service interrupts in a reasonable time, the load time from the disk (Load Page box in Fig. 12.12) must be considered. With this in mind, define an interrupt servicing routine, taking into account the level reached in the hierarchy. It may be assumed that the machine has only one user at a time.

12.4 Design and implement a firmware routine supporting the CASE SELECT construct in machine language.

CHAPTER THIRTEEN

Other Examples
of Applications

The preceding chapters introduced the most important applications of microprogramming: emulation, software support, and development of special architectures. Microprogramming has found numerous other applications, such as, in the design of control processors, specialized terminals, hardware support, and so on. This chapter presents some of these applications. The purpose of this chapter is to show the versatility of microprogramming, helping the reader to see microprogramming in a broader perspective; that is, as a flexible design tool for various applications. The first two examples illustrate the use of microprogramming for the addition of extra features to an existing computer, and the other examples illustrate the use of microprogramming in the design of specialized processors.

13.1 VIRTUAL MEMORY IMPLEMENTATION THROUGH MICROPROGRAMMING

This section is intended to provide an example of how microprogramming can be used to implement some advanced features on a machine. The example of dynamic address translation (DAT) has been chosen because it is a well-known and easily understood concept.

13.1.1. Concept of Virtual Memory

The basic concept of virtual memory is based on using auxiliary storage (disk or drum) as an extension of the main memory of a machine, thereby providing a "virtual memory" limited only by the addressing capability of the machine. In order to make the implementation details of virtual memory transparent to the users, a method is provided to map the address supplied by the programmer (virtual address) into a real address in the main memory. Various techniques exist to provide this mapping, but the most common ones use the concept of segmentation and paging [1]. It is this method that has been used in the following example. The process of accessing data in a virtual memory system consists of three main parts.

1. Converting the virtual address into the auxiliary storage address.
2. Paging into real memory the referenced page, if it is not already resident in the memory.
3. Computing the real address of the data.

The process of computing the real address from a specified virtual address is called **dynamic address translation** (DAT).

Dynamic address translation is usually performed via hardware, because this is a process used for almost every single machine-level instruction, thereby requiring a very fast execution time. However, DAT can easily be implemented via firmware in order to provide a virtual memory facility on a microprogrammable machine with an otherwise limited main memory.

13.1.2. An Example of DAT Implementation

In the example illustrated here, a dynamic address translation system was microprogrammed on the Microdata 1600 machine using auxiliary storage (up to 10 Megabytes) readily available on disk.

1. Virtual Address Structure for Microdata 1600

The Microdata 1600 uses 2 bytes for specifying a memory address; here each address is divided into three fields for the purpose of dynamic address translation: **segment number, page number,** and **displacement** (see Fig. 13.1).

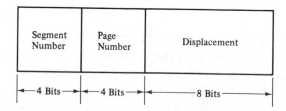

Figure 13.1 Virtual Address Structure

—The *segment number* is 4 bits long. The maximum number of segments in each program is 16.

—The *page number* is 4 bits long. There will be 16 pages in each segment.

—The *displacement* is 8 bits long. There are 256 locations within a page.

Thus a three-part address is used to locate, or reference, instructions and data.

The address has the structure (s, p, i) where:

s identifies the segment number of the location within a program's address space;

p identifies the page number (within the segment) of the location;

i points to the location being addressed within the page.

Here we assume that addresses in this format are provided in machine language by an assembler or a compiler.

2. Segment and Page Tables

In Fig. 13.2, the real storage has been partitioned into **page frames**. Every real storage page frame has the same size as a page (256 bytes). Pages are loaded from the external memory into free page frames.

The loading process is also shown in Fig. 13.2. Segments are loaded into several page frames. Tables are built to register the corresponding locations in real storage and are used by the DAT routine at execution time.

The segmentation and paging system uses one segment table for each segment in a program and several page tables.

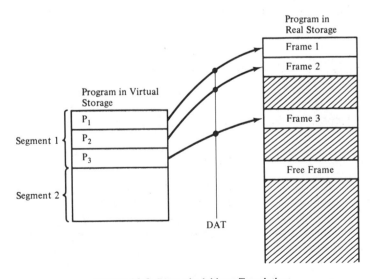

Figure 13.2 Dynamic Address Translation

—The **segment table** is built in real storage. Each entry in the segment table identifies the origin of its page table in real storage (see Fig. 13.3).

—The **page table** tells the system where a page is located in real storage (see Fig. 13.4).

Segment Number	Page Table
1	7100
2	8100
3	9300
4	9000

Figure 13.3 Segment Table

Page Number	Real Storage Address
1	1792
2	2048
3	3328
4	3840

Figure 13.4 Page Table (Address 7100)

3. Dynamic Address Translation

Consider Fig. 13.5, which contains the translation tables of the program and a relative address that references a location in its virtual space. The DAT microprogram translates virtual addresses during program execution as follows: The virtual address references a data item in Segment 1, Page 3 at location 120. The following sequence of events occurs during the DAT process.

1. A segment table origin register points to the program's segment table (7000).
2. The segment number is used to point to the corresponding segment table entry. This entry is the address of the page table for that segment (7100).
3. The page number is used to point to the page frame that contains this page (3328).
4. The displacement is added to yield the final absolute address (3448).

4. Paging

A virtual address translated into a real storage address can be used to access the required data item; however, this is true only if the page frame already contains a copy of the program's page, which is not the case unless this part of the program has been "paged in" from the auxiliary storage (that is, has already been referenced and not overlaid). An *IN* bit is added to each entry in the page table indicating if the corresponding page has been read (is

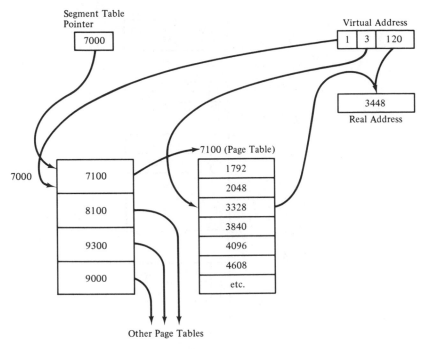

Segment Table Pointer

7000

Virtual Address

| 1 | 3 | 120 |

3448
Real Address

7100 (Page Table)

| 1792 |
| 2048 |
| 3328 |
| 3840 |
| 4096 |
| 4608 |
| etc. |

7000

| 7100 |
| 8100 |
| 9300 |
| 9000 |

Other Page Tables

Figure 13.5 Address Mapping

already in memory). If this bit is on, the real address obtained via DAT does point to the required data item; however, if the bit is off, the program's page must be read from auxiliary storage and the translated address will then point to the data item. The DAT routine uses another set of tables (external page tables) that indicates the address on auxiliary storage of each page. This address is used to read the external page into the page frame and the IN bit is turned on, since now the frame does contain the corresponding program code. If no more free frames are available, a frame is freed by copying its content onto auxiliary storage at the associated address indicated by the external page table. Note that this operation is necessary only for pages containing variables or modifiable code. In this implementation, no optimization was made on the choice of the page frame to be freed.

5. Details of the Implementation

The Microdata 1600 file register assignments are as follows (see Fig. 13.6).

—Primary File F contains the high-order part of the virtual address.
—Primary File E contains the low-order part of the virtual address.
—Secondary File 1 contains the high-order part of the segment table origin register.

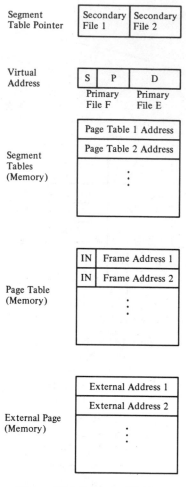

Figure 13.6 Formats of Tables

—Secondary File 2 contains the low-order part of the segment table origin Register. Secondary File Registers 1 and 2 should contain the correct information before using this program.

—Segment and all page tables reside in the main memory.

—Secondary File 3 contains the high-order part of the disk sector number.

—Secondary File 4 contains the low-order part of the disk sector number.

Note that the addresses use only 15 bits, because real storage is limited here to 16K bytes. Each page is followed by its external page table.

The DAT microprogram in this implementation translates a virtual address in 8.4 μs if the page is memory-resident, and in 13.2 μs if the page is to be brought from the disk (this does not include the I/O time, which can vary).

A flowchart summarizing this microprogram is shown in Fig. 13.7, and the microprogram is shown in Listing 13.1.

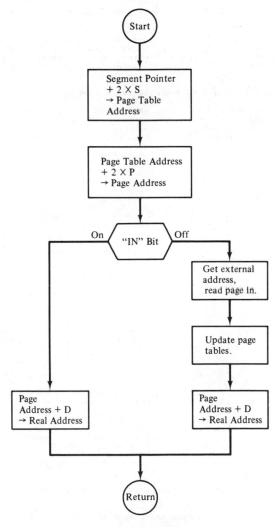

Figure 13.7 DAT Flowchart

```
                   ****************************************************************************
                   *    THIS MICROPROGRAM IMPLEMENTS THE                                      *
                   *  DYNAMIC ADDRESS TRANSLATION                                             *
                   *  ON THE  MICRODATA 1600                                                  *
                   ****************************************************************************
                   *
                   *
                   *  FILE REGISTERS 14 AND 15 CONTAIN:
                   *  AT THE BEGINNING THE VIRTUAL ADDRESS
                   *  AT THE END THE REAL ADDRESS
                   *
                   *  FILES 1 AND 2 CONTAIN THE SEGMENT TABLE ORIGIN REGISTER
                   *
                   *
                   *
0000 1040          SPF
0001 CF01          MOV     15,(T)          VIRTUAL ADDRESS (UPPER BYTE)
0002 1080          SSF
0003 8520          CPY     5,T             SAVE IN 5 AND
0004 8620          CPY     6,T             IN 6
0005 7620          SRF     6               SELECT SEGMENT NUMBER
0006 F600          SFL     6               SEGMENT # IS MULTIPLIED BY 2
0007 C201          MOV     2,(T)           SEGMENT TABLE ORIGIN REGISTER(LOW) IN T
0008 8620          ADD     6,T             POINTS TO CORRESPONDING PAGE TABLE ADDRESS
0009 C101          MOV     1,(T)           SEGMENT TABLE ORIGIN REGISTER(HIGH)
000A B7A0          CPY     7,L,T           COPY IN 7 WITH LINK UPDATE
                   *
                   * NOW 6 AND 7 POINT TO THE PAGE TABLE ADDRESS
                   *
000B 110F          LT      X'OF'           MASK TO SELECT PAGE NUMBER
000C E520          AND     5,T             SELECT PAGE NUMBER
000D 864B          ADD*    6,I,(N)         ADDRESS OF PAGE TABLE POINTER
000E A78A          RMF*    7,L,(M)         READ PAGE TABLE ADDRESS (LOW BYTE)
000F F500          SFL     5               PAGE # IS MULTIPLIED BY 2
0010 8520          ADD     5,T             INDEX PAGE TABLE
0011 C60B          MOV*    6,(N)           READ PAGE TABLE
0012 A70A          RMF*    7,(M)           ADDRESS (HIGH BYTE)
0013 B7A0          CPY     7,L,T           AND SAVE INTO 7
0014 C50B          MOV*    5,(N)           READ PAGE ADDRESS(HIGH)
0015 A70A          RMF*    7,(M)           FROM CORE
0016 1040          SPF                     RETURN TO PRIMARY FILES
0017 BF20          CPY     15,T            STORE RESULT IN FILE F
0018 4F80          TZ      15,X'80'        CHECK IF IN BIT IS ON
0019 1421          JP      R1
001A 1080          SSF
001B 854B          ADD*    5,I,(N)         READ ADDRESS (LOW BYTE)
001C A78A          RMF*    7,L,(M)         FROM CORE
001D 1040          SPF                     RETURN TO PRIMARY FILES
001E 8E20          ADD     14,T            ADD DISPLACEMENT TO LOW BYTE
001F 8F80          ADD     15,L OF PAGE ADDRESS
0020 1020          RTN
                   *
                   *
                   *
0021 1080    R1    SSF                     THIS ROUTINE TAKES CARE OF EXTERNAL
                   *                       ADDRESSES AND CALL THE READ DISK
                   *                       ROUTINE
```

```
0022 1120          LT      X'20'           ADD 32 TO POINT TO EXTERNAL TABLE
0023 852B          ADD*    5,T,(N)         READ EXTERNAL PAGE ADDRESS
0024 A78A          RMF*    7,L,(M)         (HIGH BYTE) FROM CORE
0025 B320          CPY     3,T             AND SAVE IN FILE 3
0026 1120          LT      X'20'           AGAIN
0027 856B          ADD*    5,I,T,(N)       READ EXTERNAL PAGE ADDRESS
0028 A78A          RMF*    7,L,(M)         (LOW BYTE)  FROM CORE
0029 B420          CPY     4,T             AND SAVE IN 4
002A 0100          JE      PAGIN           JUMP TO PAGING ROUTINE
                   *
                   * THE DISK READ ROUTINE GETS THE SECTOR ADDRESS IN FILES 3,4
                   * AND RETURNS THE PAGE ADDRESS IN THE SAME REGISTERS
                   *
                   *
                   *  NOW WE UPDATE THE PAGE TABLE AS A NEW PAGE CAME IN
                   *
```

Listing 13.1 Dynamic Address Translation Microprogram

```
002B  1080            SSF
002C  C301            MOV     3,(T)           PAGE ADDRESS (HIGH BYTE)
002D  C50B            MOV*    5,(N)           5 STILL POINTS TO ENTRY IN TABLE
002E  A71A            WMF*    7,(M)  UPDATE HIGH BYTE WITH IN BIT RESET
002F  1040            SPF                     AND COPY RESULT
0030  BF20            CPY     15,T            IN FILE F
0031  1080            SSF
0032  C401            MOV     4,(T)           NOW WE DC THE SAME
0033  854B            INC*    5,(N)           FOR THE LOW BYTE
0034  A79A            WMF*    7,L,(M)         OF THE PAGE ADDRESS
0035  1040            SPF
0036  8E20            ADD     14,T            STORE RESULT IN FILE 14
0037  8F80            ADD     15,L            AND UPDATE 15
0038  1020            RTN
                   *
                   *
      0100      PAGIN  EQU    X'100'          READ DISK ROUTINE
                      END     0
```

Listing 13.1 (continued)

13.2 MICRODIAGNOSTICS

13.2.1. Introduction

In the event of a hardware failure in a computer system, steps must be taken in order to ensure prompt repair and return to a normal operation.

1. Recognition of a hardware failure

This might very well be the most difficult step, especially if a failure is suspected while executing an untested piece of software, making it difficult to blame the unexpected behavior on the hardware or on the program itself. This situation can be further complicated by the fact that a fault may occur in a seldom-used hardware component, such as in the floating-point unit in a system using mainly integer arithmetic. In this case, the fault can remain undetected for quite a while, especially if the fault is intermittent. When a fault is suspected, a diagnostic program should be initiated to verify the presence of the fault. Such a program exercises all the functions of the suspected trouble area and (if well designed) indicates positively the presence or the absence of a fault in one of the components.

2. Isolation of the faulty component

If the previous step indicates that some component of the system has failed, the next step consists of pinpointing as precisely as possible which component has failed. The precision of this process depends on the characteristics of the machine and on the design of the diagnostic programs; fault isolation can be performed to the card level or the integrated circuit level, depending on the maintenance procedure and on the spare parts available. It is of course much faster to change the card containing the faulty component, thereby restoring normal operation, and then repair the card itself than it is to repair the card while the machine is down. The isolation of the malfunctioning part can be done using another diagnostic program, which will exercise the individual functions of each major component.

These two steps necessitate that the normal operation of the machine be halted and that only the diagnostic programs be run to detect and isolate the malfunction. The diagnostic programs are usually written in assembler language in order to provide control on the machine's individual components as closely as possible. However, three principal drawbacks can be identified with this procedure: The first one arises from the fact that an assembler program utilizes logical concepts which are often far removed from the real machine components. For example, if a floating-point operation is causing some trouble, the fault can lie in such areas as the ROM containing the floating-point microroutines, in the address used, or in the internal micro-registers used. Consequently, an assembler language routine cannot pinpoint very precisely the source of the fault. The second drawback arises from the fact that the machine has to be down while the diagnostics are run and the fault isolated. The third disadvantage is that the whole procedure is started when a fault is suspected; this leads to errors when an intermittent failure remains undetected.

The latter drawback is usually treated by introducing redundancy in the processing (for example, using a parity bit for memory access) and by systematic checking. When a checking process detects the presence of an error, a flag is raised (for example, a machine check or memory check), signaling the necessity to discard the recent results and to initiate the diagnostic programs.

13.2.2. Advantages of Microdiagnostics

The main advantage of writing a diagnostic program at microprogram level is the higher resolution obtained in locating a faulty component. Due to the fact that microinstructions access only a few components, a diagnostic program written in microcode can exercise individual components independently and, therefore, point to the source of the fault with much more accuracy than a machine-language diagnostic program. Furthermore, some components may be addressable (and, therefore, testable) only at microlevel and not at the machine-language level (for example, internal flags or registers). A fault in such components would cause erratic behavior that would be very difficult to isolate at the machine-language level. In this respect, microdiagnostics resolve the first drawback of the conventional diagnostic procedures mentioned earlier.

The second advantage offered by a microdiagnostic program is that it helps in reducing the down time of the machine. In some situations, this is achieved by reconfiguring the system once a malfunctioning unit has been identified; wherever possible, firmware routines are used to perform the functions of the malfunctioning unit, which is then bypassed until it is repaired. For example, a hardware floating-point unit could be turned off-line, and the floating point firmware could be used in its place once a fault is detected in the floating-point unit. This approach results in a more reliable system because it provides a firmware backup for some hardware components or functions.

Another improvement can be expected when using microdiagnostics. At the conventional machine level, diagnostics are initiated when a machine check occurs; that is, only after a fault has been detected in a component. However, with microdiagnostics the whole process of checking, detection, and reconfiguration can be automated by building it into the normal firmware interpreter. This provides for a systematic check after each significant computing sequence (for example, one machine instruction execution) and automatic reconfiguration by swapping firmware routines (in read/write control store). This will, of course, result in a slower instruction execution rate, but it will also reduce down time when errors are detected. The idea of using microdiagnostics should, however, be incorporated in the design of the whole machine architecture as these routines interact heavily with the use of the firmware. Furthermore, specially designed microinstructions for diagnostic purposes should be included in the microinstruction set.

13.2.3. Microdiagnostics Implementation

The implementation of a microdiagnostic program necessitates extra ROM and often extra writable control store for nonresident diagnostic routines, because it may be prohibitive to keep all microprograms resident in read-only memory.

Some additional hardware, such as switches for changing from the ROM containing the normal firmware to the ROM containing the diagnostics or switches for generating intentional errors in order to test the diagnostic program itself, is usually incorporated in the machine. It is also helpful to provide a single-cycle switch (for executing one microinstruction at a time) in addition to the usual single-step switch (for executing one machine language instruction at a time).

A diagnostic program can be exercised by running programs in machine language form. The interpretation of each such instruction by firmware will, in turn, execute the microinstructions implementing the diagnostics program; this method is close to the normal machine-language diagnostic procedure unless special machine-level diagnostic instructions have been designed in order to activate microdiagnostics. They can also be exercised by running microprograms directly, thereby providing all the advantages mentioned. However, this approach may use more ROM than necessary because some system components are easily tested at the machine-language level. A mixture of machine-level and microlevel diagnostics can usually perform a satisfactory job without requiring too much ROM.

13.3 FIRMWARE IMPLEMENTATION OF SOME FUNCTIONS OF A GRAPHICS TERMINAL

13.3.1. Introduction

The introduction of low-cost graphics terminals has resulted in a widespread use of computer graphics, enabling many users to afford this technology. Graphics terminals have existed since the 1950s, but their early cost was prohibitive for many applications. The utility of low-cost terminals is, however, limited because they depend almost entirely on the host computer for processing. Their processing capabilities are often limited to nothing more than displaying a line or a character. The fact that all processing has to be done on the host computer degrades the response time because of:

1. The usually slow data link between the processor and the terminal;
2. The competition between the various terminals to obtain processor attention.

If some of the processing is performed locally, there is less demand on the main computer and less data traffic on the communication line. This results in a faster response time from the graphics terminal. Furthermore, the communication line data does not have to be "low-level" data (for example, a series of x- and y-coordinates in the display of a circle); it can, instead, be "high-level" data (for example, the x-and y-coordinates of the center and the radius of a circle) that must be interpreted by the local processor in order to generate the necessary "low-level" code for display.

Graphics terminals with local processing capabilities have been implemented using various minicomputers or microprocessors [5]. In one implementation, a microcomputer was used to provide local processing capabilities and to hold the current copy of the image being displayed for easy manipulation, because this was not feasible on the storage-tube terminal that was used. Although the gains in performance obtained by the introduction of a microcomputer for local processing are very impressive, there are still some applications that cannot be fully realized due mainly to the speed of microprocessors. For example, consider an image consisting of about 100 line segments (a typical order of magnitude for many applications) that is to be rotated in a 3-dimensional space in real time. The solution of each point necessitates a 4×4 matrix multiplication that can be simplified to 9 multiplications and 6 additions (in floating-point representation), plus a sine and a cosine function computation for each angle increment. This can (in terms of orders of magnitude) be considered to represent from 15 to 20 multiplications. A total of 1500 to 2000 operations is, therefore, necessary to rotate the whole picture, and—because 30 frames per second are necessary for animation effect—about 50,000 floating-point multiplications must be performed each second, requiring a floating-point multiplication cycle time of 20 μs. If a multiplication routine consists of about 50 single instructions (see Chap. 7 for an example of floating add and subtract), then the local processor must have a maximum cycle time of 400 ns to perform this rotation. It is, therefore, clear that this type of processing can be better handled at the micropro-gramming level due to the speed available and due to the fact that very specialized instructions can be created (for example, matrix multiplication) when necessary.

13.3.2. A Microprogrammed Graphics Terminal

Figure 13.8 represents the hardware configuration of the graphics system incorporating a local microprogrammable processor. The graphics terminal communicates with the microprogrammable processor via a general-purpose, byte-oriented interface. The speed of this interface is much greater than the drawing speed of the terminal and, therefore, it does not introduce any limitations. The processor itself communicates with the host computer via a standard RS232C interface at 300 baud (limit introduced by the link and the modem used). Therefore the local processor acts as a part of the graphics terminal as far as the graphics software running on the host computer is concerned.

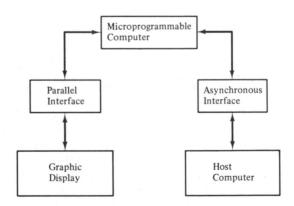

Figure 13.8 Components of the Graphics System

Figure 13.9 represents the software configuration of the graphics system. For the reader unfamiliar with computer graphics terminology, these are defined in the references [7]; however, their meanings are summarized here.

—The **viewing algorithm** consists of all the segments of the application pro-gram causing graphic processing to occur (for example, **DISPLAY LINE** or **ERASE**).

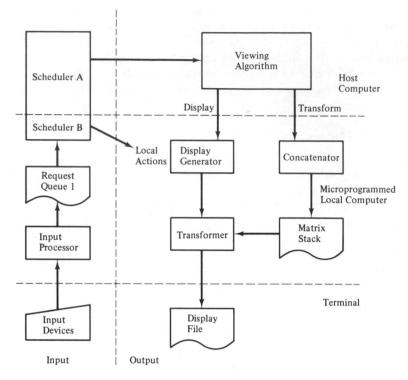

Figure 13.9 Structure of the Graphics System

—The **concatenator and the transformer** manage the geometric transformations (such as ROTATION or SCALE) of the picture.

—The **display generator** generates the machine language instructions for the graphics terminal from the orders specified by the viewing algorithm.

—The **display file** consists of the graphics terminal machine language program (that is, the program causing the actual display).

—The **input processor, scheduler, and interrupt queue** are the same elements as those used in operating systems, and they manage the input part of the system (that is, the response to the operator actions at the terminal such as light-pen interrupt).

In a graphics terminal without any local processing capabilities, all these components reside in the main computer. The only exception is the display file, which is constantly refreshed from the terminal's local memory or electronically stored on the terminal screen. Depending on the amount of local processing available, some of these components can be moved to the terminal end.

In the case where all parts of the graphics system, including the application program, are resident in the local processor, we have a stand-alone system with no link to a main computer except, eventually, for interrogation of a large data base. The elements placed in the microprogrammable processor in this example are indicated in Fig. 13.9. All these components are microprogrammed, but some functions are software-assisted in order to simplify the programming.

13.3.3. Architecture of the Graphics Terminal

Figure 13.10 shows the architecture of the graphics terminal. It contains the following elements:

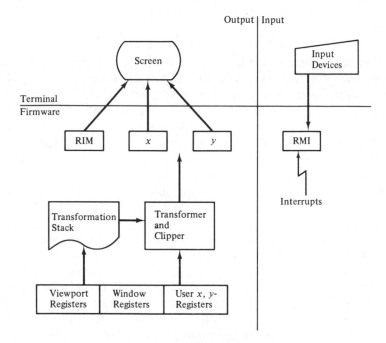

Figure 13.10 Architecture of the Graphics Terminal

1. *x- and y-registers*. These 16-bit registers contain the current *x*- and *y*-coordinates of the point on the screen (in screen coordinates); each coordinate is 10 bits in size. They are updated after the completion of a graphics instruction because interrupts are not recognized until the end of a microroutine.

2. *Transformation stack*. This stack, emulated in memory, contains up to 256 3×3 matrices for the transformations. A stack pointer is associated with this stack to indicate the current transformation.

3. *ux- and uy-registers*. These two 16-bit registers contain the *x*- and *y*-coordinates of the current point in user space (in floating-point notation).

4. *Window registers*. These two pairs (x, y) of registers contain the specifications of a 2-dimensional window as specified by the user. The coordinates are expressed in user-space units.

5. *Viewport registers.* These two pairs (x, y) of registers indicate the screen position of the viewport. These coordinates are expressed in the screen space units.

6. *Register mask for interrupts* (*RMI*). This register contains the mask for disabling or enabling the various interrupt sources (such as light pen, keyboard, or communication line).

7. *Register for image modification* (*RIM*). This register indicates the current display mode (such as alphanumeric, line, point, or dotted).

Some other components, not detailed here, are concerned with the communication between the microprogram and the terminal and are, therefore, transparent to the graphics software in the main computer.

13.3.4. Operation of the Terminal

When an opcode is received (see Table 13.1) it is interpreted as a normal machine-language instruction. For example, the instruction *Line x, y* causes a line to be displayed starting from the point with coordinates that are the current values of the *ux*-and *uy*-registers to the point with coordinates (x, y) specified by the instruction. The coordinates (x, y) are first transformed according to the matrix on the top of the stack, which yields a set (x, y) of coordinates (in user units) corresponding to the image of that point in the user screen. This point is then fed to the clipper, which determines what part of the line is seen (in the user's window) and then scaled to the viewport yielding the final (x, y)-value (in screen coordinates) that is finally sent to the terminal for display.

If an action is taken by the operator, the scheduler part which is resident in the microprogram first determines if it corresponds to an action to be passed on to the application program (in which case the other part of the scheduler will process it) or if it corresponds to an action to be processed locally (in which case the corresponding microroutine or software routine is called). An example of the former case is the input by the operator of some keyword for the application program; an example of the latter case is a local zoom operation to be performed on the picture.

This graphics terminal, where all the processing has been implemented on the Microdata 1600, provides all the capabilities that exist on more expensive hardware.

13.4 A COMMUNICATIONS CONTROLLER

13.4.1. Introduction

The relative complexity of the tasks to be performed by a communications controller makes attractive its implementation by program rather than by hardware. The programmed implementation offers other advantages as well;

flexibility, for example, makes reconfiguration an easy task—especially if it is to be done dynamically. However, programming a general-purpose computer in order to implement communications control is an approach which suffers from two main disadvantages.

1. A general-purpose instruction set is not well-suited for the operations necessary for communications control. Special-purpose instructions should be available in order to assist the programmer in this task rather than having to realize each separate hardware function with cumbersome (and inefficient) routines.
2. The use of programs to implement communications-control functions makes the execution of these functions slower than if they were implemented by hardware. This may make the management of high-speed lines difficult, while the management of low-speed lines is still easy. The slower speed will limit the number of lines that can be controlled, thereby decreasing the capacity of the controller as the available lines cannot all be made operational at the same time.

As in the other examples, microprogramming appears to be the ideal choice to implement such functions due to its position "midway" between hardware and software. In this particular case, the two drawbacks mentioned can be easily removed by using firmware. Microprogramming allows the person who designs the controller to provide very specialized instructions that do not prevent flexibility even if the firmware is implemented in ROMs; this is because a careful design of the instruction set will provide the programmer with all the necessary controls. The firmware concerns itself with providing functions such as code translation, control of serializing or deserializing, and such things as redundancy checks while leaving to the programmer control over the configuration of the network, speeds of the lines, byte formats, and choice of codes.

13.4.2. Example of a Microprogrammed Controller

This section describes a communications controller implemented on the Microdata 1600. The purpose of this implementation is both practical and pedagogical. Figure 13.11 represents the hardware configuration of the controller and the associated devices. Four communication ports are available for various purposes. Figure 13.11 shows the devices connected to these ports. These ports conform to the RS232C interface standards, and parameters such as port speed, character format, and I/O function are programmable. When operating under the controller firmware, the Microdata 1600 computer communicates with the console operator in order to establish the desired communication link (or links) at specified speeds. Once a link is established, the firmware carries on the I/O operations until an intervention from the operator terminates the communication or establishes a new one.

TABLE 13.1

GRAPHICS OPCODES

BYTE XY Y \ X	0	1	2	3	4	5	6	7
0	NOOP	START SESSION	START MESSAGE	EOM	END SESSION			RING BELL
1			START OF AN IMAGE	END OF AN IMAGE	START OF BLOC	END OF BLOC	START OF GRAPHIC SUBROUTINE	END OF GRAPHIC SUBROUTINE
2		READ FUNCTION KEYBOARD	READ ALPHANUMERIC KEYBOARD	READ LIGHT PEN	READ GRAPHIC CURSOR	READ ALPHANUMERIC CURSOR	READ TABLET	
3		INTERRUPT FUNCTION KEYBOARD	INTERRUPT KEYBOARD	INTERRUPT LIGHT PEN				
4		INKING	DRAGGING	RUBBER BAND	GRID	LIGHT POTENTIOMETER	LIGHT HANDLE	
5		TRANSFER OBJECT IMAGE	TRANSFER X, Y, Z					
6		LOAD RMI	DRAW PIF	ERASE PIF	REDRAW BLOC	ERASE BLOC	ADD BLOC	REMOVE BLOC
7								
8	INTERRUPT LOCAL PROCESSOR	SYNCHRO						
9	GRAPHIC NOOP	BRANCH					CALL SUBROUTINE	RETURN
A		LOAD RIM						
B								
C	END OF MODE	ABSOLUTE POSITION	ABSOLUTE POINT	ABSOLUTE LINE	ABSOLUTE CIRCLE			CHARACTER
D	IDENTITY	TRANSLATE	SCALE	ROTATION				RESTORE
E		LOAD RIM						
F								

Rows 0–7: COMMUNICATION INSTRUCTIONS
Rows 8–F: DISPLAY FILE INSTRUCTIONS

TABLE 13.1 (continued)

GRAPHICS OPCODES

8	9	A	B	C	D	E	F	Type
				RESET		START PROGRAM	END PROGRAM	SYSTEM
								SEGMEN-TATION
OPTION 0	READ X	READ Y	READ Z	OPTION 1	OPTION 2	OPTION 3	OPTION 4	INPUT
INTERRUPT ERROR								
								OUTPUT
								GRAPHIC PRIMITIVE
								TRANSFOR-MATION
								MODIFI-CATION
								OPTIONS
								SYSTEM
REMOVE SUBROUTINE				REMOVE PIF				SEGMEN-TATION
								INPUT
								OUTPUT
2 BYTE INSTRUCTION	RELATIVE POSITION	RELATIVE POINT	RELATIVE LINE	RELATIVE CIRCLE			CHARACTER SET #2 / CHARACTER	GRAPHIC PRIMITIVE
								TRANSFOR-MATION / MODIFI-CATION / OPTIONS

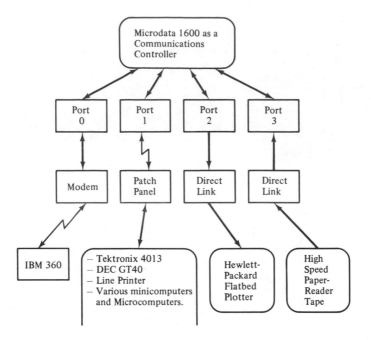

Figure 13.11 Example of the Controlled Configuration

1. Operation of the controller

Once the firmware is loaded into the WCS of the computer and its execution started, the first phase of the controller function is realized; it consists of establishing one or more links as required by the operator.

The first message sent to the operator console asks for the ports to be connected; both the controller message and operator response are shown in the following examples. The latter is underlined in order to distinguish it from the controller messages.

EXAMPLE:

CONNECT?

0 TO 2

establishes a link between ports 0 and 2. Only one port can communicate with another in order to provide two different links at the same time. In a more complex controller this need not be the case; for example, a communication could be carried out between two ports and echoed on other ports as well.

Once two lines are connected, the controller prompts the operator for the various parameters of each line.

EXAMPLE:

INIT PORT 0

SPEED	= 2400	(2400 baud)
I/O	= I	(Input Only)
STOPS	= 1	(1 Stop Bit)
DATA	= 8	(8 Data Bits)
PARITY	= NO	(No Parity Check Required)
TRANS	= NO	(No Transcoding Required)

INIT PORT 2

SPEED	= 9600	(9600 baud)
I/O	= O	(Output Only)
STOPS	= 1	(1 Stop Bit)
DATA	= 8	(8 Data Bits)
PARITY	= NO	(No Parity Generation Required)
TRANS	= NO	(No Transcoding)

After specifying all the parameters for the desired communication, the operator is prompted again to supply data for another connection. Either new data is entered if a second connection is to be established, or a "carriage return" terminates this first phase.

Before proceeding with the actual processing of the communication requirements, checks are made on the input data for possible incompatibilities (for example, two "input only" lines or an output line slower than an input line).

The second phase of the controller function consists of processing the communication requirements and is carried out without operator intervention unless a link break is required by the operator. In this particular example, this is the only way to terminate a link as signals like DTR (Data Terminal Ready) were not considered in the implementation. This processing consists of the following.

—Checking for the DATA IN status from the input port (or ports).
—Reading the data into a file register.
—Transcoding it if necessary according to one of the translate tables resident in main memory (as specified for the input port).
—Transcoding it again as specified for the output port connected to the input port, from which the data was received.

—Checking for the DATA BUFFER EMPTY status from the selected output port.
—Sending the data.

2. *Details of the implementation*

All the controller functions are carried out by microprograms using Microdata 1600 file registers as temporary storage. Due to the fact that an output device must be faster than an input device, buffering is not necessary. The only use made of main memory is to store the messages for the dialogue with the operator's console and to store the various translate tables necessary to support various terminals. The processing of control characters is determined by these translate tables and not by the firmware. The details of the firmware for communications control are shown in Listing 13.2.

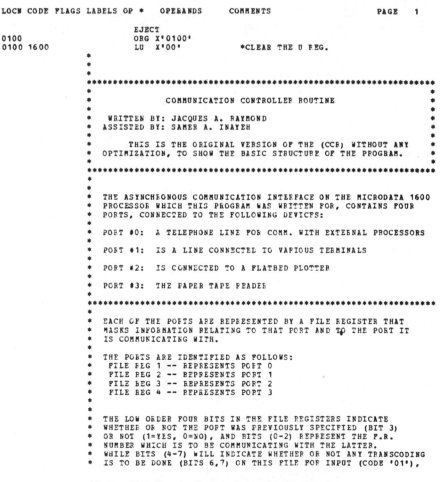

```
LOCN CODE FLAGS LABELS OP *   OPERANDS      COMMENTS                      PAGE    1

                          EJECT
0100                      ORG X'0100'
0100 1600                 LU  X'00'          *CLEAR THE U REG.
            *
            *
            *
            *****************************************************************
            *                                                             *
            *          COMMUNICATION CONTROLLER ROUTINE                    *
            *                                                             *
            *   WRITTEN BY: JACQUES A. RAYMOND                             *
            *   ASSISTED BY: SAMER A. INAYEH                               *
            *                                                             *
            *      THIS IS THE ORIGINAL VERSION OF THE (CCR) WITHOUT ANY   *
            *   OPTIMIZATION, TO SHOW THE BASIC STRUCTURE OF THE PROGRAM.  *
            *                                                             *
            *****************************************************************
            *
            *
            *   THE ASYNCHRONOUS COMMUNICATION INTERFACE ON THE MICRODATA 1600
            *   PROCESSOR WHICH THIS PROGRAM WAS WRITTEN FOR, CONTAINS FOUR
            *   PORTS, CONNECTED TO THE FOLLOWING DEVICES:
            *
            *   PORT #0:  A TELEPHONE LINE FOR COMM. WITH EXTERNAL PROCESSORS
            *
            *   PORT #1:  IS A LINE CONNECTED TO VARIOUS TERMINALS
            *
            *   PORT #2:  IS CONNECTED TO A FLATBED PLOTTER
            *
            *   PORT #3:  THE PAPER TAPE READER
            *
            *****************************************************************
            *
            *   EACH OF THE PORTS ARE REPRESENTED BY A FILE REGISTER THAT
            *   MASKS INFORMATION RELATING TO THAT PORT AND TO THE PORT IT
            *   IS COMMUNICATING WITH.
            *
            *   THE PORTS ARE IDENTIFIED AS FOLLOWS:
            *     FILE REG 1 -- REPRESENTS PORT 0
            *     FILE REG 2 -- REPRESENTS PORT 1
            *     FILE REG 3 -- REPRESENTS PORT 2
            *     FILE REG 4 -- REPRESENTS PORT 3
            *
            *
            *   THE LOW ORDER FOUR BITS IN THE FILE REGISTERS INDICATE
            *   WHETHER OR NOT THE PORT WAS PREVIOUSLY SPECIFIED (BIT 3)
            *   OR NOT (1=YES, 0=NO), AND BITS (0-2) REPRESENT THE F.R.
            *   NUMBER WHICH IS TO BE COMMUNICATING WITH THE LATTER.
            *   WHILE BITS (4-7) WILL INDICATE WHETHER OR NOT ANY TRANSCODING
            *   IS TO BE DONE (BITS 6,7) ON THIS FILE FOR INPUT (CODE '01'),
```

Listing 13.2 Communications Controller Microprogram

```
        *  OR FOR OUTPUT (CODE '10') OR FOR INP. AND OUT. (CODE '11'),
        *  OR NO TRANSCODING AT ALL (CODE '00').
        *  BITS (4,5) ARE THE PAGE NUMBER IN MEMORY OF THE TRANSCODE
        *  TABLE TO BE USED.
        *
        *
        *
LOCN CODE FLAGS LABELS OP *  OPERANDS        COMMENTS                    PAGE   2

              *
              EJECT
0101 2100     LF   1,0              *
0102 2200     LF   2,0              *CLEAR REGISTERS
0103 2300     LF   3,0              *
0104 2400     LF   4,0              *
              *
              *  THE MESSAGES TO THE TTY FOR THE USER ARE LOCATED IN MAIN
              *  MEMORY AT LOCATIONS (100 TO 1FF). A MESSAGE IS A MAXIMUM OF
              *  15 BYTES AND EACH MESSAGE IS ENDED WITH THE HEX. CODE '00'.
              *
              *
              *  SEND CONNECT AND READ PORT #
              *
0105 2510  C1 LF   5,X'10'          *ADDRESS OF MESSAGE 'CONNECT'
0106 01BF     JE   SMR    .         *SEND MESSAGE
0107 01DA     JE   RMR              *RECEIVE MESSAGE ROUTINE
0108 2503     LF   5,X'03'          *MASK CODE
0109 E521     AND  5,T(T)           *CLEAN OUT ANSWER
010A 8549     INC* 5,(T)            *TO MAP REGISTERS
010B B620     CPY  6,T              *REMEMBER IT FOR CONNECTION
010C 2520     LF   5,X'20'          *LF OPCODE
010D C52E     LOR* 5,T(U)           *LF OPCODE PLACED IN U REG
010E 1000     NOP                   *U REG DELAY
010F 0008     ELT  0,X'08'          *MARK REGISTER FOR USE
              *
              *  SEND TO AND READ PORT #
              *
0110 1600  T1 LU   X'00'
0111 2520     LF   5,X'20'          *MESSAGE 'TO'
0112 01BF     JE   SMR              *SEND IT
0113 01DA     JE   RMR              *GET ANSWER
0114 2503     LF   5,X'03'          *CLEAN OUT MASK
0115 E521     AND  5,T(T)           *CLEAN ANSWER
0116 8549     INC* 5,(T)            *MAP TO REGISTER
0117 B720     CPY  7,T              *REMEMBER FOR CONNECTION
0118 2540     LF   5,X'40'          *TZ OPCODE
0119 C52E     LOR* 5,T(U)           *TZ OPCODE PLACED IN U REG
011A 1000     NOP                   *U REG DELAY
011B 0008     ELT  0,X'08'          *CHECK IF ALREADY USED
011C 1510     JP   T1               *YES ASK AGAIN
011D 2520     LF   5,X'20'          *GET LF CODE
011E C52E     LOR* 5,T(U)           *LF OPCODE PLACED IN U REG
011F 1000     NOP                   *U REG DELAY
0120 0008     ELT  0,X'08'          *MARK FOR USE
0121 1600     LU   X'00'            *CLEAN FOR JE
0122 1000     NOP                   *U REG DEALY
0123 0158     JE   CONNECT          *CONNECT THESE PORTS
              *
LOCN CODE FLAGS LABELS OP *  OPERANDS        COMMENTS                    PAGE   3

              EJECT
0124 1600  C2 LU   X'00'
0125 2510     LF   5,X'10'          *CONNECT MESSAGE,
0126 01BF     JE   SMR              *SEND IT
0127 01DA     JE   RMR              *READ ANSWER
0128 B620     CPY  6,T              *SAVE A WHILE
0129 2573     LF   5,X'73'          *COMPLEMENT OF 8D I.E. (CR)
012A 8520     ADD  5,T              *ADD UP
012B 55FF     TN   5,X'FF'          *WAS ANSWER (CR)
012C 154F     JP   CEND             *YES GET OUT
012D C601     MOV  6,(T)            *RESTORE
012E 2503     LF   5,X'03'          *MASK CODE
012F E521     AND  5,T(T)           *CLEAN OUT
0130 8549     INC* 5,(T)            *MAP TO REGISTER
0131 B620     CPY  6,T              *REMEMBER IT
0132 2540     LF   5,X'40'          *TZ OPCODE
0133 C52E     LOR* 5,T(U)           *TZ OPCODE PLACED IN U REG
0134 1000     NOP                   *U REG DELAY
0135 0008     ELT  0,X'08'          *CHECK IF USED
```

Listing 13.2 (continued)

```
0136 1524              JP   C2                *YES RETRY
0137 2520              LF   5,X'20'           *LF OPCODE
0138 C526              LOR  5,T(U)            *LF OPCODE PLACED IN U REG
0139 1000              NOP                    *U REG DELAY
013A 0008              ELT  0,X'08'           *MARK FOR USE
013B 1600        T2    LU   X'00'             *CLEAN U
013C 2520              LF   5,X'20'           *"TO" MESSAGE
013D 01BF              JE   SMR               *SEND IT
013E 01DA              JE   RMR               *READ ANSWER
013F 2503              LF   5,X'03'           *MASK BYTE
0140 E521              AND  5,T(T)            *CLEAN OUT
0141 8549              INC* 5(T)              *MAP TO REGISTER
0142 B720              CPY  7,T               *SAVE IT FOR CONNECTION
0143 2540              LF   5,X'40'           *TZ OPCODE
0144 C52E              LOR* 5,T(U)            *TZ OPCODE PLACED IN U REG
0145 1000              NOP                    *U REG DELAY
0146 0008              ELT  0,X'08'           *TEST IF USED
0147 153B              JP   T2                *YES RETRY
0148 2520              LF   5,X'20'           *LF OPCODE
0149 C52E              LOR* 5,T(U)            *LF OPCODE PLACED IN U REG
014A 1000              NOP                    *U REG DELAY
014B 0008              ELT  0,X'08'           *MARK FOR USE
014C 1600              LU   X'00'             *CLEAN U
014D 1000              NOP                    *DELAY
014E 0158              JE   CONNECT           *CONNECT THESE TWO
```

LOCN CODE FLAGS LABELS OP * OPERANDS   COMMENTS   PAGE   4

```
                      EJECT
                 *
                 * LINES HAVE BEEN CONNECTED PROMPT FOR ALL LINES.
                 *
                 * THE FOLLOWING WILL CHECK FOR THE FOUR FILE REGISTERS
                 * TO SEE THE ONES THAT WERE ENABLED FOR ACTION,  THOSE
                 * THAT WERE ARE THEN PROMPTED FOR THE FOLLOWING REQUIRED
                 * RELEVANT INFORMATION TO ENABLE THE PROPER SETUPS.
                 *
014F 2641        CEND  LF   6,X'41'           *(TZ 1) OPCODE
0150 C606        CT    MOV  6,(U)             *PLACED IN THE U REG
0151 1000              NOP                    *DELAY
0152 00FF              ELT  0,X'FF'           *HAS PORT BEEN USED
0153 1564              JP   PROMPT            *YES GO GET PARAMETERS
0154 8640        CP    INC  6                 *NEXT PORT
0155 66BB              CP   6,X'BB'           *ALL DONE
0156 1550              JP   CT                *NO DO NEXT
0157 1C0A              JP   COMMLOOP          *YES DO COMMUNICATIONS
                 *
                 *
                 * THE FOLLOWING PROCEDURE WILL CONNECT LOGICALLY THE
                 * PORTS THAT ARE SUPPOSED TO TALK TO EACH OTHER.
                 * THIS IS DONE VIA THE FILE REGISTERS, THIS INFORMATION
                 * IS USED LATER ON IN THE PROGRAM.
                 *
0158 C601        CONNECT MOV 6,(T)            *GET 1ST PORT IN T
0159 25C0              LF   5,X'C0'           *CODE FOR LOR
015A C52E              LOR* 5,T(U)            *CODE FOR LOR IN U
015B C701              MOV  7,(T)             *GET 2ND PORT IN T
015C 0020              EOT  0,T               *CONNECT 2ND TO 1ST
015D C52E              LOR* 5,T(U)            *CODE FOR LOR IN U
015E C601              MOV  6,(T)             *GET 1ST PORT IN T
015F 1000              NOP                    *DELAY
0160 0020              EOT  0,T               *CONNECT 1ST TO 2ND
0161 1600              LU   X'00'             *CLEAN UP
0162 1000              NOP                    *DELAY
0163 1020              RTN                    *RETURN
```

LOCN CODE FLAGS LABELS OP * OPERANDS   COMMENTS   PAGE   5

```
                      EJECT
                 *
                 * PROMPTING FOR SPEED, FORMAT
                 *
0164 1600        PROMPT LU   X'00'            *CLEAN UP U
0165 133B              LN   X'3B'             *ADDRESS IN PROMPT MESSAGE
0166 1201              LM   X'01'             *MESSAGE IN PAGE ONE
0167 9649              DEC* 6,(T)             *GET PORT # COPIED INTO
0168 B720              CPY  7,T               *FILE REG 7
```

Listing 13.2 (continued)

370

```
0169 37F0                    AF  7,X'F0'           *TRANSFORM TO ASCII
016A A719                    WMF* 7,(T)            *WRITE INSIDE MESSAGE
016B F700                    SFL 7                 *TO SEND TO USER
016C F700                    SFL 7                 *FOR PORT IDENTIFICATION
016D F700                    SFL 7
016E F700                    SFL 7
016F F700                    SFL 7
             *
             *  THE MESSAGE IS JUST AN INFORMATION STEP
             *  DESIGNATING THE PORT NUMBER THE FOLLOWING
             *  QUESTIONS ARE RELATED TOO.
             *
0170 2530                    LF  5,X'30'           *MESSAGE ADDRESS
0171 01BF                    JE  SMR               *SEND IT
             *
             *  THE FOLLOWING ENABLES THE CTS (CLEAR TO SEND)
             *                     AND THE DTR (DATA TERMINAL READY)
             *
0172 28DC                    LF  8,X'DC'           *CTS COMMAND MESSAGE
0173 1101                    LT  X'01'             *ENABLE
0174 C729                    LOR* 7,T(T)           *PLACE THE PORT NUMBER INTO REG T
0175 01F2                    JE  STL               *SEND TO THE LINE
0176 28FC                    LF  8,X'FC'           *DTR COMMAND MESSAGE
0177 1101                    LT  X'01'             *ENABLE
0178 C729                    LOR* 7,T(T)           *PLACE THE PORT NUMBER INTO REG T
0179 01F2                    JE  STL               *SEND TO THE LINE
             *
             * SPEED ?
             *
017A 2540                    LF  5,X'40'           *SPEED MESSAGE
017B 01BF                    JE  SMR               *SEND IT
017C 01DA                    JE  RMR               *READ SPEED #
017D 2507                    LF  5,X'07'           *MASK CODE
017E E529                    AND* 5,T(T)           *CLEAN UP TO 3 BITS
017F C729                    LOR* 7,T(T)           *BUILD SPEED CODE INTO T
0180 283C                    LF  8,X'3C'           *SPEED INSTRUCTIONS IN 8
0181 01F2                    JE  STL               *SEND TO LINE
             *
             * STOP BITS ?
             *
0182 2550                    LF  5,X'50'           *STOP BIT # MESSAGE
0183 01BF                    JE  SMR               *SEND MESSAGE
0184 01DA                    JE  RMR               *READ NUMBER OF STOP BITS
0185 2501                    LF  5,X'01'           *MASK CODE
0186 E521                    AND 5,T(T)            *CLEAN UP TO 1 BITS
0187 F501                    SFL 5,(T)             *SET IN POSITION
0188 C721                    LOR 7,T(T)            *OR IT WITH BASE CODE
             *

LOCN CODE FLAGS LABELS OP *   OPERANDS       COMMENTS                 PAGE   6

             * DATA BITS ?
             *
0189 2560                    LF  5,X'60'           *DATA BIT # MESSAGE
018A 01BF                    JE  SMR               *SEND MESSAGE
018B 01DA                    JE  RMR               *READ NUMBER OF DATA BITS
             *
             *  THE FOLLOWING SETS UP THE NUMBER READ IN TO THE
             *  REQUIRED FORMAT TO BE SENT OUT TO THE REQUIRED
             *  PORT.  THE SETUP IS AS FOLLOWS:
             *
             *  FOR 8 DATA BITS THE CODE IS '00'
             *  FOR 7 DATA BITS THE CODE IS '10'
             *  FOR 6 DATA BITS THE CODE IS '01'
             *  FOR 5 DATA BITS THE CODE IS '11'
             *
018C B520                    CPY 5,T               *THE INPUT WILL BE CHANGED
018D 2E00                    LF  14,X'00'          *ACCORDINGLY TO THE REQUIRED
018E F520                    SFR 5                 *RESULTS REPRESENTED IN
018F FE80                    SFL 14,L              *THE TABLE MENTIONED
0190 D520                    XOR 5,T               *PREVIOUSLY
0191 F520                    SFR 5
0192 FE80                    SFL 14,L
0193 FE00                    SFL 14                *THE FINAL RESULT IS
0194 FE01                    SFL 14,(T)            *PLACED IN THE T REG
0195 C721                    LOR 7,T(T)            *THEN IT IS ORED WITH THE
             *                                     *PREVIOUS FORMAT INFORMATION
             *                                     *CALCULATED BEFORE
             *
```

Listing 13.2 (continued)

```
                    * PARITY ?
                    *
0196 2570                  LF   5,X'70'          *PARITY MESSAGE
0197 01BF                  JE   SMR              *SEND MESSAGE
0198 01DA                  JE   RMR              *READ PARITY REQUIREMENT
           *                                     *('00' = NO PARITY,
           *                                     *'01' = PARITY IS ODD,
           *                                     *'10' AND '11' = PARITY IS EVEN)
0199 2503                  LF   5,X'03'          *CLEAN MASK
019A E521                  AND  5,T(T)           *CLEAN IT
019B 5503                  TN   5,X'03'          *ANY PARITY
019C 15A2                  JP   NOPAR            *NO
019D F520                  SPR  5
019E F500                  SFL  5                *YES PROCESS IT
019F F500                  SFL  5                *POSITION THE
01A0 F500                  SFL  5                *BITS
01A1 F541                  SLI  5,(T)            *PUT PARITY INFORMATION IN T REG
01A2 C729       NOPAR      LOR* 7,T(T)           *COMBINE RESULT WITH
           *                                     *PREVIOUS CALCULATIONS
           *
           * WE HAVE ALL THE FORMAT INFORMATION NEEDED
           * THEREFORE LETS SEND IT.
           *
01A3 285C                  LF   8,X'5C'          *FORMAT INSTRUCTION IN 8
01A4 01F2                  JE   STL              *SEND TO LINE

LOCN CODE FLAGS LABELS OP *    OPERANDS      COMMENTS                      PAGE   7

                    EJECT
           *
           * THE FOLLOWING WILL PROMPT FOR INFORMATION AS TO WHETHER
           * OR NOT ANY TRANSCODING WILL BE DONE ON INPUT OR OUTPUT
           * OR BOTH.  THE CODING IS SHOWN BELOW.
           *
01A5 2580                  LF   5,X'80'          *I/O MESSAGE
01A6 01BF                  JE   SMR              *SEND MESSAGE
01A7 01DA                  JE   RMR              *READ (0=NO;1=IN;2=OUT;3=IO)
01A8 2803                  LF   8,X'03'          *SELECT 2 BITS
01A9 E821                  AND  8,T(T)           *GET THEM
01AA F800                  SFL  8
01AB F800                  SFL  8                *MAKE ROOM FOR TRANSLATE TABLE CODE
01AC 58FF                  TN   8,X'FF'          *ANY TRANSCODING
01AD 15B4                  JP   NOTRANS          *NO TRANSCODING TO BE DONE
01AE 2590                  LF   5,X'90'          *YES THEN
01AF 01BF                  JE   SMR              *SEND TRANSCODE MESSAGE
01B0 01DA                  JE   RMR              *READ TABLE PAGE NUMBER
01B1 2503                  LF   5,X'03'          *SELECT 2 BIT CODE
01B2 F529                  AND* 5,T(T)           *GET THEM
01B3 C821                  LOR  8,T(T)           *WITH I/O CODE
01B4 F800       NOTRANS    SFL  8
01B5 F800                  SFL  8
01B6 F800                  SFL  8                *ADJUST IN 8
01B7 C601                  MOV  6,(T)            *GET REG. TO BE MODIFIED
01B8 2507                  LF   5,X'07'
01B9 E529                  AND* 5,T(T)           *GET REGISTER #
01BA 25C0                  LF   5,X'C0'          *GET LOR OPCODE
01BB C526                  LOR  5,T(U)           *PUT LOR FILL IN U
01BC F801                  SFL  8,(T)            *GET CODE TO SEND THERE
01BD 0020                  EOT  0,T              *OR INTO REGISTER
01BE 1554                  JP   CP               *RETURN

LOCN CODE FLAGS LABELS OP *    OPERANDS      COMMENTS                      PAGE   8

                    EJECT
           *
           *     (SMR) SEND MESSAGE ROUTINE
           *
           * A BYTE OF THE MESSAGE IS SEND TO THE CONSOLE
           *
01BF 1120       SMR        LT   X'20'            *GET STATUS
01C0 7090                  COX  0                *SEND CODE
01C1 1201                  LM   X'01'            *CLEAR M
01C2 15C3                  JP   *+1              *DELAY
01C3 7080                  CIO  0
01C4 70F0                  DIX  0                *STATUS PLACED IN T REG
01C5 1000                  NOP
01C6 1000                  NOP
```

Listing 13.2 (continued)

```
01C7 BA20              CPY  10,T           *PLACE STATUS IN FILE REG 10
01C8 7080              CIO  0              *CLEAR THE I/O
01C9 5A04              TN   10,X'04'       *CHECK FOR INPUT READINESS
01CA 15BF              JP   SMR            *NOT READY
01CB A5C3              RMF  5,I(N)         *READ DATA FROM MEMORY
01CC BA20              CPY  10,T
01CD 5AFF              TN   10,X'FF'       *CHECK FOR NULL CHARACTER
01CE 1020              RTN                 *YES RETURN
01CF 1100              LT   X'00'          *NO THEN SEND OUT
01D0 7090              COX  0              *CODE TO THE CONSOLE
01D1 1000              NOP                 *FOR CONTINUATION OF THE
01D2 15D3              JP   *+1            *MESSAGE REQUESTED
01D3 7080              CIO  0              *CLEAR THE I/O
01D4 CA01              MOV  10,(T)         *MOVE THE DATA INTO THE T REG
01D5 70A0              DOX  0              *SEND OUT THE DATA
01D6 1000              NOP
01D7 1000              NOP
01D8 7080              CIO  0
01D9 15BF              JP   SMR            *CONTINUE

LOCN CODE FLAGS LABELS OP *   OPERANDS       COMMENTS                          PAGE   9

                       EJECT
               *
               *    (RMR) READ MESSAGE ROUTINE
               *
               *    A SINGLE BYTE IS READ FROM THE CONSOLE
               *
01DA 1120      RMR     LT   X'20'          *GET STATUS
01DB 7090              COX  0              *SEND CODE
01DC 1000              NOP
01DD 1000              NOP
01DE 7080              CIO  0
01DF 70E0              DIX  0              *STATUS PLACED IN T REG
01E0 1000              NOP
01E1 1000              NOP
01E2 BA20              CPY  10,T           *PLACE STATUS IN FILE REG 10
01E3 7080              CIO  0              *CLEAR I/O
01E4 5A02              TN   10,X'02'       *CHECK FOR OUTPUT READINESS
01E5 15DA              JP   RMR            *NOT READY
01E6 1100              LT   X'00'
01E7 7090              COX  0
01E8 1000              NOP
01E9 1000              NOP
01EA 7080              CIO  0
01EB 70E0              DIX  0              *READ BYTE FROM CONSOLE
01EC 1000              NOP
01ED 1000              NOP
01EE B520              CPY  5,T            *PLACE BYTE IN FILE REG 5
01EF 7080              CIO  0              *CLEAR I/O
01F0 C501              MOV  5,(T)          *PLACE THE BYTE INTO REG T
01F1 1020              RTN

LOCN CODE FLAGS LABELS OP *   OPERANDS       COMMENTS                          PAGE  10

                       EJECT
               *
               *    (STL) SEND TO LINE ROUTINE
               *
               *    A BYTE IS SEND TO THE DESIGNATED PORT
               *
01F2 BA20      STL     CPY  10,T           *SAVE T (THE DATA BYTE)
01F3 C801              MOV  8,(T)          *GET COMMAND BYTE
01F4 7090              COX  0
01F5 1000              NOP
01F6 1000              NOP
01F7 7080              CIO  0
01F8 CA01              MOV  10,(T)         *PUT BACK DATA BYTE INTO T REG
01F9 70A0              DOX  0              *SEND OUT THE DATA BYTE
01FA 1000              NOP
01FB 1000              NOP
01FC 7080              CIO  0
01FD 1020              RTN
               *
               *    (IFL) INPUT FROM LINE ROUTINE
               *
               *    A BYTE IS READ FROM THE DESIGNATED PORT
               *
```

Listing 13.2 (continued)

```
01FE C801      IFL       MOV  8,(T)         *MOVE COMMAND BYTE TO T REG
01FF 7090                COX  0
0200 1000                NOP
0201 1000                NOP
0202 7080                CIO  0
0203 70E0                DIX  0             *GET THE REQUIRED DATA BYTE
0204 1000                NOP
0205 1000                NOP
0206 B820                CPY  8,T           *PLACED IT IN FILE REG 8
0207 7080                CIO  0             *CLEAR THE I/O
0208 C801                MOV  8,(T)         *PUT DATA BYTE BACK INTO THE T REG
0209 1020                RTN
```

LOCN CODE FLAGS LABELS OP *   OPERANDS   COMMENTS   PAGE 11

```
                         EJECT
               *
               * COMMUNICATION LOOP
               *
               *  THIS IS THE COMMUNICATION LOOP FOR ALL THE PORTS.
               *  ALL THE PORTS ARE ENABLED FOR INPUT THEN THE PROCESSOR
               *  GOES INTO A WAIT STATE FOR ANY ONE OF THE PORTS TO
               *  REQUEST SERVICING.  THEN ONCE A PORT HAS REQUESTED A SERVICE
               *  THE PORT NUMBER IS IDENTIFIED FROM THE STATUS BYTE
               *  FILE REGISTERS (1-4) THE OTHER PORT NUMBER IS RETRIEVED
               *  THUS THE INPUT BYTE IS READ, THIS OTHER PORT IS THEN
               *  ENABLED FOR OUTPUT, A STATUS IS CHECKED FOR OUTPUT READINESS
               *  THEN THE PORT IS DISABLED FOR OUTPUT AND THE BYTE IS PASSED
               *  OUT TO THE PORT. FINALLY THE PROCESSING ENTERS THE WAIT
               *  STATE AGAIN AWAITING THE NEXT REQUEST FOR INPUT.
               *
020A 1600      COMMLOOP LU  X'00'
               *
               *  ENABLE ALL PORTS FOR INPUT
               *
020B 287C                LF   8,X'7C'       *REQUEST MASK
020C 1102                LT   X'02'         *REQUEST INPUT LINE 0
020D 01F2                JE   STL
020E 1122                LT   X'22'         *REQUEST INPUT LINE 1
020F 01F2                JE   STL
0210 1142                LT   X'42'         *REQUEST INPUT LINE 2
0211 01F2                JE   STL
0212 1162                LT   X'62'         *REQUEST INPUT LINE 3
0213 01F2                JE   STL
               *
               *  WAIT UNTIL A REQUEST FOR INPUT IS MADE
               *
0214 285C      WAIT      LF   8,X'5C'       *SERVICE FLAG CODE
0215 01FE                JE   IFL           *READ FROM LINE
0216 BA20                CPY  10,T          *GET SERVICE FLAG
0217 5A01                TN   10,X'01'
0218 1C14                JP   WAIT          *NO REQUEST
               *
               *  REQUEST IS MADE THEN READ STATUS
               *
0219 283C                LF   8,X'3C'       *STATUS READ CODE
021A 01FF                JE   IFL
021B BA20                CPY  10,T
               *
               * GET REQUESTING PORT # IN R10 AND THE DATA
               *
021C 7A20                SRF  10
021D FA20                SFR  10            *ALIGN PORT #
021E 1103                LT   X'03'         *MASK
021F EA20                AND  10,T
0220 8A40                INC  10            *HERE IT IS
0221 281C                LF   8,X'1C'       *INPUT CODE
0222 01FF                JE   IFL           *READ IT
0223 BB20                CPY  11,T          *DATA IN 11
```

LOCN CODE FLAGS LABELS OP *   OPERANDS   COMMENTS   PAGE 12

```
                         EJECT
               *
               * PROCESS BYTE
               *
0224 11C0                LT   X'C0'         *'MOVE' OPCODE
```

Listing 13.2 (continued)

```
0225 CA26              LOR   10,T(U)           *'MOVE' OPCODE IN U
0226 1000              NOP
0227 0001              EOT   0,(T)             *COPY PORT REG
0228 BA20              CPY   10,T              *COPY CONTENT OF PORT REG IN 10
0229 1107              LT    X'07'             *TO SELECT CONNECTED PORT
022A EA29              AND*  10,T(T)           *GET CONNECTED PORT #
022B BD20              CPY   13,T              *SAVE INTO 13 FOR ENABLING LATER
022C 2CC0              LF    12,X'C0'          *MOVE OPCODE
022D CC26              LOR   12,T(U)           *MOVE OPCODE IN U
022E 1000              NOP
022F 0001              EOT   0,(T)             *COPY CONNECTED PORT REG IN T
0230 BC20              CPY   12,T              *COPY CONTENT OF CONNECTED
           *                                   *PORT REG INTO FILE REG 12
0231 1600              LU    X'00'
0232 5A40              TN    10,X'40'          *TRANSCODING
0233 1C3A              JP    NOIT              *NO INPUT TRANSCODING
           *
           * INPUT TRANSCODING
           *
0234 CB03              MOV   11,(N)            *GET LOW ADDRESS OF TRANSLATED BYTE
0235 7A20              SRF   10
0236 1113              LT    X'13'             *TO CLEAN I/O
0237 EA22              AND   10,T(M)           *GET TABLE ADDRESS
0238 A000              RMF   0                 *READ TRANSLATED BYTE
0239 BB20              CPY   11,T              *INTO 11
           *
023A 5C80      NOIT    TN    12,X'80'          *ANY TRANSCONDING IN OUTPUT?
023B 1C42              JP    NOOT              *NO
           *
           * OUTPUT TRANSCODING
           *
023C CB03              MOV   11,(N)            *GET LOW ADDRESS
023D 7C20              SRF   12
023E 1113              LT    X'13'             *CLEAN 12
023F EC22              AND   12,T(M)           *GET TABLE ADDRESS
0240 A000              RMF   0                 *READ TRANSLATED BYTE
0241 BB20              CPY   11,T              *INTO 11
           *
0242 287C      NOOT    LF    8,X'7C'           *REQUEST TO ENABLE
0243 9D40              DEC   13                *TO ADJUST
0244 FD00              SFL   13
0245 FD00              SFL   13
0246 FD00              SFL   13
0247 FD00              SFL   13
0248 FD00              SFL   13                *SHIFT IT TO THE TOP
0249 1112              LT    X'12'             *CODE FOR OUTPUT ENABLING
024A CD29              LOR*  13,T(T)           *INTO T
024B 01F2              JE    STL               *SEND ENABLE CODE


LOCN CODE FLAGS LABELS OP *  OPERANDS     COMMENTS                    PAGE  13

                       EJECT
           *
           * READ SERVICE FLAG FOR OUTPUT READINESS
           *
024C 285C      TS1     LF    8,X'5C'
024D 01FE              JE    IFL
024E BA20              CPY   10,T
024F 5A01              TN    10,X'01'          *IS PORT READY FOR OUTPUT
0250 1C4C              JP    TS1               *NOT READY
           *
           * YES PORT IS READY THEN DISABLE THE PORT FOR OUTPUT
           *
0251 287C              LF    8,X'7C'           *REQUEST TO DISABLE
0252 1110              LT    X'10'             *DISABLE CODE
0253 CD29              LOR*  13,T(T)
0254 01F2              JE    STL               *DISABLE
           *
           * FINALLY SEND THE DATA BYTE OUT TO THE PORT
           *
0255 281C              LF    8,X'1C'           *SEND OUT DATA CODE
0256 CB01              MOV   11,(T)            *GET DATA
0257 01F2              JE    STL               *SEND OUT
0258 1C14              JP    WAIT              *GO BACK AND WAIT FOR NEXT REQUEST
                       END
```

Listing 13.2 (continued)

REFERENCES

[1] SHAW, ALAN C., *The Logical Design of Operating Systems*, (Englewood Cliffs, N.J.: Prentice-Hall, Inc., 1974), pp. 112–16.

[2] NOLET, N., and T. PHAM, "Dynamic Address Translation for the Microdata 1600," Internal Report 4200, Computer Science Department, University of Ottawa, 1974.

[3] RAMAMOORTHY, C. V., and L. C. CHANG, "System Modeling and Testing Procedures for Microdiagnostics," *IEEE Transactions on Computers*, C–21, no. 11 (November 1972), pp. 1169–83.

[4] JOHNSON, A. M., "The Microdiagnostics for the IBM System 360 Model 30," *IEEE Transactions on Computers*, C–20, no. 7 (July 1971), pp. 798–803.

[5] RAYMOND, J., and D. K. BANERJI, "Using a Microprocessor in an Intelligent Graphics Terminal," *IEEE Computer Magazine*, 9, 4 (April 1976), pp. 18–25.

[6] KERR, H. D., "A Microprogrammed Processor for Interactive Computer Graphics," *Proceedings of the Second Annual Symposium on Computer Architecture*, January 20–22, 1975, pp. 28–33.

[7] NEWMAN, W. M., and R. F. SPROULL, *Principles of Interactive Computer Graphics*, (New York: McGraw-Hill Book Company, 1972).

FURTHER READINGS

1. CAILLOUET, L. P., JR., and SHRIVER, B. D., "An Integrated Approach to the Design of Fault Tolerant Computing Systems," *Preprints of the Seventh Annual Workshop on Microprogramming*, Palo Alto, Ca. (October 1974), pp. 12–24.

2. CANADAY, C. H., and others, "A Back-end Computer for Data Base Management," *Comm. of the ACM*, 17, no. 10 (October 1974), 575–82.

3. CHOQUET, M. F., and NUSSBAUMER, H. J., "Microcoded Modern Transmitters," *IBM Journal of Research and Development*, 18 (July 1974), 338–51.

4. DEMORI, R., RIVOIRA, S., and SERRA, A., "A Special Purpose Computer for Digital Signal Processing," *IEEE Trans. Comput.*, C–24, 12 (December 1975), 1202–11.

5. DROMARD, F., "Design of a Microprogrammed Alphanumeric Terminal," *Preprints of the Seventh Annual Workshop on Microprogramming*, Palo Alto, Ca. (October 1974), pp. 128–34.

6. HARTENSTEIN, R. W., and MUELLER, K. O., "A Microprogrammed Display Processor Concept for 3D Dynamic Interactive Computer Graphics," *SIGMICRO Newsletter* 4, no. 1 (April 1973), 30–35.

7. HWANG, K., "Design of Fault-Tolerant Microprogrammed Digital Controllers with Partitioned Hybrid Redundancy," *IEEE Computer Society Repository*, R75–281, 28 pages.

8. KEHL, T. H., MOSS, C., and DUNKEL, L., "LM²—A Logic Machine Minicomputer," *Computer*, 8, no. 11 (November 1975), pp. 12–22.

9. KRATZ, G. L., SPROUL, W. W., and WALENDZIEWICZ, E. J., "A Microprogrammed Approach to Signal Processing," *IEEE Trans. Comput.*, C–23, no. 8 (August 1974), 808–17.

10. KRUSE, B., "A Parallel Picture Processing Machine," *IEEE Transactions on Computers*, C–22, no. 12 (December 1973), 1075–87.

11. LIDINSKY, W. O., "Mirage, A Microprogrammable Interactive Raster Graphics Equipment," *Proceedings of the 1971 IEEE International Computer Society Conference*, Boston, Ma. (September 1971), pp. 15–16.

12. MACRES, P., and COULOURIS, G. F., "A Microprogrammed Storage Management System for a Paged Stack Machine," *Preprints of the Seventh Annual Workshop on Microprogramming*, Palo Alto, Ca.: (October 1974), pp. 122–27.

13. MARVEL, O. E., "SPEAC, Special Purpose Electronic Area Correlator," *Proceedings of the Second Annual Symposium on Computer Architecture*, January 20–22, 1975, pp. 91–94.

14. MEZZALIRA, L., and SCHREIBER, F. A., "A Microcomputerized Interface for Computer Communication," *EUROMICRO Newsletter*, 1, no. 4, (July 1975), pp. 37–46.

15. RAUSCHER, T. G., "Microprogramming the AN/UYK–17 (XB–1) (V) Signal Processing Element Signal Processing Arithmetic Unit," *SIGMICRO Newsletter*, 5, no. 26 (July 1975), pp. 29–63.

16. RAUSCHER, T. G., and AGRAWALA, A. K., "Developing Application-Oriented Computer Architectures on General Purpose Microprogrammable Machines," *AFIPS Conference Proceedings*, 45 (1976 NCC), 715–22.

17. SCHWOMEYER, W. A., "Verification of a Virtual Storage Architecture on a Microprogrammed Computer," *AFIPS Conference Proceedings* 42 (1973 NCC), 401–406.

18. SILTON, W. G., and WEAR, L. L., "A Virtual Memory System for the Hewlett-Packard 2100A," *Preprints of the Seventh Annual Workshop on Microprogramming*, Palo Alto, Ca. (October 1974), pp. 119–21.

19. VAN DAM, A., "Microprogramming for Computer Graphics," *SIGMICRO Newsletter* 3, no. 1 (April 1972), 3–7.

20. WU, Y. S., "Microprogramming Applications to Signal Processing Architectures," in *Microarchitecture of Computer Systems*, ed. R. W. Hartenstein and R. Zaks. Amsterdam: North-Holland/American Elsevier, 1975, pp. 263–273.

EXERCISES

13.1 Rework the virtual address DAT algorithm using a 24-bit word as a virtual address (16M bytes virtual memory). The real address space is 64K bytes and the page size is 4K bytes.

13.2 Rewrite the ADD instruction microprogram presented in Chap. 7 to provide diagnostics for the 8-bit adder. The diagnostics could be carried out, for example, by performing the addition by two different methods and comparing the results.

13.3 Write a microprogram implementing the instruction CIRCLE (X'C4') from Table 13.1. The format of the instruction is:

8	10	10	10
C4	Radius	X of center	Y of center

Assume the graphics terminal plots lines when receiving a sequence of 10 bits each for x and y-coordinates. An 8-bit control character X'00' preceding an x, y pair positions the spot without plotting.

13.5 Microprogram a communications controller similar to the example given, allowing two ports to communicate. One port is input only and the other one is output only. They both have the same byte format but the output line speed is 300 baud, whereas the input line speed is 600 baud. Messages received by the input line do not exceed 1024 characters in length and are always separated by delay of a few seconds.

APPENDIX A

The Nova Computer*

The types of functions performed by instructions in most computers are the following.

1. Move data between memory and the operating registers.
2. Modify memory, usually in conjunction with a test to determine whether to alter the program sequence.
3. Alter the program sequence by jumping to a new location.
4. Perform an arithmetic or logical operation.
5. Test the value of a word or flag, or one word against another, to determine whether to alter the program sequence.
6. Transfer data to or from the peripheral equipment.

In many computers the first and fourth and the third and fifth groups overlap. In the Nova-line, Groups 1 and 3 are unique. But Groups 4 and 5 coincide: every arithmetic and logical instruction can test the result for a skip.

*Reproduced by permission of Data General Corporation from their manual entitled "How to Use the NOVA Computers." NOVA is a registered trademark of Data General Corporation, Southboro, Mass.

The following lists the registers that must be specified and the functions performed by the various instruction classes in the Nova-line computers.

Move data
: One memory location, one accumulator. Either may be the source of the operand, the other is the destination.

Modify memory
: One memory location. Increment or decrement contents; skip if result is zero.

Jump
: One memory location from which the next instruction is taken. A return address can be saved in AC3.

Arithmetic and logic
: Two accumulators. One or both may be source of operand(s). Perform arithmetic or logical function, with a Bit-0 carry affecting the carry flag as indicated. If desired, swap halves of answer or rotate it with carry 1 place right or left, load result into either accumulator, and skip on condition specified for result or carry.

Input-output
: One accumulator, one I/O device. Transfer word in either direction between any accumulator and one of up to 3 registers in up to 62 devices. Also operate device as specified.

(*Note.* A subclass of these instructions executes no transfer and specifies only a device. The instruction either operates the device or skips on a selected condition in it.)

ADDRESSING

Instructions in the first three classes must address a memory location. Each instruction word contains information for determining the effective address, which is the actual address used to fetch or store the operand or alter program flow. The instruction specifies an 8-bit displacement, which can directly address any location in 4 groups of 256 locations each. The displacement can be an absolute address; that is, it may be used simply to address a location in page zero, the first 256 locations in memory. But it can also be taken as a signed number that is used to compute an absolute address by adding it to a 15-bit base address supplied by an index register. The instruction can select AC2 or AC3 as the index register; either of these accumulators can thus be used as an ordinary index register to vary the address computed from a constant displacement, or as a base register for a set of different displacements. The program can also select PC as the index register, so any instruction can address 256 words in its own vicinity (relative addressing).

Now the computed absolute (15-bit) address can be the effective address. However, the instruction can use it as an indirect address; that is, it can specify a location to be used to retrieve another address. Bits 1 through 15 of the word read from an indirectly addressed location can be the effective address or they can be another indirect address.

AUTOMATIC INCREMENTING AND DECREMENTING

The program can make use of an automatic indexing feature by indirectly addressing any memory location from 00020 to 00037 (addresses are always octal numbers). Whenever one of these locations is specified by an indirect address, the processor retrieves its contents, increments or decrements the word retrieved, writes the altered word back into memory, and uses the altered word as the new address, direct or indirect. If the word is taken from locations 00020–00027, it is incremented by one; if taken from locations 00030–00037, it is decremented by one.

A.1 INSTRUCTION FORMATS

There are four basic formats for instruction words. In all but the arithmetic and logical instructions, Bit 0 is zero. If Bits 1 and 2 are also 0, Bits 3 and 4 specify the function (jump or modify memory) and the rest of the word supplies information for calculating the effective address. Bits 8 through 15 are the displacement, Bits 6 and 7 specify the index register if any, and Bit 5 indicates the type of addressing, direct or indirect.

ADDRESS TYPE

0 0 0	FUNCTION	\	INDEX	DISPLACEMENT
0	2 3	4 5 6	7 8	15

JUMP AND MODIFY MEMORY FORMAT

If Bits 1 and 2 differ they specify a move data function. Bits 3 and 4 address an accumulator, and the rest of the word is as above.

ADDRESS TYPE

0	FUNCTION 01 OR 10	AC ADDRESS	\	INDEX	DISPLACEMENT
0 1	2 3	4 5 6	7 8		15

MOVE DATA FORMAT

If Bits 1 and 2 are both 1, an in/out instruction is indicated. In this case the function is specified by Bits 5 through 9, of which Bits 5 through 7 indicate the direction of transfer and select one of three registers in the device. The transfer takes place between the accumulator addressed by Bits 3 and 4 and the device selected by Bits 10 through 15. Bits 8 and 9 of the function part specify an action to be performed, such as starting the deivce. If Bits 5 through 7 are all zero or all 1, there is no transfer and Bits 8 and 9 specify a control or skip function, respectively.

0 1 1	AC ADDRESS	FUNCTION TRANSFER	CONTROL	DEVICE CODE

| 0 | 2 3 | 4 5 | 7 8 | 9 10 | 15 |

IN/OUT FORMAT

If Bit 0 is 1, Bits 5 through 7 specify an arithmetic or logical function. One operand is taken from the accumulator addressed by Bits 1 and 2; a second operand, if any, from that addressed by Bits 3 and 4. The rest of the word specifies the other functions that can be performed, including whether or not the result is to be loaded into the destination accumulator.

1	AC SOURCE ADDRESS	AC DESTINA-TION ADDRESS	FUNCTION	SECONDARY FUNCTIONS ROTATE, SWAP, CARRY, NO LOAD, SKIP

| 0 1 | 2 3 | 4 5 | 7 8 | 15 |

ARITHMETIC AND LOGIC FORMAT

A.2 MEMORY

From the addressing point of view, the entire memory is a set of contiguous locations with addresses ranging from zero to a maximum dependent upon the capacity of the particular installation. In a system with the greatest possible capacity, the largest address is octal 77777 or decimal 32,767. But the memory is actually made up of a number of core memory modules, each with a capacity of 1024, 2048, 4096, or 8192 words, and can also contain read-only memory modules. The latter may be used for storage of pure (unalterable) programs and constants; they contain 256, 512, or 1024 words. The Supernova may also operate with semiconductor random access memory modules; these are available in units of 256, 512, and 1024 words. An address supplied by the program is actually decoded in two parts, the more significant to select a memory module and the less significant to select a location within that module, but this need not concern the programmer. From the point of view of the programmer, memory-module size is irrelevant, and read-only memory differs from the others only in that its contents cannot be altered electrically. Common arithmetic and in/out routines are available in standard read-only memory modules; others are available on a custom basis.

Memory Restrictions. The use of certain locations is defined by the hardware.

0–1	Program interrupt locations.
20–27	Autoincrementing locations.
30–37	Autodecrementing locations.

A.3 MEMORY REFERENCE INSTRUCTIONS

Bits 5 through 15 have the same format in every memory reference instruction whether the effective address is used for storage or retrieval of an operand or

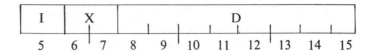

to alter program flow. Bit 5 is the indirect bit, Bits 6 and 7 are the index bits, and Bits 8 through 15 are the displacement. The effective address E of the instruction depends on the values of I, X, and D. If X is 00, D addresses one of the first 256 memory locations; that is, D is a memory address in the range 00000–00377. This group of locations is referred to as page zero.

If X is nonzero, D is a displacement that is used to produce a memory address by adding it to the contents of the register specified by X. The displacement is a signed binary integer in 2's complement notation. Bit 8 is the sign (0 positive, 1 negative), and the integer is in the octal range −200 to +177 (decimal −128 to +127). If X is 01, the instruction addresses a location relative to its own position; that is, D is added to the address in PC, which is the address of the instruction being executed. This is referred to as *relative addressing*. If X is 10 or 11 respectively, it selects AC2 or AC3 as a base register, to which D is added.

X	*Derivation of address*
00	Page zero addressing. D is an address in the range 00000–00377.
01	Relative addressing. D is a signed displacement (−200 to +177) that is added to the address in PC.
10	Base register addressing. D is a signed displacement (−200 to +177) that is added to the address in AC2.
11	Base register addressing. D is a signed displacement (−200 to +177) that is added to the address in AC3.

If I is 0, addressing is direct, and the address already determined from X and D is the effective address used in the execution of the instruction. Thus a memory reference instruction can directly address 1024 locations: 256 in page zero, and three sets of 256 in the octal range 200 less than to 177 greater than the address in PC, AC2 and AC3. If I is 1, addressing is indirect, and the processor retrieves another address from the location specified by the address

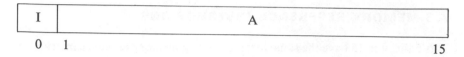

already determined. In this new word, Bit 0 is the indirect bit: Bits 1 through 15 are the effective address if bit 0 is 0; otherwise they specify a location for yet another level of address retrieval. This process continues until some referenced location is found with a zero in Bit 0; Bits 1 through 15 of this location are the effective address E.

If at any level in the effective address calculation an address word is fetched from locations 00020–00037, it is automatically incremented or decremented by 1, and the new value is both written back in memory and used either as the effective address or for the next step in the calculation depending on whether Bit 0 is zero or 1. Addresses taken from locations 00020–00027 are incremented, those from locations 00030–00037 are decremented.

The set of all addresses is cyclic with respect to the operations performed in an effective address calculation; regardless of the true sum or difference in any step, only the low-order 15 bits are used as an address. Hence the next address beyond 77777 is 00000 and the next below 00000 is 77777.

LDA   Load Accumulator

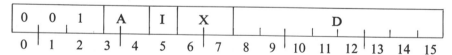

Load the contents of location E into accumulator A. The contents of E are unaffected and the original contents of A are lost.

STA   Store Accumulator

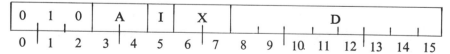

Store the contents of accumulator A in location E. The contents of A are unaffected and the original contents of E are lost.

ISZ   Increment and Skip if Zero

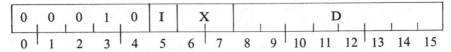

Add 1 to the contents of location E and place the result back in E. Skip the next instruction in sequence if the result is zero.

DSZ   Decrement and Skip if Zero

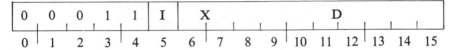

Subtract 1 from the contents of location E and place the result back in E. Skip the next instruction in sequence if the result is zero.

JMP   Jump

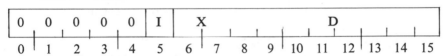

Load E into PC. Take the next instruction from location E and continue sequential operation from there.

JSR   Jump to Subroutine

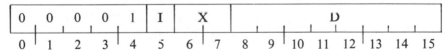

Load an address one greater than that in PC into AC3 (hence AC3 receives the address of the location following the JSR instruction). Load E into PC. Take the next instruction from location E and continue sequential operation from there.

A.4 ALU INSTRUCTIONS

A.4.1. Carry, Shift and Skip Functions

An instruction that has a 1 in Bit 0 performs one of 8 arithmetic and logical functions as specified by Bits 5 through 7 of the instruction word. The function, which may be anything from a simple move to a subtraction, always uses the contents of the accumulator specified by Bits 1 and 2; and if a second operand is required, it comes from the accumulator addressed by Bits 3 and 4.

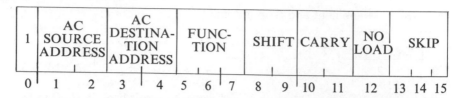

1	AC SOURCE ADDRESS	AC DESTINA- TION ADDRESS	FUNC- TION	SHIFT	CARRY	NO LOAD	SKIP
0	1 2	3 4	5 6 7	8 9	10 11	12	13 14 15

The instruction also supplies a carry bit to the shifter with the result. Bits 10 and 11 specify a base value to be used in determining the carry bit. The instruction supplies either this value or its complement depending upon both the function being performed and the result it generates. The mnemonics and bit configurations and the base values they select are as follows.

Mnemonic	Bits 10–11	Base value for carry bit
	00	Current state of carry.
Z	01	Zero.
O	10	One.
C	11	Complement of current state of carry.

The three logical functions simply supply the listed values as the carry bit to the shifter. The five arithmetic functions supply the complement of the base value if the operation produces a carry out of Bit 0; otherwise they supply the value given. The carry bit can be used in conjunction with the sign of the result to detect overflow in operations on signed numbers. But its primary use is as a carry out of the most significant bit in operations on unsigned numbers, such as the lower order parts in multiple precision arithmetic.

The 17-bit word consisting of the carry bit and the 16-bit result is operated on by the shifter as specified by Bits 8 and 9.

Mnemonic	Bits 8–9	Shift operation
	00	None.
L	01	Left rotate one place. Bit 0 is rotated into the carry position and the carry bit into Bit 15.

$$\boxed{C} \longleftarrow \boxed{0\text{--}15} \longleftarrow$$

| R | 10 | Right rotate one place. Bit 15 is rotated into the carry position and the carry bit into Bit 0. |

$$\boxed{C} \longrightarrow \boxed{0\text{--}15} \longrightarrow$$

S   11   Swap the halves of the 16-bit result. The carry bit is not affected.

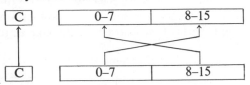

The 17-bit output of the shifter is loaded into carry and the accumulator addressed by Instruction Bits 3 and 4, provided Bit 12 is zero. A 1 programmed in Bit 12 inhibits the loading and prevents the instruction from affecting carry or the accumulator. Note that it is the shifted result that is loaded: AC receives the result of the function and carry the carry bit only if Bits 8 and 9 are zero.

The shifter output is also tested for a skip according to the condition specified by Bits 13–15. The processor skips the next instruction if the specified condition is satisfied.

Bit	*Effect of a 1 in the bit*
13	Selects the condition that the low-order 16 bits of the shifter output are all zero.
14	Selects the condition that the bit in the carry position of the shifter output is zero.
15	Inverts the conditions selected by Bits 13 and 14. In other words, a 1 in Bit 15 causes 1's in the other bits to select nonzero conditions.

The combined effects of Bits 13 through 15 taken together and the mnemonics for the various bit configurations are as follows.

Mnemonic	*Bits 13–15*	*Skip function*
	0	Never skip.
SKP	1	Always skip.
SZC	2	Skip on zero carry.
SNC	3	Skip on nonzero carry.
SZR	4	Skip on zero result.
SNR	5	Skip on nonzero result.
SEZ	6	Skip if either carry or result is zero.
SBN	7	Skip if both carry and result are nonzero.

A.4.2. Arithmetic and Logical Functions

The eight functions are selected by Bits 5 through 7 of the instruction word. For convenience, the source and destination accumulators addressed by the S and D parts of the instruction are referred to as ACS and ACD, respectively.

COM   Complement

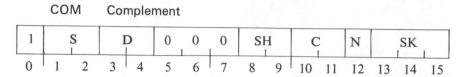

Place the (logical) complement of the word from ACS and place the carry bit specified by C in the shifter. Perform the shift operation specified by SH. Load the shifter output in carry and ACD unless N is 1. Skip the next instruction if the shifter output satisfies the condition specified by SK.

NEG   Negate

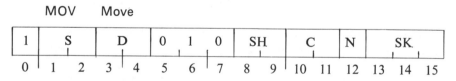

Place the 2's complement of the number from ACS into the shifter. If ACS contains zero, supply the complement of the value specified by C as the carry bit; otherwise supply the specified value. Perform the shift operation specified by SH. Load the shifter output in carry and ACD unless N is 1. Skip the next instruction if the shifter output satisfies the condition specified by SK.

MOV   Move

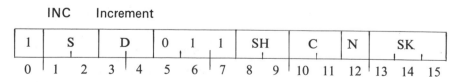

Place the contents of ACS and the carry bit specified by C in the shifter. Perform the shift operation specified by SH. Load the shifter output in carry and ACD unless N is 1. Skip the next instruction if the shifter output satisfies the condition specified by SK.

INC   Increment

Add 1 to the number from ACS and place the result in the shifter. If ACS contains $2^{16} - 1$ (signed $- 1$), supply the complement of the value specified by C as the carry bit; otherwise supply the specified value. Perform the shift operation specified by SH. Load the shifter output in carry and ACD unless N is 1. Skip the next instruction if the shifter output satisfies the condition specified by SK.

SUB   Subtract

1	S	D	1	0	1	SH	C	N	SK

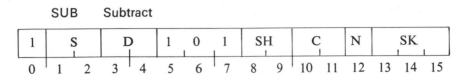

0   1   2   3   4   5   6   7   8   9   10 11 12 13 14 15

Subtract by adding the 2's complement of the number from ACS to the number from ACD, and place the result in the shifter. If ACD $\geq$ ACS (unsigned), supply the complement of the value specified by C as the carry bit; otherwise supply the specified value. Perform the shift operation specified by SH. Load the shifter output in carry and ACD unless N is 1. Skip the next instruction if the shifter output satisfies the condition specified by SK.

ADC   Add Complement

1	S	D	1	0	0	SH	C	N	SK

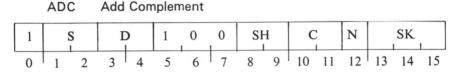

0   1   2   3   4   5   6   7   8   9   10 11 12 13 14 15

Add the (logical) complement of the number from ACS to the number from ACD, and place the result in the shifter. If ACD $>$ ACS (unsigned), supply the complement of the value specified by C as the carry bit; otherwise supply the specified value. Perform the shift operation specified by SH. Load the shifter output in carry and ACD unless N is 1. Skip the next instruction if the shifter output satisfies the condition specified by SK.

ADD   Add

1	S	D	1	1	0	SH	C	N	SK

0   1   2   3   4   5   6   7   8   9   10 11 12 13 14 15

Add the number from ACS to the number from ACD, and place the result in the shifter. If the unsigned sum is $\geq 2^{16}$, supply the complement of the value specified by C as the carry bit; otherwise supply the specified value. Perform the shift operation specified by SH. Load the shifter output in carry and ACD unless N is 1. Skip the next instruction if the shifter output satisfies the condition specified by SK.

(*Note*: For signed numbers the carry condition is that both summands are negative, or their signs differ and their magnitudes are equal or the positive one is the greater in magnitude.)

AND   And

1	S	D	1	1	1	SH	C	N	SK
0	1	2	3	4	5	6	7	8	9	10	11	12	13	14	15

Place the logical AND function of the word from ACS and the word from ACD in the shifter. Supply the value specified by C as the carry bit. Perform the shift operation specified by SH. Load the shifter output in carry and ACD unless N is 1. Skip the next instruction if the shifter output satisfies the condition specified by SK.

A.5 INPUT/OUTPUT

Instructions in the in/out class govern all transfers of data to and from the peripheral equipment, and also perform various operations within the processor. An instruction in this class is designated by 011 in Bits 0 through 2. Bits 10 through 15 select the device that is to respond to the instruction. The format thus allows for 64 codes of which 62 can be used to address devices (octal 01–76). The code 00 is not used, and 77 is used for a number of special functions including reading the console data switches and controlling the program interrupt.

Every device has a 6-bit device selection network, an *interrupt disable* flag, and *busy* and *done* flags. The selection network decodes Bits 10 through 15 of the instruction so that only the addressed device responds to signals sent by the processor over the in/out bus. The *busy* and *done* flags together denote the basic state of the device. When both are clear the device is idle. To place the device in operation, the program sets *busy*. If the device will be used for output, the program must give a data-out instruction that sends the first unit of data—a word or character depending on how the device handles information. (The word *output* used without qualification always refers to the transfer of data from the processor to the peripheral equipment; *input* refers to the transfer in the opposite direction.) When the device has processed a unit of data, it clears *busy* and sets *done* to indicate that it is ready to receive new data for output, or that it has data ready for input. In the former case the program would respond with a data-out instruction to send more data; in the latter with a data-in instruction to bring in the data that is ready. If the *interrupt disable* flag is clear, the setting of *done* signals the program by requesting an interrupt; if the program has set *interrupt disable*, then it must keep testing *done* or *busy* to determine when the device is ready.

In all in/out instructions, Bits 8 and 9 either control or sense *busy* and *done*. In those instructions in which Bits 8 and 9 specify a control function, the mnemonics and bit configurations and the functions they select are as follows.

Mnemonic	Bits 8–9	Control function
	00	None.
S	01	Start the device by clearing *done* and setting *busy*.
C	10	Clear both *busy* and *done*, idling the device.
P	11	Pulse the special in/out bus control line—the effect, if any, depends on the device.

The overall sequence of *busy* and *done* states is determined by both the program and the internal operation of the device.

NIO   No IO Transfer

0	1	1	0	0	0	0	0	F		D			
0	1	2	3	4	5	6	7	8	9	10	11	12	13	14	15

Perform the control function specified by F in Device D.

SKPBN   Skip if Busy is Nonzero

0	1	1	0	0	1	1	1	0	0		D			
0	1	2	3	4	5	6	7	8	9	10	11	12	13	14	15

Skip the next instruction in sequence if the *busy* flag in Device D is 1.

SKPBZ   Skip if Busy is Zero

0	1	1	0	0	1	1	1	0	1		D			
0	1	2	3	4	5	6	7	8	9	10	11	12	13	14	15

Skip the next instruction in sequence if the *busy* flag in Device D is 0.

SKPDN   Skip if Done is Nonzero

0	1	1	0	0	1	1	1	1	0		D			
0	1	2	3	4	5	6	7	8	9	10	11	12	13	14	15

Skip the next instruction in sequence if the *done* flag in Device D is 1.

SKPDZ   Skip if Done is Zero

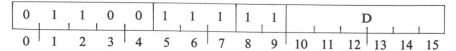

Skip the next instruction in sequence if the *done* flag in Device D is 0.

DIA   Data In A

Move the contents of the A-buffer in device D to Accumulator AC and perform the function specified by F in Device D.

DOA   Data Out A

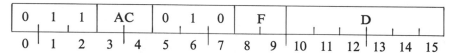

Send the contents of Accumulator AC to the A-buffer in device D and perform the function specified by F in Device D.

DIB   Data in B

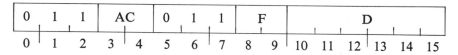

Move the contents of the B-buffer in device D to Accumulator AC and perform the function specified by F in Device D.

DOB   Data Out B

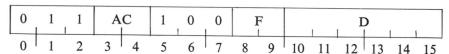

Send the contents of Accumulator AC to the B-buffer in device D and perform the function specified by F in Device D.

DIC   Data in C

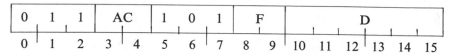

Move the contents of the C-buffer in device D to Accumulator AC and perform the function specified by F in Device D.

DOC   Data Out C

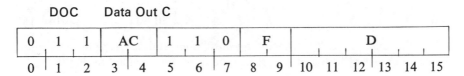

Send the contents of Accumulator AC to the C-buffer in Device D and perform the function specified by F in Device D.

NIOS CPU   Interrupt Enable

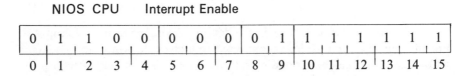

Set the *interrupt on* flag to allow the processor to respond to interrupt requests

DIB–,CPU   Interrupt Acknowledge

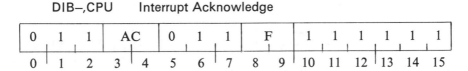

Place in AC Bits 10 through 15 the device code of the first device on the bus that is requesting an interrupt (*first* means the one that is physically closest to the processor on the bus). Perform the function specified by F.

NIOC CPU   Interrupt Disable

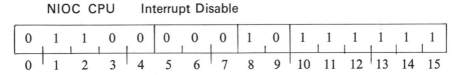

Clear the *interrupt on* flag to prevent the processor from responding to interrupt requests.

DIA–,CPU   Read Switches

0	1	1	AC	0	0	1	F	1	1	1	1	1	1
0	1	2	3	4	5	6	7	8	9	10	11	12	13	14	15

Read the contents of the console data switches into AC and perform the function specified by F.

DIC 0,CPU   Clear IO Devices

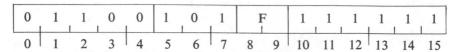

Clear the control flip-flops, including *busy, done* and *interrupt disable*, in all devices connected to the bus. Perform the function specified by F.

DOB–,CPU   Mask Out

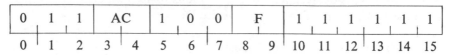

Set up the *interrupt disable* flags in the devices according to the mask in AC. For this purpose each device is connected to a given data line, and its flag is set or cleared as the corresponding bit in the mask is 1 or zero. Perform the function specified by F.

SKPBZ CPU   Skip if Interrupt On is Zero

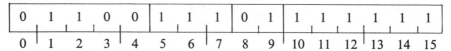

Skip the next instruction in sequence if *interrupt on* is 0.

SKPBN CPU   Skip if Interrupt On is Nonzero

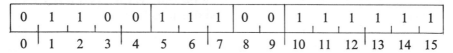

Skip the next instruction in sequence if *interrupt on* is 1.

SKPDZ CPU   Skip if Power Failure is Zero

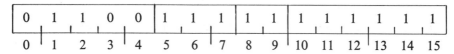

Skip the next instruction in sequence if the *power failure* flag is 0.

SKPDN CPU   Skip if Power Failure is Nonzero

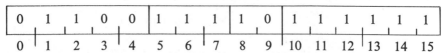

Skip the next instruction in sequence if the *power failure* flag is 1.

DOC 0,CPU   Halt

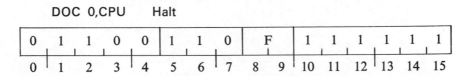

0	1	1	0	0	1	1	0	F	1	1	1	1	1	1
0	1	2	3	4	5	6	7	8	9	10	11	12	13	14	15

Perform the function specified by F and then halt the processor. When the processor stops, the instruction and data lights display the halt instruction, the address lights point to the location following the halt instruction.

APPENDIX B

The Microdata 1600

The appendix lists selected microinstructions of the Microdata 1600 with brief explanations of their uses. The appendix is intended as a guide for the examples presented in various chapters, especially Chap. 7. More details can be found in the manufacturer's literature.*

The r-field for all instructions is specified as follows.

FIELD DESTINATION REGISTER DESIGNATORS

BIT CONFIGURATION	DESIGNATOR	REGISTER DESIGNATED
000		None
001	T	T-Register
010	M	M-Register
011	N	N-Register
100	L	L-Register (Adds 200 ns)
101	K	K-Register (Adds 200 ns)
110	U	U-Register
111	S	U-Register; logical OR performed between the upper 8 bits of commands with opcodes 8 through F, and U-register.

*The material in this appendix is based on the *Microprogramming Handbook* and is reprinted with the permission of Microdata Corporation, Irvine, California.

B.1 EXECUTE COMMANDS*

The two EXECUTE commands are special commands that cause a logical OR to be performed between the U-Register and the 8 high-order bits of control memory output. The OR operation is performed before the command is gated into the R-register. The actual command executed is a combination of the bits in the U-register and those read out of control memory. The EXECUTE command is designated by zeros in the 4 high-order bits of the command in control memory. An effective command with zeros in these bits is a JUMP EXTENDED. The 12 remaining bits of the EXECUTE command can be coded as needed. The effect of the EXECUTE command can be obtained by coding destination-register 7 on operate commands.

EOT   Execute, Operate Type

0	f	C	* r

The 8-bit contents of the U-register are ORed with the 8 high-order bits of the command to form an effective command, which is then executed. The f-, C-, *, and r-fields are used as described for the desired effective command. In coding the C-field bits, any modifier may be used.

ELT   Execute, Literal Type

0	f	Literal

The 8-bit contents of the U-register are ORed with the 8 high-order bits of the command to form an effective command, which is then executed. The f- and literal fields are used as described for the desired effective command.

JE   Jump Extended

0	Address

The contents of the 12-bit address field are placed in the L-register. If an inhibit L-register save command has not been executed since the last JUMP EXTENDED, the following operation will also take place. The old contents of the L-register are stored in the L-save register or, when the L-save stack option is present, the L-register is stored in the 12 low-order bits of the current stack level and the contents of the control memory bank-select register are stored in the upper 3 bits of the current stack level. A JUMP EXTENDED command requires 400 ns to execute.

The JUMP EXTENDED command permits jumping anywhere within 4096 words of control memory in the basic machine. When the L-save stack

*Reprinted with permission of Microdata Corporation, Irvine, California.

and extended control memory options are included, this command controls jumping anywhere within the current selected 4096-word bank of control memory.

The JUMP EXTENDED command is assigned an operation code of zero and is a special form of the EXECUTE command which performs a logical OR between the contents of the U-register and the 8 high-order bits of the command. In order to obtain an operation code of zero in the R-register, the 4 high-order bits of the U-register must be set to zero. If desired, the 4 low-order bits of the U-register may be used to set Bits 8 through 11 of the L-register; otherwise they should also be set to zero.

B.2 LOAD ZERO INSTRUCTIONS*

B.2.1. General Format

LZ   Load Zero Control

10	Literal

The 8-bit literal field of the load-zero control command is used to specify combined operations of the load-zero group of generic instructions. If the literal field is 00, no operation (NOP) occurs. When multiple bits are specified, the designated control functions will execute.

This single command in a "vertical" sequence of microprogramming contains "horizontal" microprogramming characteristics, with the ability to perform multiple operations in a single 200-ns clock interval.

B.2.2. Examples

NOP   No Operation

1000

This command does not perform any operation and can be used to insert a delay of 200 ns.

RTN   Return

1020

The contents of the L-save register are placed in the L-register or, when the L-save stack option is present, the 12 low-order bits of the current stack level are placed in the L-register and the 3 high-order bits of the current stack level are placed in the control memory bank-select register. Execution requires

*Reprinted with permission of Microdata Corporation, Irvine, California.

600 ns and the inhibit L-save mode is cleared, if set, causing further JUMP EXTENDED commands to save the current contents of the L-register.

SPF   Select Primary File

This command causes the primary file of registers to be selected for further file-register operations. The primary file is also selected after a "power on" or by pressing the master reset on the front panel.

SSF   Select Secondary File

This command causes the secondary file of registers to be selected for further file-register operations. This set will remain selected until the execution of a SELECT PRIMARY FILE command or the occurrence of a master reset.

B.3 LOAD REGISTER INSTRUCTIONS*

LT   Load T

11	Literal

The contents of the 8-bit literal field are placed in the T-register. The condition flags and LINK are not affected.

LM   Load M

12	Literal

The contents of the 8-bit literal field are placed in the M-register at a time when the memory is not busy. The condition flags and LINK are not affected.

LN   Load N

13	Literal

The contents of the 8-bit literal field are placed in the N-register and the

*Reprinted with permission of Microdata Corporation, Irvine, California.

M-register is cleared at a time when the memory is not busy. The condition flags and LINK are not affected.

JP Jump

14 | 15 | 1C | 1D	Address

The contents of the 8-bit address field are placed in the 8 low-order bits of the L-register and Bits 8 and 11 of the command are placed in Bits 8 and 9 of the L-register, respectively. Bits 10 through 12 of the L-register and the optional control memory bank-select register remain unchanged. The location of the next command is the address specified by the new contents of the L-register. These jump commands provide for jumping within a 4-page block of 1024 words with starting address zero modulo 1024. The assembler selects the proper command code from the address, which must be in the 1024-word block containing the command. The command executes in 400 ns.

LU Load U

16	Literal

The contents of the 8-bit literal field are placed in the U-register. The condition flags and LINK are not affected. Due to the look-ahead access method of the control memory, the new contents of the U-register are not available for command modification during the machine cycle immediately following the LU command.

B.4 LOAD SEVEN INSTRUCTIONS*

B.4.1. General Format

17	Literal

The individual bits of the literal field control independent functions. Any number of bits in the literal field may be 1's.

B.4.2. Examples

DEI Disable External Interrupts

1704

The command causes the external interrupt system to be disabled.

*Reprinted with permission of Microdata Corporation, Irvine, California.

Interrupts are not lost when the interrupt system is disabled, but they cannot be recognized by the processor.

EEI   Enable External Interrupts

1708

The external interrupt system is enabled, allowing the processor to recognize external interrupts.

DRT   Disable Real-Time Clock

1710

The real-time clock and interrupt are disabled.

ERT   Enable Real-Time Clock

1720

The real-time clock and interrupt are enabled. The first interrupt will occur after a full interrupt interval.

HLT   Halt

1780

The processor is halted, stopping all microcommand execution. However, the direct memory access (DMA) channel, if activated, will continue its operation until completion.

B.5 VARIOUS CONTROL INSTRUCTIONS*

RLT   Return and Load T

19	Literal

This command combines the functions of Return (RTN) and Load T (LT) and executes in 600 ns.

MLC   Modify Lower Command

1A00

*Reprinted with permission of Microdata Corporation, Irvine, California.

This command performs the logical AND between the contents of the output data buffer and the 8 low-order bits of the next command accessed from the control memory. If the IC register is set to zero, the contents of the output data buffer will be the same as the T-register. If the IC register is not set to zero, the output data buffer will contain the value that was in the T-register at the time the IC register was set to a nonzero value.

ILS   Inhibit L-Save

1B00

This command inhibits the saving of the L-register in the L-save register or the saving of the bank-select register and the L-register in the current level of the L-save stack until the execution of a RETURN command.

ISP   Increment Stack Pointer

1B01

The contents of the 4-bit stack pointer register are incremented by 1 to select the next level in the stack for saving the contents of the L-register during the next JUMP EXTENDED. If the modified contents of the register are greater than 15, Bit 6 in File 0 will be set; otherwise it will be reset.

DSP   Decrement Stack Pointer

1B02

The contents of the 4-bit stack pointer register are decremented by 1 to select the previous level in the stack for a return operation. If the modified contents of the register are less than zero, Bit 6 in File 0 will be set; otherwise it will be reset.

B.6 FILE REGISTER INSTRUCTIONS*

LF   Load File Register

2	f	Literal

The contents of the 8-bit literal field are placed in the file register designated by f. Since File Register 0 is not used for general storage, it is not to be loaded by this command. The condition flags and LINK are not affected.

*Reprinted with permission of Microdata Corporation, Irvine, California.

AF   Add to File Register*

3	f	Literal

The contents of the 8-bit literal field are added to the contents of the file register designated by f. Since File Register 0 is not used for general storage, it is not altered by this command. Two's complement subtraction may be performed by placing the 2's complement of the operand in the literal field. The condition flags and LINK are not affected.

TZ   Test If Zero

4	f	Literal

If, for all the 1-bits in the literal field, the corresponding bits of the file register designated by f are zero, the next command is not executed. This command performs the logical product of the literal field and the contents of the file register and tests for zero result. The condition flags, LINK, and the designated file register are not affected.

TN   Test If Not Zero

5	f	Literal

If, for any 1-bit in the literal field, the corresponding bit of the file register designated by f is also a 1, the next command is not executed. This command performs a logical product of the literal field and the contents of file register and tests for a nonzero result. The condition flags, LINK, and the designated file register are not affected.

CP   Compare

6	f	Literal

If the sum of the contents of the literal field and the file register designated by f is greater than 255, the next command is not executed. The condition flags and the designated file register are not affected. The LINK stores the carry out of the adder. This means that if the skip is not taken, the content of LINK will be a zero; if the skip is taken, the content of LINK will be a 1.

*Reprinted with permission of Microdata Corporation, Irvine, California.

B.7 COMMAND SEVEN INSTRUCTIONS*

All forms of Command 7 unconditionally update the arithmetic condition codes in File 0 but do not affect the LINK. A destination register designation of 7 is undefined for these commands. In other words, the U-register may not be used to modify the command. All permissible variations of the basic Command 7 are explained.

The following four commands provide special data flow operations.

ESS   Enter Sense Switches

7	f	1	* r

The status of the 4 console sense switches, with 4 low-order 1's appended, are placed in the file register designated by f if * is zero and in the register designated by r. The status of a switch is a 1 when the switch is set.

SRF   Shift Right Four

7	f	2	* r

The 4 high-order bits of the file register designated by f are placed in the 4 low-order bits of that file if * is zero and in 4 low-order bits of the register designated by r. The 4 high-order bits of the result are set to 1's.

EIS   Enter Internal Status

7	f	4	* r

The 8 internal status bits are placed in the file register designated by f if * is zero and in the register designated by r. The internal interrupt flag in File 0 is reset by this command, along with the console interrupt, real-time clock, and power-fail/restart status bits. The console step flag is reset upon release of the console switch and spare bits are controlled according to their individual implementation in hardware.

ECS   Enter Console Switches

7070

A logical AND is performed between the contents of the 8 low-order console command switches and the 8 low-order bits of the next command. The value of a switch is a 1 when the switch is set. If the switch is either not

*Reprinted with permission of Microdata Corporation, Irvine, California.

set or, as in the case of a basic panel, is not there, its value is a zero. File Register 0 and destination register 0 must be selected because data movement is not permitted.

The command could be used to implement 8 additional sense switches. This is done by following the ENTER CONSOLE SWITCHES command with a LOAD REGISTER or LOAD FILE command that has a literal value of all 1's.

B.8 I/O INSTRUCTIONS*

CIO   Clear I/O

7	f	8	* r

A value of zero is placed in the I/O control register (IC), which removes all control signals from the I/O bus. This places the bus in the no-activity mode. All standard Microdata peripheral controllers require the K-register to return to the zero state after each nonzero setting. When the current contents of the IC register are 0, 1, 2, or 3, the file register designated by f is moved to the register designated by r. When the current contents of the IC Register are 4, 5, 6, or 7, a logical AND is performed between the contents of the input bus and the file register designated by f. The result is placed in the file register if * is zero and in the register designated by r.

COX   Control Output

7	f	9	* r

A value of 1 is placed in the IC register, which enables the control output signal until it is removed by a CLEAR I/O command. The contents of the file register designated by f are moved to the register designated by r.

DOX   Data Output

7	f	A	* r

A value of 2 is placed in the IC register, which enables the data output signal until it is removed by a CLEAR I/O command. The contents of the file register designated by f are moved to the register designated by r.

IAK   Interrupt Acknowledge

7	f	D	* r

*Reprinted with permission of Microdata Corporation, Irvine, California.

A value of 5 is placed in the IC register, which enables the interrupt acknowledge signal until it is removed by a CLEAR I/O command. Upon removal of this signal, the requesting controller will reset the external interrupt request flag bit in File 0. The contents of the file register designated by f are moved to the register designated by r.

DIX   Data Input

7	f	E	* r

A value of 6 is placed in the IC register, which enables the data input signal until it is removed by a CLEAR I/O command. The contents of the file register designated by f are moved to the register designated by r.

B.9 ARITHMETIC INSTRUCTIONS*

For these instructions, the following modifiers apply.

T   *Select T:* The contents of the T-register or the input bus are selected as the B-bus operand. If this bit is off, the operand is zero.

C   *Condition Flag Update:* The condition flags are updated according to the result of the current operation.

*   *File Write Inhibit:* The result is not placed in the file register designated by f.

ADD   Add

8	f	LITC	* r

The sum of the contents of the file register designated by f and the selected operand is formed. The sum is placed in the file register if * is zero and in the register designated by r. The state of the carry out of the high-order bit position of the adder is placed in LINK. The modifier bits perform the following control.

L   *Link Control:* The content of LINK is added to the sum. When this flag is a 1, the zero-condition flag can be reset but not set. This allows for propagation of the zero test over multiple byte operations, the first of which would have this bit off.

I   *Increment:* One is added to the sum.

SBT   Subtract (2's Complement)

9	f	L0TC	* r

*Reprinted with permission of Microdata Corporation, Irvine, California.

The 2's complement difference of the contents of the file register designated by f and the selected operand is formed. The difference is placed in the file register if * is zero and in the register designated by r. The state of the carry out of the high-order bit position of the adder is placed in LINK. The modifier bits perform the following control.

L *Link Control:* The content of LINK is added to the 1's complement difference. When this flag is a 1, the zero-condition flag can be reset but not set. This allows for propagation of the zero test over multiple byte operations, the first of which would have this bit off.

SBO   Subtract (1's Complement)*

9	f	L1TC	* r

The 1's complement difference of the contents of the file register designated by f and the selected operand is formed. The difference is placed in the file register if * is zero and in the register designated by r. The state of the carry out of the high-order bit position of the adder is placed in LINK The modifier bits perform the following control.

L *Link Control:* The content of LINK is added to the difference. When this flag is 1, the zero-condition flag can be reset but not set. This allows for propagation of the zero test over multiple byte operations, the first of which could have this bit off.

DEC   Decrement

9	f	010C	* r

The contents of the file register designated by f are decremented by 1 and the result is placed in the file register if * is zero and in the register designated by r. The state of the carry out of the high-order bit position of the adder is placed in LINK.

INC   Increment

8	f	010C	* r

This command is a form of the ADD command. The contents of the file register designated by f are incremented by 1 and the result is placed in the file register if * is zero and in the register designated by r. The state of the carry out of the high-order bit position of the adder is placed in LINK.

*Reprinted with permission of Microdata Corporation, Irvine, California.

ZOF   Zero File*

| B | f | 000C | * r |

A value of zero is placed in the file register designated by f if * is zero and in the register designated by r. The LINK is not affected.

POF   Plus One to File

| B | f | 010C | * r |

A value of $+1$ is placed in the file register designated by f if * is zero and in the resister designated by r. The LINK is not affected.

CPY   Copy

| B | f | LITC | * r |

The selected operand is placed in the file register designated by f if * is zero and in the register designated by r. The LINK is not affected.

L   *Link Control:* The content of LINK is added to the operand. When this bit is a 1, the zero-condition flag can be reset but not set. This allows for propagation of the zero test over multiple byte operations, the first of which would have this bit off.

I   *Increment:* One is added to the operand.

B.10 MEMORY REFERENCE

B.10.1. First Phase: Common to All Memory Reference Instructions

The contents of the file register designated by f in unaltered, incremented, or decremented form as determined by *m* are placed in the file register if * is zero and in the register designated by r. The condition flags and LINK are not affected.

m

No flag 00   The contents of the selected file register are transferred unaltered to the specified destination register.

D   01   *Decremented:* The contents of the file register minus 1 are routed as specified unless the M-register is specified to receive the result. When the M-register is selected, the contents of the file register, minus 1, plus the content of LINK are routed.

L   10   *Add Link:* The content of LINK is added to the contents of the file register and the sum is routed as specified.

I   11   *Increment:* The contents of the file register are incremented by 1 and the result is routed as specified.

*Reprinted with permission of Microdata Corporation, Irvine, California.

B.10.2. Second Phase:

RMF   Read Memory, Full Cycle*

A	f	m00	* r

A full-cycle memory read is initiated at the location specified by the contents of the M- and N-registers. Command execution is delayed if the memory is busy when the command is accessed. The T-register is set to zero and the accessed data is placed into it 400 ns after the command is executed. The addressed memory location is left unaltered.

RMH   Read Memory, Half Cycle

A	f	m10	* r

A half-cycle memory read is initiated at the location specified by the contents of the M- and N-registers. Command execution is delayed if the memory is busy when the command is accessed. The T-register is set to zero and the accessed data is placed into it 400 ns after the command is executed. The memory location is left in an all 1's condition.

WMF   Write Memory, Full Cycle

A	f	m01	* r

A full-cycle memory write operation is initiated at the location specified by the contents of the M- and N registers. Command execution is delayed if the memory is busy when the command is accessed.

The data to be written must be in the T-register at the time the command is executed or must be entered into the T-register with the next command. The T-register may be used for other purposes with the second command after the WMF.

WMH   Write Memory, Half Cycle

A	f	m11	* r

A half-cycle memory write operation is initiated at the location specified by the contents of the M- and N-registers. Command execution is delayed if the memory is busy when the command is accessed. The data to be written must be in the T-register when the command is executed. The contents of the addressed memory location must be all 1's for a proper write to take place, because a logical AND is performed between the original contents of the

*Reprinted with permission of Microdata Corporation, Irvine, California.

memory location and the contents of the T-register. The T-register may be used for other purposes with the first command after WMH.

B.11 LOGICAL INSTRUCTIONS*

The result of the specified logical operation between the contents of the file register designated by f and the selected operand is placed in the file register if * is zero and in the register designated by r. The LINK is not affected. The 5 modifier bits perform the following control.

L   *Link Control:* When this bit is a 1, the zero-condition flag can be reset but not set. This allows for propagation of the zero test over multiple byte operations, the first of which would have this bit off.

F   *Select T-Complement:* The 1's complement of the contents of the T-register or input bus are selected as the B-bus operand. If the T-register is also selected, the effective operand contains all 1's.

T   *Select T:* The contents of the T-register or the input bus are selected as the B-bus operand. If both the T- and F-bits are off, the selected operand is zero.

C   *Condition Flag Update:* The condition flags are updated according to the result of the current operation.

*   *File Write Inhibit:* The result of the operation is not placed in the file register.

AND   And

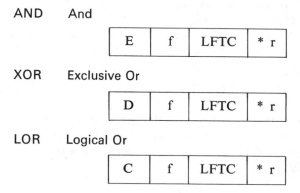

| E | f | LFTC | * r |

XOR   Exclusive Or

| D | f | LFTC | * r |

LOR   Logical Or

| C | f | LFTC | * r |

For the following instructions, the 3 modifier bits perform the following control.

L   *Link Control:* The LINK content is shifted into the low-order bit of the result. When this bit is a 1 the zero-condition flag can be reset but not set. This allows for propagation of zero test over multiple byte operations, the first of which would have this bit off.

C   *Condition Flag Update:* The condition flags are updated according to the result of the current operation.

*   *File Write Inhibit:* The shifted register contents are not placed in the file register.

*Reprinted with permission of Microdata Corporation, Irvine, California.

MOV   Move*

C	f	L00C	* r

The contents of the file register designated by f are moved to the register designated by r. The LINK is not affected.

SFL   Shift Left

F	f	L00C	* r

The contents of the file register designated by f are shifted 1 bit position to the left and placed in the file register if * is zero and in the register designated by r. The high-order bit which is shifted out is placed in LINK. A zero or the content of LINK is shifted into the vacated bit position as determined by the L-modifier bit.

SFR   Shift Right

F	f	L01C	* r

The contents of the file register designated by f are shifted 1 bit position to the right and placed in the file register if * is zero and in the register designated by r. A zero or the content of LINK is shifted into the vacated bit position as determined by the L-modifier bit. The low-order bit which is shifted out is placed in LINK.

SRI   Shift Right and Insert

F	f	011C	* r

The contents of the file register designated by f are shifted 1 bit position to the right and placed in the file register if * is zero and in the register designated by r. A 1 is inserted into the vacated high-order bit position. The low-order bit which is shifted out is placed in LINK.

SLI   Shift Left and Insert

F	f	010C	* r

The contents of the file register designated by f are shifted 1 bit position to the left and placed in the file register if * is zero and in the register designated by r. The high-order bit which is shifted out is placed in LINK. A 1 is inserted in the vacated low-order bit position.

*Reprinted with permission of Microdata Corporation, Irvine, California.

B.12 MICROASSEMBLER SYNTAX*

The microinstructions have one of the following formats.

LITERAL COMMANDS:
> OPCODE   file register, literal
>
> OPCODE   literal

OPERATE COMMANDS:
> OPCODE   file register, modifier, destination register

GENERIC COMMAND:
> OPCODE

B.12.1. OPCODE

OPCODE is a mnemonic as specified in the preceding sections. If followed by *, it indicates that the modifier bit * is on.

EXAMPLES:
> ADD
>
> SRF*
>
> INC

B.12.2. File Number

The file number is a number between 0 and 15. This field can be a decimal constant or a label.

EXAMPLES:

	AF	2, X'00'
TWO	EQU	2
	AF	TWO, X'00'

B.12.3. Literal

The literal is a hexadecimal or a decimal constant.

EXAMPLES:
> 10
>
> 3
>
> X'1A'
>
> X'05'

*Reprinted with permission of Microdata Corporation, Irvine, California.

B.12.4. Modifier*

The modifier field consists of several coded characters indicating the binary value of the C-field, as follows.

Code	Definition	Binary value
C	Modify condition code.	0001
T	Select T.	0010
F	Select T-complement.	0100
I	Increment.	0100
D	Decrement.	0100
L	Link control.	1000

EXAMPLES:

CT	0011
LI	1100

B.12.5. Destination Register

This field specifies the destination register for the result of the operation as follows.

(T)	T-register
(M)	M-register
(N)	N-register
(L)	L-register (even)
(K)	L-register (odd)
(U)	U-register
(S)	OR U with command

EXAMPLES:

ADD   2, IT, (T)

will select T, increment it, add contents of File 2 and store the result in T and in File 2.

ADD*   2, IT, (T)

will do the same operations, but the result goes into T only.

ADD   2, T, (M)

adds the contents of File 2 and the contents of T and stores the sum in M and in File 2.

*Reprinted with permission of Microdata Corporation, Irvine, California.

APPENDIX C

Nova* Emulator

```
LOCN CODE FLAGS LABELS OP *    OPERANDS    COMMENTS                        PAGE   1
                        *
                        *
                        *                   NOVA EMULATOR
                        *                   ON MICRODATA 1600/30
                        *
                        *
          0000  F0      EQU  0              MICRODATA CONDITION FLAGS.
          0001  F1      EQU  1              (BIT 1) CARRY BIT.
          0002  IU      EQU  2              UPPER BYTE OF INST. REG..
          0003  IL      EQU  3              LOWER BYTE OF INST. REG..
          0004  LL      EQU  4              LOWER BYTE OF PROGRAM COUNTER.
          0005  LU      EQU  5              UPPER BYTE OF PROGRAM COUNTER.
          0006  A0L     EQU  6              LOWER BYTE OF AC0.
          0007  A0U     EQU  7              UPPER BYTE OF AC0.
          0008  A1L     EQU  8              LOWER BYTE OF AC1.
          0009  A1U     EQU  9              UPPER BYTE OF AC1.
          000A  A2L     EQU  10             LOWER BYTE OF AC2.
          000B  A2U     EQU  11             UPPER BYTE OF AC2.
          000C  A3L     EQU  12             LOWER BYTE OF AC3.
          000D  A3U     EQU  13             UPPER BYTE OF AC3.
          000E  OL      EQU  14             LOWER BYTE OF OPERAND REG..
          000F  OU      EQU  15             UPPER BYTE OF OPERAND REG..
                        *
                        *  INITIALIZATION:-
                        *
0000 113C               LT   X'3C'          * SILENT 700 DATA TERMINAL BAUD RATE CONTROL.
0001 0189               JE   COX
0002 1103               LT   X'03'          * SET BAUD RATE TO 300 BPS.
0003 0192               JE   DOX
0004 115C               LT   X'5C'          * SILENT 700 DATA TERMINAL CHARACTER FORMAT CONTROL.
0005 0189               JE   COX
0006 1112               LT   X'12'          * CHARACTER FORMAT SETTING: EVEN PARITY,
0007 0192               JE   DOX            * 1 STOP BIT, 8 BITS CHARACTER LENGTH.
```

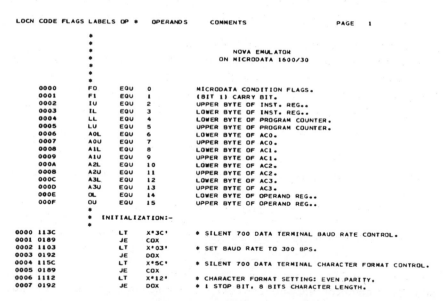

Appendix C Nova Emulator Microprogram

*Nova is a registered trademark of Data General Corporation, Southboro, Mass.

```
0008 113C        LT    X'3C'       * PAPER TAPE READER BAUD RATE CONTROL.
0009 0189        JE    COX
000A 1164        LT    X'64'       * SET BAUD RATE TO 1200 BPS.
000B 0192        JE    DOX
000C 115C        LT    X'5C'       * PAPER TAPE READER CHARACTER FORMAT CONTROL.
000D 0189        JE    COX
000E 1172        LT    X'72'       * CHARACTER FORMAT SETTING : EVEN PARITY, 1 STOP BIT,
000F 0192        JE    DOX         *                            8 BITS CHARACTER LENGTH.
0010 117C        LT    X'7C'       * SET' PAPER TAPE READER DATA READY MASK.
0011 0189        JE    COX
0012 1162        LT    X'62'
0013 0192        JE    DOX
0014 11FC        LT    X'FC'       * SET DATA TERMINAL READY CONTROL.
0015 0189        JE    COX
0016 1101        LT    X'01'
0017 0192        JE    DOX
0018 119C        LT    X'9C'       * ARM THE ASYNCHRONOUS MODEM INTERFACE INTERRUPT.
0019 0189        JE    COX
001A 018E        JE    DIX
001B 1708        EEI               * PROCESSOR INTERRUPT ENABLE.
001C 1080        SSF               * EMULATED SYSTEM (NOVA) INITIALIZATION:
001D 21B2        LF    1,X'B2'     * CLEAR ALL DEVICES' CONTROL FLAGS,  AND INTERRUPT
001E 028F        JE    CLEAR       * DISABLE FLAGS.
```

LOCN CODE FLAGS LABELS OP * OPERANDS   COMMENTS   PAGE 2

```
001F 2108        LF    F1,X'08'    * LOAD THE STARTING ADDRESS INTO PC COUNTER THROUGH
0020 2F04        LF    OU,X'04'    * KEY BOARD INPUT.
0021 1D5C        JP    ECP
            *
            * FETCH NOVA INST. FROM MEMORY AND STORE IN INST. REG..
            * THIS REQIRES 2 MEMORY READS.
0022 C401  FET   MOV   LL,(T)      * THE CONTENTS OF PROGRAM COUNTER ARE MOVED TO
0023 BE20        CPY   OL,T        * OPERAND REG..
0024 C501        MOV   LU,(T)
0025 BF20        CPY   OU,T
0026 002F        JE    MAP         * CALL SUBROUTINE MAP.
0027 A000        RMF   FO          * LOAD THE LOWER BYTE OF NOVA INST. IN IL REG..
0028 B320        CPY   IL,T
0029 CE03        MOV   OL,(N)      * LOAD THE UPPER BYTE OF NOVA INST. IN IU REG..
002A AF02        RMF   OU,(M)
002B B220        CPY   IU,T
            *
            * INST. CLASS SEPARATION : INST. SET WITH MEMORY REFERENCE(I.E.  JMP,
            * STA, LDA ETC.), ONE WITHOUT (I.E. INPUT/OUTPUT INST., ARITH. AND LOGIC
            * INST.. THE OP. CODE OF THOSE INST. IS GREAT THAN 3.),
            * AND JUMP TO THE DESIGNATED SUBROUTINE.
002C 62A0        CP    IU,X'A0'    * SKIP; IF OP. CODE <3.
002D 1434        JP    MRE         * ELSE GO TO MRE ROUTINE.
002E 14A8        JP    IOA         * CONTINUE AT IOA ROUTINE.
            *
            * MEMORY MAPPING: NOVA'S MEMORY IMAGE TO BE MAPPED TO MICRODATA'S MEMORY.
            *
002F FE00  MAP   SFL   OL          * OPERAND REG. CONTAINS THE NOVA INST. ADDRESS.
0030 FF80        SFL   OU,L        * ACCORDING TO THE MEMORY MAPPING EQUATION:
0031 8E4B        INC*  OL,(N)      * THE CORRESPONDING MICRODATA MEMORY LOCATION =
0032 8F8A        ADD*  OU,L,(M)    * ( OPERAND REG. )*2.
0033 1020        RTN               * LOAD THE LOWER BYTE NOVA INST. ADDRESS IN M,N REG..
            *
            * MEMORY REFERENCE INST. DECODING AND OPERAND ADDRESS CALCULATION.
            * (PAGE ZERO, RELATIVE, OR BASE REG. ADDRESSING.)
            *
0034 2F00  MRE   LF    OU,X'00'    * CLEAR OU REG..
0035 C301        MOV   IL,(T)
0036 BE20        CPY   OL,T        * LOAD THE LOWER BYTE NOVA INST. INTO OL REG..
0037 5203        TN    IU,X'03'    * SKIP, IF RELATIVE OR BASE REG. ADDRESSING.
0038 144A        JP    DID         * ELSE GO TO DID ROUTINE(PAGE ZERO ADDRESSING).
            *
            * ADDRESS CALCULATION FOR RELATIVE AND BASE REG. ADDRESSING.
            *
0039 4380        TZ    IL,X'80'    * CHECK DISPLACEMENT SIGN BIT. POSITIVE INTERGER?
003A CF60        LOR   OU,T,F      * NO, EXTEND DISPLACEMENT SIGN BIT TO OU REG..
003B 1103        LT    X'03'       * DISTINGUISH THE TYPE OF ADDRESSING (BASE OR RELATIVE)
003C E229        AND*  IU,T,(T)    * AND LOAD  THE INDEX IN IL REG..
003D B320        CPY   IL,T
003E F300        SFL   IL          * INDEX REG. MAPPING.
003F 33C2        AF    IL,X'C2'
0040 4202        TZ    IU,X'02'    * RELATIVE ADDRESSING ?
0041 3304        AF    IL,X'04'    * NO, BASE ADDRESSING.
0042 C306        MOV   IL,(U)      * COPY  THE CONTENTS OF THE SPECIFIED INDEX REG. TO
0043 0001        ELT*  FO,X'01'    * OPERAND REG..
```

LOCN CODE FLAGS LABELS OP * OPERANDS   COMMENTS   PAGE 3

```
0044 8E20        ADD   OL,T
0045 0101        ELT*  F1,X'01'
0046 8FA0        ADD   OU,L,T
0047 1600        LU    X'00'
0048 117F        LT    X'7F'
0049 EF20        AND   OU,T
            *
```

Appendix C (continued)

```
                 *  EFFECTIVE ADDRESS CALCULATION. (DIRECT, INDIRECT, OR AUTO INCREMENT/DECREMENT
                 *  ADDRESSING )
                 *  ADDRESS CALCULATION FOR PAGE ZERO OR AUTO INCREMENT/DECREMENT ADDRESSING.
                 *
004A  5204   DID   TN    IU.X'04'       * SKIP, IF INDIRECT ADDRESSING.
004B  1471         JP    SEP            * ELSE GO TO SEP ROUTINE(DIRECT ADDRESSING).
004C  4F7F   CKR   TZ    OU.X'7F'       * YES, CHECK FOR AUTO INCREMENT/DECREMENT ADDRESSING.
004D  146A         JP    IDT            * (WHETHER THE MEMORY LOCATION IS IN THE RANGE OF 20-37)
004E  4EE0         TZ    OL.X'E0'
004F  146A         JP    IDT
0050  5E10         TN    OL.X'10'
0051  146A         JP    IDT
0052  2380         LF    IL.X'80'       * MANIPULATION OF AUTO INCREMENT/DECREMENT ADDRESSING.
0053  4E08         TZ    OL.X'08'       * SET INCREMENT/DECREMENT INDEX IN IL REG.
0054  2390         LF    IL.X'90'
0055  002F         JE    MAP            * MEMORY MAPPING.
0056  005C         JE    MID            * ADDRESS CALCULATION.
0057  4F60   OVK   TZ    OU.X'60'       * TRANSFER TO OVF ROUTINE
0058  15E0         JP    OVF            * IF MEMORY OVERFLOW OCCURS.
0059  5F80   REP   TN    OU.X'80'       * SKIP, IF INDIRECT ADDRESSING.
005A  1471         JP    SEP            * ELSE GO TO SEP ROUTINE.
005B  144C         JP    CKR            * CONTINUE AT CKR ROUTINE.
                 *
                 *  MEMORY CONTENTS INCREMENT OR DECREMENT SUBROUTINE.
                 *
005C  C306   MID   MOV   IL.(U)         * IL REG. CONTAINS THE INCR./DECR. INDEX CODE .
005D  A020         RMH   FO             * RETRIEVE THE CONTENTS OF THE SPECIFIED MEMORY
005E  8320         CPY   IL.T           * LOCATION (20-37) AND INCR. OR DECR. THE WORD
005F  0351         ELT   IL.X'51'       * RETRIEVED. THEN WRITE THE ALTERED WORD BACK INTO THE
0060  A030         WMH   FO             * SAME LOCATION.
0061  CE03         MOV   OL.(N)
0062  BE20         CPY   OL.T
0063  AF22         RMH   OU.(N)
0064  B320         CPY   IL.T
0065  0391         ELT   IL.X'91'
0066  A030         WMH   FO
0067  BF20         CPY   OU.T
0068  1600         LU    X'00'
0069  1020         RTN
                 *
                 *  ADDRESS CALCULATION FOR DIRECT OR INDIRECT ADDRESSING.
                 *
006A  002F   IDT   JE    MAP            * MEMORY MAPPING AND RETRIEVE THE LOWER AND UPPER
006B  A000         RMF   FO             * BYTE OF NOVA ADDRESS WORD FROM MEMORY AND LOAD
006C  CE03         MOV   OL.(N)         * THEM IN OPERAND REG..
006D  BE20         CPY   OL.T
006E  AF02         RMF   OU.(N)
006F  BF20         CPY   OU.T
0070  1457         JP    OVK            * TEST MEMORY OVERFLOW.
                 *


     LOCN CODE FLAGS LABELS OP *   OPERANDS      COMMENTS                PAGE   4

                 *  MEMORY REF. INST. DECODING. (LDA, STA, JMP, JSR, ISZ, DSZ.)
                 *
0071  4260   SEP   TZ    IU.X'60'       * SKIP, IF MEMORY REF. WITHOUT ACC.
0072  1474         JP    LST            * ELSE GO TO LST ROUTINE.
0073  1491         JP    JID            * CONTINUE AT JID ROUTINE.
                 *
                 *  MEMORY REF. WITH ACCUMULATOR INST. DECODING.
                 *
0074  1118   LST   LT    X'18'          * EXTRACT  THE ACC. ADDRESS FROM NOVA INST. AND
0075  E229         AND*  IU.T.(T)       * LOAD IT IN IL REG..
0076  8320         CPY   IL.T           * REG. MAPPING
0077  F320         SFR   IL
0078  F320         SFR   IL
0079  002F         JE    MAP            * MEMORY MAPPING.
007A  4240         TZ    IU.X'40'       * SKIP, IF LDA INST..
007B  1484         JP    STA            * ELSE GO TO STA ROUTINE.
                 *
                 *  LDA INSTRUCTION EXECUTIVE ROUTINE.
                 *
007C  A000         RMF   FO             * LDA INST. EXECUTION.
007D  33B6         AF    IL.X'86'       * LOAD DATA FROM MEMORY TO THE SPECIFIED ACC..
007E  C306         MOV   IL.(U)
007F  0020         ELT   FO.X'20'
0080  CE03         MOV   OL.(N)
0081  AF02         RMF   OU.(N)
0082  0120         ELT   F1.X'20'
0083  148E         JP    LUP
                 *
                 *  STA INSTRUCTION EXECUTIVE ROUTINE.
                 *
0084  33C6   STA   AF    IL.X'C6'       * STORE DATA FROM THE SPECIFIED ACC. INTO MEMORY.
0085  C306         MOV   IL.(U)
0086  0001         ELT   FO.X'01'
0087  A010         WMF   FO
0088  CE03         MOV   OL.(N)
0089  0101         ELT   F1.X'01'
008A  AF12         WMF   OU.(N)
008B  148E         JP    LUP
                 *
```

Appendix C (continued)

```
                  *  PC COUNTER UPDATING.
                  *
008C 8440   SKP   INC   LL           *  INCREMENT PC COUNTER BY 2
008D 8580         ADD   LU,L         *  IF SKIP OPERATION.
008E 8440   LUP   INC   LL           *  ELSE INCREMENT BY 1.
008F 8580         ADD   LU,L
0090 15A4         JP    INT
                  *
                  *  MEMORY REF. WITHOUT ACCUMULATOR INST. DECODING.
                  *  JMP AND JSR INST. DECODING AND EXECUTION.
                  *
0091 4210   JID   TZ    IU,X'10'     *  MODIFY MEMORY INST. ?
0092 14A0         JP    IDS          *  YES. JUMP TO IDS ROUTINE.
0093 5208         TN    IU,X'08'     *  JSR INST. ?
0094 149B         JP    JMP          *  NO. JUMP TO JUMP ROUTINE.
0095 8449         INC*  LL,(T)       *  JSR INST. EXECUTION.
0096 BC20         CPY   A3L,T        *  PLACE THE  RETURN ADDRESS INTO ACC 3.
0097 8589         ADD*  LU,L,(T)
```

```
0098 BD20         CPY   A3U,T
0099 117F         LT    X'7F'        *  ENSURE 15-BIT EFFECTIVE ADDRESS.
009A ED20         AND   A3U,T
009B CE01   JMP   MOV   OL,(T)       *  MOVE THE OPERAND ADDRESS TO PC COUNTER.
009C B420         CPY   LL,T
009D CF01         MOV   OU,(T)
009E B520         CPY   LU,T
009F 15A4         JP    INT
00A0 2380   IDS   LF    IU,X'80'     *  MODIFY MEMORY INST. DECODING AND EXECUTION.
00A1 4208         TZ    IU,X'08'     *  SET ISZ/DSZ INDEX  CODE IN IL REG..
00A2 2390         LF    IL,X'90'
00A3 002F         JE    MAP          *  MEMORY MAPPING.
00A4 005C         JE    MID          *  MEMORY CONTENTS INCREMENT/DECREMENT.
00A5 5004         TN    F0,X'04'     *  RESULT=0 ?
00A6 148E         JP    LUP          *  NO. GO TO LUP.
00A7 148C         JP    SKP          *  YES. GO TO SKP.
                  *
                  *  NON MEMORY REF. INST. DECODING.
                  *  ARITHMETIC & LOGICAL INST. DECODING.
                  *
00A8 5280   IOA   TN    IU,X'80'     *  ARITH. AND LOGIC INST. ?
00A9 155A         JP    IOI          *  NO. JUMP TO I/O ROUTINE.
00AA F120         SFR   F1           *  LOAD CARRY BIT INTO A TEMPORARY LOCATION
00AB 5101         TN    F1,X'01'     *  (BIT 0 OF FILE REG. 1).
00AC 14E0         JP    CRS
00AD F140         SLI   F1
00AE 5330   CCR   TN    IL,X'30'     *  C BIT INITIATE.
00AF 148C         JP    ACD          *  USE CURRENT C BIT STATE.
00B0 2E01         LF    OL,X'01'     *  SET UP MODIFIER IN OL AND OU REG. ACCORDING TO
00B1 2FC1         LF    OU,X'C1'     *  C BIT = Z EXECUTE AND MICRO INST.
00B2 5310         TN    IL,X'10'     *            O EXECUTE LOR MICRO INST.
00B3 14B9         JP    SEC          *            C EXECUTE XOR MICRO INST.
00B4 3F10         AF    OU,X'10'
00B5 4320         TZ    IL,X'20'
00B6 14B9         JP    SEC
00B7 2EFE         LF    OL,X'FE'
00B8 3F10         AF    OU,X'10'
00B9 CF06   SEC   MOV   OU,(U)       *  UPDATE TEMPORARY CARRY BIT.
00BA CE01         MOV   OL,(T)
00BB 0020         ELT   F0,X'20'
00BC 2E60   ACD   LF    OL,X'60'     *  EXTRACT  ACC SOURCE ADDRESS AND PLACE IN OL REG..
00BD C201         MOV   IU,(T)
00BE EE20         AND   OL,T
00BF 7E20         SRF   OL
00C0 3E10         AF    OL,X'10'
00C1 2F18         LF    OU,X'18'     *  EXTRACT ACC DESTINATION ADDRESS AND PLACE IN OU REG..
00C2 EF20         AND   OU,T
00C3 FF20         SFR   OU
00C4 FF20         SFR   OU
                  *
                  *  FUNCTION DECODING.
                  *
00C5 3EC6         AF    OL,X'C6'     *  ACC ADDRESS MAPPING.
00C6 CE06         MOV   OL,(U)       *  MOVE THE CONTENTS OF THE SPECIFIED ACC TO T REG..
00C7 0001         ELT   F0,X'01'
00C8 4204         TZ    IU,X'04'     *  SKIP. IF FUNCTION CODE RANGE FROM 0 TO 3.
00C9 14E5         JP    B20          *  ELSE GO TO B20 (FUNCTION CODE = 4 TO 7).
```

```
00CA 3F06         AF    OU,X'06'     *  DEST. ACC ADDRESS MAPPING.
00CB 4202         TZ    IU,X'02'     *  SKIP. IF COM /NEG INST..
00CC 14E2         JP    B10          *  ELSE GO TO B10 (MOV/INC INST.).
00CD 3E10         AF    OL,X'10'     *  ONE'S COMPLEMENT OF THE CONTENTS
00CE CE06         MOV   OL,(U)       *  OF SOURCE ACC.
00CF 0079         ELT   F0,X'79'
00D0 BE20         CPY   OL,T
00D1 01F9         ELT   F1,X'F9'     *  TEST FOR EVEN OR ODD NO. FUNCTION CODE.
00D2 F230   SAM   SFR   IU,C         *  THEN LOAD THE UPPER BYTE OF RESULT
00D3 B220         CPY   IU,T
```

Appendix C (continued)

```
00D4  1600        LU    X'00'     * INTO IU REG..
00D5  5001        TN    FO.X'01'  * SKIP IF ODD NO. FUNCTION CODE(01/11).
00D6  1506        JP    CHS       * ELSE GO TO CHS ROUTINE.
00D7  8E40        INC   OL        * INCREMENT RESULT BY 1.
00D8  8290        ADD   IU.L.C
00D9  F1A0   UDC  SFR   F1.L      * SKIP , IF OVERFLOW OCCURS.
00DA  F190        SFL   F1.L.C    * ELSE GO TO CHS ROUTINE.
00DB  5001        TN    FO.X'01'
00DC  1506        JP    CHS
00DD  1101        LT    X'01'     * UPDATE THE CONTENTS OF TEMPORARY CARRY
00DE  D120        XOR   F1.T      * (BIT 0 OF FILE REG. 1).
00DF  1506        JP    CHS
00E0  F100   CRS  SFL   F1
00E1  14AE        JP    CCR
      *
      * MOV & INC INSTRUCTION EXECUTIVE ROUTINE.
      *
00E2  BE20   B10  CPY   OL.T      * COPY THE CONTENTS OF SOURCE ACC TO DEST. ACC.
00E3  0101        ELT   F1.X'01'
00E4  14D2        JP    SAM       * CONTINUE TO DECODE MOV OR INC FUNCTION.
      *
      * ADC SUB ADD & AND INSTRUCTION DECODING AND EXECUTIVE ROUTINE.
      *
00E5  4202   B20  TZ    IU.X'02'  * SKIP, IF ADC OR SUB INST..
00E6  14FA        JP    ADN       * ELSE GO TO ADN ROUTINE.
00E7  3F96        AF    OU.X'96'  * ONE'S COMPLEMENT DIFFERENCE OF
00E8  CF06        MOV   OU.(U)    * THE CONTENTS OF THE SOURCE ACC
00E9  0079        ELT   FO.X'79'  * FROM THE DEST. ACC.
00EA  CE06        MOV   OL.(U)
00EB  BE20        CPY   OL.T
00EC  0101        ELT   F1.X'01'
00ED  CF06        MOV   OU.(U)
00EE  01F9        ELT   F1.X'F9'
00EF  F1A0        SFR   F1.L
00F0  F190        SFL   F1.L.C
00F1  5001        TN    FO.X'01'  * SKIP, IF UNDERFLOW OCCURS.
00F2  14D2        JP    SAM       * ELSE CONTINUE AT SAM TO DECODE
00F3  F130        SFR   F1.C      * ADC OR SUB FUNCTION.
00F4  5001        TN    FO.X'01'  * UPDATE THE VALUE OF TEMPORARY CARRY.
00F5  14F8        JP    CAD
00F6  F100        SFL   F1
00F7  14D2        JP    SAM
00F8  F140   CAD  SLI   F1
00F9  14D2        JP    SAM
      *
      * AND & ADD INSTRUCTION EXECUTIVE ROUTINE.
      *
```

```
00FA  3F86   ADN  AF    OU.X'86'  * IF ADD FUNCTION EXECUTE ADD MICRO-ROUTINE
00FB  4201        TZ    IU.X'01'  * TO ADD THE NO. FROM SOURCE ACC TO
00FC  3F60        AF    OU.X'60'  * THE NO. FROM DESTINATION ACC.
00FD  CF06        MOV   OU.(U)    * IF AND FUNCTION EXECUTE AND MICRO-ROUTINE
00FE  0039        ELT   FO.X'39'  * TO LOGICAL AND THE WORD FROM SOURCE ACC AND
00FF  CE06        MOV   OL.(U)    * THE WORD FROM DESTINATION ACC.
0100  BE20        CPY   OL.T
0101  0101        ELT   F1.X'01'
0102  CF06        MOV   OU.(U)
0103  01B9        ELT   F1.X'B9'
0104  B220        CPY   IU.T
0105  14D9        JP    UDC       * CONTINUE TO DECODE AND OR ADD FUNCTION.
      *
      * SHIFT FUNCTION DECODING AND EXECUTIVE ROUTINE.
      *
0106  4380   CHS  TZ    IL.X'80'  * SKIP, IF LEFT SHIFT OR NO SHIFT.
0107  1514        JP    SRS       * ELSE PERFORM RIGHT SHIFT OR SWAP.
0108  5340        TN    IL.X'40'  * SKIP, IF LEFT SHIFT.
0109  152A        JP    LAC       * ELSE GO TO LAC ROUTINE.
010A  1190        LT    X'90'     * RESULT LEFT ROTATE ONE POSITION WITH CARRY.
010B  F120        SFR   F1
010C  16F0        LU    X'F0'
010D  1A00        MLC
010E  0EFF        ELT   OL.X'FF'
010F  1A00        MLC
0110  02FF        ELT   IU.X'FF'
0111  F180        SFL   F1.L
0112  1600        LU    X'00'
0113  152A        JP    LAC       * CONTINUE.
0114  4340   SRS  TZ    IL.X'40'  * SKIP, IF RIGHT SHIFT.
0115  151F        JP    SWP       * ELSE GO TO SWP ROUTINE.
0116  11B0        LT    X'B0'     * RESULT RIGHT ROTATE ONE POSITION WITH CARRY.
0117  F120        SFR   F1
0118  16F0        LU    X'F0'
0119  1A00        MLC
011A  02FF        ELT   IU.X'FF'
011B  1A00        MLC
011C  0EFF        ELT   OL.X'FF'
011D  F180        SFL   F1.L
011E  152A        JP    LAC       * CONTINUE.
011F  CE01   SWP  MOV   OL.(T)    * SWAP THE HALVES OF THE 16 BIT RESULT.
```

Appendix C (continued)

418

```
0120 1080          SSF
0121 B120          CPY    1.T
0122 1040          SPF
0123 C201          MOV    IU.(T)
0124 BE20          CPY    OL.T
0125 1080          SSF
0126 C101          MOV    1.(T)
0127 1040          SPF
0128 B220          CPY    IU.T
0129 152A          JP     LAC        * CONTINUE.
                *
                * INHIBIT LOAD FUNCTION EXECUTIVE ROUTINE.
                *
012A 4308   LAC    TZ     IL.X'08'   * SKIP, IF TO LOAD THE RESULT TO THE DEST. ACC.
012B 153F          JP     CSK        * ELSE GO TO CSK ROUTINE.
012C F138          SFR*   F1.C       * LOAD TEMPORARY CARRY INTO CARRY BIT.
```

LOCN CODE FLAGS LABELS OP * OPERANDS COMMENTS PAGE 8

```
012D 5001          TN     F0.X'01'   * SKIP, IF TEMPORARY CARRY = 1.
012E 153C          JP     LCR        * ELSE GO TO LCR ROUTINE.
012F 1102          LT     X'02'      * SET CARRY BIT = 1.
0130 C120          LOR    F1.T
0131 0F69   LAD    XOR*   OU.F.T.(T) * RESTORE ACC DEST. ADDRESS.
0132 3F10          AF     OU.X'10'   * LOAD THE RESULT INTO THE DEST. ACC.
0133 8F29          ADD*   OU.T.(T)
0134 EF20          AND    OU.T
0135 CE01          MOV    OL.(T)
0136 3FB0          AF     OU.X'B0'
0137 CF06          MOV    OU.(U)
0138 0020          ELT    F0.X'20'
0139 C201          MOV    IU.(T)
013A 0120          ELT    F1.X'20'
013B 153F          JP     CSK        * CONTINUE SKIP FUNCTION DECODING.
013C 11FD   LCR    LT     X'FD'      * CLEAR THE CARRY BIT.
013D E120          AND    F1.T
013E 1531          JP     LAD        * CONTINUE LOAD FUNCTION EXECUTION.
                *
                * SKIP OPERATION DECODING AND EXECUTIOVE ROUTINE.
                *
013F CE10   CSK    MOV    OL.C       * TEST THE RESULT STATUS.
0140 C290          MOV    IU.L.C
0141 1650          LU     X'50'      * SET U REG. := TN OPERATION CODE.
0142 4301          TZ     IL.X'01'   * SKIP, IF SZC, SZR, SEZ, OR NOP.
0143 1553          JP     B15        * ELSE GO TO B15(DECODE SKIP, SNC, SNR, OR SBN).
0144 5304   CRC    TN     IL.X'04'   * DECODE THE BITS CONFIGURATIONS AND
0145 154D          JP     CCY        * EXECUTE ACCORDINGLY:
0146 0004          ELT    F0.X'04'   *  MNEMONIC         FUNCTION
0147 1557          JP     B14        *    SZC     010 SKIP ON ZERO CARRY.
0148 5301          TN     IL.X'01'   *    SNC     011 SKIP ON NONZERO CARRY.
0149 148C          JP     SKP        *    SZR     100 SKIP ON ZERO RESULT.
014A 5302          TN     IL.X'02'   *    SNR     101 SKIP ON NONZERO RESULT.
014B 148C          JP     SKP        *    SEZ     110 SKIP ON EITHER CARRY OR RESULT IS ZERO.
014C 154F          JP     SBN        *    SBN     111 SKIP IF BOTH CARRY CARRY & RESULT ARE
014D 5302   CCY    TN     IL.X'02'   *                NONZERO.
014E 148E          JP     LUP
014F F138   SBN    SFR*   F1.C
0150 0001          ELT    F0.X'01'
0151 148C          JP     SKP
0152 148E          JP     LUP
0153 1640   B15    LU     X'40'      * SET U REG. := TZ OPERATION CODE.
0154 4306          TZ     IL.X'06'   * SKIP IF SKIP OPERATION.
0155 1544          JP     CRC        * ELSE GO TO CRC ROUTINE.
0156 148C          JP     SKP        * INCREMENT PC COUNTER BY 2.
0157 5301   B14    TN     IL.X'01'
0158 154D          JP     CCY
0159 148E          JP     LUP
                *
                * INPUT/OUTPUT INST. DECODING AND EXECUTION.
                *
015A 2F3F   IOI    LF     OU.X'3F'   * EXTRACT DEVICE CODE AND LOAD INTO OU REG..
015B C301          MOV    IL.(T)
015C EF20          AND    OU.T
015D 2E07          LF     OL.X'07'   * EXTRACT THE TRANSFER FUNCTION FIELD AND
015E C201          MOV    IU.(T)     * LOAD INTO OL REG..
015F EE20          AND    OL.T
```

LOCN CODE FLAGS LABELS OP * OPERANDS COMMENTS PAGE 9

```
0160 6FC1          CP     OU.X'C1'   * SKIP, IF DEVICE CODE = 77.
0161 1583          JP     NCPU       * TRANSFER TO NCPU ROUTINE.
                *
                * SPECIAL FUNCTION INST. HANDLING ROUTINE.
                *
0162 6EF9          CP     OL.X'F9'   * SKIP, IF TRANSFER FUNCTION = 7.
0163 1574          JP     CPD        * OTHERWISE. JUMP TO CPD ROUTINE.
0164 5380          TN     IL.X'80'   * SKIP, IF TEST FOR POWER FAILURE STATUS.
0165 156C          JP     SKINT
0166 1641          LU     X'41'      * CONTROL FUNCTION   SKP-- CPU
0167 5340          TN     IL.X'40'   *      10              SKIP IF POWER FAILURE IS NONZERO
```

Appendix C (continued)

```
0168 1651          LU    X'51'     *   11          SKIP IF POWER FAILURE IS ZERO
0169 0040          ELT   0.X'40'
016A 148E          JP    LUP
0168 148C          JP    SKP
      *
      * INTERRUPT ON FLAG STATUS TEST AND SKIP ROUTINE.
      *
016C 164C   SKINT  LU    X'4C'     *   00          SKIP IF INTERRUPT ON IS NONZERO
016D 5340          TN    IL.X'40'  *   01          SKIP IF INTERRUPT ON IS ZERO
016E 165C          LU    X'5C'
016F 1080          SSF
0170 0080          ELT   0.X'80'
0171 1DC4          JP    JLUP
0172 1040          SPF
0173 148C          JP    SKP
      *
      * CONTROL FIELD DECODING(SET/RESET INTERRUPT ON FLAG) FOR I/O INST. WITH
      * DEVICE CODE = 77.
      *
0174 4380   CPD    TZ    IL.X'80'  * SKIP. IF ENABLE INTERRUPT.
0175 157D          JP    DEI
0176 5340          TN    IL.X'40'  * IF CONTROL CODE = 00 JUMP TO DCPU ROUTINE.
0177 1C88          JP    DCPU
0178 1080          SSF             * SET IF. AND NI FLAGS ON THE SECONDARY FILE REG. 12.
0179 11C0          LT    X'C0'
017A CC20          LOR   12.T
017B 1040   EEI    SPF
017C 1C88          JP    DCPU
017D 4340   DEI    TZ    IL.X'40'  * SKIP. IF DISABLE INTERRUPT.
017E 1C88          JP    DCPU      * GO TO DCPU ROUTINE. (CONTROL CODE = 11.)
017F 1080          SSF             * RESET IF AND NI FLAGS  ON THE SECONDARY FILE REG. 12.
0180 113F          LT    X'3F'
0181 EC20          AND   12.T
0182 157B          JP    EEI
      *
      * EXTERNAL DEVICE DECODING AND EXECUTION.
      * (DEVICE CODE = 01 TO 76 )
      *
0183 4F30   NCPU   TZ    OU.X'30'  * TRANSFER TO UDN ROUTINE. FOR I/O INST. WITH
0184 15D6          JP    UDN       * DEVICE CODE OTHER THAN 10. 11. 12. 14
0185 5F08          TN    OU.X'08'
0186 15D6          JP    UDN
0187 3FF0          AF    OU.X'F0'  * TRAP TO THE DEVICE CODE JUMP TABLE.
0188 CF05          MOV   OU.(K)
      *
      * BASIC INPUT OUTPUT SUBROUTINE.

LOCN CODE FLAGS LABELS OP *   OPERANDS      COMMENTS                      PAGE  10

      *
0189 7090   COX    COX   0         * CONTROL OUTPUT ROUTINE. SEND THE CONTROL CODE
018A 1000          NOP
018B 158C          JP    CIO       * TO A DEVICE CONTROLLER.
018C 7080   CIO    CIO   0
018D 1020          RTN
018E 70E0   DIX    DIX   0         * DATA INPUT ROUTINE. INPUT  DATA FROM A DEVICE
018F 1590          JP    ELT       * AND LOAD INTO THE TEMPARY STORAGE(FILE REG. 1).
0190 B120   ELT    CPY   1.T
0191 158C          JP    CIO
0192 70A0   DOX    DOX   0         * DATA OUTPUT ROUTINE. OUTPUT DATA TO A DEVICE.
0193 158C          JP    CIO
      *
      * DATA TRANSFER ROUTINE.
      *
0194 1040   IDATO  SPF             * LOAD DATA FROM FILE REG. TO ACC. AS SPECIFIED
0195 3FB6          AF    OU.X'B6'  * IN OU REG..
0196 CF06          MOV   OU.(U)
0197 0020          ELT   0.X'20'
0198 0100          ELT   1.X'00'
0199 1600          LU    X'00'
019A 1020          RTN
      *
      * CLEAR I/O DEVICE  EXECUTIVE ROUTINE.
      *
019B 1080   CLIO   SSF             * SET REAL TIME CLOCK FREQ. TO AC LINE FREQ. (50 HZ.).
019C 246C          LF    4.X'6C'   * CLEAR ALL CONTROL FLAGS.
019D 256C          LF    5.X'6C'
019E 21B9          LF    1.X'89'
019F 028F          JE    CLEAR
01A0 148E          JP    LUP
      *
      * HALT INST. EXECUTIVE ROUTINE.
      *
01A1 8440   HALT   INC   LL        * UPDATE PROGRAM COUNTERAND STOP THE PROCESSOR.
01A2 8580          ADD   LU.L
01A3 1780          HLT
      *
      * INTERNAL HOUSE KEEPING ROUTINE.
      *
01A4 1600   INT    LU    X'00'     * CHECK SYSTEM CONDITION.
01A5 1080          SSF             * TRANSFER TO PFR. IF INTERNAL INTERRUPT.
01A6 4010          TZ    0.X'10'   * (RTC OR POWER FAIL)
```

Appendix C (continued)

```
01A7 1DAE          JP    PFR       * ELSE SKIP TO NEXT INST..
01A8 5080    MAIN  TN    0.X'80'   * SKIP IF EXTERNAL INTERRUPT.
01A9 1C43          JP    TTY       * ELSE JUMP TO TTY ROUTINE.
01AA 032B          JE    IAK       * INTERRUPT ACKNOWLEDGE.
01AB 1C00          JP    CDC       * GO TO CDC ROUTINE TO EXAMINE DEVICES' CONDITION.
             *
             * ERROR ROUTINE FOR UNEXPECTED DEVICE REQUESTS FOR SERVICE
             * IN ASYNCHRONOUS INTERFACE.
             *
01AC 111C    ERA   LT    X'1C'     * SEND CONTROL BYTE TO DEVICE INTERFACE.
01AD 0189          JE    COX
01AE 5110          TN    1.X'10'   * SKIP IF OUTPUT SUB-CHANNEL.
01AF 1583          JP    ERI       * ELSE GO TO ERI ROUTINE.
01B0 1100    ERO   LT    X'00'     * OUTPUT DATA AND DISCARD.
```

LOCN CODE FLAGS LABELS OP *   OPERANDS   COMMENTS   PAGE 11

```
01B1 0192          JE    DOX
01B2 1C43          JP    TTY       * CONTINUE IN TTY ROUTINE.
01B3 018E    ERI   JE    DIX       * INPUT DATA AND DISCARD.
01B4 1C43          JP    TTY       * CONTINUE IN TTY ROUTINE.
             *
             * ACC ADDRESS DECODING ROUTINE.
             *
01B5 2F18    ACA   LF    OU.X'18'  * EXTRACT AC ADDRESS AND LOAD INTO OU REG..
01B6 C201          MOV   IU.(T)
01B7 EF20          AND   OU.T
01B8 FF20          SFR   OU
01B9 FF20          SFR   OU
01BA 1020          RTN
             *
             * INTERRUPT ACKNOWLEDGE EXECUTIVE ROUTINE.
             *
01BB 01B5    INA   JE    ACA       * DECODE AND MAP THE AC ADDRESS.
01BC 3FB6          AF    OU.X'B6'
01BD 1080          SSF
01BE CC01          MOV   12.(T)    * PLACE THE DEVICE STATUS INTO TEMPARARY STORAGE
01BF B120          CPY   1.T       * (FILE REG. 1).
01C0 DA69          XOR*  10.T.F.(T)
01C1 E120          AND   1.T       * DETERMINE THE UNMASKED AND DONE FLAG SET DEVICES.
01C2 5104          TN    1.X'04'   * SKIP. IF REAL TIME CLOCK INTERRUPT.
01C3 15CA          JP    PTT
01C4 110C          LT    X'0C'     * LOAD DEVICE CODE '0C'.
01C5 1040    ACK   SPF             * INTO THE SPECIFIED AC .
01C6 CF06          MOV   OU.(U)
01C7 0020          ELT   0.X'20'
01C8 0100          ELT   1.X'00'
01C9 148E          JP    LUP
01CA 5110    PTT   TN    1.X'10'   * SKIP. IF PTR INTERRUPT.
01CB 15CE          JP    IOT
01CC 110A          LT    X'0A'     * LOAD DEVICE CODE '0A'.
01CD 15C5          JP    ACK
01CE 5102    IOT   TN    1.X'02'   * SKIP. IF TTI INTERRUPT.
01CF 15D2          JP    TYO
01D0 1108          LT    X'08'     * LOAD DEVICE CODE '08'.
01D1 15C5          JP    ACK
01D2 1100    TYO   LT    X'00'     * IF TTO INTERRUPT, LOAD DEVICE CODE '09' INTO
01D3 4101          TZ    1.X'01'   * THE SPECIFIED ACC. OTHERWISE LOAD '00'.
01D4 1109          LT    X'09'
01D5 15C5          JP    ACK
             *
             * UNDEFINED (NOT IMPLEMENTED) DEVICE'S I/O INST. EXECUTIVE ROUTINE.
             *
01D6 6EF9    UDN   CP    OL.X'F9'  * SKIP IF SKIP INST..
01D7 15DB          JP    UIN       * ELSE GO TO UIN ROUTINE.
01D8 5340          TN    IL.X'40'  * INCREMENT PROGRAM COUNTER BY 2.
01D9 148E          JP    LUP       * IF BUSY OR DONE FLAG = 0.
01DA 148C          JP    SKP       * ELSE INCREMENT BY 1.
01DB 5E01    UIN   TN    OL.X'01'  * SKIP IF DATA INPUT INST..
01DC 148E          JP    LUP       * ELSE GO TO LUP ROUTINE.
01DD 01B5          JE    ACA
01DE 029B          JE    CAC       * CLEAR THE ADDRESSED ACC.
01DF 148E          JP    LUP       * CONTINUE IN LUP ROUTINE.
01E0 119F    OVF   LT    X'9F'     * MEMORY CYCLIC.
```

LOCN CODE FLAGS LABELS OP *   OPERANDS   COMMENTS   PAGE 12

```
01E1 EF20          AND   OU.T
01E2 1459          JP    REP
01E3 117C    ERPT  LT    X'7C'     * RESET SEND BUFFER-EMPTY MASK.
01E4 0189          JE    COX
01E5 1110          LT    X'10'
01E6 0192          JE    DOX
01E7 111C          LT    X'1C'     * SEND CONTROL BYTE TO ASYN. INTERFACE.
01E8 0189          JE    COX
01E9 4110          TZ    1.X'10'   * SKIP . IF SEND SUBCHANNAL.
01EA 15B0          JP    ERO       * ELSE GO TO ERO ROUTINE.
01EB C601          MOV   6.(T)     * OUTPUT 'NULL' TO SILENT 700
01EC 0192          JE    DOX       * TO RELEASE SCANNER.
01ED 1C43          JP    TTY       * CONTINUE AT TTY ROUTINE.
01EE 1780    ICDR  HLT             * ILLEGAL REQUEST HALT PROCESSOR.
```

Appendix C (continued)

```
01EF 4340      HZ2  TZ    IL,X'40'    * SKIP IF IDLE RTC.
01F0 148E           JP    LUP
01F1 1100           LT    X'00'       * CLEAR RTC BUSY-DONE FLAGS.
01F2 1710           DRT               * DISABLE RTC.
01F3 1DEF           JP    HZ3
             *
             * ILLEGAL TTO INSTRUCTION ROUTINE.
             *
01F4 5201      U15  TN    IU,X'01'    * SKIP IF INPUT DATA TRANSFER.
01F5 1CE1           JP    NO1         * ELSE GO TO NO1.
01F6 0298           JE    CAC         * CLEAR THE ADDRESSED ACC.
01F7 1CE1           JP    NO1         * PERFORM THE CONTROL FUNCTION.
             *
             * IMPLEMENTED DEVICES' JUMP TABLE.
             *
01F8 1CA8           JP    TTI         * TELETYPE INPUT.
01F9 1C00           JP    TTO         * TELETYPE OUTPUT.
01FA 1CF5           JP    PTR         * PAPER TAPE READER.
01FB 15D6           JP    UDN         * UNUSED.
01FC 1DCE           JP    RTC         * REAL TIME CLOCK.
01FD 15D6           JP    UDN         * UNUSED.
01FE 15D6           JP    UDN         * UNUSED.
01FF 15D6           JP    UDN         * UNUSED.
             *
             * CHECK DEVICE CONDITION. PERFORM THE DATA TRANSFER IF REQUIRE
             * AND UPDATE THE DEVICE'S STATUS.
             *
0200 113E      CDC  LT    X'3E'       * GET DEVICE NUMBER.
0201 E120           AND   1.T         * SKIP IF ASYNCHRONOUS INTERFACE (DN = 1C) REQUEST
0202 61C8           CP    1,X'C8'     * FOR SERVICE. ELSE GO TO ICDR ROUTINE.
0203 15EE           JP    ICDR
0204 113C           LT    X'3C'       * INPUT STATUS BYTE FROM ASYNCHRONOUS INTERFACE.
0205 0189           JE    COX
0206 018E           JE    DIX
0207 11F0           LT    X'F0'       * TRANSFER TO ALP ROUTINE IF CHANNEL 0
0208 E120           AND   1.T         * REQUEST SERVICE.
0209 61EF           CP    1,X'EF'     * ELSE CONTINUE.
020A 1C25           JP    ALP
020B 61A0           CP    1,X'A0'     * SKIP IF PTR REQUEST SERVICE(CHANNEL NO. = 3).
020C 15AC           JP    ERA         * ELSE GO TO ERA ROUTINE.
020D 117C           LT    X'7C'       * SEND INTERRUPT MASK CONTROL BYTE.
020E 0189           JE    COX
020F 1172           LT    X'72'       * SET SEND-BUFFER-EMPTY MASK BIT.

LOCN CODE FLAGS LABELS OP *  OPERANDS     COMMENTS                    PAGE  13

0210 0192           JE    DOX
0211 111C           LT    X'1C'       * INPUT DATA FROM PTR AND
0212 0189           JE    COX         * STORE DATA IN PTR BUFFER (FILE REG. 8).
0213 018E           JE    DIX
0214 C101           MOV   1,(T)
0215 8820           CPY   8.T
0216 117C           LT    X'7C'       * SEND INTERRUPT MASK CONTROL BYTE.
0217 0189           JE    COX
0218 1170           LT    X'70'       * RESET DATA READY MASK BIT.
0219 0192           JE    DOX
021A 111C           LT    X'1C'       * DISCONNECT PTR (SET READER NOT READY).
021B 0189           JE    COX
021C 1193           LT    X'93'
021D 0192           JE    DOX
021E 4881           TZ    11,X'81'    * TRANSFER TO TTY ROUTINE IF BOTH PTR
021F 1C21           JP    GCON        * BUSY DONE FLAGS ARE RESET.
0220 1C43           JP    TTY         * ELSE GO TO GCON ROUTINE.
0221 2801      GCON LF    11,X'01'    * SET PTR DONE FLAG.
0222 1110           LT    X'10'       * UPDATE DEVICES' DONE-FLAG STATUS IN FILE REG. 12.
0223 CC20           LOR   12.T
0224 1C43           JP    TTY         * CONTINUE AT TTY ROUTINE.
0225 111C      ALP  LT    X'1C'       * SEND ASYN. INTERFACE CONTROL BYTE.
0226 0189           JE    COX
0227 5110           TN    1,X'10'     * SKIP, IF SEND SUBCHANNEL REQUEST FOR SERVICE.
0228 15B3           JP    ERI         * ELSE GO TO ERI ROUTINE.
0229 7110           ESS   1
022A 4110           TZ    1,X'10'     * SKIP, IF TTO ECHO ON SILENT 700 DATA TERMINAL.
022B 15E3           JP    ERPT        * ELSE GO TO ERPT ROUTINE.
022C 5F80           TN    15,X'80'    * SKIP, IF TTO BUSY FLAG ON.
022D 15E3           JP    ERPT        * ELSE GO TO ERPT ROUTINE.
022E 117C           LT    X'7C'       * RESET SEND BUFFER-EMPTY MASK.
022F 0189           JE    COX
0230 1110           LT    X'10'
0231 0192           JE    DOX
0232 111C           LT    X'1C'       * OUTPUT DATA TO SILENT 700 DATA TERMINAL.
0233 0189           JE    COX
0234 C601           MOV   6,(T)
0235 0192           JE    DOX
0236 F310           SFL   3.C         * TEST TIME OUT FOR CR CHARACTER.
0237 5004           TN    0,X'04'     * SKIP , IF END OF TIME OUT OR NON CR CHAR.,
0238 1C7F           JP    TD1         * ELSE GO TO TD1 ROUTINE.
0239 117F           LT    X'7F'       * TRANSFER TO TD2 ROUTINE
023A E620           AND   6.T         * IF OUTPUT CHARACTER := CR.
023B 11F3           LT    X'F3'
023C 8630           ADD   6.T.C
```

Appendix C (continued)

```
023D 4004          TZ    0,X'04'
023E 1C7E          JP    TD2
023F 2600          LF    6,X'00'    * CLEAR TTO A BUFFER.
0240 2F01          LF    15,X'01'   * SET TTO DONE FLAG.
0241 1101          LT    X'01'      * UPDATE DEVICES' DONE-FLAG STATUS IN FILE REG. 12.
0242 CC20          LOR   12,T
0243 1120   TTY    LT    X'20'      * INPUT TTY STATUS.
0244 0189          JE    COX
0245 018E          JE    DIX
0246 C101          MOV   1,(T)      * STORE STATUS BYTE INTO FILE REG. 1 & 9.
0247 B920          CPY   9,T
0248 5902          TN    9,X'02'    * SKIP IF TTI DATA READY.


LOCN CODE FLAGS LABELS OP *  OPERANDS     COMMENTS                      PAGE  14

0249 1C52          JP    ITO        * ELSE GO TO ITO ROUTINE.
024A 1100          LT    X'00'      * INPUT DATA FROM TTY.
024B 0189          JE    COX
024C 018E          JE    DIX
024D C101          MOV   1,(T)      * STORE DATA INTO TTI BUFFER (FILE REG. 7).
024E B720          CPY   7,T
024F 1102          LT    X'02'      * SET TTI DONE FLAG.
0250 CC20          LOR   12,T       * UPDATE DEVICES' DONE FLAG STATUS.
0251 2E01          LF    14,X'01'
0252 5F80   ITO    TN    15,X'80'   * SKIP IF TTO BUSY FLAG ON.
0253 1C61          JP    DINT       * ELSE GO TO DINT ROUTINE.
0254 7110          ESS   1
0255 5110          TN    1,X'10'    * SKIP, IF TTO ECHO ON CRT.
0256 1C61          JP    DINT       * ELSE GO TO DINT ROUTINE.
0257 5904          TN    9,X'04'    * SKIP IF TTY SEND BUFFER EMPTY ON.
0258 1C61          JP    DINT       * ELSE GO TO DINT ROUTINE.
0259 1100          LT    X'00'      * SEND DATA TRANSFER CONTROL CODE
025A 0189          JE    COX        * TO TTO INTERFACE.
025B C601          MOV   6,(T)
025C 0192          JE    DOX
025D 2600          LF    6,X'00'    * CLEAR TTO BUFFER.
025E 2F01          LF    15,X'01'   * SET TTO DONE FLAG.
025F 1101          LT    X'01'      * UPDATE DEVICES' DONE FLAG STATUS.
0260 CC20          LOR   12,T
             *
             * EMULATED INTERRUPT EXECUTIVE ROUTINE.
             *
0261 5C80   DINT   TN    12,X'80'   * SKIP IF INTERRUPT ENABLE FLAG ON.
0262 1C7C          JP    IFT        * ELSE GO TO IFT ROUTINE.
0263 4C40          TZ    12,X'40'   * SKIP, IF NI FLAG IS SET.
0264 1C7A          JP    CIT        * ELSE GO TO CIT ROUTINE.
0265 113F          LT    X'3F'      * TRANSFER TO IFT ROUTINE IF UNMASKED
0266 EC29          AND*  12,T,(T)   * DEVICE REQUEST FOR SERVICE.
0267 B120          CPY   1,T
0268 DA69          XOR*  10,T,F,(T)
0269 E120          AND   1,T
026A 513F          TN    1,X'3F'
026B 1C7C          JP    IFT
026C 117F          LT    X'7F'
026D EC20          AND   12,T
026E 1040          SPF
026F 1300          LN    X'00'      * STORE RETURN ADDRESS AT MEMORY LOCATION 0.
0270 A511          WMF   LU,(T)
0271 1301          LN    X'01'
0272 A411          WMF   LL,(T)
0273 1302          LN    X'02'      * LOAD THE CONTENTS OF MEMORY LOCATION 1
0274 A000          RMF   0          * (ADDRESS OF INTERRUPT HANDLING ROUTINE)
0275 B520          CPY   LU,T       * INTO PROGRAM COUNTER.
0276 1303          LN    X'03'
0277 A000          RMF   0
0278 B420          CPY   LL,T       * CONTINUE NEXT INSTRUCTION'S DECODING AND
0279 1422          JP    FET        * EXECUTIVE OPERATIONS.
027A 118F   CIT    LT    X'8F'      * CLEAR NI BIT.
027B EC20          AND   12,T
027C 1040   IFT    SPF              * CONTINUE IN FET ROUTINE.
027D 1422          JP    FET
027E 23F0   TD2    LF    3,X'F0'    * SET TIME OUT COUNTER(FILE REG. 3).


LOCN CODE FLAGS LABELS OP *  OPERANDS     COMMENTS                      PAGE  15

027F 117C   TD1    LT    X'7C'      * SET SEND BUFFER-EMPTY MASK.
0280 0189          JE    COX
0281 1112          LT    X'12'
0282 0192          JE    DOX
0283 1C43          JP    TTY        * CONTINUE AT TTY ROUTINE.
             *
             * MASK OUT INST. EXECUTIVE ROUTINE.
             *
0284 01B5   MASK   JE    ACA        * EXTRACT ACC ADDRESS.
0285 3FC6          AF    OU,X'C6'
0286 CF06          MOV   OU,(U)
0287 0001          ELT   FO,X'01'   * LOAD THE MASK PATTERN FROM THE SPECIFIED ACC TO THE
0288 1080          SSF              * MASK REG. (FILE REG. 10).
0289 BA20          CPY   10,T
028A 1DC4          JP    JLUP       * JUMP TO PROGRAM COUNTER UPDATING ROUTINE.
```

Appendix C (continued)

```
                  *
                  * SPECIFIED I/O FUNCTION INST. DECODING ROUTINE. (WITH DEVICE CODE = 77 ).
                  *
028B 6EFF    DCPU   CP    OL.X'FF'
028C 148E           JP    LUP        * TRANSFER TO LUP ROUTINE FOR NO I/O TRANSFER.
028D 3EA0           AF    OL.X'A0'
028E CE04           MOV   OL.(L)     * TRAP TO THE SPECIAL FUNCTION INST. JUMP TABLE.
                  *
                  * CLEAR A BAND OF FILE REGISTERS (FROM THE SPECIFIED FILE REG. TO FILE REG. 15).
                  *
028F C106    CLEAR  MOV   1.(U)      * CLEAR ALL THE CONTROL FLAGS.
0290 0000           ELT   0.X'00'
0291 8140           INC   1
0292 6140           CP    1.X'40'
0293 1C8F           JP    CLEAR
0294 1600           LU    X'00'
0295 1040           SPF
0296 1020           RTN
                  *
                  * ILLEGAL TTI INSTRUCTION ROUTINE.
                  *
0297 5201    U14    TN    IU.X'01'   * SKIP IF INPUT DATA TRANSFER.
0298 1CC2           JP    NIO        * ELSE GO TO NIO
0299 029B           JE    CAC        * CLEAR THE ADDRESSED ACC.
029A 1CC2           JP    NIO        * PERFORM THE CONTROL FUNCTION.
                  *
                  * CLEAR THE SPECIFIED ACCUMULATOR.
                  *
029B 3FB6    CAC    AF    OU.X'86'
029C CF06           MOV   OU.(U)
029D 0000           ELT   0.X'00'
029E 0100           ELT   1.X'00'
029F 1600           LU    X'00'
02A0 1020           RTN
                  *
                  * SPECIAL FUNCTION INSTRUCTION JUMP TABLE ( DEVICE CODE = 77 ).
                  *
02A1 1D5A           JP    SWT        * READ SWITCHES
02A2 148E           JP    LUP        * UNUSED
02A3 15BB           JP    INA        * INTERRUPT ACKNOWLEDGE
02A4 1C84           JP    MASK       * MASK OUT
02A5 1598           JP    CLIO       * CLEAR I/O DEVICE


LOCN CODE FLAGS LABELS OP *  OPERANDS     COMMENTS              PAGE  16

02A6 15A1           JP    HALT       * HALT
02A7 148E           JP    LUP        * UNUSED
                  *
                  * TELETYPE INPUT INSTRUCTION EXECUTIVE ROUTINE.
                  *
02A8 6EF9    TTI    CP    OL.X'F9'   * SKIP IF SKP INST..
02A9 1CBA           JP    T14        * ELSE GO TO T14.
02AA 1080           SSF
02AB CE01           MOV   14.(T)     * COPY TTI BUSY-DONE STATUS TO T REG..
                  *
                  * SKIP DEVICE BUSY-DONE STATUS ROUTINE.
                  *
02AC 1040    CBD    SPF
02AD BF20           CPY   OU.T       * COPY BUSY-DONE STATUS TO OU REG..
02AE 1130           LT    X'30'      * SET T REG. = 30 IF SKPDN/SKPDZ.
02AF 5380           TN    IL.X'80'   * ELSE SET T REG. = 10.
02B0 1110           LT    X'10'
02B1 2E40           LF    OL.X'40'   * SET OL REG. = 40 IF SKPBN/SKPDN.
02B2 4340           TZ    IL.X'40'   * ELSE SET OL REG. = 50.
02B3 3E10           AF    OL.X'10'
02B4 1A00           MLC
02B5 FF30           SFR   OU.C       * SHIFT LEFT IF TEST BUSY CONDITION.
02B6 CE06           MOV   OL.(U)     * ELSE SHIFT RIGHT.
02B7 0001           ELT   0.X'01'
02B8 148C           JP    SKP        * PERFORM SKIP/NONSKIP OPERATION.
02B9 148E           JP    LUP
                  *
                  * TTI DATA INPUT INSTRUCTION (DIA - TTI) EXECUTIVE ROUTINE.
                  *
02BA 01B5    T14    JE    ACA        * GET ACC ADDRESS.
02BB 4206           TZ    IU.X'06'   * SKIP IF LEGAL TTI INST..
02BC 1C97           JP    U14        * ELSE GO TO U14.
02BD 6EFF           CP    OL.X'FF'   * SKIP IF DATA INPUT.
02BE 1CC2           JP    NIO        * ELSE GO TO NIO.
02BF 1080           SSF
02C0 C701           MOV   7.(T)      * INPUT DATA FROM TTI BUFFER
02C1 0194           JE    IDATA      * TO THE SPECIFIED ACC.
                  *
                  * TTI CONTROL FUNCTION DECODING.
                  *
02C2 4380    NIO    TZ    IL.X'80'   * SKIP IF 'S' FUNCTION.
02C3 1CCB           JP    CLP        * ELSE GO TO CLP.
02C4 5340           TN    IL.X'40'   * SKIP IF START THE DEVICE (TTI).
02C5 148E           JP    LUP
02C6 1080           SSF
02C7 2E80           LF    14.X'80'   * SET TTI BUSY FLAG.
```

Appendix C (continued)

424

```
02C8 11FD    SIM   LT    X'FD'      * RESET TTI DONE FLAG
02C9 EC20    RSI   AND   12,T       * IN THE DEVICES' DONE FLAG STATUS BYTE.
02CA 1DC4          JP    JLUP       * ( FILE REG. 12 )
02CB 4340    CLP   TZ    IL,X'40'   * SKIP IF IDLE THE DEVICE.
02CC 148E          JP    LUP
02CD 1080          SSF
02CE 2E00          LF    14,X'00'   * CLEAR TTI BUSY AND DONE FLAGS.
02CF 1CC8          JP    SIM
             *
             * TELETYPE OUTPUT INSTRUCTION EXECUTIVE ROUTINE.
             *
```

LOCN CODE FLAGS LABELS OP * OPERANDS   COMMENTS   PAGE 17

```
02D0 6EF9    TTO   CP    OL,X'F9'   * SKIP IF SKP INST..
02D1 1CD5          JP    T15        * ELSE GO TO T15.
02D2 1080          SSF
02D3 CF01          MOV   15,(T)     * COPY TTO BUSY-DONE STATUS INTO T REG..
02D4 1CAC          JP    CBD        * GO TO SKIP CONDITION DECODING ROUTINE.
             *
             * TTO DATA OUTPUT INSTRUCTION (DOA - TTO) EXECUTIVE ROUTINE.
             *
02D5 0185    T15   JE    ACA        * GET ACC ADDRESS.
02D6 4205          TZ    IU,X'05'   * SKIP IF LEGAL TTO INST..
02D7 15F4          JP    U15        * ELSE GO TO U15.
02D8 6EFF          CP    OL,X'FF'   * SKIP IF DATA OUTPUT ,
02D9 1CE1          JP    NO1        * ELSE GO TO NO1.
02DA 3FC6          AF    OU,X'C6'   * COPY THE CONTENTS OF SPECIFIED ACC
02DB CF06          MOV   OU,(U)     * INTO TTO BUFFER.
02DC 0001          ELT   0,X'01'
02DD 1600          LU    X'00'
02DE 1080          SSF
02DF 8620          CPY   6,T
02E0 1040          SPF
             *
             * TTO CONTROL FUNCTION DECODING.
             *
02E1 4380    NO1   TZ    IL,X'80'   * 'C'/'P' OPERATION ?
02E2 1CF0          JP    CL1        * YES, GO TO CL1.
02E3 5340          TN    IL,X'40'   * SKIP IF START THE DEVICE.
02E4 148E          JP    LUP
02E5 1080          SSF
02E6 7110          ESS   1          * TRANSFER TO BD1 ROUTINE
02E7 4110          TZ    1,X'10'    * IF TTO ECHO ON CRT.
02E8 1CED          JP    BD1        * CONTINUE AT BD1 ROUTINE.
02E9 117C          LT    X'7C'      * SET SEND BUFFER EMPTY MASK.
02EA 0189          JE    COX
02EB 1112          LT    X'12'
02EC 0192          JE    DOX
02ED 2F80    BD1   LF    15,X'80'   * SET TTO BUSY FLAG.
02EE 11FE    PNO   LT    X'FE'      * RESET THE TTO DONE FLAG IN
02EF 1CC9          JP    RSI        * THE DEVICES' DONE FLAG STATUS BYTE.
02F0 4340    CL1   TZ    IL,X'40'   * SKIP IF IDLE THE DEVICE.
02F1 148E          JP    LUP
02F2 1080          SSF
02F3 2F00          LF    15,X'00'   * CLEAR TTO BUSY-DONE FLAGS.
02F4 1CEE          JP    PNO
             *
             * PAPER TAPE READER INSTRUCTION EXECUTIVE ROUTINE.
             *
02F5 6EF9    PTR   CP    OL,X'F9'   * SKIP IF SKP INST..
02F6 1CFA          JP    T11        * ELSE GO TO T11.
02F7 1080          SSF
02F8 CB01          MOV   11,(T)     * COPY PTR BUSY-DONE STATUS TO T REG..
02F9 1CAC          JP    CBD        * GO TO SKIP CONDITION DECODING ROUTINE.
             *
             * PTR DATA INPUT INSTRUCTION (DIA - PTR) EXECUTIVE ROUTINE.
             *
02FA 0185    T11   JE    ACA        * GET ACC ADDRESS.
02FB 4206          TZ    IU,X'06'   * SKIP IF LEGAL PTR INST..
02FC 1DC6          JP    U11        * ELSE GO TO U11.
```

LOCN CODE FLAGS LABELS OP * OPERANDS   COMMENTS   PAGE 18

```
02FD 6EFF          CP    OL,X'FF'   * SKIP IF DATA.INPUT.
02FE 1D02          JP    NO5        * ELSE GO TO NO5.
02FF 1080          SSF
0300 C801          MOV   8,(T)      * INPUT DATA FROM PTR BUFFER
0301 0194          JE    IDATA      * TO THE SPECIFIED ACC.
             *
             * PTR CONTROL FUNCTION DECODING.
             *
0302 4380    NO5   TZ    IL,X'80'   * 'C'/'P' OPERATION ?
0303 1D26          JP    TR1        * YES, GO TO TR1.
0304 5340          TN    IL,X'40'   * SKIP IF START THE DEVICE.
0305 148E          JP    LUP
0306 1080          SSF
0307 117C          LT    X'7C'      * SEND BUFFER EMPTY MASK.
0308 0189          JE    COX
0309 1172          LT    X'72'
030A 0192          JE    DOX
```

Appendix C (continued)

```
030B 5080    STM    TN    0,X'80'       * SKIP IF EXTERNAL INTERRUPT. ELSE WAIT.
030C 1D0B           JP    STM
030D G32B           JE    IAK           * INTERRUPT ACKNOWLEDGE.
030E 113E           LT    X'3E'         * GET DEVICE CODE.
030F E120           AND   1,T
0310 61C8           CP    1,X'C8'       * SKIP IF 8 CHANNEL ASYCHONOUSE INTERFACE.
0311 1780           HLT                 * ELSE HALT PROCESSOR.
0312 113C           LT    X'3C'         * INPUT STATUS BYTE.
0313 0189           JE    COX
0314 018E           JE    DIX
0315 11F0           LT    X'F0'         * TRANSFER TO EEE ROUTINE IF CHANNEL 0
0316 E120           AND   1,T           * (TTO) REQUEST FOR SERVICE.
0317 61EF           CP    1,X'EF'
0318 1D31           JP    EEE
0319 6190           CP    1,X'90'       * SKIP IF SEND BUFFER EMPTY.
031A 1D55           JP    NOG           * ELSE GO TO NOG.
031B 117C           LT    X'7C'         * CLEAR SEND BUFFER EMPTY MASK.
031C 0189           JE    COX
031D 1170           LT    X'70'
031E 0192           JE    DOX
031F 111C           LT    X'1C'         * READY PTR.
0320 0189           JE    COX
0321 1191           LT    X'91'
0322 0192           JE    DOX
0323 2880           LF    11,X'80'      * SET PTR BUSY FLAG.
0324 11EF    TR2    LT    X'EF'         * RESET PTR DONE FLAG IN THE
0325 1CC9           JP    RSI           * DEVICES' DONE FLAG STATUS BYTE.
0326 4340    TR1    TZ    IL,X'40'      * SKIP IF IDLE THE DEVICE.
0327 148E           JP    LUP
0328 1080           SSF
0329 2B00           LF    11,X'00'      * CLEAR PTR BUSY-DONE FLAGE.
032A 1D24           JP    TR2
032B 70D0    IAK    IAK   0             * SEND INTERRUPT ACKNOWLEDEGE CONTROL ORDER,
032C 1000           NOP
032D 1D2E           JP    CIAK          AND RECEIVE THE DEVICE NO. IN FILE REG 1.
032E B120    CIAK   CPY   1,T
032F 7080           CIO   0
0330 1020           RTN
0331 5110    EEE    TN    1,X'10'       * SKIP IF SEND SUBCHANNEL REQUEST
0332 1D51           JP    INE           * FOR SERVICE. ELSE GO TO INE ROUTINE.
```

```
LOCN CODE FLAGS LABELS OP *   OPERANDS     COMMENTS                    PAGE  19

0333 117C           LT    X'7C'         * RESET SEND BUFFER-EMPTY MASK.
0334 0189           JE    COX
0335 1110           LT    X'10'
0336 0192           JE    DOX
0337 111C           LT    X'1C'         * OUTPUT DATA TO SILENT 700 DATA TERMINAL.
0338 0189           JE    COX
0339 C601           MOV   6,(T)
033A 0192           JE    DOX
033B 5F80           TN    15,X'80'      * SKIP . IF TTO BUSY FLAG ON.
033C 1D0B           JP    STM           * ELSE GO TO STM ROUTINE.
033D F310           SFL   3,C           * TEST TIME OUT FOR CR CHARACTER.
033E 5004           TN    0,X'04'       * SKIP, IF END OF TIME OUT OR NON CR CHAR..
033F 1D4C           JP    TD3           * ELSE GO TO TD3 ROUTINE.
0340 117F           LT    X'7F'         * TRANSFER TO TD4 ROUTINE
0341 E620           AND   6,T           * IF OUTPUT CHAR. := CARRIAGE RETURN.
0342 11F3           LT    X'F3'
0343 8630           ADD   6,T,C
0344 4004           TZ    0,X'04'
0345 1D4B           JP    TD4
0346 2600           LF    6,X'00'       * CLEAR TTO A BUFFER.
0347 2F01           LF    15,X'01'      * SET TTO DONE FLAG.
0348 1101           LT    X'01'         * UPDATE DEVICES' DONE FLAG STATUS IN FILE REG. 12.
0349 CC20           LOR   12,T
034A 1D0B           JP    STM           * CONTINUE AT STM ROUTINE.
034B 23F0    TD4    LF    3,X'F0'       * SET TIME OUT COUNTER(FILE REG. 3).
034C 117C    TD3    LT    X'7C'         * SET SEND BUFFER-EMPTY MASK.
034D 0189           JE    COX
034E 1112           LT    X'12'
034F 0192           JE    DOX
0350 1D0B           JP    STM           * CONTINUE AT STM ROUTINE.
0351 111C    INE    LT    X'1C'         * INPUT DATA AND DISCARD.
0352 0189           JE    COX
0353 018E           JE    DIX
0354 1D08           JP    STM           * CONTINUE AT STM ROUTINE.
0355 111C    NOG    LT    X'1C'         * OUTPUT 'NULL' CHAR. TO FREE SCANNER.
0356 0189           JE    COX
0357 1100           LT    X'00'
0358 0192           JE    DOX
0359 1D0B           JP    STM
          *
          * READ SWITCH INST. DECODING AND EXECUTIVE ROUTINE.
          *
035A 01B5    SWT    JE    ACA           * EXTRACT AND MAP AC ADDRESS.
035B 3F06           AF    0U,X'06'
035C 1120    ECP    LT    X'20'         * CLEAR THE ADDRESSED AC.
035D 8F2E           ADD*  0U,T,(U)
035E 0000           ELT   0,X'00'
035F 0100           ELT   1,X'00'
```

Appendix C (continued)

426

```
0360 1600          LU    X*00*
0361 1153          LT    X*53*        * SET T REG. := 'S'.
0362 1080          SSF
0363 297F          LF    9,X*7F*      * SET INPUT INDICATOR.
0364 7110   CCP    ESS   1            * TRANSFER TO EPT ROUTINE IF ECHO ON
0365 5110          TN    1,X*10*      * SILENT 700 DATA TERMINAL.
0366 1DA7          JP    EPT          * ELSE ECHO ON CRT.
0367 B120          CPY   1,T
0368 1100          LT    X*00*
```

```
0369 0189   SWE    JE    COX
036A C101          MOV   1,(T)
036B 0192          JE    DOX          * OUTPUT DATA ON CRT SCREEN.
036C F950          SLI   9,C          * UPDATE INPUT INDICATOR.
036D 4001          TZ    F0,X*01*     * WAIT FOR KEYBOARD INPUT?
036E 1D79          JP    CDAT         * NO, INPUT DATA READY.
036F 1120   AGAIN  LT    X*20*        * CHECK TTY STATUS.
0370 0189          JE    COX
0371 018E          JE    DIX
0372 5102          TN    1,X*02*      * KIP, IF INPUT DATA READY.
0373 1D6F          JP    AGAIN
0374 1100          LT    X*00*        * INPUT KEYBOARD DATA.
0375 0189          JE    COX
0376 018E          JE    DIX
0377 C101          MOV   1,(T)
0378 1D64          JP    CCP          * INPUT DATA CHECKING AND DISPLAY.
               *
               * KEYBOARD INPUT DATA CHECKING ROUTIN.
               *
0379 F100   CDAT   SFL   1
037A 111A          LT    X*1A*
037B 9138          SBT*  1,T,C
037C 5004          TN    F0,X*04*     * SKIP, IF CARRY RETURN.
037D 1D8E          JP    CKD          * CHECK FOR LEGAL DIGIT.
037E 7110          ESS   1            * TRANSFER TO ECRT ROUTINE IF TTO ECHO ON CRT.
037F 4110          TZ    1,X*10*      * ELSE CONTINUE.
0380 1D89          JP    ECRT
0381 117C          LT    X*7C*        * RESET SEND BUFFER-EMPTY MASK.
0382 0189          JE    COX
0383 1110          LT    X*10*
0384 0192          JE    DOX
0385 111C          LT    X*1C*        * OUTPUT 'NULL' CHAR. TO SILENT 700 DATA TERMINAL.
0386 0189          JE    COX
0387 1100          LT    X*00*
0388 1192          LT    DOX
0389 1040   ECRT   SPF
038A 5108          TN    F1,X*08*     * SKIP, IF SYSTEM INITIALIZATION.
038B 148E          JP    LUP
038C 2100          LF    F1,X*00*     * RESET SYSTEM START BIT.
038D 15A4          JP    INT          * GO TO INT ROUTINE.
               *
               * INPUT DATA CHECKING ROUTINE.
               *
038E 61A0   CKD    CP    1,X*A0*      * IF DATA IS LEGAL OCTUAL DIGIT LOAD DATA
038F 1092          JP    BEGIN        * INTO THE SPECIFIED ACC;
0390 6191          CP    1,X*91*      * OTHERWISE, RE-START THE OPERATION.
0391 1D94          JP    SHB
0392 1040   BEGIN  SPF
0393 1D5C          JP    ECP
               *
               * STACK INPUT DIGITS INTO THE SPECIFIED ACC.
               *
0394 F121   SHB    SFR   1,(T)        * USED IL AS A COUNTER.
0395 1040          SPF                * SHIFT THE ADDRESSED AC LEFTWISE 3 POSITIONS.
0396 B220          CPY   IU,T
0397 23C0          LF    IL,X*C0*
0398 11F0   SHA    LT    X*F0*
```

```
0399 8F2E          ADD*  OU,T,(U)
039A 0000          ELT   0,X*00*
039B 0180          ELT   1,X*80*
039C F310          SFL   IL,C
039D 4001          TZ    F0,X*01*
039E 1D98          JP    SHA
039F 11C0          LT    X*C0*        * ADD THE LEAST SIGNIFICANT 3 BITS OF INPUT DATA
03A0 8F2E          ADD*  OU,T,(U)     * TO THE LOWER 3 BIT POSITIONS OF THE SPECIFIED AC.
03A1 1107          LT    X*07*
03A2 E221          AND   IU,T,(T)
03A3 0020          ELT   0,X*20*
03A4 1600          LU    X*00*
03A5 1080          SSF
03A6 1D6F          JP    AGAIN        * WAIT FOR ANOTHER INPUT DIGIT FROM KEYBOARD.
03A7 B120   EPT    CPY   1,T          * SET SEND BUFFER-EMPTY MASK.
03A8 117C          LT    X*7C*
03A9 0189          JE    COX
03AA 1112          LT    X*12*
03AB 0192          JE    DOX
```

Appendix C (continued)

427

```
03AC 111C          LT    X'1C'
03AD 1D69          JP    SWE          * CONTINUE AT SWE ROUTINE.
                *
                * INTERNAL INTERRUPT DECODING AND EXECUTIVE ROUTINE.
                *
03AE 7140    PFR   EIS   1            * INPUT INTERNAL STATUS BYTE.
03AF 5184          TN    1,X'84'      * SKIP IF POWER FAIL OR RTC INTERRUPT.
03B0 1780          HLT                * ELSE HALT THE SYSTEM.
03B1 5180          TN    1,X'80'      * SKIP IF POWER FAIL INTERRUPT.
03B2 1DB7          JP    IRT          * ELSE GO TO RTC INTERRUPT ROUTINE.
03B3 1140          LT    X'40'        * SET POWER FAIL FLAG.
03B4 1040          SPF
03B5 C120          LOR   F1,T
03B6 1080          SSF
03B7 5104    IRT   TN    1,X'04'      * SKIP IF RTC INTERRUPT.
03B8 15A8          JP    MAIN         * ELSE GO TO MAIN ROUTINE.
03B9 8450          INC   4,C          * INCREMENT RTC COUNTER BY 1.
03BA 5001          TN    0,X'01'      * SKIP IF OVERFLOW OCCURS.
03BB 15A8          JP    MAIN         * ELSE GO TO MAIN ROUTINE.
03BC 5D80          TN    13,X'80'     * SKIP IF RTC BUSY BIT WAS SET.
03BD 1DC1          JP    NEG          * ELSE GO TO NEG ROUTINE.
03BE 1104          LT    X'04'        * SET RTC DONE FLAG.
03BF CC20          LOR   12,T         * AND UPDATE DEVICES' DONE FLAG STATUS.
03C0 2D01          LF    13,X'01'
03C1 C501    NEG   MOV   5,(T)        * RESET RTC COUNTER.
03C2 B420          CPY   4,T
03C3 15A8          JP    MAIN         * CONTINUE AT MAIN ROUTINE.
03C4 1040    JLUP  SPF
03C5 148E          JP    LUP
                *
                * ILLEGAL PTR INSTRUCTION EXECUTIVE ROUTINE.
                *
03C6 5201    U11   TN    IU,X'01'     * SKIP, IF INPUT DATA TRANSFER.
03C7 1D02          JP    NO5          * ELSE GO TO NO5.
03C8 0298          JE    CAC          * CLEAR THE ADDRESSED ACC.
03C9 1D02          JP    NO5          * PERFORM THE CONTROL FUNCTION.
                *
                * ILLEGAL RTC INSTRUCTION EXECUTIVE ROUTINE.

LOCN CODE FLAGS LABELS OP *  OPERANDS      COMMENTS                    PAGE  22
                *
■ 03CA 5201  U13   TN    IU,X'01'     * SKIP, IF INPUT DATA TRANSFER.
  03CB 1DEA        JP    NO3          * ELSE GO TO NO3.
  03CC 0298        JE    CAC          * CLEAR THE ADDRESSED ACC.
  03CD 1DEA        JP    NO3          * PERFORM THE CONTROL FUNCTION.
                *
                * REAL TIME CLOCK INSTRUCTION EXECUTIVE ROUTINE.
                *
  03CE 6EF9  RTC   CP    OL,X'F9'     * SKIP IF SKP INST..
  03CF 1DD7        JP    T13          * ELSE GO TO T13.
  03D0 1080        SSF                * COPY RTC BUSY-DONE STATUS TO T REG.
  03D1 CD01        MOV   13,(T)
  03D2 1CAC        JP    CBD          * GO TO SKIP CONDITION DECODING ROUTINE.
  03D3 1176  HZ1   LT    X'76'        * LOAD THE INITIAL RTC COUNTER VALUE:
  03D4 4E01        TZ    OL,X'01'     * SET T = 76 IF 100 HZ (10)
  03D5 117F        LT    X'7F'        *     T = 7F    1000 HZ (11)
  03D6 1DE5        JP    SCT          * GO TO RTC FREQ. SETTING ROUTINE.
                *
                * RTC INSTRUCTION EXECUTIVE ROUTINE.
                *
  03D7 4205  T13   TZ    IU,X'05'     * SKIP, IF LEGAL RTC INST..
  03D8 1DCA        JP    U13          * ELSE GO TO U13.
  03D9 6EFF        CP    OL,X'FF'     * SKIP IF DATA OUTPUT.
  03DA 1DEA        JP    NO3          * ELSE GO TO NO3.
  03DB 01B5        JE    ACA          * GET ACC ADDRESS.
  03DC 3FC6        AF    OU,X'C6'     * ACC ADDRESS MAPPING, AND
  03DD CF06        MOV   OU,(U)       * DETERMINE THE CLOCK FREQENCE.
  03DE 0001        ELT   0,X'01'      * LOAD THE CONTENTS OF ADDRESSED ACC
  03DF BE20        CPY   OL,T         * INTO OL REG..
  03E0 4E02        TZ    OL,X'02'     * SKIP IF 50/10 HZ.
  03E1 1DD3        JP    HZ1          * ELSE GO TO HZ1.
  03E2 111C        LT    X'1C'        * LOAD THE INITIAL RTC COUNTER VALUE:
  03E3 5E01        TN    OL,X'01'     * SET T = 6C IF 50 HZ (00)
  03E4 116C        LT    X'6C'        *     T = 1C    10 HZ (01)
  03E5 1080  SCT   SSF                * LOAD THE INITIAL FREQ. VALUE
  03E6 8520        CPY   5,T          * INTO RTC COUNTER.
  03E7 B420        CPY   4,T
  03E8 1720        ERT                * ENABLE RTC .
  03E9 1040        SPF
  03EA 4380  NO3   TZ    IL,X'80'     * TRANSFER TO HZ2 IF C/P RTC FUNCTION.
  03EB 15EF        JP    HZ2
  03EC 5340        TN    IL,X'40'     * SKIP, IF RTC START FUNCTION.
  03ED 148E        JP    LUP          * ELSE GO TO LUP ROUTINE.
  03EE 1180        LT    X'80'        * SET RTC BUSY FLAG.
  03EF 1080  HZ3   SSF                * RESET THE RTC DONE FLAG IN
  03F0 BD20        CPY   13,T         * THE DEVICES' DONE FLAG STATUS BYTE.
  03F1 11FB        LT    X'FB'
  03F2 EC20        AND   12,T
  03F3 1DC4        JP    JLUP         * CONTINUE OPERATION.
                   END
```

Appendix C (continued)

428

VALUE	SYMBOL	REFERENCED													
0006	AOL														
0007	AOU														
0008	A1L														
0009	A1U														
000A	A2L														
000B	A2U														
000C	A3L	0096													
000D	A3U	0098	009A												
01B5	ACA	01BB	01DD	0284	02BA	02D5	02FA	035A	03DB						
00BC	ACD	00AF													
01C5	ACK	01CD	01D1	01D5											
00FA	ADN	00E6													
036F	AGA	0373	03A6												
0225	ALP	020A													
0157	B14	0147													
0153	B15	0143													
00E2	B10	00CC													
00E5	B20	00C9													
02ED	BD1	02E8													
0392	BEG	038F													
029B	CAC	01DE	01F6	0299	03C8	03CC									
00F8	CAD	00F5													
02AC	CBD	02D4	02F9	03D2											
0364	CCP	0378													
00AE	CCR	00E1													
014D	CCY	0145	0158												
0379	CDA	036E													
0200	CDC	01A8													
0106	CHS	00D6	00DC	00DF											
032E	CIA	032D													
018C	CIO	018B	0191	0193											
027A	CIT	0264													
038E	CKD	0370													
004C	CKR	005B													
02F0	CL1	02E2													
028F	CLE	001E	019F	0293											
019B	CLI	02A5													
02CB	CLP	02C3													
0189	COX	0001	0005	0009	000D	0011	0015	0019	01AD	01E4	01E8	0205	020E	0212	0217	021B	0226
		022F	0233	0244	024B	025A	0280	02EA	0308	0313	031C	0320	0334	0338	034D	0352	0356
		0369	0370	0375	0382	0386	03A9								
0174	CPD	0163													
0144	CRC	0155													
00E0	CRS	00AC													
013F	CSK	0128	013B												
0288	DCP	0177	017C	017E											
017D	DEI	0175													
004A	DID	0038													
0261	DIN	0253	0256	0258											
018E	DIX	001A	01B3	0206	0213	0245	024C	0314	0353	0371	0376				
0192	DOX	0003	0007	000B	000F	0013	0017	01B1	01E6	01EC	0210	0219	021D	0231	0235	025C	0282
		02EC	030A	031E	0322	0336	033A	034F	0358	036B	0384	0388	03AB		
035C	ECP	0021	0393												
0389	ECR	0380													
0331	EEE	0318													
017B	EEI	0182													

VALUE	SYMBOL	REFERENCED														
0190	ELT	018F														
03A7	EPT	0366														
01AC	ERA	020C														
01B3	ERI	01AF	0228													
01B0	ERO	01EA														
01E3	ERP	0228	022D													
0001	F1	001F	0045	0082	0089	00AA	00AB	00AD	00D1	00D9	00DA	00DE	00E0	00E3	00EC	00EE	00EF
		00F0	00F3	00F6	00F8	0101	0103	0108	0111	0117	011D	012C	0130	013A	013D	014F	038A
		038C	03B5													
0022	FET	0279	027D													
0000	F0	0027	0043	005D	0060	0066	006B	007C	007F	0086	0087	00A5	00BB	00C7	00CF	00D5	00DB
		00E9	00F1	00F4	00FE	012D	0138	0146	0150	0287	036D	037C	039D			
0221	GCO	021F														
01A1	HAL	02A6														
03D3	HZ1	03E1														
01EF	HZ2	03EB														
03EF	HZ3	01F3														
032B	IAK	01AA	030D													
01EE	ICD	0203														
0194	IDA	02C1	0301													
00A0	IDS	0092														
006A	IDT	004D	004F	0051												
027C	IFT	0262	0268													
0003	IL	0028	0035	0039	003D	003E	003F	0041	0042	0052	0054	005C	005E	005F	0064	0065	0076
		0077	0078	007D	007E	0084	0085	00A0	00A2	00AE	0082	0085	0106	0108	0114	012A	0142
		0144	0148	014A	014D	0154	0157	0158	0164	0167	016D	0174	0176	017D	01D8	01EF	02AF
		0282	02C2	02C4	02CB	02E1	02E3	02F0	0302	0304	0326	0397	039C	03EA	03EC	
01BB	INA	02A3														
0351	INE	0332														
01A4	INT	0090	009F	038D												
00A8	IOA	002E														

Appendix C (continued)

```
015A   IOI   00A9
01CE   IOT   01CB
03B7   IRT   03B2
0252   ITO   0249
0002   IU    002B  0037  003C  0040  004A  0071  0075  007A  0091  0093  00A1  00A8  008D  00C8  00CB
             00D2  00D3  00D8  00E5  00FB  0104  0110  011A  0123  0128  0139  0140  015E  01B6  01F4  0297
             02BB  02D6  02FB  0396  03A2  03C6  03CA  03D7
0091   JID   0073
03C4   JLU   0171  028A  02CA  03F3
009B   JMP   0094
012A   LAC   0109  0113  011E  0129
0131   LAD   013E
013C   LCR   012E
0004   LL    0022  008C  008E  0095  009C  01A1  0272  0278
0074   LST   0072
0005   LU    0024  008D  008F  0097  009E  01A2  0270  0275
008E   LUP   0083  0088  00A6  014E  0152  0159  016A  01A0  01C9  01D9  01DC  01DF  01F0  028C  02A2  02A7
             02B9  02C5  02CC  02E4  02F1  0305  0327  0388  03C5  03ED
01A8   MAI   0388  038B  03C3
002F   MAP   0026  0055  006A  0079  00A3
0284   MAS   02A4
005C   MID   0056  00A4
0034   MRE   002D
0183   NCP   0161
03C1   NEG   038D
```

VALUE SYMBOL REFERENCED   PAGE   25

```
02C2   NIO   0298  029A  028E
02E1   NOI   01F5  01F7  02D9
03EA   NO3   03CB  03CD  03DA
0302   NO5   02FE  03C7  03C9
0355   NOG   031A
000E   OL    0023  0029  002F  0031  0036  0044  004E  0050  0053  0061  0062  006C  006D  0080  0088  0098
             00B0  0087  008A  008C  008E  008F  00C0  00C5  00C6  00CD  00CE  00D0  00D7  00E2  00EA  00EB
             00FF  0100  010E  011C  011F  0124  0135  013F  015D  015F  0162  0106  01D6  0288  028D  028E
             02A8  0281  02B3  02B6  02BD  02D0  02D8  02F5  02FD  03CE  03D4  03D9  03DF  03E0  03E3
000F   OU    0020  0025  002A  0030  0032  0034  003A  0046  0049  004C  0057  0059  0063  0067  006E  006F
             0081  008A  009D  00B1  0084  0088  0089  00C1  00C2  00C3  00C4  00CA  00E7  00E8  00ED  00FA
             00FC  00FD  0102  0131  0132  0133  0134  0136  0137  015A  015C  0160  0183  0185  0187  0188
             0195  0196  01B5  01B7  01B8  01B9  01BC  01C6  01E1  0285  0286  0298  029C  02AD  02B5  02DA
             02DB  0358  035D  0399  03A0  030C  03DD
01E0   OVF   0058
0057   OVK   0070
03AE   PFR   01A7
02EE   PNO   02F4
02F5   PTR   01FA
01CA   PTT   01C3
0059   REP   01E2
02C9   RSI   02EF  0325
03CE   RTC   01FC
00D2   SAM   00E4  00F2  00F7  00F9
014F   SBN   014C
03E5   SCT   03D6
0089   SEC   00B3  0086
0071   SEP   004B  005A
0398   SHA   039E
0394   SHB   0391
02C8   SIM   02CF
016C   SKI   0165
008C   SKP   00A7  0149  014B  0151  0156  0168  0173  01DA  0288
0114   SRS   0107
0084   STA   0078
030B   STM   030C  033C  034A  0350  0354  0359
0369   SWE   03AD
011F   SWP   0115
035A   SWT   02A1
02FA   T11   02F6
03D7   T13   03CF
02BA   T14   02A9
02D5   T15   02D1
027F   TD1   0238
027E   TD2   023E
034C   TD3   033F
034B   TD4   0345
0326   TR1   0303
0324   TR2   032A
02A8   TTI   01F8
02D0   TTO   01F9
0243   TTY   01A9  0182  0184  01ED  0220  0224  0283
01D2   TYO   01CF
03C6   U11   02FC
03CA   U13   03D8
0297   U14   028C
```

VALUE SYMBOL REFERENCED

```
01F4   U15   02D7
00D9   UDC   0105
01D6   UDN   0184  0186  01FB  01FD  01FE  01FF
01D8   UIN   01D7
```

Appendix C (continued)

430

Index

A

Action table, 186–89
Adaptive compiler, 259, 260
Adaptive optimization, 258, 259
ADD instruction, 5
  logic, 8
  microprogram representation, 11
  timing sequence, 7
Agerwala, 102, 190
Agrawala, 127
Alterable control memory, 20
ALU, 4, 5, 26
APL, microprogrammed implementation, 261–63
APL Assist, 261–63
APLEC instruction, 262
Assembler, 122
Assembly process, 122–23

B

Banerji, 102, 103
Base register, 29
Basu, 103
Bauer, 253

Bit-slice microprocessors (*see* Microprogrammable microprocessor)
Bus:
  ALU input, 28
  ALU output, 28

C

CDC, 130
Channel enhancement, 254
Chattergy, 250
Choudhury, 103
Communications controller (*see* Microprogrammed implementation, communications controller)
Compatibility, at software level, 13
Compilation, 254
Conditional assembly, 124
Control, levels of, 78–82
Control flip-flops, 26, 36, 40–50
Control matrix, 17
Control memory:
  address decoder, 18
  address register, 18, 67
  cover table, 102
  defined, 10

Control memory (*cont.*):
  extension, 180–84
  location counter, 67
  optimization, 176–80, 184–90
  sequencing, 67–69
  technology, 71–77
Control registers, 26
Control store (*see* Control memory)
Control unit, function, 5
Conventional control, 5
CPU:
  function of, 26
  organization, 26, 27
  registers, 26
Cross microassembler, 123
Cyclic redundancy check, 146, 150, 152–53

D

Das, 102, 103
Dasgupta, 103, 104
Data General, 20, 206, 379
Data path, width, 28
DELtran, 260, 261
DeWitt, 130
Diagonal microinstruction, 89
  execution, 97
Digital Equipment Corporation, 20
Dijkstra, 253
Directly executable language, 257
Displacement field, 30
DMA:
  concept, 47
  controller, 48
  flip-flop, 47
Dynamic address translation:
  concept, 348
  implementation, 348–55

E

Eckhouse, 128
Effective address, 30
EMMY, 260, 261
Emulation, 21
  APL, 261–63
  CPU functions, 202–6
  defined, 199
  flowchart, 212
  front panel operation, 234
  interrupt systems, 218–19
  I/O functions, 213, 216–18
  Nova computer (*see* Nova computer, emulation
    of non I/O functions)
  trade-offs in, 232–33
Emulator, 13, 21, 199
  for Nova computer (listing), 414–29
EROM, 117
Euler, microprogrammed implementation of,
  257–58
Execution optimization, of microprograms,
  190–94

F

Firmware, 113–15, 117–19
Firmware implementation of structured programming (*see* Microprogrammed implementation, block-structured programming)

Flynn, 105, 260, 261
FORTRAN, microprogrammed implementation,
  260–61
Functional specialization, 259

G

General purpose registers, 26, 30
Glushkov, 184, 185
Gonzales, 190
Graphics terminal, microprogrammed implemen-
  tation of functions (*see* Microprogrammed
  implementation, graphics functions)
Grasselli, 100, 101, 102

H

Hardwired control, 5
Hassitt, 261, 262, 263
Hewlett-Packard, 20
High-level language, for microprogramming,
  125–31
High-level languages, microprogramming support
  for (*see,* Microprogramming support, for
  high-level languages)
Hoevel, 256–57
Honeywell, 19
Horizontal microinstruction, 87
  execution, 97
Host machine, 21, 199
Husson, 3, 19, 200

I

IBM, 19, 21, 22, 51, 131, 153, 154, 155, 253
Ideal DEL, 257
In-circuit emulator, 21, 322
Index register, 28
Input/output:
  interrupt-driven, 44
  programmed, 44
  register, 26, 32
Input/output device, communication, 32
Instruction:
  classification, 52
  fetch and execution, 37–39
  field, 29
  format, 29, 33–36
  functions performed, 53–60
  mask, 58
  mode field, 33
  opcode, 29
  operand, 29
  type, 33–36
Instruction register, 5, 26
Instruction units, 261
Intel Series 3000:
  components, 275
  CPE, 276, 288–97
    functional description, 290–97
    organization, 288–90
  cross microprogramming system, 297–321
    microprogramming techniques, 313–21
    XMAP language, 298, 312
    XMAS language, 297–312
  function bus, 275
  in-circuit emulator, 321–22
  MCU, 277–88
    extended addressing, 287–88

Intel Series 3000 (*cont.*):
  functional description, 280–88
  jump function bus, 279
  organization, 277–80
  microinstruction format, 277
  microprogram memory, 275, 280–83
  typical configuration, 276
Intermediate code, 254
Interpretation, 254
Interrupt:
  flip-flop, 42
  input/output, 44
  mechanism, 42
  priority, 42
  service time, 47
  stack, 46
  types, 42
Interrupts, emulation of, 218–19
I/O system:
  emulation (*see* Emulation, I/O functions)
  of Nova (*see* Nova computer, I/O system)

J

Jackson, 104
Jayasri, 103

K

Kleir, 186, 189

L

Liskov, 252
Lyon, 261, 262, 263

M

Macroinstruction, 124
Mallach, 199
Memory address register, 26, 28
Memory data register, 26, 28
Microassembler language, 120–25
Microcode, 20
Microcommand, 10
  compatibility, 101
  compatibility class, 101
  maximal compatibility class, 101
  prime compatibility class, 101
Microdata, 20
Microdata 1600:
  description, 138–41
  device address, 158
  device order, 158
  internal status byte, 164–65
  interrupt system, 163–66
  I/O system, 156–59
  microassembler syntax, 412–13
  microinstruction formats, 140–41
  microinstructions, 396–411
    arithmetic type, 406–8
    command seven type, 404–5
    control type, 401-2
    execute type, 397
    file register type, 402–3
    I/O type, 405–6
    load register type, 399–400
    load seven type, 400–401

Microdata 1600 (*cont.*):
  load zero type, 398–99
  logical type, 410–11
  memory reference type, 408–10
  registers, 138–40
  status byte, 158
Microdiagnostics, 355–57
Microinstruction, 9
  bit minimization, 100–105
  buffer register, 68
  cycle, 93
  defined, 86
  design considerations, 98-106
  encoding, 92
  execution, 93
    monophase, 93
    polyphase, 93–96
  formats, 87–93
  modification, 71
  optimization (*see* Microinstruction, bit minimization)
  register, 67
Microoperating system, 131
Microoperation, 10
Microprogram:
  absolute coding, 113-15
  action table, 186
  assembly language coding, 120–23
  for communications controller, 368–75
  conditional branching, 19
  defined, 10
  for dynamic address translation, 354–55
  execution optimization, 190–94
  for Nova emulator, 414–29
  storage optimization (*see* Control memory, optimization)
  testing, 115–19
Microprogrammable microprocessor, 20, 272 (*see* also Intel Series 3000)
  advantages, 272
  an example (*see* Intel Series 3000)
  microprogram control unit, 272–73
  processor section, 273–74
Microprogrammed control, 10
  hardware, 66–67
  schematic, 66
Microprogrammed implementation:
  ADD instruction, 141–42
  block-structured programming, 324–46
    control program instructions, 331–44
    at machine level, 325–31
  communications controller, 362–75
  conditional branch, 143
  convert to binary instruction, 143–45
  cyclic redundancy check, 146, 150, 152–53
  floating add and subtract, 146–50
  functions, 137
  graphics functions, 358–62
  I/O instructions, 156–62
  I/O interrupt handling, 169
  output data instruction, 158, 160
  print instruction, 161–62
  program interrupt processing, 167–69
  read and echo instruction, 160–61
  real-time clock, 166–67
  stack processing, 169–71
  TRT instruction, 153–55
  virtual memory, 347–55
    dynamic address translation, 348–55
Microprogrammed interrupt handling, 162–69
Microprogramming:
  advantages, 12–14
  concepts, 9, 10
  disadvantages, 14–15

Microprogramming (*cont.*):
  history, 19–22
Microprogramming support:
  for high-level languages, 254–63
    different approaches, 256
    examples, 257–63
  for operating systems
    examples, 248–54
    general considerations, 242–44·
    implementation, 244–48
    improvements expected, 241–42
    OS concepts, 239–40
    OS overhead, 241
Montanari, 100, 101, 102
MTOS, 251

N

Nanoprogramming, 82
Nova computer:
  ALU instructions, 385–90
  arithmetic unit, 206
  emulation of non I/O functions, 209–13
  emulator microprogram, 414–29
  general description, 206–9, 379–81
  instruction formats, 207–8, 381–82
  I/O instructions, 390–95
  I/O system, 220–23
  I/O system emulation, 223–31
  mapping of registers, 209–10
  memory addressing, 208–9, 380–81, 382–83
  memory reference instructions, 383–85
  memory word mapping, 210–11, 213

O

Operating systems:
  microprogramming support for (*see*
        Microprogramming support, for
        operating systems)
  overhead, 241
  primitives, 245
    maxiprimitives, 245
    midiprimitives, 245
    miniprimitives, 245
  review, 239–40
  schematic diagram, 240
Optimization, of microprograms (*see* Control
        memory, optimization)
OS/360, 245
Overlays, in control memory, 182–84

P

PC (*see* Program counter)
Perkin-Elmer, 20
Polyphase microinstruction, minimization, 103–4
Privileged instruction, 57
Program counter, 26
  function, 28
Programmed interrupt, 51
Program store, 11
PROM, 75–77
Pseudo instruction, 121, 123, 124

R

Ramamoorthy, 98, 130, 186, 189, 190
Random access memory, 20

RCA, 19
Read-only memory, 12, 20, 72
  simulator, 21, 118, 119
Relocatable code, 124
Resident microassembler, 123
Residual control, 71
Robertson, 105

S

Scheduler, microprogramming of, 248–50
Schwartz, 100
Sequencing matrix, 17
Simulation, 200
Sinha, 103
Srimani, 103
Stack:
  LIFO, 32
  POP operation, 32
  PUSH operation, 32
  return-address, 26, 33
Stack pointer, 31
Stack processing, by microprograms, 169–71
Surrogate, for source program, 254
Syllables, 261
System 360/30, 257, 258
System 370/145, 261, 262, 263

T

Target machine, 21, 199
Tartar, 103, 104
Tomasulo, 186, 188
TOS, 251
Trap flip-flop, 50
Traps, 50–51
TSS enhancement, 253
Tsuchiya, 98, 130, 190

U

Univac, 20
Universal host, 81, 233
User microprogramming, 20

V

Venus operating system, 252–53
Vertical microinstruction, 88
  execution, 96–97
Virtual control store, 182
Virtual machine, 137, 199
Virtual memory, microprogrammed implementa-
        tion (*see* Microprogrammed implementa-
        tion, virtual memory)

W

WCS (*see* Writable control store)
Weber, 257, 258
Werkheiser, 245
Wilkes, 3, 17, 127
Writable control store, 20, 117
Wulf, 258, 259